MICHAEL COLLINS
The Lost Leader

MICHAEL COLLINS
The Lost Leader

MARGERY FORESTER

GILL AND MACMILLAN

Published in Ireland by
Gill and Macmillan Ltd
Goldenbridge
Dublin 8
with associated companies throughout the world
© Margery Forester 1971 and 1989
0 7171 1711 1
First published 1971 by
Sidgwick and Jackson Ltd

A catalogue record is available
for this book from the British Library.

3   5   7   6   4

To the host of the O'Coileain
whose hospitable troop
it has been my good fortune to encounter

Contents

Preface to the 1989 Edition   ix

List of Illustrations   xi

Acknowledgements   xiii

PART ONE

Something Expected

1 Woodfield (1890–1906)   3
2 London (1906–1915)   18
3 The Rising   34
4 Internment   50

PART TWO

Carrying the Long Day

5   Readjustment (1917)   65
6   Resurgence (1918)   81
7   Sinn Fein (1919)   97
8   The Irish Volunteers (1919)   114
9   The Black and Tans (January–June 1920)   132
10 The Changing Order (July–September 1920)   149
11 A Hell to Live In (October–December 1920)   164
12 The Terror Ends (January–July 1921)   180

PART THREE

The Day Came so Strenuous

13 Truce   201
14 London (October 1921)   217
15 The Treaty   233

Contents

16 The Questioning   258
17 Provisional Government (January–March 1922)   275
18 Resistance (April–June 1922)   295
19 Eruption (June–August 1922)   315
20 The Last Journey South   326
21 Epilogue   340

    Bibliography   351

    Glossary   354

    Index   358

Preface to the 1989 Edition

This book, first published in 1971, is re-issued to coincide with the centenary of Michael Collins's birth in 1890.

It is, therefore, nearly twenty years since its first appearance. In that time the exposition and reinterpretation of Irish history has continued at a vigorous pace. The debate between what might broadly be called the nationalist and the revisionist views of Irish history has been urgent and stimulating, an energetic feature of Irish intellectual life. Yet where Collins's life is concerned the known facts stand largely as they were when this book was first published. No new papers or documents touching directly on Collins have emerged. The papers of General Richard Mulcahy have been catalogued and are available to scholars in the Archives Department of University College Dublin; they are invaluable as a primary source for the study of the period from 1919 to 1923. As far as Collins is concerned, however, they corroborate what was known before rather than adding much that is new. Dr Leon O Broin has edited a selection of the correspondence between Collins and his fianceé, Kitty Kiernan, which was originally made available to me. It reveals not only their mutual love but also the intolerable pressure under which Collins lived the last year of his short life.

As to the manner of his death, an element of controversy will always remain. Several books and articles have appeared, ranging in their degrees of speculation from the intriguing to the bizarre, without seriously advancing knowledge on what actually happened. One can still say only that Michael Collins was most probably killed by a ricochet bullet fired from the Republican side at Beal na mBlath. While this absorption with the mystery surrounding his death is understandable, I have always felt that the question of who fired the petty bullet has little relevance to any enquiry into Collins's life and achievements. My own speculation is that he himself would not have wanted it dwelt on: he was too big-minded, essentially concerned with building, not destruction, and things of good report.

I have amended my original text in two or three places where errors of fact have been brought to my attention. Few of the many participants in the events chronicled who generously shared their recollections with me are now alive. They brought to my youthful researches a distillation of wisdom and, with few exceptions, a tolerance that surprised me. I have since concluded that many of them may have felt that these might well be their last words on such matters, and that they were anxious to have them set down free of past rancour. My judgements then were formed in large part as a result of these conversations, and I have no mind to change what I wrote, or to be less grateful to all who helped me. The bibliography has, however, been revised and expanded to take account of the many outstanding books published since. Although no claim is made as to its completeness, it is hoped that it will prove a useful guide to further reading.

In Ireland the period since the first publication of the book has been dominated by the continuing conflict in Northern Ireland. Inevitably, the echoes of the first 'troubles', in which Collins played so vital a part, have been loud and have contributed to speculation about what would have happened had Collins lived. At the end of the book I quote a Republican officer saying sadly that 'Collins was the ideal man to bring the North in somehow.' That 'somehow' speaks volumes, yet all such speculation is, of course, fruitless. It has to be enough that Collins lived, was as he was and did what he did. That is all a biographer can record.

List of Illustrations

The following illustrations are groupd in one section between pages 196 and 197.

Michael Collins at Christmas 1916.

One of the company mobilisation orders issued to the Irish Volunteers prior to the Easter Rising of 1916.

Collins as Minister for Finance in the Dail government.

Members of the first Dail outside the Mansion House, 21 January 1919.

The first meeting of Dail Eireann in the Round Room of the Mansion House, 21 January 1919.

Arthur Griffith.

Michael Collins and Harry Boland at Croke Park, 1921.

Members of the Black and Tans.

Wedding party, 22 November 1920, the morning after 'Bloody Sunday'.

Collins at Arthur Griffith's graveside.

Collins and General Richard Mulcahy marching in Arthur Griffith's funeral procession.

O'Connell Street during the Civil War.

Following the Treaty, troops of the provisional government of the Irish Free State replaced the British Army.

Sean Collins beside his brother's coffin.

xi

Acknowledgements

Many of those who have helped in supplying material for this book have asked that their names should not be mentioned: my debt to them is none the less deep. Many more, though unable to give information themselves, have gone out of their way to find others who could. Without all of these there would, quite simply, have been no book.

Among those who have helped me are: Brother William P. Allen of the O'Connell School, Dublin; Mrs H. L. Barniville; Mr Robert Barton; Mr Earnan de Blaghd; Senator Gerald Boland; Comdt W. J. Brennan-Whitmore; Colonel Eamon Broy; Comdt Vincent Byrne; Mrs Kathleen Clarke; Mr Maurice Collins; Mr W. T. Cosgrave; Mr Felix Cronin; Mr Sean Culhane; Professor Thomas Dillon and Mrs Dillon; Mr Joseph Dolan; Mrs Sheila Donovan; Miss Mary Flood; Mr Oliver D. Gogarty, S.C.; Miss Aine Goodwin; Professor Michael Hayes; Mr Sean Kavanagh; Mr Charles S. P. Kelly, P.C.; Fr P. Kiely; Sister Eithne Lawless; Colonel J. V. Lawless; the Rt Hon. the Earl of Longford; Judge Fionan Lynch; Mr Ned Lynch; Mrs C. Leigh Doyle; Dr Brigid Lyons-Thornton; Mr Alex McCabe; Mr Eugene MacCarthy; Mr Denis McCullough; Lt-General Sean MacEoin; Mr Joseph McGrath; Mr Liam McNeive; Mr Patrick Moylett; Mr Eoin Neeson; Mr Dave Neligan; Mr Sean Nunan; Professor Liam O Briain; Miss Eileen O'Connor; Frank O'Connor; Mrs J. A. O'Donovan; Miss Eileen O'Donovan; Miss Peg O'Donovan; Mrs Diarmuid O'Hegarty; Mr Dick O'Hegarty; Mr Padraig O'Keeffe; Mr Colm O Lochlainn; Dr M. W. O'Reilly; Fr Gearoid O'Sullivan, C.M.; Mr John Power; Desmond Ryan; Dr James Ryan; Mr Luke Smith; Maj-General Joseph A. Sweeney; Mr Frank Thornton.

I am also very thankful to the following persons and bodies for permission to quote from documents: the Trustees of the National Library of Ireland; the Deputy Keeper, the Public Record Office of Ireland; the National Museum of Ireland; the Kilmainham Restoration Committee, and in particular Mr James Brennan and Mr Eamonn de Barra; the Minister for Defence, Ireland. Thanks are also due to Lady Rachel Sturgis, the Public Record Office and the British Home Office for permission to quote the diaries of Sir Mark Sturgis; to Mr. Laurence P. Scott for allowing me to quote the diaries of C. P. Scott, now in the British Museum. Transcripts of Crown-copyright records in the Public Record Office appear by permission of the Controller of H.M. Stationery Office.

Quotation from Dail Eireann debates is made by permission of the Irish Stationery Office. Extracts from Professor Crane Brinton's *The Anatomy of Revolution* are quoted by permission of Prentice-Hall, Inc. The quotation from Allen Curnow's *Landfall in Unknown Seas* is made with acknowledgement to the New Zealand Government Department of Internal Affairs.

The biography of President de Valera by Lord Longford and Mr Thomas P. O'Neill was first published while this book was in proof. I am most grateful to the authors for their helpful advice.

Where the Collins family is concerned, any attempt to make adequate acknowledgement of their help and encouragement must fail lamentably. I hope the dedication will go a little way towards showing my thanks.

PART ONE

Something Expected

CHAPTER ONE

Woodfield

(1890–1906)

I

The Collinses of Woodfield may be said to have had as long a tradition of inherited dispossession as any other family of native stock in Ireland. Despite the warning of the ancient saying, *A great host with whom it is not fortunate to contend, the battle-trooped host of the O Coileain,* part of their ancestral clan was driven from its stronghold in Co. Limerick in the days of Strongbow when the great upheaval in the Irish national way of life first began. The extended wanderings which brought West Cork its present strength of Collinses culminated for one family at Sam's Cross, a small scattering of farms which lies inland and surrounded by hills halfway between the towns of Rosscarbery and Clonakilty. They were to farm there, at Woodfield, for about seven generations.

They were, of course, tenant farmers, since to be Catholic and Irish was synonymous with tenancy of a more or less precarious kind. They held their acres of scattered land, surviving the vicissitudes of penal law and eviction, famine and emigration that became the traditional birthright of the native Irish.

By the middle of the 19th century three unmarried Collins brothers, Patrick, Tom, and Michael, were living at Woodfield. Patrick had been born about 1798, a year which might have altered the course of European history had Napoleon not kept one finger on the map of the Nile while he listened to Wolfe Tone's ideas for an extensive French campaign in Ireland.

The brothers remained firmly within the nationalist tradition that had consistently withstood both assimilation and oppression. In 1850 Patrick and Tom drove out two members of the landlord class who were hunting over the farm without any regard for the crops. For this embryonic rising the two brothers spent a year in Cork gaol. Michael made the journey on horseback to visit them as often as the authorities allowed. No doubt this experience influenced him when the Fenian Brotherhood was formed a few years later, for he joined its secret ranks.

Neither Patrick nor Tom married, and it was not until 1875, when he was sixty, that Michael brought a young bride to Woodfield. Despite the forty years' difference in their ages their life was happy. Mary Anne O'Brien brought a woman's hand to what had for so long been a bachelor establishment, and Woodfield throve. Their first child, Margaret, was born in 1877, followed by John, Johanna (Hannie), and Mary.

These were the years of the Land League and the rise of Parnell. Harvest failures, while they were in no way as devastating in their consequences as those of the Great Starvation years earlier in the century, served to point the arguments of those who demanded land reform as the only solution to the chronic discontents of Ireland. Yet, though poverty and social distress were the results of English rule, they were not the causes of resistance to it. The failure of successive British Governments to grasp this was as much their country's tragedy as Ireland's.

By 1887 three more children had been born to Michael and Mary Anne Collins: Helena, Patrick, and Katie. The older children were by now becoming conscious of the ceaseless undercurrent of politics which ran through, and were an integral part of Irish life; now and then surging up to flood one part or another of the country with periods of unrest which were generally bloody and always had at their source the question of land possession.

With the Land War prices of produce fell alarmingly, and neighbours gathered at Woodfield to discuss the age-old problems of rent payment and eviction. To the children the ominous word 'hanging-gale' sounded an almost monotonous note of terror. Even while they understood little of this sickening method of reversed hire-purchase, by which an extra half-year's rent in advance was demanded, they comprehended the fear of a possible inability to meet it in the neighbours' voices, the fear of a bad harvest, of loss of cattle, the knowledge that to improve one's land invited eviction in favour of a tenant able to pay a higher rent. They were spared the hunger known to other Irish children of their generation, whose slice of bread for lunch would be eaten before the first field was passed on their way to school; nevertheless, they accepted without question that any silver coin presented by a more prosperous relative must be handed over for the rent, though pennies might be kept for themselves.

The *Weekly Freeman* was always in the house, and those of the family who were unable to read the latest news of the land struggle absorbed what they could from its cartoons.

The two much-loved uncles were now dead. Michael Collins himself, one of his children was to write, 'never looked an old man and never had an old age'. When he was seventy-five his eighth and last child, a son, was born in the early hours of Thursday, 16 October 1890.

It was customary at that time for children to be baptized on the day of their birth. His father favoured calling him James after an elder brother. The rest of the family, however, recalling the Gaelic tradition that named the third son for his father, insisted on Michael. Perhaps this early controversy was the origin of Michael's adolescent affectation of the signature 'M. J. Collins', for since their father believed that one Christian name was sufficient for each of his children there could be no compromise. Sheer weight of opinion prevailed, and it was Michael that Father Peter Hill duly baptized the baby that day at Rosscarbery Church.

II

The way of life at Woodfield in which Michael Collins was to spend his childhood is the key to all that he was later to become. No other single influence was to lie closer to his heart. The Woodfield acres were few to have contained a vision as broad as he possessed, yet to the end of his life they filled it completely.

For centuries his people had lived close to the earth in one particular district, bounded by the customs of their own small world. Even where the extremity of hardship had brought emigration like spreading blight across that way of life, the reports of the New World – all too seldom brought back in person by those who had gone – came only as bewildering and unreal travellers' tales. They had no impact on the integrated life of rural Ireland.

Though Michael was born into a generation that moved out and away from that life, he never denied the deep-rooted instinct that it was the only lasting foundation upon which the necessary changes of the modern world could be successfully grafted. All his actions were to be guided by the yardstick of the preservation and greater well-being of Sam's Cross.

This close community life could have bred no finer sense of citizenship. The social injustices of Irish life had for so long been inevitable as to be almost unquestioned. Where no help had ever come none was expected; these men and women relied solely on God and each other. It was not superstition but this sense of utter dependence on the only source of relief that blessed the crops, mixed holy water with the wheat before sowing, or sprinkled it upon the mare about to foal. Any loss might mean ruin; yet it was the same acceptance of the inevitability of their lot that met disaster with a quiet *Dé bheatha, toil Dé* – Welcome be God's will.

Woodfield in that last decade of the 19th century was almost entirely self-supporting. Mary Anne Collins grew her own flax and wove her linen for the spotless sheets and shirts which she spread out in the bleaching field. She spun her wool, which was then sent for carding to the local mill, and from which she would knit stockings and woollen underclothes. She baked bread from the Woodfield corn which was ground at the mill. Wasting nothing, she fed the bran to the calves, plucked her geese, cut seed potatoes, and set her milk, scouring the pans with heather and salt and scalding them with water from the well when the rain butts ran low in dry weather. No speck of dust might enter the dairy where, on Thursday nights, the children would help churn the butter ready for market the following day.

The care of the smaller children, particularly Michael, devolved upon the older girls. It is the inevitable, and often deeply resented, way with large families; yet from the first they lavished affection upon him. 'We thought he had been invented for our special edification', is Miss Hannie Collins's comment.

Two things were apparent about him from the first: he had an overwhelming generosity, and no conception of fear.

Like all small children he had his share of near disasters. Seen in the light of his later adventures they suggest an aura of special protection which he was to carry with him into manhood. In his crawling days he was taken by his sisters up to the loft of the house from which, via the trapdoor, he fell, surprised but un-injured, down to the kitchen below. At the age of two he wan-dered away one morning and was not missed for some hours. His brother Johnny, hearing uneasy snorting, glanced into the stall of a particularly vicious horse which only his father could approach. The animal's forelegs were braced gingerly apart; between them Michael lay curled up, fast asleep.

A sturdy, fair little boy, he took after his father in looks. Later, his hair would take the dark brown, almost black in some lights, sheen that predominates in the south of Ireland : the colour of the reed beds when the wind bends them. His eyes were grey with hazel flecks in them. The squarely-set jaw gave promise that later its owner might prove a very determined young man indeed. He laughed most of the time, flew into rages and out of them again as suddenly. If he thought anyone else had been hurt he wept bitterly.

Although his mother had to leave much of his care to the older children her influence was a gentle and stimulating one. One of his earliest memories must have been of standing near as she milked the cows, singing the old songs in the Irish she had learnt from her grandmother, a fluent speaker of the language.

Life was hard for the women of those times. In the evening hours before Michael's birth, limping from a broken and badly-set ankle, Mary Anne Collins had done the milking, pouring it out for setting from heavy pails, and doing the baking for the next day. Yet she was by no means a mere household drudge, being alive to the affairs of the community and quick of intellect.

Michael's father was the supreme being in his life. From the time Michael could walk, father and son would go about the farm together. The elder Michael Collins studied the needs of his land. The small boy would watch the dried sea-weed and sand for top-dressing being spread over some of Woodfield's sixty acres, or listen to his father's stories as he cut the *saileach*, or osiers, in the sally gardens for the panniers which he wove in the autumn to hold cattle fodder. As he fashioned farm gates, a new cow stall, or displayed his meticulous craftsmanship in some piece of furniture for the house, the old man, stern, thought-

ful, and somewhat aloof from his other children, told Michael
something of his country's history and of the recurring theme,
the land for the people.

He would often quote lines in praise of nationalism. In later
years, when all memory of his father's appearance had faded
from the boy's mind, these stories and quotations were the recollections of his father which stayed with him.

He was as straight a man as ever lived, and his children revered
him. 'I was afraid to be mean in his presence', wrote one of them,
many years afterwards. He once allowed himself to be taken
to court by a Clonakilty tradesman for alleged non-payment of
a debt. Only when the magistrate demanded it did he produce
the plaintiff's receipt for the amount. The shopkeeper had known
him all his life : his word should have been evidence enough
of payment.

Humanity to man and beast was another of the father's
qualities to be inherited by the son. No animal might be ill-
treated, nor a nest in the rookery near the farm buildings touched.
His influence on Michael's character and outlook was profound.
From him, too, Michael seems to have inherited his most pronounced traits of bearing and intellect.

Bright, and with a boundless energy, he was to the fore in all
activities. When he was four the elders of the family went off
to a fair, leaving him to the care of his sister Mary. She mentioned that they would need some potatoes; shortly afterwards
she found him in the garden, scarlet of face and dragging a large
bucketful with the triumphant cry of 'I have them nearly
dug !'

At other times he would insist on joining fishing expeditions
to the Owenahincha river, at that time a broad-flowing stream
some hundreds of yards below the house. No attempt to 'spear'
a fish could be made without Michael's hand on the pike. With
the need to be in the forefront of everything he had a deep kindness
of heart. No effort which he felt merited praise went unnoticed.
'Well done, old fellow !' he would cry, regardless of the age or
sex of the doer.

Even in matters of religion he showed an early independence.
Mary prepared him for his first confession, pointing out that
this must include telling the priest how often he had helped

himself surreptitiously to sugar or jam. Michael was horrified. 'If I tell him that he'll think I'm a thief!' he protested.

In the evenings the women of Sam's Cross would gather in each other's kitchens to sew and spin, to quilt the hoods of their heavy black cloaks, or to make up their frieze cloth into working garments for the men. The men came there also, to turn to such tasks as the making of the *súgáin*, the straw ropes with which they would secure the reeks of hay in the fields, since barns were few, anchoring them with stones to the ground.

At such times the kitchen of Woodfield became the scene of patriotic discussion. The elder Michael Collins would speak of O'Connell and Thomas Davis and make the children repeat the poetry of nationalism. Their uncle, Dan O'Brien, sang rebel songs. The young Michael, like his father, had no singing voice, though he loved music. His own choice was usually *Deep in Canadian Woods*. It was then, grouped in the dusk about the big open fireplace before the lamps were lit, that the tales would also be told. The bad times of the past, never far from the Irish consciousness, rose vividly before the mind's eye, as such things must when no one knows if tomorrow they may not return. His grandmother, Johanna McCarthy O'Brien, would tell of how, going to Clonakilty on a fair day in the famine times, she had seen people lying dead of starvation by the roadside, unable to complete their journey to the workhouse to beg for food.

More than a million people had died of starvation and disease in the famine years, well within the elder Michael Collins's lifetime. Over a million more had fled to America. Skibbereen, one of the worst stricken areas, lay a matter of miles west of Sam's Cross. The realization of these things was seared across the young Michael's mind, as it was across the mind of his race. With it festered the bitter knowledge that had it not been for the British Government's obduracy in clinging to inadequate economic policies, and the influence of rent-anxious landlords in the face of human misery, the blight that had overtaken the potato crop in Ireland need never have overtaken the Irish people.

Always to Islanders danger is what comes over the sea.[1] The

[1] Allen Curnow *Landfall in Unknown Seas*, quoted in *A Book of New Zealand Verse 1923–45* (Christchurch, N.Z. 1945).

Starvation of Ireland had brought indelibly home to her people that Britain lay beyond the Irish Sea. The decimation of a people is not easily forgotten by those who survive it. Nor can there be any wish to forget until its causes are eradicated.

British governments of more recent times had, indeed, tried to grapple with what they termed the Irish Question. They might have made better progress if they had not always approached it with an English answer totally at variance with that supplied by the Irish themselves.

Gladstone worked selflessly and honourably for the pacification of Ireland. Once British governments accepted direct responsibility for the relief of poverty a great deal of good work was done by the Congested Districts Board, established in 1891. Even Balfour, one of the few but distinguished men upon whom Ireland has bestowed the title of 'Bloody', was prepared, once coercion had done its work of restoring order, to bring in ameliorative measures.

Balfour applied the remedy to the wrong ill, as Irish separatists, then in a minority, realized. Though most Irishmen regarded severance from England as being impossible of attainment, even if desirable, for those who trod in the Fenian tradition it was the only solution.

There were other events besides the trauma of famine so close as to be recalled by even the young generation round the Woodfield hearth. At nine years of age Johnny had seen an eviction. A battering ram was used to level the mud-walled home of the expelled tenant. The family had stood there bewildered, the children shivering in the raw November afternoon, the man sullen and afraid to show any fight.

Perhaps he should have fought. They remembered the Plan of Campaign and its influence on the passing of the Land Act of 1887. 'Britain never gave a thing without violence being shown first' was the conclusion drawn by Michael Collins's elders. If proof was wanted it came not long after. A man was evicted as he lay on his deathbed, and one of his sons in a fury put a pitchfork through the agent's eye. It was the last eviction in the district.

Michael had his own reason for disliking agents. On the day of his own death he was to recall how, his father being ill, he had been sent to pay the rent, £4 6s. 8d. On the way he saw, and passionately longed for, a football in a shop window for one shilling. Perhaps the agent would give back a shilling discount for prompt payment, as had very occasionally happened. But the man took the whole sum with a sharp: 'Tell your father he's a fool to trust such a small lad with so much money.' There would be no agents in Ireland once Michael could have a say in the matter.

In March 1897, when Michael was six, his father died. As he lay dying his words echoed the hope that had been handed down through years of repression and rebellions that rose slowly and were swiftly crushed: 'I shall not see Ireland free, but in my children's time it will come, please God.'

III

Before Michael was five he began to go to school at Lisavaird, about two miles from Woodfield. Denis Lyons was to prove as influential in moulding his capabilities in class as his father was in his home environment. At Lisavaird the boy received the grounding without which he might well never have developed the will to learn, the impetus of which drove him forward for the rest of his days. From the first he showed his father's flair for mathematics, and the love of reading which no one living at Woodfield could well avoid inheriting.

Generally speaking, the National Schools of that day were run on the policy of weaning their pupils from any element of nationalism that might have crept into their early upbringing. Fate had an eye to Michael's future when she put him in the hands of Denis Lyons. An old Fenian like Michael's father, he not only believed in that organization's policy of separation, to be achieved if necessary by physical force, but proclaimed his belief. There must have been an extraordinary presence and determination about the man, for he was never replaced by anyone considered more doctrinally sound by the authorities.

All his life Michael was to cling lovingly to the turns of speech of his own country people, so that they remained as vital a part of him as the soft, intensely expressive Cork accent which no length of exile ever stole from him.

Yet one subject that was not taught in school was Irish. Though an ever-growing number of enthusiastic students all over the country flocked to the Gaelic League's classes in Irish it remained a closed book to the Collins children and this despite their own parents' proficiency in the language. The truth was that for their father the speaking of Irish remained, as it had been in his youth, synonymous with poverty, showing a lack of the desire to aspire to independence, though this aspiration was in fact eventually to become the avowed purpose of the Gaelic League. As yet it remained a strictly non-political organization : perhaps another reason for the old Fenian's indifference to it.

As Michael grew he began to excel in outdoor activities, especially those which aroused his competitive instincts. On the way home from school he would practise with his cousins the illegal but widely condoned sport of bowling. He always used the heavier, 8-ounce ball, insisting that it would develop his muscles better for the day when he was big enough to use the full 16-ounce weight. His great ambition was to be a champion bowler.

Football, jumping, wrestling, and particularly running and hurling later became his favourites. With his muscles he also developed the spectacular, lightning-flash temper to arouse which was the delight and terror of his friends and which, coupled with his aggressive, half-teasing manner, was to make him many enemies.

Her husband's death left Mary Anne Collins to manage Woodfield alone. The old home, too small for such a large family, dissatisfied her, and she set about having a new house built beside it, and laid out a flower garden. The house was finished about the turn of the century. Michael's room looked out between hills and trees to Knockfeen, northward from the stream below. Its only decorations were books and a verse, carefully framed in passe-partout, entitled *Moonlight in my Prison Cell*. He disliked over-ornamentation.

Michael took his share of the farm work. He rode with more balancing ability than finesse, galloping about on the white mare, Gypsy, and driving his mother and sisters in the trap. In the evenings he would escort his grandmother back to her home by Sam's Cross, listening to her with the solemn attention he would always give to old people. Independent to a degree, he responded to firm discipline, transferring something of the reverence he had shown for his father to his brother Johnny, twelve years his senior, doing his bidding without question.

The family was beginning to go its inevitably separate ways. More fortunate than many, the Collinses lost only one son, Patrick, to America. He left early in the new century, never to return. Each departure was another wrench at the fabric of the life Michael loved so passionately that he might almost have known how short a time he himself was to spend at Woodfield. When Helena left to join a convent in England her last sight was of Michael running after her as far as he could down the road, waving and waving until she was gone.

His affection for his family extended to all living things on the farm. That strongly protective impulse which was later to inspire the implicit trust of fighting men is apparent in the child. He kept hidden from even his closest companions the birds' nests he had found, lest they might disturb or steal the eggs. Only to Hannie, home on holiday, he showed the nests, empty now. 'Every one of them has flown away and the world is full of small birdeens', he said triumphantly.

The house was filled with books as the old one, now used as a farm building, had been. Michael embarked upon Lamb's *Tales*, duly succeeded by Shakespeare proper; poetry was always to remain his special love. His catholic taste ranged widely from the English classics to the stirring and usually sentimental ballads of the minor Irish writers of his day. Fiction of every description engrossed him. A favourite novel was *The Mill on the Floss*. He once confided to Katie, the close companion of these early years : 'We're like Tom and Maggie Tulliver.' When she protested that he could never be cruel like Tom he admitted, after a pause, 'I could be worse.' Perhaps he was already sensing within himself the ruthlessness which, though it was devoid of cruelty, the events of his adult life were to call forth.

The patriotic writers of Ireland's past supplied a deeper part of his reading : tales of Tone and Emmet and the novels of Kickham, which drew angry tears. Thomas Davis he not only read but studied. Davis, more than any other writer, was to influence his future conception of Ireland's course. If he was to follow where Arthur Griffith led it was because, in common with Griffith, his early guide had been Davis. Davis 'preached education, knowledge, toleration, unity, self-reliance, all fused by love of country . . . including and uniting every race and every class and every creed'[2] : and Michael Collins heard.

In adolescence he would go for long walks through the soft green and purple countryside, brooding, we may surmise, on that most ancient and compelling of causes, the matter of Ireland; passing the grazing cattle in the swampy, lush fields, and often climbing on, up the hills that surrounded his home valleys. At such times, alone under the racing, rain-swept sky, the silence broken only by an occasional curlew's cry, itself a traditional reminder of secret gatherings by night, of pikes and skirmishes, there must have grown in him that awareness of racial destiny which comes only with long thinking close to its native earth.

These days of his awakening sense of nationalism were a time when the processes of revolution were already beginning to stir, though to outward appearances it might seem that the very opposite was the case.

The preliminary symptoms of revolution, we are told,[3] include: economic incentive, the transfer of the allegiance of the intellectuals, and what the French writer, Sorel, called 'the social myth' and which in Ireland's case may best be summed up as the vision of Old Ireland Free. The conditions for revolt were to come, not in an Ireland so crushed by repression as to be too weak to rise, but where that first symptom, economic incentive, had now appeared.

Balfour's first Land Act of 1887 had been followed by others designed progressively to enable tenant farmers to purchase their holdings. Both the rural and urban populations were able, as never before, to lift their heads and look about them. The conditions they had existed under hitherto now appeared intolerable. Could not still better things be expected? As the pressure from above was lifted the hopes of the formerly repressed began to rise.

[2] P. S. O'Hegarty *A History of Ireland Under the Union 1801–1922* (London 1952) pp.220 and 221

[3] Lyford P. Edwards *The Natural History of Revolution* (Chicago 1927)

Left to itself, this stirring to life might never have found the tongue to speak and be heard had not that other, all-important symptom of things to come, the support of the intellectuals, rallied to its aid.

What D. P. Moran in the *Leader* was doing for industry, and Sir Horace Plunkett, with the enthusiastic if erratic help of George Russell ('AE'), was doing for agriculture, Yeats and his fellow-organizers of the Irish Literary Theatre now achieved in the cultural sphere. Defining the Abbey Theatre movement as 'a return to the people', Yeats brought the voice of nationalism to a society anglicized to the point of boredom. The Gaelic League fired people of widely-varying interests with a kindred enthusiasm. The Gaelic Athletic Association, formed before any of them, continued increasingly to make the playing fields of Ireland the venue for the expression of solely nationalistic energy.

As de Tocqueville had observed, a bad government's most dangerous moment comes when it studies to reform. In addition, however, to the incentives to eventual revolution which the policy of 'killing Home Rule by kindness' engendered, there were what might be termed 'irritants' : the running sore of emigration and, above all, the continued refusal to grant Home Rule on any terms; acting as goads to remind Ireland that she still stood very far below the summit of her aspirations.

From Lisavaird Michael had passed on to Clonakilty National School. Already it was apparent that thoughts of Ireland's political future were activating his mind. He had weighed up the policies of both the Irish Nationalist Party and Arthur Griffith and come down heavily in favour of Griffith.[4] No doubt he was influenced by the more mature judgements of those about him who, like Griffith himself, had no faith in those leaders who had deserted Parnell and, by the ensuing split, weakened the Nationalist Party at Westminster.

Whoever may have influenced Michael, it is interesting to see that he had already, in advance of all but a handful of his countrymen, chosen his leader, and this at a time when the Irish Party, reunified and given, for the time being, a new lease of life, was entering upon its final years of domination of Irish politics.

[4] Rex Taylor *Michael Collins* (London 1958) p. 43

The cause of nationalism, however, had no part in Mary Anne Collins's consideration of how Michael should earn his living in the future. She was in poor health and anxious to see him settled. 'He is head of his class and I am afraid he will get into mischief', she told one of his sisters. The master at Clonakilty, Mr John Crowley, had a wide reputation for preparing successful candidates for the British Civil Service examinations. His mother determined that Michael should follow Hannie to the Post Office Savings Bank in London. Accordingly he began studying for the examinations that would qualify him for a Post Office Boy Clerkship. Indeed there seemed little choice. For a promising boy of his class at that time the only alternatives to the civil service were the Royal Irish Constabulary (R.I.C.) or emigration to America.

In Clonakilty Michael lodged by the week with his eldest sister, Margaret O'Driscoll. On Saturday mornings he would be off over the four miles of country roads that rise and fall gently westwards, turning off by the small Curragh Lough and so down beside the fields to the thatched white cottages of Sam's Cross and home to Woodfield.

At fourteen years of age he had his first bicycle, a means of transport on which he would one day conduct a war. With Katie he would go to such favourite haunts as Castlefreke or the Red Strand on the indented, up-and-down coastline of West Cork where cliffs give way to fields that carry the harvest right down to the edge of the sea.

He spent most of his holidays with his boon companion, Sean Hurley. They stayed in each other's homes, wrestling, helping with farm work, or discussing the tireless subject, Ireland's freedom. The general feeling in the country was, as always, that it would be a long time coming. Michael was less pessimistic. Passing the home of a formerly prominent evicting landlord he once cried to his disbelieving cousin : 'When I'm a man we'll have him and his kind out of Ireland!'

When he was fifteen he passed his Post Office entrance, and in July 1906 left Sam's Cross for the first time in his life to take up a position as a Temporary Boy Clerk in the West Kensington Post Office where Hannie had already been for some years.

He went at a time when a milestone in Ireland's history had

just been reached. For years Ireland's political voice had not been that of her most vital political thought. The Irish independence movement had lacked a political framework on which to build its challenge to the stagnating Irish Party.

In 1905 Arthur Griffith founded Sinn Fein (We Ourselves).

CHAPTER TWO

London

(1906–1915)

I

For the next nine and a half years Michael was to live with Hannie in West Kensington at 5 Netherwood Road. For the first four of them he was employed, like her, in the Post Office Savings Bank. Like any other lad of his age he drank in all that he saw of London, for he had the imagination which sees history as the actions of men and women living through the everyday struggles of existence, often unaware of their import. He was never to lose the sense that he too was living in history.

His circumstances were hardly propitious. For someone with so pronounced a sense of destiny an immense self-confidence was needed if the prospects of a Temporary Boy Clerk in a Post Office were not to point implacably to nothing better than the next desk up. He knew it was not his world : it was nevertheless the real world for the time being. Some intimation that to cease driving himself now would be to lose the impetus for greater things made him knuckle down to the work before him and learn all that he could while waiting for the right hour to bring him to the right task.

He had been only six months in London when his mother's health worsened, and in March 1907 she died. If her influence upon him remains less clear-cut for us than that of others, many of the qualities that were to become manifest in him can be traced back to Mary Anne Collins : a great kindness towards all in need; and a tolerance of outlook which overrode the then still potent barriers of creed in favour of Christian charity so that on the night of her death it was her Protestant neighbours who came to her bedside, and many more to her funeral.

In Hannie, now his counsellor and confidant, another influence was shaping Michael. For many Irish lads the leaving of Ireland meant also the leaving of a way of life in which family ties were strong and restrictive. Casually drifting about the widely-flung areas of Irish London they suffered an Irish Sea-change; reacting, if usually only in adolescence, into a hard-drinking, anti-clerical antithesis of what life at home had been.

Hannie ensured that Michael was not flung headlong into the potent influences of this section of the London-Irish colony. She could not save him altogether from anti-clericalism. It caught him like a bad attack of measles, but without the complication of atheism. In time he would return, having made his own reassessment, to the things he had been taught to value. Now, however, the absence, generally speaking, of clerical support for Ireland's national struggle in the past was a weighty accusation against the Church in Michael's eyes. He addressed a paper on the Catholic priesthood's part in Irish history to a startled Sinn Fein branch meeting, which is said to have concluded with the words 'Exterminate them!'[1]

He drew to him many friends, most of them the Irish denizens of the Savings Bank, and these learnt early that his was a friendship to rely upon. No length of separation ever altered it. If they grew away from him in years of changed interests and environment he was the first to try to regain the old footing, the one to be hurt by failure to do so. It was no one's fault; human relationships cannot be made immutable with the best will in the world, but because his own loyalty was an invariable he brought to every such alteration over the years the terrible vulnerability of a child.

The young Irishmen who met him in these days were struck by one outstanding trait: his Cork clannishness. If they hailed from Cork his devotion to them knew no bounds. If they did not, he hardly went so far as to tell them it was their own fault, but at the same time they were made to understand that they could scarcely claim to be proper Irishmen.

His generosity was resplendent. 'The most unselfish man I ever knew' has often been said of him. One had only to submit to his essentially predominating rôle in friendship – and those who did not found him intensely unlikeable – to discover that one had gained a fully paid up insurance against all kinds of hardship.

[1] Desmond Ryan *Remembering Sion* (London 1934) p. 235

Michael was now attending evening classes at King's College, working for Civil Service examinations in Customs and Excise. His essays reveal him battling to clothe his ideas in phrases after his masters, Addison, Goldsmith, and Locke.

Did Napoleon as a boy ever chew his pen and write on the future of Europe? Michael Collins turned a boyish eye on the British Empire. He would have been astounded had he foreseen what he was to write on the same subject little more than a decade later, for his vision of the Empire then showed him only an expanse of forcibly acquired territories, held in the military subjection that enabled their affairs to be mismanaged. It is an understandable view, for to him the British Empire was Ireland. His conclusion was a shout of defiance after Parnell: 'Every country has a right to work out its own destiny in accordance with the laws of its being. . . . The first law of nations is self-preservation, and let England be wise and not neglect it. . . .'[2]

His tutor can hardly have foreseen the day when his pupil would find a more effective means of writing the argument than with his pen, and would take it from the lowest means of entry to the Board of Trade to Downing Street itself.

Formal schooldays had been over at fifteen, but the craving for knowledge would never be slaked. He carried with him a small brown notebook in which he jotted down facts and figures in whatever haphazard juxtaposition he had snatched them from their widely varied sources: geometrical calculations, observations on the Plateau of Iran, biographical details of such Irishmen as O'Connell and Parnell.

In London he began what had until now been denied him, the study of the Irish language. In the pages of O'Growney and Dinneen he entered a world strange yet hearteningly familiar. Words, at first sight unknown, transformed themselves miraculously into well-loved expressions gleaned in childhood as he played near the farm workers in the stubble fields at Sam's Cross. This half-recollected tongue of his race divulged to him something of the indefinable thing which could be summed up, though never fully comprehended, as love of country; which for him also meant love of his origins, in which lay his understanding of himself.

[2] National Library of Ireland MS 13329

Under Hannie's encouraging eye he ranged widely through English literature : Scott and Dickens of the great novelists, and among writers of his own time Chesterton, Arnold Bennett, and H. G. Wells. He read the Talbot Press editions of the Abbey Theatre plays, which he would later see performed whenever possible. He read and saw the plays of J. M. Barrie, but his first love in the theatre was Shaw, and he copied extracts from *The Man of Destiny* to place in his wallet.

It was an exuberant necessity of his nature to be forever on the rampage, wrestling, throwing his weight about, or, failing any other outlet for his teeming brain which needed as prodigious an amount of exercise as his body, lighting upon impulsive, frequently destructive, practical jokes for which he would be penitent when it was too late. At home, where the necessity to push the claims of Michael Collins the leader of men could be hung up with his hat – when he bothered to wear one – the tornado would abate, and he would settle down to Swinburne or Yeats, or, one of his favourites, Padraig Colum's *Wild Earth*. There was little money for books, but a Carnegie Library was nearby and he went through it avidly, if still without discrimination.

When his brother Patrick sent money from America at Christmas he bought Whitman's *Leaves of Grass*. It stirred him profoundly, and he marked such passages as :

> I exist as I am, that is enough,
> If no other in the world be aware I sit content,
> And if each and all be aware I sit content

and wrote in pencil at the end of the book a quotation from Colonel Robert Ingersoll (whose views on religion may, incidentally, have influenced his own at this time) : 'This book was and is the true transcript of a soul.'

He never chafed at these evenings spent at home. One of the tragedies of his later years was to be that, devoted to home and family life, he would have neither, a visitor always at others' firesides.

One thing Hannie did for him was the negation of all the Irish nationalist influences then at work upon him. She took him into the homes of her English friends, who became his friends. Irish London emphasized above all else the need to eliminate all that was English if Ireland was to regain her independence and native way of life. Hannie saw to it that Michael at least understood the English. When war came he would fight ruthlessly, in hatred of the bigotry and indifference that lay behind the ancient quarrel; but he would fight without hatred of the English people who he knew possessed other qualities than these.

His nationalism, like everything else about him, was extreme, but he knew that he could achieve nothing alone. The weakness of Ireland's bids for freedom in the past had lain in the lack of a unity of purpose in her people. Now, wherever he found a group formed whose aim was to build up that strength of purpose among the ordinary people of Ireland, he joined it.

A born athlete, he joined the Gaelic Athletic Association soon after his arrival in London. His club was the Geraldines, and he played in its hurling team, usually in mid-field or back. A member of a rival team, Ned Lynch, remembers him as an effective though not particularly polished player, a good sportsman as long as the game was fair, but liable to fly into a temper if he suspected foul play. On the hurling field, as elsewhere, he liked things to go his way. This trait was not a universally endearing one, as evidenced by the keen competition he faced when, at seventeen, he was elected Hurling Vice Captain. Once on the committee, however, he stayed there, becoming a delegate to the London County Board of the G.A.A. in January 1909.

These were days of controversy, when the question of whether other than Gaelic sports should be allowed on the playing field became a fierce issue, Michael naturally taking up his position on the furthest ditch. It was about this time that he was elected to the secretaryship of the club which he was to hold for the rest of his time in London. His first half-yearly report was a trenchant one, for the Geraldines were undergoing one of their less happy periods.

'Our internal troubles were saddening, but our efforts in football and hurling were perfectly heartbreaking. . . . In conclusion I can only say that our record for the past half-year leaves no scope for self-congratulation. Signs of decay are unmistakable, and if members are not prepared in the future to act more harmoniously together and more self-sacrificingly generally – the club will soon have faded into an inglorious and well-deserved oblivion.'[3]

In July once more : 'The Secretary read his report. It was not flattering to the members.' The Collins of the future was already finding his form. He was also, it seems, attracting something of that extraordinarily magnetized devotion which he was later to inspire. The report was adopted on this occasion 'after the exhibition of marked enthusiasm by a few members'.

Running and jumping in sports held under G.A.A. auspices were the activities at which he excelled, in Ireland as well as in London. All his holidays were spent at Woodfield. Johnny had married Katty Hurley, the sister of Michael's great friend Sean, and home remained for him a place of comfort where he could enjoy the company of small children, to whom he was unashamedly devoted.

Gathered with old friends in the evenings he would exchange with them the long thoughts of days spent in the fields, regaining in their down-to-earth discussion of affairs, which ranged far beyond the immediate horizons of Sam's Cross, the straightforward reasoning which the frantic commerce of London had enervated.

The changes which had begun in the years before he left Ireland were now more marked. The Land Act of 1903 had brought a greater measure of self-sufficiency to tenant landholders than any of its predecessors. This much at least George Wyndham, perhaps the only Chief Secretary who gave his whole heart to Ireland, had been able to leave her as his memorial. Under the annuity system of payments Woodfield was at last coming under Collins ownership in law as well as of right. More than half a century later John Collins was to recall the relaxed well-being of those days when a new pride of possession invigorated every Irish farmer.

At evening gatherings in neighbouring farmhouses or in his cousin Jerry Collins's little pub, the Five Alls, at Sam's Cross,

[3] National Library of Ireland MS 13329

Michael could always be relied upon to round off the night's entertainment with a rousing recitation of *Kelly and Burke and Shea* :

> 'I wish 'twas in Ireland, for there's the place,'
> Said Burke, 'that we'd die by right,
> In the cradle of our soldier race,
> After one good stand-up fight.'[4]

Broad-shouldered, alert of eye, his head thrown back except when the chin jutted forward in a quick downward thrust of emphasis, he would give it to them in the rich West Cork accent that had a ringing conviction compellingly his own.

The need to earn his living took him back to London. The call to 'one good stand-up fight' in Ireland was not yet. Until it should come – and at times he must have wondered, as past generations had done, if it would indeed come in his lifetime – he did not confine himself to rendering patriotic verse. Ireland must at all costs be rid of the British administration : she must also have a native system ready to replace it. Michael recognized in Sinn Fein a similarly pragmatic approach to the achievement of his own ideals. He joined the movement soon after his arrival in London. The manœuvrings of politics as such he would always view with impatient antipathy. The economics behind them were his paramount concern.

II

'If the eyes of the Irish Nation are continually focused on England, they will inevitably acquire a squint', wrote Griffith in the first issue of the *United Irishman*. In Sinn Fein he founded a movement which should bring the centre of focus back to Ireland.

The resurgent nationalism had been brought into one broad stream, the various bodies which it had comprised being amalgamated with Sinn Fein, whose name they officially took in 1908; to what channel its policy could be most effectively committed remained uncertain. Physical force was impracticable even if the

[4] The full text of the poem, by J. I. C. Clarke, may be found in Frank O'Connor (ed.) *A Book of Ireland* (London 1959)

separatist element in Ireland which advocated it could have counted on more than fractional support. Imperial Parliamentarianism Griffith saw as a mildewed growth, barren of results. He looked to European history for a parallel to Ireland's predicament and in 1904 published his pamphlet, *The Resurrection of Hungary*, in which he traced that country's successful struggle for independence under a dual-monarchy. Here was a path Ireland might follow.

The first step must be to gain administrative control on Irish soil at local government level and stimulate a consciousness of nationality as the starting points for ultimate independence. Sinn Fein made its first parliamentary challenge in 1907 in the North Leitrim by-election.

Michael Collins viewed the struggle with enthusiasm. He wrote in his notebook, apparently at a Sinn Fein meeting: 'That 5 shillings be sent (for the N. Leitrim fight) from the funds of the Branch and 5s more raised here tonight by the members'. That his enthusiasm was shared by his fellow members is apparent from the addition of the laconic statement: 'Done. £2'.

North Leitrim was lost, but Sinn Fein polled one third of the votes.

Michael's enthusiasm for the extreme of every national cause was not universally applauded. It was overlarded with an adolescent bombast which nettled the older men and those of a more sober temperament. He was the young cub who scoffs at the old wolf's caution; the junior who tells the oldest member just what is wrong with the club. He laced his remarks with language more suited to the docks than the drawing-room. He never outgrew this schoolboy accomplishment, but swore with a rich splendour and variety of expletive, yet always, unless he were really in a fury, with a lift to the corner of the mouth and a light of devilry in the eye that turned the oaths almost to caresses.

While this wild colt behaviour made him an unmitigated affliction to more staid men, others saw in it the promise of leadership and an underlying grasp of affairs which time would develop and control. He was a frequent visitor at the home of the great nationalist, Dr Mark Ryan, whose 'sunny blend of Gaelic qualities', as W. P. Ryan wrote of him, influenced so much of young Ireland in London. Sam Maguire, that stalwart Post

Office man whose convictions were always expressed in positive action, watched him also for his own purposes.

Michael continued to read anything and everything that he could lay hands on that dealt with Irish politics and economics. He kept a wallet into which he tucked newspaper cuttings: statements by Winston Churchill on Liberal intentions towards Ireland, and others by Redmond on the Irish Party's intentions at Westminster. He carried leaflets setting out the objects of Sinn Fein, articles by Griffith, and extracts from R. Barry O'Brien's *Life of Parnell*. Parnell had never overestimated the effective action that could be carried out at Westminster. Michael copied Parnell's words as they might have been his own: 'We must show them that Ireland supports us and defies their House', and again, 'If we had not the people behind us we could do nothing'.

At home he seemed forever immersed in statistics. In his notebook he wrote the depressing figures of Irish emigration – nearly 50,000 in the first ten months of 1906, over 60,000 for the same period in the following year. How could Ireland hope to regain her national way of life, let alone her independence, while this remorseless drain on her youth and labour force was allowed to continue, the ebbtide of potential prosperity? Constitutional methods were those of a long-term policy; Sinn Fein admitted it. Yet was there any reason why its aims should not be hastened by the time-honoured methods of the past, those of Tone and Emmet, advocated more recently by Denis Lyons and his own father?

His dedication to Irish ideals, his enthusiasm, intelligence, and obvious integrity had brought him to the notice of another organization which lay behind every national movement in Ireland. In November 1909 Sam Maguire swore him into the Irish Republican Brotherhood.

The oft-repeated conclusion drawn at the Woodfield hearth that 'Britain never gave a thing without violence being shown first' echoed that of Parnell: 'I have long ceased to believe that anything but force of arms will ever bring about the redemption of Ireland.'

Long before Parnell the same belief had brought about the formation of the Irish Republican Brotherhood, a secret, oath-bound society, pledged to achieve Ireland's independence by physical force. The greatest and least sectarian of a long succession of secret societies, it had been founded in Dublin in 1858 and maintained with intermittent financial help from America where the Fenian movement, from which it took its own more familiar title, had been organized.

Contrary to the widespread impression that the Fenians were an unscrupulous and bloodthirsty band given to shooting policemen without provocation, membership of the I.R.B. was in fact as exclusive as that of the Knights of the Round Table, or the Red Branch warriors of Irish legend. Its members, as its Constitution (1914) makes clear, might only include 'every Irishman, irrespective of class or creed, whose character for patriotism, truth, valour, sobriety, and obedience to superior officers can bear scrutiny. . . .'[5] They were drawn from the small farmer and labouring classes in the country and the shop assistants and working people of the towns.[6]

The first rising organized by the I.R.B. in 1867 had failed. Since then it had been behind every other movement in Ireland that either shared its separatist ideals or had objectives which would favour Irish independence. It lacked, however, the necessary vitality that must come from the top if any organization is to succeed.

In 1908 Thomas Clarke, one of the most active Fenians before his imprisonment for fifteen years, returned from America. Under his influence the tenuously strung links of the I.R.B. were drawn together anew. The Organization, as it was known by its members, was at this stage of dawning revival when Michael Collins joined it.

In 1911 a youthful element, with Sean MacDiarmada foremost among them, rallied behind the symbolic leadership of Tom Clarke and gained control of the Supreme Council of the I.R.B. Henceforward the organization's aim was no longer to be merely support for other national movements, but to gain their direction so that it should become the spearhead of the resistance to England which diffusion of endeavour had weakened in the past.

The limitations which face all underground movements ine-

[5] National Library of Ireland, Ministry of Defence Archives
[6] O'Hegarty *Ireland Under the Union* p. 445

vitably hampered its progress. There is a limit to the effective military activity that can be carried out in secret, and this was particularly true of Ireland, where the police traditionally formed a highly effective intelligence network and the mass movement of men in country areas was as hard to conceal as the rising of the moon.

This problem was solved in an unexpected quarter. The answer came, as it had done in the days of Wolfe Tone and the United Irishmen, from Belfast.

Sinn Fein at this time had entered the doldrums. Unable to make effective headway with its economic programme, lacking funds to sustain its propagandist paper which would have kept it, at least in part, in the public eye, its heaviest blow came in 1910 when the Irish Party which it had hoped to oust, and to which it had once seemed a potential menace, regained its balancing position in the saddle of British politics and brought the Liberals again to that Becher's Brook of their fortunes, the question of Home Rule. Yet the Irish Party's aims were moderate. To throw the Empire into convulsions was no part of its plan, but merely to set the Irish house in order within the bounds of Empire.

Asquith was to introduce his Home Rule Bill in 1912. Though it now appears a damp squib indeed to have set off such a train of explosives, Redmond, the leader of the Irish Party, in the name of nationalist Ireland, called it a full and final settlement of Irish claims. In North-East Ulster its fullness and finality were also so apparent that over 219,000 men covenanted to oppose it under the leadership of Sir Edward Carson. At the end of 1912 the Ulster Volunteers were formed to withstand, with force of arms if need be, its entry onto the Statute Book.

Where an independent parliament for Ireland had once been won by the raising of an armed force of volunteers, Carson proposed to prevent it. He had no illusions : 'The Volunteers are illegal and the Government know they are illegal, and the Government dare not interfere with them. . . . Don't be afraid of illegalities.'[7]

His advice was taken in Dublin : the I.R.B. moved.

In November 1913 the Irish Volunteers were inaugurated,

[7] Speech at Newry, 7 September, 1913. Quoted in Dorothy Macardle *The Irish Republic* 4th edition (Dublin 1951) pp. 89–90

with Eoin MacNeill, Professor of Early Irish History at University College, Dublin, as their originator and titular head. Behind him, though he did not know it, stood the I.R.B. Now it had an open military organization with which to press towards an independent Ireland. A government that had allowed the Ulster Volunteers to organize and shake a defiant fist under its nose could hardly object to the formation of a similar body in the South to uphold its own Act of Parliament.

Because their separatist foundations were unperceived the Irish Volunteers were allowed to stand. North-East Ulster had armed her Volunteers extensively, with the connivance of the authorities. It was a different matter in the South. On 26 July 1914 Erskine Childers sailed his yacht *Asgard* into Howth harbour with a cargo of 900 Mauser rifles and ammunition. The Irish Volunteers were waiting. They were met by the police with military support on their return journey. The marching Volunteers, after a scuffle and the loss of a few rifles, carried the gun-running to a successful conclusion, but the Dublin populace who had crowded Bachelor's Walk to see what was afoot, was less fortunate. Stones were thrown and the troops opened fire, killing and wounding some of the crowd.

The first rounds had been fired in a struggle that was to continue with increasing horror for another seven years.

Michael Collins became an Irish Volunteer in No. 1 Company, London, on 25 April 1914. He was enrolled by Sean Hurley, and at once began the weekly contributions that would one day make him the owner of a rifle. Drilling was carried out in the German gymnasium at King's Cross, where he manœuvred in company with Padraig O Conaire the writer, their weapons sawn-off Martini-Henry rifles which they hired.

In June Asquith moved the partition of Ireland. It was designed as the only possible solution to an intolerable situation that would otherwise have resulted in civil war in Ireland. Yet that situation was of Asquith's own making. His refusal to move promptly at the first defiance from Belfast nearly three years before had now brought Ireland to this near impasse.

The crisis was to pale for the moment, swallowed up in a greater one. As Erskine Childers sailed on his way to Howth he passed through the Spithead Review. For a brief moment both

the vital issues which were to be England's preoccupation in the
coming years came together unnoticed. *Asgard* was to sail on
with the guns for Ireland's renewed fight for independence. The
fleet was to sail to Scapa Flow, ordered there by Churchill in
preparation for the struggle that was soon to engulf large independent nations and small subject ones alike.

Soon after war was declared the Home Rule Act came onto
the Statute Book, its operation suspended while hostilities should
last. Carson refused to commit one Ulster Volunteer to the conflict until they might march under their own banner of the
Red Hand; Redmond, however, pledged the South to defend
Ireland in support of England. He did so without reference to the
Irish Volunteers, of whom he had gained partial control.

By this gesture, more gallant than strategic, he offered to England as a token of his faith in her intentions what it was not his to
give – Ireland's allegiance. In so doing he lost Home Rule, the
last chance of a peaceful settlement, his never very decisive hold
on the Volunteers, and, ultimately, the leadership of the Irish
people. In the race for the freedom of small nations Ireland was
already officially out of the running.

It was a time of high emotion. Even so, the House of Commons
caught its breath and was moved where it had not expected to
be moved. From Ireland, where it had most feared trouble, it
was apparently being offered a gentleman's agreement, something
England had never tried to make with Ireland before. It caused
Sir Edward Grey to see in the dark days ahead that 'the one
bright spot is Ireland'. He did not recognize it for what it was,
the brightness of red sky at dawning.

III

In April 1910 Michael had left the Post Office, taking a clerical
job with the stockbroking firm of Horne & Co. in Moorgate,
where he was in charge of messengers. Soon after the outbreak of
war he changed his job again, becoming a Labour Exchange
clerk in Whitehall at £70 a year. In his application he wrote :
'The trade I know best is the financial trade, but from study and
observation I have acquired a wider knowledge of social and

economic conditions and have specially studied the building trade and unskilled labour.'[8] He also mentioned being proficient in typewriting and the double-entry system and making trial balances. It is interesting to find that he gave his date of birth as 16 October 1889 and not 1890. Perhaps his youthful appearance demanded such redressing of the balance.

He had already met several of those who were to bear him company on the road he waited to tread. Diarmuid O'Hegarty was one. On the day war was declared Michael was in Liverpool, playing for London against Scotland in the final of the Hurling Championship of Great Britain. There at Greenwich Park he met one of the Liverpool Irish, Frank Thornton. Even then, seen in a crowd, he stood out in Thornton's eyes. If events cast their shadows before we may assume that in 1911 young Joe O'Reilly had also turned to look again when Collins first confronted him.

Another who first noticed him in these days was Peadar Kearney, author of *The Soldier's Song*, one day to win its battle-honours and become the national anthem of the Irish Republic. Kearney has described the 'tall, good-humoured boy, who gave no indication of the road before him',[9] seen for brief moments in the Shamrock Bar in Fetter Lane, mostly with his fellow Corkmen, under the kindly but restraining eye of Sam Maguire.

He had a robustness that demanded notice. Where others approached with circumspection, he was born to tease. Religious discrepancies provided an irresistible butt. He would square up to the quietly-amused Sam Maguire with 'You bloody South of Ireland Protestant!' At Irish Literary Society meetings his greeting to Robert Lynd, then writing for the *Daily News* was usually: 'And how is the non-conformist conscience today?' He was still what he was to remain, the schoolboy looking for a rise. When he got it he was delighted. On the occasions when real offence was taken he would be penitent. But he never comprehended any need to explain his contrition – or his forgiveness.

The advent of war increased his inner turmoil. To fight for England in a conflict not Ireland's was unthinkable. The good stand-up fight in Ireland was his whole desire; passive resistance would have been a toxin in his belligerent blood. If conscription

[8] Public Record Office of Ireland
[9] Seamus de Burca *The Soldier's Song* (Dublin 1957) p. 65

came, the only solution might well be America. His brother Pat in Chicago urged this course upon him : 'If you don't take a chance you will never get anywhere', he wrote early in 1915. 'A little nerve is all that's necessary.'[10]

Pat also wrote to Katie, sending her Michael's fare to the States. He foresaw trouble in Ireland – England's difficulty was notoriously Ireland's opportunity. But a warning like this was the last to persuade Michael to emigrate. He had the money returned. If there was to be trouble he would be in it. It was the first hint most of his family had of his nationalist activities.

Nevertheless he took one precautionary step. In April 1915 he found a new job with the Guaranty Trust Company of New York in its London Office. If the worst happened a transfer across the Atlantic might be possible.

In Dublin, the step that in London was more of a pipe dream than a probability had been decided upon within three weeks of the declaration of war. Asquith had used the war as an excuse for shelving the Irish problem. Why should the Irish not use it as an excuse for reviving it? Ireland would rise against England during the course of the war.

The I.R.B. took more definite steps. Its Executive placed the working out of detailed plans for a rising in the hands of a Military Council. The Gaelic League had already come under I.R.B. control; now the Brotherhood also regained that of the Irish Volunteers, though the majority, styling themselves the National Volunteers, followed Redmond and his call to join the British forces.

Michael Collins as usual brought his own forthright methods to the support of the smaller but more integrated and determined remnant of the Irish Volunteers. At a meeting in St George's Hall in Southwark the backer of a Redmondite nominee for office finished an eloquent speech with the words : 'He is a man I would go to hell and back with'. The unmistakable accent of West Cork came swiftly from the rear of the hall : 'I'd not trouble about the return portion of the ticket'.

A restless fear assailed him that opportunities of striking a blow for Ireland were being allowed to slip away unchallenged. His only chances of action were mere gestures – he was even

[10] National Library of Ireland MS 13556

reduced to pulling the needles out of Hannie's knitting for British soldiers.

By the latter part of 1915 the growing certainty of conscription became an urgent problem to those Irishmen in Britain who saw fighting for her as a betrayal of Ireland. Some slipped away to Ireland, picking up jobs where they could. Michael saw them go and drew his own conclusions. Were they merely evading combat, or going home to prepare for one as certain, about which he had been kept in the dark? He hurried over to Dublin late in 1915 and, through the I.R.B., made contact with Tom Clarke and Sean MacDiarmada. Whatever it was he heard from them sent him back to London in a very different frame of mind.

Conscription came. A few days later Michael attended a Volunteer meeting, held to discuss what should be done. Liam MacCarthy, who presided, was a London County Councillor and, as such, in no position to advise conscription evasion, but he left at least one of his hearers in no doubt. 'If you come from Clonakilty it is obvious where you must go', he said.

As yet no one outside the inner councils of the I.R.B. knew when Ireland would strike, but Michael knew now it would be soon. He resigned his job, packed his bags and caught the boat for Dublin. Despite his elation he parted from Hannie with a heavy heart. The days of preparation in London had not lacked their pleasant times; the future was dark with uncertainty.

CHAPTER THREE

The Rising

I

The Conscription Act came into force on 16 January 1916. On the previous night Michael left England. His first letter to Hannie is dated 17 January, and the brief phase of homesickness which usually afflicted him is apparent. Dublin was, after all, less familiar to him than London and he was alone. 'I have arrived safely and am looking round here for the present. . . . See J[ack] H[urley] this morning. . . . Not feeling at all happy, lonely you know.'

He quickly found his feet however, and, resisting the temptation to slip off to Woodfield, he took temporary lodgings with relatives at Inchicore and set about finding himself a job. Ten days later he wrote again to Hannie :

'I'm still in Dublin doing a very little bit. Working three days a week 10 to 4 as financial adviser to Count Plunkett for which I get lunch each day & £1 a week. . . .

'This place has many advantages over London in spite of everything. It's just lovely to see the mountains of a morning. My present job is at Kimmage far out – seems to be as remote as Woodfield but it's only a short walk & a penny tram from the Emerald pasture of College Green.'

Later he wrote :

'There are quite a few of my old associates here and life passes just so – weather rather fearsome but yesterday morning it was simply splendid to look across the river and the park from the bedroom here short lived though that splendour was and the slush afterwards was unspeakable.'

He was filled with the anticipation that pervaded those little pockets of Irish life which waited impatiently for revolution. He no longer hid his hopes of being involved in such an event and his letters, though they contained only a bare mention of 'something expected' which might turn up, returned always to his need to break all connection with the old life which might yet drag him back to face conscription. Aware that even a circular sent on might give him away he warned: 'eat them or do anything with them but don't for goodness sake send them on to this address'. Already he was learning the wisdom of having poste restante addresses here and there about the city.

He might have been living in two worlds, each reflecting the Ireland of that time. On the one hand were the relatives with whom he lodged, well-meaning, as he himself was quick to admit, and anxious to persuade him to remain with them; yet they were part of the predominantly complacent Irish life which, if it grumbled at the rising cost of living, found the living itself well enough to its liking. It preferred Baden-Powell's Boy Scouts to the Fianna boys, the nationalist youth movement now organizing so militantly under the rebel daughter of Gore-Booth, the Countess Markievicz; it cheered its sons as they went off in British uniforms to France and turned from the window when the Irish Volunteers swung past on a weekend route march.

Michael chafed at talk of joining the Army and earning an honest living. He rumpled his aunt's cushions, ate more than his share of cake, and caught 'a frightful cold since I came here – nearly pegged out in fact. . . . I still have one of those *coffs* you used to know. However while there's life there's hope!' Later he moved to new lodgings at 16 Rathdown Road.

There was nothing to depress him in his other world, however. His job at Countess Plunkett's property, Larkfield, at Kimmage brought him into one of the centres of revolutionary preparation. When the Countess went abroad Miss Geraldine Plunkett needed a clerk to attend to her mother's property accounts, and asked her brother Joseph to find someone trustworthy. Presumably it was the London I.R.B. who recommended Michael, who was duly given the job – hardly that of 'financial adviser to Count Plunkett', their father. He was not yet so self-confident that he could forbear attempts to impress.

Miss Plunkett found that although he had no experience of the particular work she now gave him, Michael handled it very efficiently. He had, she also observed, a business manner and a social manner. The business manner was very correct; the social manner was not. He had a brusqueness, due perhaps to his having spent his impressionable years in the hurly-burly of London office life instead of with more sophisticated associates. Nevertheless, abruptness masked sensitivity, and his boyish humour and eagerness to be up and at whatever came to hand aroused the interest of those who were now wholly engaged in planning the coming insurrection. Michael might well write : 'From my political point of view there is also no reason for despondency, in fact there is every excuse for satisfaction'.

Joe Plunkett recognized the potential revolutionary in the restless young man who joined them at meals, though he was surprised at what he considered Michael's ignorance of such basic principles as the need to keep spies out of the movement. London had been too much cut off from the mainstream of separatist thinking in Dublin. His ideas were revolutionary; his background was not. As a gentle hint on the subject of spies Joe Plunkett lent him Chesterton's *The Man who was Thursday*. Whatever else Michael gleaned from the bizarre doings of the Central Council of European Anarchists one interesting point may be noted : their President's belief that 'if you didn't seem to be hiding nobody hunted you out'. One can only speculate whether it was Chesterton who suggested the policy of bluff which was to save Michael so often in later days. If so, it is ironical that it should have been the cryptic Plunkett who planted the seed.

Plunkett, delicate, much-travelled, and having a taste for the strange and colourful that might have pertained to a Moorish prince, wrote 'of terrible and splendid things' – he is the only one of the poets of the Rising to have a place in the *Oxford Dictionary of Quotations*. Yet beneath the *poseur* the doer of those things was at work with a clear head and the courage of a lion. It was to be his insurrection as much as any other man's.

From the first the Rising had been conceived only as a gesture, a blood sacrifice to startle Irishmen from their apathy. If arms from abroad were forthcoming, it might result in a *coup d'état*; if they were not, the gesture would have been made and, as those who planned it believed, not in vain.

Devoted as he was to Joseph Plunkett, whose health deteriorated steadily as 1916 passed into spring, Michael was to claim two other men as his masters in insurrection. One of them was Sean MacDiarmada; the other, Tom Clarke, he saw as master of all.

Tom Clarke had upheld the young men of the I.R.B. in their struggle for power against his own contemporaries who saw in-action as discretion. He continued to guide and encourage, a kindly, bespectacled, grey-moustached man who gave more away in emboldening philosophy than he sold in tobacco or newspapers in his busy little shop in Great Britain Street. Dublin Castle, stronghold of the British administration, deeply suspicious, yet lulled by a belief in the ineffectiveness of the Irish Volunteers, saw his shop merely as the centre of a potentially dangerous spider's web, with the slight, drooping figure of Tom Clarke spinning endless treasonable sedition.

Sean MacDiarmada was a man on fire, who kindled all those who came near his radiance. His dark eyes burn even in photo-graphs. No set-back daunted him. He had taken the lion's share of the work for Sinn Fein in the lost Leitrim election, and the painstaking labour of reviving the I.R.B. had been his also, though it cost him his health and left him a cripple. He was gay, generous, gentle, dedicated, and tireless, and if he had any faults they have not been recorded. Barely thirty, he was leader to all the young men who waited about Dublin for the 'some-thing expected' to turn up. It was MacDiarmada who won Michael's deepest love and who seems to have introduced him to most of those whom he met at this time, at the Keating Branch of the Gaelic League or in pubs in Lower Abbey Street or along the quays. MacDiarmada too might have been spinning a web of enchantment to bind those who he foresaw would take over the struggle when he was gone.

At the Keating Branch Michael's closest companions were, inevitably, his fellow Corkmen, Gearoid O'Sullivan and Diar-muid O'Hegarty, though he met a hundred others. A scarcely less active centre was Larkfield.

Late in 1915 it had been decided to transfer the Liverpool company of the Irish Volunteers to Dublin as a body, since any individual return to their own homes would only result in the local R.I.C. swooping on them as evaders under the Conscription Act. In mid-January the drift to Dublin in twos and threes began.

Larkfield was used by the 4th Battalion of the Volunteers as their headquarters and drill ground. They were now joined not only by the 'Liverpool Lambs' but also by others from London, Manchester, and Glasgow.

The chief activity at Larkfield, apart from intensive drilling and rifle practice, was the making of munitions, though bayonets and even pikes were also manufactured. Dr Thomas Dillon became the Volunteers' adviser on explosives and hand grenades and bombs made in biscuit tins. To him came Michael, who was an enthusiastic extern member of the Kimmage garrison, bringing for inspection samples of munitions made in their spare time by Dublin factory workers. A balance of 6s. 3d. still stands to Michael's credit on a ledger sheet of a firm of Dublin ironfounders from whom, a week before the Rising, he purchased two dozen 'washers' – in reality iron castings for use in making munitions.[1]

On 23 February Michael took a temporary job with the firm of chartered accountants, Craig, Gardner & Co., in Dame Street. Jobs were not easy to come by. When Ned Lynch, now back from London and living in Clare, wrote to ask Michael if there was any prospect of work in Dublin, his reply was short and to the point : 'If you can get enough to eat at home, stay put.' At Kimmage he was regarded with some envy since he was earning thirty shillings a week.

Office hours cramped his superabundant energies, and on arrival at the camp he might well wade into the first man he met and start a wrestling match. Mostly he made friends, some of them visitors to the camp like himself. Padraig O'Keeffe, Sinn Fein's imperishable General Secretary in the days ahead, met him here, bearing bundles of old clothes for the more destitute members of the garrison. Colm O Lochlainn encountered him too, though at first he was unaware of Collins's identity, for Joe Plunkett introduced the young Corkman by a grandiloquent Spanish name of his own devising. Another whom he met and came to know well in these weeks before the Rising was Rory O'Connor.

O'Connor was a Home Ruler at this time. He did not join the Volunteers, but helped Dr Dillon in his fine-chemicals venture

[1] National Museum of Ireland

at Larkfield, and stayed to assist with Volunteer activities when the camp swung into commission.

O'Connor was a cultured, musical young man, saturnine in appearance until one caught the gleam of humour, thin-cheeked, light of build. He and Collins soon became close friends. O'Connor's devotion to Collins, indeed, was such that he declared there was no one at Kimmage to equal him. Their different make-ups were to prove an explosive mixture for a close friendship. O'Connor was a highly sensitive man, unable to admit faults in what he saw as the ideal of himself. Collins, younger, and capable of far greater mental development, had an abruptness in dismissing ideas he had outworn that left the impression, however erroneous, of contempt for those who still clung to them. In too many ways Collins laid himself open to misunderstanding.

II

Holy Week came. All over the country the Volunteers were in a state of battle alert after weeks of drilling, route marches, and tactical exercises. To all appearances they were a united force, lacking only any intention of moving and an adequate supply of arms.

Only the Military Council of the I.R.B. and the Clan na Gael leaders in America knew that the appearance of purposeless activity was an illusion. Insurrection was to begin on Easter Sunday, 23 April 1916.

In February the Chief Secretary of Ireland, Augustine Birrell, had told Sir John French that he did not expect a 'rising' so much as 'secret outrages' of the bombs and dynamite variety. Dublin and Cork he regarded as the danger spots.[2] It was a shrewd enough observation. The farmers were doing well out of the war. Any agitation to revolt in the cities was unlikely to find much support in the country districts.

The apparent lack of arms was all too real. The German arms ship *Aud*, the only source of supply and the only reason for Eoin MacNeill's eventual acquiescence in allowing the Rising,

[2] Hon. Gerald French *Life of Field-Marshal Sir John French* (London 1931) p. 338

was destined to lie before Good Friday was over at the bottom of the sea outside Cobh harbour, a dozen miles from where the *Lusitania* had gone down a year before with heavy loss of life.

The antithesis of the mystic-minded Pearse, eager to sweep ahead with the Rising in all its symbolism, MacNeill saw Ireland as 'the Irish nation, which is a concrete and visible reality' and not as 'a poetical abstraction'. He declared: 'There is no such person as Caitlín Ní Uallacháin or Roisín Dubh or the Seanbhean Bhocht, who is calling upon us to serve her.'[3]

The young poets, Pearse, Plunkett, MacDonagh, had heard her calling all too clearly and rose up impatiently to answer, armed or not.

Michael Collins, like all the rest of the Volunteers, who with the other militant organizations, the Citizen Army and Cumann na mBan, had part in the preparations for the coming insurrection, had his own orders to carry out during Holy Week. Sean MacDiarmada had made him party to the plan to put the Cahirciveen wireless station out of action, thereby cutting off telegraphic communication with the outside world.

Five men were deputed to carry out the scheme, one of them being Colm O Lochlainn. Early on Good Friday Michael met him on Aston's Quay, handed him the train tickets to Kerry, took charge of his bicycle (which he was to contribute a few days later on O Lochlainn's behalf to a barricade at Abbey Street corner), and waved him onto a tram for Kingsbridge. O Lochlainn himself had no idea that anything beyond an arms landing was contemplated.

The light-hearted beginning to the day's adventures was to end in the tragic drowning of two of the five, and the operation was not carried out.

Joseph Plunkett, to whom Collins was attached as one of his several aides-de-camp, had returned from Switzerland for an operation for tuberculosis of the throat and was now in a private nursing home. Some time during Good Friday Michael assisted him thence to the Metropole Hotel, and waited upon him intermittently thereafter.

Saturday brought Michael varying emotions. He cannot have

[3] Rev. F. X. Martin O.S.A. 'Eoin MacNeill on the 1916 Rising' *Irish Historical Studies* vol. XII, 1960–1

failed to be depressed by the disasters on the Kerry coast. Con Keating, one of those drowned on the Cahirciveen mission, had been one of the London-Irish: the death of those he knew always grieved Collins deeply. Yet he must also have been elated by what the next day seemed bound to bring forth. His heroes since childhood had been the men of '98. Of the generations since, his was to be the one that should rise again. During the day he met his cousin, Nancy O'Brien,[4] on O'Connell Bridge. Unwontedly, he shook hands, seeming glad to see one of his own people. One of his hands was bandaged, the result of what he described vaguely as 'an experiment' at Kimmage. In his usual teasing way he asked why she wasn't on her way home to Sam's Cross. When she replied that she would have to be back at work in the Post Office on Tuesday he laughed: 'Ah, you'll have longer than that.'

He had no illusions about the success of the Rising. 'If we had not the people behind us we could do nothing', Parnell had said. The people of Ireland were wholeheartedly not behind them now. With the hope of an arms landing gone, Michael knew it was to be a gesture only. To his practical mind gestures, however well-planned, were no substitute for the upsurge of a guided nation. Nevertheless he was only too ready to join battle. There was another side to his nature that saw the historic link with the past inherent in the whole idea of the Rising. On the Saturday evening he was bubbling over with anticipation. Alex McCabe who saw him then remembers him as 'jocular and fooling about as usual'.

Sunday was a day of supreme inaction in Dublin, or so it seemed, for I.R.B. and Castle executives alike moved on tiptoe to allay each other's suspicions that either was moving at all. MacNeill's resistance to the I.R.B. leaders' plans had now resulted in the postponement of the Rising until Easter Monday. The British, who saw the loss of the *Aud* as the deathblow to any possible insurrection, were nevertheless preparing for widespread arrests of Sinn Feiners next day, by which time the Home Secretary's permission for such a move should have been obtained.

The Volunteers throughout the country, faced with the bewil-

[4] Later to become one of his most trusted fellow-workers in the War of Independence, Miss O'Brien afterwards married his widowed brother, Sean

dering series of orders and counter-orders which followed the scuttling of the *Aud* and the capture of Roger Casement, and believing MacNeill to be their undisputed leader, had dispersed on his orders. Here and there, notably in Galway and Wexford, sporadic resistance was to occur. Essentially, however, the Rising was to be Dublin's alone.

III

Mobilization was ordered for 10 a.m. on Easter Monday, 24 April 1916. Michael Collins appeared promptly in staff captain's uniform. Plunkett introduced him to one of his fellow aides-de-camp, Brennan-Whitmore, who found his hand seized in a bone-shaking grip. Collins's natural exuberance had given way to concentration on the job in hand and he maintained a grim and somewhat disconcerting silence. Plunkett, however, a sick man indeed, appeared to draw strength from his rugged vitality.

In his room in the Metropole Plunkett gave Michael the keys to a cabin trunk, bidding him take out three automatics and three watches. They prepared to descend. The hotel was spilling over with British officers bound for the Fairyhouse races. Plunkett warned that a small, dark-haired, stout man might attempt to stop them : if so, he must be shot immediately. He sounded just the type of British Intelligence officer who would be shadowing the enigmatic Plunkett. Sure enough, there he was at the foot of the stairs. Hands in pockets, Brennan-Whitmore and Collins slipped the safety catches of their heavy automatics, but with a 'Good day to you, gentlemen', he let them pass.

The British officers departed shortly also. As Lord Wimborne reported afterwards to the Commission of Inquiry into the Rebellion, insurrections simply do not happen after the hour of noon. He forgot that the Irish are notoriously late risers.

At Liberty Hall Plunkett, Connolly, the Labour leader, and Pearse conferred in a small room, Collins, still silent and observant, in attendance. Just before noon the Volunteer column formed up and moved off, the three leaders at its head, Collins a couple of paces behind on the left flank. In his grey-green uniform he no longer swaggered, but moved with a lightness of foot that showed the perfect balance of his big, well-proportioned body. Those without uniforms looked enviously at him. Nor did they forbear to comment, nor he to rise to their sallies.

They marched along Lower Abbey Street and into O'Connell Street, where the General Post Office lay. When they were opposite the Post Office, they charged across at Connolly's order and entered. The Irish Volunteers and Connolly's Citizen Army had lost their separate identities: in Connolly's phrase, they were now the Irish Republican Army.

Though Michael Collins was part of Easter Week, with the lack of hind-sight that does not recognize destiny until its proper hour is come, hardly anyone remarked him. With Brennan-Whitmore he dealt with Lieutenant Chalmers, the unfortunate British officer who had chosen that time of day to buy a stamp, dumping him in a telephone booth and scornfully assuring a nervous Dublin Metropolitan policeman that they did not shoot their prisoners.

Later, his mood of taciturn determination gone, Collins joined those who were shattering and barricading the windows, gaily wielding a telephone handset and laughing at the cries of consternation outside as the glass crashed.

Plunkett, exhausted and scarcely able to stand at times, went upstairs to rest during the afternoon. Collins took his turn at the operations table in the main office, plotting positions elsewhere in the city on a map as reports came in, and keeping the Commanding Officers informed. He also spent a good deal of time upstairs in the instrument room. At a time when confusion seemed to prevail, while everyone sorted out what was to be done, Collins, the inevitable notebook in his hand, purposefully listed the names and addresses of the men in his Company.

Little more is recorded of him in those days of Ireland's most richly recorded week. The impression left by him on those who did notice him is one of efficiency; the organizer at work.

At times he was serious-minded, as when he scathingly remarked that if there must be singing there was a piano in the next room; at others, giving vent to his boyish love of play, he joined in the same singing, or, with Gearoid O'Sullivan when the fighting was at its fiercest, gravely asked Pearse's leave to go out, as they had previously made a date with some girls and didn't like to let them down. Even the careworn Pearse smiled gratefully at that.

Relatively little is remembered of Michael Collins in those days under fire in the Headquarters of the Provisional Government because this scene belongs to other men. Here and there those who would one day step with him into the limelight come and go in the lesser parts of Easter Week: Gearoid O'Sullivan, his most constant companion in the G.P.O., who, as the youngest officer present, raised the first flag over its roof. Joe O'Reilly, Collins's 'guardian angel' in later days, Frank Thornton of his Intelligence, and W. T. Cosgrave, that steadfast man who would one day lead Ireland, were also in the fighting; Diarmuid O'Hegarty and Fionan Lynch, Collins's close friends in the years ahead, over in North King Street. Out in the country at Ashbourne Thomas Ashe, Collins's future inspiration and guide, and his second in command, Richard Mulcahy, rounded up policemen in the kind of warfare that scorned static battles and the holding of isolated key points and was one day to sweep Ireland to a position of reckoning.

Another for whom Easter Week was not the major act of his life, though it was very nearly to prove so, was Commandant Eamon de Valera. In the Boland's Mills area, like many other teachers of his generation whose world until then had been almost exclusively academic, he was coping with a new dimension of reality, the officering of men in a front-line battle position. As with Pearse, also a teacher, though unsustained by his mysticism, he experienced the heightened sense of responsibility of the leader concerned for the ordinary citizens caught up in the conflict. He brooded; gave orders in a situation for which his experience had not prepared any nervous resistance; and worried over his men. His eye for effective deployment, his reckless unconcern for personal safety, above all his striking appearance and air of being far ahead to lead men on, held his men's imaginations and their loyalty.

To one man this week did belong, though he was to share the later fight too until another week, in another time of war, ended the dedication manifested here. Behind a barrier in the South Dublin Union, Cathal Brugha sang defiance as he held the British at bay single-handed, despite a score of wounds. They would

spare his life afterwards because they judged it a lost thing anyway – to their cost.

The chief architects of this week watched in the G.P.O. as it
ran its course : James Connolly, the big, resolute Labour leader,
giving the words of command and moving among those who
obeyed them, until wounds made him rally them from a stretcher
instead; Padraig Pearse, who had for years supplied the necessary
idealism behind the realities of insurrection, austere, a little apart,
reading the charter of the Republic to its citizens, though as
is usual with poets he comprehended their dignities better than
they did; Sean MacDiarmada, limping across the street in an
attempt to prevent the neglected hordes of the slums from dis-
honouring those dignities in a shrieking orgy of looting. Ironically it was to these alone, who cared nothing for it, that the
Republic brought something of the millenium which its adherents
dreamt it should usher in.

Joseph Plunkett was there, sabred and accoutred, personifying
the high romance of such desperate stands : 'The first capital to
be burned since Moscow!' Yet he was as down-to-earth as the
most seasoned strategist, respected even by the enemy.

Tom Clarke stood quietly where he had longed to be, at the
heart of the renewed struggle for Irish freedom. Those who had
led the way in that struggle before him to scaffold or prison had
inspired him, as he himself wrote, 'with sufficient courage to
walk part of the way along that path with an upright head'. His
was the first of the seven signatures on the proclamation of the
Republic, as his was to be one of the first names on the court-mar-
tial list for execution. Some sixteen years' apprenticeship in English
prisons had brought him this final honour, and he was content.

The long week of fighting and conflagration passed until,
about noon on Friday, the Admiralty vessel *Helga* found her
range and the first incendiary shell struck the G.P.O. By evening
the order to evacuate had been given.

Michael Collins emerges again, briefly, in the confusion of
those moments. In the glare of the blazing building and the
devastated streeet beyond he appeared at the head of the group
of men lined up at the Henry Street exit as if, as one of them put
it afterwards, they were in a children's game waiting for the word
'Go'. Revolver in hand, his breeches scorched by burning debris,

he 'cheered them on. He ran along Henry Street, blotted out in smoke, found cover for them in Moore Street, and finally joined up with the rest of the garrison who had tunnelled into No. 16, a grocery shop.

Early on Saturday it was planned to press on through the old markets to set up new headquarters in the Four Courts. There the fighting had been fierce. Among those who lay dead, shot down while attempting to recapture a forward barricade, was Michael's friend and kinsman, Sean Hurley.

No such sortie was made, for the time for surrender had come. Characteristically, Pearse made his decision as much from horror of the further slaughter of civilians as from a desire to save his men from eventual annihilation.

Down Moore Street the exhausted men marched behind white banners, proudly held. Here and there a lone cheer was raised to die behind them. Mostly the crowd jeered. No one really comprehended what the insurrection had all been about.

Out to O'Connell Street they marched, past Nelson high on his pillar, whose prayer in the last hours before Trafalgar had been that humanity might predominate in time of victory.

Watched by rank upon rank of military drawn up beyond the Parnell monument, the handful of the Irish Republic's defenders stepped forward five paces and laid down their arms. Yet for those who saw it as the end of a brief upsurge of defiance the legend above still stood : *No man has the right to fix the boundary to the march of a nation.*

Sir John Maxwell, the newly-appointed Commander-in-Chief of Ireland, heeded neither prayer nor pronouncement. The men and women over whom he now held power of life and death huddled together in the small green space in front of the Rotunda Hospital through the remainder of Saturday and the following night and all Sunday as well. Enclosed by a ring of bayonets, under drenching cold rain and an intense sun they waited.

The soldiers generally treated their prisoners with respect. 'Gentlemen, you fought a clean fight!', cried a sergeant in Moore Street; an officer turned in fury on a soldier who rough-handled a prisoner. But Collins watched as a private from among their guards was prevented from giving water to his thirsty prisoners; nearby, Sean MacDiarmada had his stick struck from him with a taunt and a rough jostle. Years afterwards Collins was to record this incident as his outstanding memory of the scene. His own staff-captain's insignia was ripped off with a bayonet, providentially, as it transpired.

Late on Sunday they were marched away to Richmond Barracks, past the G.P.O. where a flag still floated proudly, along Dame Street and James's Street, MacDiarmada toiling painfully behind as best he could.

At least two men among the military, police, and detectives who waited for them there were to feel themselves uneasily in the wrong rôle: Joe Kavanagh a detective in the G Division of the D.M.P., and the Irish officer, Robert Barton, invalided home to new duties which he would soon exchange for ones less equably viewed by the British authorities.

The majority were out to unearth their prey, the known instigators of the rebellion. They prowled round the big gymnasium, pouncing here and there amongst the men crowded round the walls. Sometimes they seized the wrong man; they rarely missed the right one. Yet the one man they could least afford to let pass was one of these. Many of them would one day pay for their error with their lives. Michael Collins, unknown, all identification of rank gone, was herded off with the rest.

Sean MacDiarmada nearly went with them. He was already limping into line when the tall, grim-faced detective, Hoey, dragged him back. Collins turned away and went with the others under guard to a cattle boat at the North Wall, and thence back to England.

IV

All Ireland lay under martial law; the centre of Dublin lay in ruins. Sir John Maxwell had once pointed out to Lord Kitchener that Good Friday was 'a specially appropriate day for an act of liberation'.[5] Easter Monday, apparently, was not. The majority of the Irish people agreed with him. Their hostile reaction had been clearly foreseen by Pearse. Indeed, had it not been so, there would have been no need of a rising to bring national awareness back to the people. 'They don't take plebiscites *before*

[5]Sir George Arthur *General Sir John Maxwell* (London 1932) p. 56

revolutions', observes Professor Crane Brinton.[6] Pearse had no
need of such things. First, he knew, would come the recriminations; later, understanding.

Trials by Field General Courts-Martial were held in secret.
On 3 May the men and women held prisoner in Kilmainham
Gaol were awakened at dawn by three volleys. These, with those
that followed in the long-drawn-out tally of executions, were to
startle Ireland into the awakening planned by those who died.
Britain would have done well to remember, as the men of 1916
did, that no man yet died for Ireland but she honoured him
in long memory.

A curious change in the climate of opinion was to follow the
restoration of law and order. Some truth had quickened in the
mind of Ireland's prophets, born in that poeticism which Mac-
Neill had denied, and had burst forth when they were crushed.
How far, each Irishman asked himself, had he, by indifference
or blind hostility, been responsible for that murder of the prophets?

W. B. Yeats, deploring the passing of 'all that delirium of the
brave', had sought to revive the romantic nationalism of Ireland's
past. Now, like his fellow-poet Pearse, he found himself brought
face to face with reality, a dabbler in sorcery whose spell has
suddenly worked. Stricken, he could only wonder

> Did that play of mine send out
> Certain men the English shot?

To many people in or outside the national movement, as to
Yeats, a 'terrible beauty' had been born. For the majority there
was as yet no purpose behind it. Time and the nourishment of
English coercion would complete the task begun by the dead
prophets. The British authorities promptly imprisoned Eoin Mac-
Neill and Arthur Griffith with all the rest, soon to become identified in the public mind as the leaders of the true Ireland in her
struggle to free herself.

An ironic touch came from the Irish Nationalist Party. To
speed Sinn Fein, once its serious rival, to its grave, it had con-
temptuously fastened the name of Sinn Fein to any action that
smacked of the unconstitutional. Now, overnight, Sinn Fein

[6] Crane Brinton *The Anatomy of Revolution* (London 1953) p. 280

found itself, all unwittingly, the parent of a Rebellion. All those who had taken up arms or were suspected of sympathizing with them were branded Sinn Feiners.

The fostering of the Rising on Sinn Fein was not entirely inapt; its aims, though not its methods, were essentially those of the I.R.B. which was the true and self-acknowledged source of the Rising. It may be claimed, if one sets aside the human incalculabilities of envy, loyalty, principle, and pride, that this very real difference of method lay behind all the triumph and tragedy of Ireland that was to follow. It is the age-old difference between the sword and the Standing Orders: one or other must prevail for either finally to succeed.

Such things lay in the future. The leaders of Sinn Fein proper and those who were left of the I.R.B. and the Volunteers were, practically to a man, in prison.

CHAPTER FOUR

Internment

I

The 289 untried Irish prisoners deported to Stafford Detention Barracks on 30 April 1916 arrived there the following morning. Michael Collins, now Irish Prisoner No. 48F, found the greatest discomfort of the journey the loss of his handkerchief, taken from him at Richmond Barracks with all his other possessions.

For the first three weeks they lived in solitary confinement, seeing each other only briefly in the exercise yard. In the cell next to Michael Dr Jim Ryan tried to establish some sort of communication, not very successfully. These men were new to prison life, their attempts to come to terms with it amateurish as yet, though for many gaol conditions would become a familiar background, efficiently mastered.

From the occasional smuggled paper and from snatched whispers with new arrivals those confined learnt of the executions in Dublin.

On 16 May Michael wrote to Hannie:

'Here I am fairly well in health & not more low-spirited than the circumstances compel. We have only just been given permission to write & naturally I choose you as the victim of my production. . . . Positively you have no idea of what it's like – the dreadful monotony, the heart-scalding eternal brooding on all sorts of things, thoughts of friends dead & living – especially those recently dead – but above all the time – the horror of the way in which it refuses to pass. However I suppose things might be a great deal worse; so let us be duly thankful for that fact. . . .

'Perhaps you would kindly send me a few good (& long) novels in cheap editions, and, if still at the flat, Heath's *Practical French Grammar* or some such text book. . . . All letters will be censored. . . .

'It is only with the utmost effort that I can concentrate my thoughts or be at all rational – you see I seem to have lost acquaintance with myself and with the people I knew. Wilde's *Reading Gaol* keeps on coming up. You remember "All that we know who be in gaol" &c. . . .'

After three weeks the cell doors were opened and the men mixed freely from early morning to late in the evening, receiving political prisoners' treatment. Much of the time was passed out of doors. Football matches took place in the barrack yard between the inmates of the two wings of the gaol, and bouts of furious wrestling.

Two things only about Michael Collins impressed themselves on the majority of his fellows who noticed him at this time: his dominatingly cheerful energy and his hair-trigger temper. Baiting him was a sport in itself. A game known as 'weak horses', a two-team version of leap-frog, would galvanize him from the one mood into the other. One team presented a line of backs which the others leaped over in turn, trying to 'break' them. Whichever side Collins was on, he was certain to find ranged against him the three heavyweights, Mort O'Connell, Denis Daly, and Jim Ryan. Inevitably, under the rough pressure spared more equable men, it was Collins's back which 'broke', losing his side the game and earning him the gleeful title of 'weak sister'. The splendour of his ensuing rage lightened for many the purposelessness of life in Stafford.

A handful of his companions saw another Collins. Desmond Ryan, then unknown to him, was vouchsafed a glimpse of the thoughtful student hidden from his more boisterous tussling partners when he asked for a book that Ryan was carrying, and read from it with quick comments.[1] Few recognized the sensitivity beneath the hearty casualness of manner.

In matters of prison routine he learned quickly, as always, to adapt himself to his environment. He soon learnt too the advisability of cultivating those of his guards who would respond to such attention. When Hannie visited him she noticed how one warder in particular could not do enough for him. Perhaps here in Stafford the first recruit to Collins's underground army of the future had already been enrolled.

[1] Ryan *Remembering Sion* p. 215

Those untried prisoners considered most likely to spread disaffection were sent to Reading Gaol. Among them went Arthur
Griffith. Of the rest, nearly 2,000 Irishmen had been imprisoned
in Knutsford, Wandsworth, Glasgow, and Wakefield, as well as
Stafford. After two months, rumours of an imminent move were
confirmed. They were taken from their prisons and spilled together in a vast concourse from North, South, East, and West
such as the most nationally-minded could never have hoped in
their wildest dreams to have gathered together in Ireland. The
place chosen for this recruiting centre of Irish nationalism was
the internment camp at Frongoch, near Bala in North Wales.

II

'Irish Prisoner No. 1320
Hut 7, Upper Internment Camp
Frongoch, Bala.

My dear Hannie,
Arrived here yesterday after a journey thro' a most engaging
country which was the only pleasant part of the proceeding. It
is not nearly so good as Stafford and you know what I thought
of that. . . .'

As usual, Michael took a little time to settle into his new
surroundings though, characteristically, when he did so he made
himself completely at home. For the moment, viewing the assortment of draughty wooden huts, each holding thirty men, which
constituted the living quarters of the North Camp at Frongoch,
his first appeal was for a woollen vest and a pair of very heavy
strong boots, size nine, with nails in them.

The North Camp was in reality the overflow of the main or
South Camp. Both were separated by a road lined with barbed-
wire entanglements. The South Camp, built in a valley, consisted
of what had once been distillery buildings, all more or less bleakly
adapted for more than a thousand prisoners.

Beyond the camp to the south flowed the river Tryweryn with
Bala and its lake two miles away. Rising away to the north in the
wild beauty of the Welsh countryside moorland peaks with names

like Carnedd-y-Filast and Cader Benllyn reminded the Irish
exiles that here lived a people whose country and language were
in many ways as remote from England as Ireland itself.

The Irishmen were allowed the prisoner-of-war privilege of
running the camp under their own executive. M. W. O'Reilly,
another of Plunkett's aides-de-camp, was the North Camp's first
commandant. Out of the seven or eight hundred men there he
noticed the energetic young Corkman who dominated the recrea-
tion field. He for one found Collins more than friendly, cheerful,
and affable of manner.

One could hardly help noticing Collins, though not always
for his affability. Among those thrown into contact with him
there were, however, plenty of his own mind. These, if unconsciously as yet, began to recognize in him their future leader. The
youthful Joe Lawless, who had won his spurs at Ashbourne, first
met Collins in Frongoch. He noticed that when Collins joined
any group 'there was a feeling that something big had come into
the place'.

He was an ebullient companion in the less restrictive environment of Frongoch. Dr Jim Ryan, sharing a hut with him, found
him inevitably able to see the funny side of the ups and downs
of their enforced communal life – sure test of any man's basic
ability to get on with his fellows.

He also had a reputation for a 'no holds barred' love of fighting. Brennan-Whitmore, who came to know him well later and
discovered in him a kindness of heart and gentleness as great
as that of any man, noticed that any show of toughness called
forth an answering toughness on Collins's part. Wrestling with
Mick Collins was no joke. He would go into a bout with a
friendly determination. Grimness would begin to rise later, particularly if he was closely matched, and the contest would end
in a heated and often bloody fracas.

He had as fiercely urgent a need for the isolation and peace
which would give him time to study and think. His brain, no less
than his body, needed outlets for its inexhaustible energy. During
much of the day he threw himself into Irish history and the
intricacies of his native language. Moreover, he had early realized that the enforced sojourn in Frongoch must not be wasted
if the work started in Easter Week was to be continued.

The sentries, with their insignia of *Georgius Rex*, were either elderly or otherwise unfit for active service. These 'Gorgeous Wrecks', as they were unkindly if tolerantly known, had been warned that the men they guarded were dangerous insurgents who might wickedly tempt them with German gold. Wistful glances at those who passed so innocently within the wire were the inevitable result. Padraig O'Keeffe, strolling along one August morning, was surprised by a furtive assurance that if he were 'one of the boys with all the money' then that guard was his man. O'Keeffe, amused, reported the incident to friends. Later he was summoned to another hut, to be confronted by four men, of whom Michael Collins was one. These, it transpired, had constituted themselves a committee to plan re-organization of the military arm of the national movement on their release. O'Keeffe obligingly identified the soldier for them. That same night letters were smuggled out. It was the start of the Collins Intelligence Service.

The camp inhabitants had now been reduced to about 650 and the North Camp was therefore closed and all those in it moved to the South Camp. Michael was not pleased by the change in sleeping conditions. The granary floors had been converted into dormitories in which the men were confined from 7.30 in the evening until 6.15 the following morning. 'When one wakes the oppressive atmosphere is really quite terrible', Michael wrote. 'In some unfavoured spots breathing is almost difficult in the mornings. Luckily I myself am at a window so don't suffer as much in this respect as others but then the other night which was wild & wet my bedclothes got very damp indeed.'[2]

Wartime conditions made the problem of feeding the internees a critical one, as they understood, if it did not mollify them. Michael's letter continues: 'With the exception of Fridays when we get uneatable herrings the food never varies. Frozen meat, quite frequently bad, & dried beans, are the staple diets. The potato ration is so small that one hardly notices it. Mind you I'm not grumbling in the strict sense. . . .'

With the removal of most of those scooped up in panic haste after the Rising who had taken no part in it, the remaining men

[2] Letter to Miss Johanna Collins dated 25 August 1916

in Frongoch now sorted themselves into productive activity. The mornings were spent in military drill; in the afternoons and evenings the many highly-qualified men amongst them gave lectures on such subjects as Irish history and language, Spanish, French, Latin, and even Welsh, shorthand, and book-keeping. Professor Liam O'Briain recalls Michael 'slaving away at Irish by himself' between lectures.

Well might Tim Healy, contemplating 'Frongoch University', hail the Home Secretary as the Father of the Sinn Fein movement.[3] Other preparations were afoot of which the Camp authorities knew nothing. In Dublin steps had already been taken to reorganize the Volunteers on a fighting basis in the event of a general release. Diarmuid O'Hegarty, released in May, with others who followed him, had made contact with Frongoch.

Senior Volunteer officers in Frongoch met in secret to receive military instruction and to study how to apply suitable strategy and tactics to the requirements of the Irish terrain. In any future combat there would be no tall buildings to be held by proud, outnumbered men in uniform; only the lightning stroke, the unseen recoil and reforming before the next blow in another, unsuspected, quarter. Guerilla warfare was as yet only a growing thought in men's minds. Only the actual necessities of time and place could give it complete shape. In the meantime the rudiments must be mastered. Preparations were made to set up training camps all over Ireland after their release.

Michael was not entitled to join the lectures on these methods of fighting as he held no position in the camp to warrant his inclusion. He knew his own necessities too well, however, to be denied. He pleaded for permission to attend and, by persistence, finally won his point.

He was already involved in other underground pursuits. Although the I.R.B., its leaders gone, had no consciousness of itself as an organization in Frongoch, those who remained of its ranks, Michael the chief among them, continued to watch for suitable future recruits and took care that its doctrine should fall on any ground likely to prove fertile. The I.R.B. men percolated quietly through the camp, the most potent force at work there.

Meanwhile Michael studied a map of Dublin and wrote names

[3] House of Commons Debates, vol. 84, col. 1765

and addresses in a notebook. No one knew how long this ideal
opportunity for contact-making would last.

Most of his letters – at least of his twice-weekly ones that
went by official channels – had been returned to him. Writing to
Hannie on 25 August 1916 he mourned:

> 'It's a great pity I can't do something to please the censor's
> department – but I'm not going to even at the risk of being
> cut off altogether especially when things are as they are
> at present. It's hard to imagine anything in the shape of a man
> being more like a tyrannical old woman than the commandant
> in charge of this place. . . . Some time ago here we were given
> an offer of quarrying work at the rate of 5¼d. or 5½d. per hour
> with a deduction of 3d. per hour for upkeep as well as train
> fares. It is hardly necessary to say that this was refused, but
> I think the authorities here considered it a rebuff – as it was –
> and took it very badly. Soon afterwards a man of our number
> was wanted and it is alleged he refused to answer his name
> when called. As a result the whole camp had their letters,
> visits, and newspapers stopped for a week. Obviously every-
> body could not have known the particular man and in any
> case it is not very just to attempt make prisoners identify
> a fellow prisoner. On the same day another man was sentenced
> to cells with bread and water for forgetting to say 'sir' to an
> officer. This practice of confining to cells for trivial things
> is a thing which the commandant glories in. It is a custom
> to appoint a fatigue of 8 men every day, for general
> scavenging & removing ashes, *inside the wires*. About 8 or 10
> days ago the particular party that was on for the day was
> ordered outside the wires to do scavenging &c for the soldiers.
> Of course they refused. They were immediately sent to cells and
> since then have been interned in the northern portion of this
> camp being deprived of their letters, newspapers, smoking
> materials. Every day since 8 men have been given the same
> treatment, & the affair still goes on.'

This was the 'ash-pit' incident which was to prove the *esprit
de corps* of the internees in their determination to make the
authorities honour their prisoner-of-war status. It was to go on
until there were over a hundred men in the North Camp. Collins

was a prime mover in keeping open the channels of communication between both camps.

Early in October the 'Frongoch Sports' were held. Michael competed in the weight-throwing with his friend and fellow-Corkman, Sean Hales, who was the Munster champion. They were the only two who could throw the 56 lb weight, and Michael lost by a few yards. He was more successful in other directions.

In the Commons the sports were used as evidence that complaints about the food supplied to the internees, the occasion for constant harrying on the part of the Irish Nationalist members, were without foundation. On 18 October Major John R. P. Newman pointed out: 'Only a few days ago at Frongoch internment camp the interned prisoners had a course over which they did a 100 yard sprint . . . and they had hop, skip, and jump, and other sports.'[4]

The winner of the 100 yards sprint wrote indignantly to Hannie on 28 October:

'Major Newman said he noticed we held sports here and that the 100 yards was won in $10\frac{3}{4}$ seconds ($10\frac{4}{5}$ was correct by the way) which didn't seem to show any neglect in the way of feeding etc. Naturally he doesn't think of all the parcels one gets and what one spends in the canteen. Actually there isn't a solitary man here of no matter how slender an appetite who could live on the official ration. You know there are two or three committees supplying us with additional vegetables and sometimes apples & cocoa. . . . Of course all the M.P.'s are only on for trying to make capital out of us.'

By mid-October the Home Office had grown tired of the 'ash-pit' affair and intervened. No more men were removed for punishment, all privileges were restored, and the occasion was allowed to fade out as 'a trifling matter'. The internees felt they had won a moral victory.

All the remaining prisoners were now transferred to the North Camp, to Michael's satisfaction. He wrote to Hannie:

'On the whole I think the huts are better in any case they're more desirable and there's a fire. There are only 29 in each

[4] House of Commons Debates, vol. 86, col. 669

now & we have a nice crowd in ours. A few good readers & widely read too. Between us we haven't a bad library. A most weird collection though. To give you an idea – Service, Swinburne, Shaw, Kipling, Conrad, Chesterton, lots of Irish Broadsheet stuff, etc etc. We had Service last night and I was put through it for Dangerous Dan McGrew & some others. There is an excellent collection of American verse in a very large volume from the Quays. The variety in the way of raggedness cheap binding & fairly good binding is unique. Would be very glad to receive *Punch* each week.'

Considering the editorial outlook of *Punch* at that time, with its sarcasms at the expense of 'collapsible risings' and those who took part in them, a more partisan man might well have desired *not* to receive it. In later years Collins himself was to be the butt of several Partridge cartoons. England was to deny that he had a sense of humour. Yet have one he did, and it was to allay much bitterness in later days of delicate readjustment.

He was reading one of his other favourites, Thomas Hardy, at this time. 'Isn't "Tess" wonderful?' he wrote. 'I haven't decided yet whether it's more poignant even than "Jude" – in some ways yes.'

Autumn had arrived with constant rain.

'What kind is *your* weather. You never saw anything like *ours* here. The mud is with us again in great style, but nothing could be as bad as the horrible stuffiness of the other place. By the way though the rain comes through most of the huts – in a couple of places in our particular one.'

The arrival of 'a very pleasant pair of socks' could not compensate for the inadequacy of all attempts to cope with the churned-up morass of the North Camp. 'If I could only get puttees!' he lamented.

A far more serious situation was now approaching its climax in Frongoch. The Sankey Commission, sitting in London, had not been entirely successful in determining the extent of every internee's involvement in the Rising. Many had refused to appear before it until forced, or, doing so, would answer no questions. They had good reason for this for, apart from the question of principle in recognizing the British Commission, the more men who remained unidentified the harder would be the authorities' task of deciding who was liable for conscription.

Conscription in any army inevitably results in a certain number of disgruntled men wearing their country's uniform under protest. The British Government lost sight of common-sense in deciding to enforce the conscription of those Irishmen who, formerly resident in Britain, had unmistakably proved that they regarded the uniform they were expected to wear as that of an enemy.

Early in September the first Frongoch 'refugee' from conscription had allowed himself to be taken to avoid trouble for his companions, and was imprisoned for refusing to be conscripted. Others met to consider whether to follow his example. Michael Collins, now recognized as the leader of the 'refugees', urged them to preserve their anonymity and fight it out.[5]

Long-drawn-out efforts to segregate those liable to conscription were thwarted. The prisoners had undeniably gained the upper hand. By keeping both camps occupied they ensured that their guards would get as little respite as possible. Despite attempts to break all contact between North and South Camps a constant smuggling service was soon in full operation, with Collins once again ensuring that the channels of communication remained open and effective.

A publicity campaign had been started long before to keep the internees and the whole question of English policy towards Ireland before the eyes of the world, and those of America in particular, then hovering so providentially for Ireland over participation in the war. As long as England was fighting as the champion of small nations' freedom, Irish nationalists had a trump card which they lost no opportunity to play. Nationalist M.P.s were supplied with details of every incident in Frongoch that might embarrass the Government. It was a campaign in which Michael played his full part. Scrupulous attention was paid to accuracy in all reports, which filtered out despite every attempt to dam them up. The skilful propagandist has no need, or, if he is wise, use for exaggeration.

Early in December, to still all doubts the Home Office sent

[5] Piaras Beaslai *Michael Collins and the Making of a New Ireland* (Dublin 1926) vol. I, pp. 114–15

an official to investigate conditions in the camp. Michael was one of the four internees who appeared before him to lay their complaints. Inadequacy of diet was high on their list. After listening patiently to a seemingly endless tally of figures and instances the official, Sir Charles Cameron, asked despairingly if there was anything of which they got enough. Collins answered that there was : salt.

Though the men snatched chances for light relief from the grimness of their circumstances, tragedy took its toll. Men lost their reason; a British doctor took his own life. On 21 December the Chief Secretary for Ireland admitted that the risk of keeping the untried prisoners any longer in detention appeared greater than that of releasing them. There were too many Irish soldiers giving voluntary service in Flanders, whose eyes might turn homewards and wonder to which small nation they owed loyalty; there were too many questions being asked in England; above all, there was too much at stake in the attitude of America.

The following day unconditional release for all was announced. Names and addresses were requested for the purpose of issuing travel warrants, but Michael Collins was taking no chances. Though he had never been given an official position he was now, by common agreement, the spokesman of the 'refugees'. He refused to submit any names until the adjutant, in exasperation, told them to make out their own lists.

They left Frongoch next day, travelling by train to the boat for Ireland. To prove that their spirit remained unbroken they got out at Chester and sang *Deutschland uber Alles*. 'Most of us were anti-German really', one of them recalls. 'The British are a patient people. They took no notice.'

III

Asquith had now given place as Prime Minister to Lloyd George. Labelled as 'pro-Boer' in earlier, opposition days, Lloyd George's sympathies might have been expected to lie with the Irish nationalists. Men in power, however, cannot afford sympathies that conflict with political responsibilities, and Lloyd George, whose concern was less for Ireland than for untangling Gordian knots, had two pressing reasons in his Cabinet alone for attempting no solution that would antagonize Ulster : Sir Edward Carson and Bonar Law.

The sentenced prisoners remained in England. Sir John Maxwell had been recalled from Ireland in November, taking martial law with him, and the release of the internees augured some lessening of the restrictive atmosphere of the months since the Rising.

Michael returned to Clonakilty the day after his release and set off to walk the last miles home to Woodfield. Eight months had passed since he had last seen Ireland; they had shaped him as a lifetime of less tempering experience could never have done. He was twenty-six. He knew, as at twenty-five he had not, how men reacted to the shocks of fire and bullet and the more insidious testing of moral fibre by rigorous confinement. What he had hoped to find in himself of integrity and resistance and the ability to master an adverse situation he had found. No less important, in Frongoch he had proved these things to others as well and they had accepted him. While only the forward-looking extremist contingent had done so, they were the men he would have chosen to be his companions in the fight that lay ahead.

He stayed at Woodfield for about three weeks, 'drinking Clonakilty Wrastler on a Frongoch stomach' as he described it rather depressingly, and noticing the reactions of the quiet country people to the events in which he had taken part. Not surprisingly, perhaps, the enthusiasm for the executed leaders that had swept Ireland had not yet, in these remoter regions, become enthusiasm for their cause. For centuries the farmers had been badly off until the war brought them prosperity. They had no relish for wild young men who might upset their profits. Michael complained that only two people in Clonakilty shook his hand on his return. Like a prophet who has received the traditional treatment in his own country he wrote : 'From the National point of view I'm not too impressed with the people here. Too damn careful & cautious. A few old men aren't too bad but most of the young ones are the limit. The little bit of material prosperity has ruined them.'[6]

[6] Letter to Miss Johanna Collins dated 29 December 1916

Time was to amend this sweeping condemnation. Leaders of revolutions invariably find that those who follow them lag somewhat on the road; they reach the goal nevertheless. The people needed not only the call to arms of Easter Week, but also a sound argument behind it that would convince each of them that his liberties were at stake. The British, so far, had avoided providing that argument. 'If they don't make peace Conscription is certain for this country', Michael wrote in his letter of 29 December. The sooner the argument was supplied, in his view, the better.

In Dublin the mood of reaction was far in advance of that of the slower-moving agricultural communities, and Michael knew that his business was not now in his loved West Cork. Apart from the need to press on with sowing the favourable ground prepared by the Rising he did not want, for once, to linger at home. 'I think poor Sean Hurley's mother felt his loss more keenly when I came home than at any other time', he wrote to Hannie. The returning men, too, needed time for readjustment.

Already the Military Service Act was pressing on his heels, as it had done in Frongoch. R.I.C. men came in search of him, ostensibly about disturbances in Cork city, in which he had in fact taken no part. They came too late, however, as they would always come. He slipped them at Glanmire and took the train from Blarney for Dublin.

PART TWO

Carrying the Long Day

CHAPTER FIVE

Readjustment

(1917)

I

Michael's arrival in Dublin was very unlike that of a year before. He was now well-known, at least in the circles in which he would have wished to be known. He found lodgings at 44 Mountjoy Street, the home of Miss MacCarthy, that staunch succourer of young revolutionaries, with whom he was to remain while he could safely do so – and his standards of safety were elastic – for much of the rest of his life.

He wrote to Hannie on 23 January 1917: 'It is only since being released that I'm feeling to the full all that we have lost in the way of men and workers'. All were infected with an up-surge of purposefulness. Arthur Griffith, now released from Reading, was already preparing to resume publication of *Nationality*, to channel this flood into progressive fields.

Though the various nationalist groups had been scattered after the Rising, there was now one reunifying force at work: the Irish National Aid and Volunteer Dependents' Fund. Apart from its charitable cause it had another, unproclaimed, objective.

Mrs Tom Clarke, leaving her husband for the last time in the hours before his execution, had walked the long road back from Kilmainham. In that dawn she had remembered his words that this had been only the beginning of the fight; Ireland would never lie down again until she obtained her full freedom. Mrs Clarke determined to see that the next blow was struck.

She founded the Volunteer Dependents' Fund. Amalgamated with the Irish National Aid Fund, it was to become, with American help, the salvation of those to whom the aftermath of Easter Week would have meant destitution. By the beginning of 1917 it was also the potential means of drawing those whose spirit was that of 1916 together in readiness for the next fight.

The National Aid was 'respectable'. Prominent people of

nationalist sympathies could contribute to it without being suspected of revolutionary tendencies. Now that Ireland had been flooded with returning deportees its resources had to expand enormously, and someone with a firm hand was needed to administer them. He must also have the initiative to use his position to further the separatist cause. The 'Frongoch group' put forward the name of Michael Collins.

Mrs Clarke interviewed him and was struck immediately by a resemblance to Sean MacDiarmada : perhaps it was the same burning enthusiasm, the ability to inspire others with his own fervour. 'If he's another Sean he'll be all right', she thought.

Before his death Tom Clarke had given her a list of I.R.B. members if the Executive were swept clean. All of these were in prison, however, as were any who might have known as much of the I.R.B.'s intentions as she herself did. She had to make her own choice of men to carry on. She now decided that Collins should be one of them. She recalls : 'I was never sorry for this. I gave all that information to Mick. It gave him the leeway to get ahead, and he had the ability and the force and the enthusiasm and drive that very few men had to work on that.'

Collins combined with accountancy the hitherto honorary position of secretary at a salary of £2 10s. a week, starting on 19 February 1917. Joe McGrath, from whom he took over his new duties, found him 'a ball of fire, very quick on the uptake, rarely, if ever, missing a point and a good listener where learning the job was concerned'.

The National Aid office was at 10 Exchequer Street, a couple of corners round from Dublin Castle. Not that this detail worried Michael; the farmer's son knew that if you cannot avoid a kicking cow entirely it is best to step as close to it as possible. He concentrated on learning his way about. Soon it would be said of him that he knew every chimney-pot in Dublin.

Collins's first action on taking over his job had been to rent a clubroom for the returning men. Inevitably a few of these, out of work and happy to remain so as long as the Fund would support them, decided that their lot needed improving – at others' expense. One of them appeared dramatically in the Association's boardroom and put this point of view, highwayman-fashion, with a revolver, to Alderman Corrigan, its President. Collins was working at the far end of the room. He advanced on the intruder, snatched his gun, and with a brief 'Get to hell out of this' pushed him through the door. There was a noise as of an involuntary and swift descent of the stairs. Collins returned alone, threw down the gun, growled 'Those bloody fellows', and resumed his work.

Genuine cases of hardship he met with immediate understanding. A man with doctor's bills to meet, or needing a holiday, would receive a grant with an appreciative letter from Collins that made him feel less an object of charity than a hero reaping just reward.

He reserved this delicacy of feeling for those who he sensed needed it. His fellow-workers found him less considerate. Women in particular discovered that he did not study niceties of manner. Being essentially a shy man, he put up a guard of ungraciousness until he came to know them better, when he expected them to take him for granted anyway. Yet, if they were ill or in trouble, he was the first to visit them and use his own slender resources to see that they needed for nothing.

He liked nothing better than to rouse tempers. There was a heated exchange one evening when, leaving his office after the day's work, he was stopped by a lady worker in a National Aid area. She needed money for a man whose livelihood depended on his buying a horse. 'It's after hours. I'm off home', Collins stormed. When she angrily replied that for her National Aid work began when her day's job was over and was then done voluntarily, Collins walked off without a word. Yet next day, when she went out to the man's farm, the money for his horse had already reached him.

Collins's capacity for work was beginning to impress all who came into contact with him. Some also noticed that if he indulged in wild horse-play of an evening he did a full day's work first, getting through as much as two less galvanized men, yet never losing his concentration or appearing to tire.

He was incredibly methodical. Others might mislay documents: Collins could lay his hand on the most trifling bit of paper instantly. While they forgot or were late for appointments he would appear almost to the second. In after years they would wonder whether this dynamic energy was not a subconscious trait in a man to whom little time was to be given.

There was a magnetism about him, as if so much energy could not be contained in one body but must flow out of him like electrical impulses. 'The quickest intellect and nerve that Ireland bred', Oliver St John Gogarty wrote of him. He could never be still, whether he were tossing the dark brown hair back from his eyes in the familiar, quick gesture, or restlessly throwing himself about in a chair, unable to curb the necessity to be forever on the move. Yet for so big a man he had much grace of movement. Gogarty, with his doctor's eye that was also a poet's, has recorded that he had beautiful hands like those of a woman, and a smooth skin like undiscoloured ivory.[1] If he were finely cut he had also a massive splendour. There were no half-measures about him in anything, mental or physical.

The National Aid bore fruit abundantly. Men coming up from the country carried back advice for reorganization as well as the money they would distribute to the men waiting at home; men who, like themselves, were often 'graduates' of Frongoch. Most important of all in terms of Collins's future, these members of the movement that was to re-emerge throughout the length and breadth of Ireland were coming to know him, and he them.

He was active in fields other than the National Aid, though in that alone he wrote of himself as 'kept going from morning till night & usually into the next morning'.[2] He wrote constantly to those still in prison, cheering them and keeping them informed of developments at home. To do so he often sat up to the early hours, the fire out long since, before snatching perhaps three or four hours' sleep and hurrying out once more to work.

At the beginning of February a by-election took place in North Roscommon, on the death of the Irish Party member, unopposed since the turn of the century. Those who no longer had any faith in Redmond or Westminster chose their own candidate for the fight, Count Plunkett.

It was a choice that relied rather on sentiment than on the Count's own political convictions, for on polling day itself not even his supporters knew whether the Count, if elected, would take up the Sinn Fein policy of abstention from Westminster;

[1] Oliver St John Gogarty *As I was going down Sackville Street* (London 1937) p. 171
[2] Letter to Miss Johanna Collins dated 12 March 1917

yet nationalists worked tirelessly for him throughout the campaign.

Collins was one of them. It was at his suggestion that each car used in the campaign had a broad strip of paper stuck across it with the words – *Plunkett is winning.* He flung himself into the work of canvassing, tramping about Roscommon, which was snowed up as polling day arrived, urging the cause for which Plunkett's son had been executed.

The Count won the election with over 3,000 votes, over 1,300 more than the Irish Party candidate. T. P. O'Connor saw the result correctly as 'Ireland's answer to the executions'.

Michael wrote to Hannie on 24 February: 'Had a great time down at the North Roscommon election. The crowds were splendid. It was really pleasing to see so many old lads coming out in the snow and voting for Plunkett with the greatest enthusiasm. Practically all the very old people were solid for us and on the other end the young ones.'

He was under no illusion, however, that with so many flocking to the Sinn Fein banner the cause was won. 'I haven't the prevailing belief in the many conversions to our cause', he wrote on 31 March, 'and as you may imagine have incurred a good deal of unpopularity through telling people so'.

Nevertheless he was proud of his countrymen's response to the call of patriotism. He wrote of the National Aid Fund: 'Here's a glorious point. Ireland itself has subscribed as much as all the rest of the world put together. It would surprise you though the places we've had money from. Barcelona, Madrid, China, Japan! But the small & remote parishes in Ireland with their £50 & £80 – great.'

Dublin Castle could not suppress the upsurge of national consciousness: it could hustle its most active exponents out of the way for a time at least. Shortly after the North Roscommon verdict, Michael, announcing his intention of remaining indefinitely in Dubin – 'If I'm left unmolested' – added:

'A lot of my friends have been taken up – for what reason I don't know. No charge is made against them, but they're being forced to banish themselves from Ireland to some part of England which will be chosen for them & theyre [*sic*] they'll have to support themselves though how some of them will do it God knows. There are all sorts of rumours today about more arrests. . . .'[3]

Britain's strongest arm in Ireland for generations had been the Royal Irish Constabulary in the country districts, the Dublin Metropolitan Police in the capital. They have been defined rather as 'an army of occupation with police functions'.[4] They were trained in the use of arms which, admittedly seldom used, were stored in barracks all over Ireland. They watched the movements in and out of the smallest village of those known or suspected as nationalists and reported their activities daily.

In Dublin itself the Government's eyes and ears was the G Division of the D.M.P. At detective headquarters all the information collected by R.I.C. men was carefully filed away under area and name.

As long ago as 1795 Grattan had described British rule in Ireland as 'a monarchy of clerks, a government carried on by post and under the dominion of spies';[5] Birrell, formerly Chief Secretary, announced to the Commission of Inquiry after the Rising : 'Ireland lives under the microscope'.

The day would come when Michael would turn his own microscope on those who now peered so suspiciously at the activities in which he was taking an increasingly salient part.

No amount of Castle activity could deflect him from living as he chose. He hurried about Dublin, usually accompanied by his fellow-Corkmen, the cheerfully energetic Gearoid O'Sullivan and Diarmuid O'Hegarty, brilliant, sensitive, and the gentlest of the three. He was constantly in and out of the Keating Branch of the Gaelic League, though his energies here were probably directed more towards enrolling his fellow-members in schemes other than the study of Irish for which he had, to his regret, little time now to spare. He picked up a book whenever he could, and went to see *Man and Superman* at the Abbey – 'on the whole a really creditable performance'.

Secret societies are formed only when their objectives have proved unattainable by open methods. The sole aim of the I.R.B.

[3] Letter to Miss Johanna Collins dated 24 February 1917
[4] E. Strauss *Irish Nationalism and British Democracy* (London 1951) p. 99
[5] Quoted in Strauss *Irish Nationalism* p. 37

was the establishment of an Irish Republic. Collins and most of the remnant of the Brotherhood saw it as the obvious body to work for the achievement of the Republic which was the absolute aim of nationalist Ireland.

Collins gained a place on the temporary Supreme Council of the I.R.B. early in 1917. He was apparently co-opted as a member because of his influence with the Frongoch group.

A notable absentee from its councils was Cathal Brugha. Slightly built, physically wrecked by that blizzard of bullets in Easter Week, yet wiry as a Yorkshire terrier, from which county one of his parents came, there was nothing crippled in his spirit. He had a dogged devotion to Irish Republicanism that deviated not an inch for any man's opinion.

By 1917 the methods of the I.R.B. were no longer those Brugha advocated. He saw the revived Irish Volunteers as the proper medium to free Ireland. He was to remain a bitter opponent of the resurgent I.R.B., in time reserving the bulk of his antagonism for Collins, though in these days he must have regarded Collins chiefly for his nuisance value. At Gaelic League meetings the Cork trio would bedevil him with hair-splitting queries, usually about the accounts, for the impish delight of seeing him embark on a humourless explanation. One day Brugha would get his own back on Collins for those accounts with a vengeance; now it was all harmless enough.

The I.R.B. was to be the soul of the Irish Volunteers, though it exerted no direct control over them. The reconstitution of the Volunteer body had been the burning issue with militant thinkers almost from the time of the Easter Week surrender.

Before the general release of December 1916 a Provisional Volunteer Executive had been elected to direct the preliminaries of starting recruitment again. Early in 1917 another Provisional Convention was held and Michael Collins was also elected to the Volunteer Provisional Executive. All over the country where companies had once existed the word was sent to take up the task of reforming.[6] Since early in the war the plug had providentially been forced into the emigration drain, thousands of young Irishmen remaining at home, potential fighters for Irish freedom. With the resurgent spirit abroad and conscription an

[6] National Library of Ireland: Ministry of Defence Archives

ever-darkening menace the odds on their seizing that opportunity were indeed favourable to the Volunteers.

Torpedoes were taking their toll of ships off the Irish coast and many of these carried arms. Michael arrived for a visit to Clonakilty in 1917 to find that a ship had been blown up off that part of the coast and that its cargo, an oddly mixed lading of bathing-caps and arms, had been salvaged by the local people. He took a cart and drove off to procure, as best he could, the arms part of the consignment; even Michael's resourceful brain could visualize no national use for the rest of the cargo. The salvager, however, refused to sell. Collins, reflecting that he had offered a fair price, made other arrangements, and that night the arms were quietly abstracted from their câche and successfully distributed.

He made periodic trips to London, organizing a system of gun-running and information with the assistance of Sam Maguire. During the war a number of Irishmen were kept on in the Post Office. Maguire swore all those suitable into the I.R.B. and set them to work on the mails. 'Government carried on by post' presents certain advantages after all. Maguire had a resourceful audacity. He is said to have approached an official about some Post Office rifles which were stored in a corner and suggested that it would be wiser to shift them : the unscrupulous Sinn Feiners were known to be active. The official ignored the advice, but two nights later the rifles were duly shifted – to Dublin.

Throughout 1917 the Volunteer movement gradually gathered momentum. Re-established companies held regular parades in the hills with whatever arms they were able to unearth. Their chief activity was in the political field, however, lending practical support to Sinn Fein.

From the start of Ireland's resurgence the interests of her military arm were closely involved in those of her political one. Unlike the armies of more democratically governed countries, Ireland's Volunteer Army had politics as its *raison d'être*; indeed, those who wore her uniform were very often those who decided her nationalist policies. The advantage was absence of rivalry between the two wings of the independence movement. The disadvantage was that any political cross-current could cause the disintegration not merely of one wing but of the whole structure.

I I

At the beginning of 1917 Griffith was one of the few men to whom Sinn Fein was still a movement which aimed at the restoration of the pre-Union constitution of the King, Lords, and Commons of Ireland, though with a parliament more truly representative than Grattan's had ever been.

If one stands back from Griffith's character the predominating quality that remains clear is integrity. His was granite-like, indestructible. A short man but extremely powerful, bespectacled and moustached, he gave an impression of aloofness and lack of humour. Yet he was the best of companions to the numerous friends who were devoted to him. A journalist to the core, he had poured forth pamphlets, articles, and paper after paper, daily or weekly, all preaching the gospel of self-reliance and consciousness of country, each one as it was suppressed by the authorities being replaced by another, different in name but identical in purpose. He had opposed any rising, not because he had no use for physical force but because he believed that its use at that time would jeopardize the true Sinn Fein programme of gradual development towards autonomy along constitutional lines. As the publicist of nationalism (why, we may wonder, did they not arrest Yeats also?) he had known that he would certainly be charged with implication in the changeling Sinn Fein rebellion; in due course he had been arrested and deported.

Now he set to work once more to preach Sinn Fein as he had conceived it. Sinn Fein had a head start on all the other nationalist movements. It alone had not lost its leader, and was in the unusual position of having captured strong public support before it had set out anew to do so.

Collins viewed Sinn Fein with mixed feelings. He was entirely at one with its doctrine of self-reliance and separatism on the economic level; with its purpose of achieving those ends by political rather than physical force methods he was not. He was, however, aware that physical force was not enough. To harass the British out of Ireland by force of arms would be useless if it left an administrative vacuum behind. There must be a second line of men armed with pens and sound economic policies waiting when the British were gone. In the elected representatives of Sinn Fein this civil rearguard would find its leaders.

Even before Roscommon Collins had given earnest consideration to the future course of Sinn Fein, though his reputation as an out-and-out Republican gave little hint of it. Mr Patrick Moylett remembers a meeting early in 1917 at which Collins, standing near the table, listened so intently to the lengthy proceedings that Mr Moylett asked of his neighbour, 'Who's the young Dan O'Connell?'

In May 1917 a by-election in South Longford was narrowly won by Joseph McGuinness, then in Lewes prison, on the Sinn Fein ticket of abstention from Westminster. McGuinness had, in fact, refused to stand in any election held under the British administrative machinery; but Collins, who had picked him for his separatist convictions, was a practical patriot. Others might disdain to fight Britain with her own weapons on the idealistic grounds that she should not have brought them to Ireland in the first place. Collins saw no reason why he should not pick them up to hit back with, and he went down to Longford with the same enthusiasm as he had taken to Roscommon.

Sinn Fein's opponents were forced to admit it as a serious threat to the Irish Party. Lloyd George had for some time been anxious to patch up a settlement before those more likely to co-operate in a measure tolerable to the North-East lost their authority to do so. The result was his much-bruited Irish Convention. Sinn Fein, however, dubious of a body largely constituted of men inimical to advanced nationalist thought, refused to accept the five per cent representation allotted to it.

The Convention was thus, unrealized by its backers, doomed before it met on 25 July 1917. It was not, however, without significance for Sinn Fein. As a gesture of good faith all the Irish prisoners convicted after the Rising were released.

III

Collins was responsible for seeing to the prisoners' travel arrangements for destinations all over the country. For most of them this was their first glimpse of the young man who had been unknown when they left Ireland. Now he was spoken of everywhere as the man to get things done.

Not all were favourably impressed by him. Robert Brennan has written of how, meeting him that first day in Dublin, he took an instant dislike to Collins which, despite his later appreciation of his capacity for work and organization, he never entirely overcame. 'Perhaps,' he writes, 'it was because he was ruthless with friend and foe; because he could brook no criticism or opposition. He drove everyone hard, but none harder than he drove himself.'[7]

Another man who was not initially impressed by him was W.T. Cosgrave, who as yet saw only the brusqueness of manner. Later he came to see Collins as a man who worked harder and longer than other men, and did better work. Another of his qualities was an almost infallible gift for selecting men for any given work.

Many of the released men took immediately to Collins. Harry Boland, debonair, reckless, and a hard worker, found him a man after his own heart. Fionan Lynch shared Michael's room at 44 Mountjoy Street. Being freshly out of prison, Lynch preferred to rise at a more leisurely hour than his room-mate, who would be up and away with derisive comment and, not infrequently, a freshener in an upturned jug of cold water: a true test of a friendship that yet remained firm.

He was gaining a reputation among the younger men for forceful leadership and that hallmark of his activities, the concise grasp of every essential detail. Dick O'Hegarty, Diarmuid's younger brother, discovered this one Sunday morning early, when a blustering young man strode into his room, shook him violently, and asked what he was doing in bed on such a lovely morning. Did he know the way to Maynooth? 'No.' 'A nice Volunteer you are,' and Collins proceeded to detail the route, including where he would stop for Mass, checking the time on his watch. He gave him a message to deliver, shouted a final instruction, and was gone.

Thomas Ashe and Diarmuid Lynch in particular valued Collins's preliminary work in reorganizing the I.R.B. When a permanent Supreme Council was established he became its secretary. When

[7] Robert Brennan *Allegiance* (Dublin 1950) p. 152

the draft of a revised Constitution was drawn up, Collins, with Diarmuid Lynch, further revised it.[8] The result was a tightening of discipline coupled with intensified recruitment.

While the members of Lloyd George's Convention deliberated insolubles in Trinity College, Sinn Fein was organizing. It did so to the accompaniment of increasing repression by the authorities who hoped that 'disaffection' might thus be prevented from spreading. They might as well have tried to siphon a tidal wave into buckets. The Irish rallied to parades of uniformed Volunteers armed with sticks, flew the tricolour, and elected de Valera and W. T. Cosgrave to the vacant seats of Clare and Kilkenny.

Sinn Fein meetings were proclaimed in the vicious circle of move and counter-move that had now begun. On 15 August Austin Stack, Fionan Lynch, and numerous others were arrested for making 'speeches calculated to cause disaffection' or for drilling. Thomas Ashe was to travel south with Collins to address a Sinn Fein meeting at Skibbereen on 26 August. He was, however, arrested on 20 August. Collins, about to leave for Clonakilty, wrote more grimly than he knew to Hannie that day : 'Tom Ashe has been arrested so that fixes him.'

In Mountjoy, under the direction of Austin Stack as senior Volunteer officer, the men began anew the fight for recognition as political prisoners. Their resistance met only with increased punishment and they went on hunger-strike on 20 September. Ashe was already suffering the effects of lying for more than two days and nights on a cold floor without bedding or boots. Now forcible feeding was adopted.

On 25 September Fionan Lynch saw Ashe being carried down a prison corridor on his way to undergo this treatment. 'Stick it, Tom, boy,' he called. 'I'll stick it, Fin,' was the answer. When they carried him back he was blue in the face and deeply unconscious. Later, a horrified warder whispered that Ashe was dead.

An electrical storm appeared to burst over Ireland. Ashe, young, handsome, an Easter Week Commandant, and Sinn Fein's most effective public speaker, was a fitting recruit to the ranks of Pearse, MacDonagh, and MacDiarmada. Thousands flocked

[8] Diarmuid Lynch *The I.R.B. and the 1916 Insurrection* (Cork 1957) p. 32

to where he lay in state in Volunteer uniform. All Ireland seemed
to be represented at his burial. Ashe had shown an early appreciation of Collins, who had become his friend; it was Collins
who had given the Volunteer shirt in which he lay; Collins who,
when the volleys and the Last Post had rung out, stood at the
graveside in his Vice-Commandant's uniform, flanked by the
green of the Dublin Brigade, and spoke Ashe's brief *vale* in Irish
and English.

The Volunteers marched unmolested home. Collins was observed by a companion to be weeping bitterly.

This was probably the last occasion on which he wore Volunteer uniform in public, save in one brief and brilliant moment
of defiance nearly two years later. Realization was dawning that
the fight must be underground if it were to succeed.

Now, as always, he translated his grief into action, continuing
to speak vigorously at the Sunday Sinn Fein meetings which had
become part of a nation-wide campaign. Earlier in August he
had spoken in places as far apart as Armagh and Carrick-on-
Shannon. At the Skibbereen meeting to which Ashe should have
accompanied him he had urged his listeners not to bewail their
patriot dead; these were assured immortality; for the living there
was work to do. A week later he had spoken at a large meeting
in Bantry, and in the following weeks in various centres in Leinster – Ballymahon, Drumraney, Granard, Ballinalee. On 8
October he wrote to Hannie:

'You have no idea of how busy I've been. For about a fortnight I've been up almost alternate nights but hope to get
some rest during the coming week. Yesterday I was speaking
down at Ballinalee – the place where Tom Ashe made the
speech for which they arrested & finally killed him. In the
circumstances I came out on the strong side "as you may
understand". However all well so far although at the meeting
there was a bit of unpleasantness with a policeman who was
taking notes. Eventually though he gave up his book quietly.'

The time had come when a definition of Sinn Fein policy was
imperative. The national banner had many devices interwoven
upon it. To achieve unity of purpose these must be replaced by
a single emblem, agreeable to all national ways of thought. A

Sinn Fein Convention (Ard Fheis) was therefore announced for 25 October to approve a new Constitution and elect a President.

While the economic objectives of Sinn Fein were accepted by all, the constitutional status of a free Ireland remained in dispute. The Republicans adhered to the Easter Week Proclamation of an Irish Republic. At the other extreme Arthur Griffith still believed that a monarchy promised better stability than a republic. Between these two diametrically opposed concepts de Valera now emerged.

In Lewes, de Valera had urged that all national declarations of aim should be for nothing less than a Republic.[9] It was now essential to persuade all those in whose hands the national movement rested to agree to a formula that would embrace all points of view. He was not yet an elected leader, but it is significant that it was de Valera who was now able to draw the opposing factions together.

The meeting called to discuss such a formula opened with Brugha hardly willing to sit in the same room as Griffith. It continued with Michael Collins and Rory O'Connor walking out and being fetched back by de Valera. It ended in the small hours of the morning with what had appeared an inevitable split averted and with an agreed objective: 'Sinn Fein aims at securing the International recognition of Ireland as an independent Irish Republic. Having achieved that status the Irish people may by referendum freely choose their own form of Government.'

This formula, if it was no more than a papering over of the cracks, was the only possible adhesive that could have been applied at that time. Ireland was now to tread the republican road where unity of direction was more important than unity of destination. Had she trodden any other might she not, after all, have fallen by the wayside almost before she had set out?

The statement had its inherent weaknesses. In laying down the achievement of international recognition for the Republic as its prior essential it ignored the obvious in that, if Britain won the war, no nation was likely to recognize for Ireland a status of greater independence than Britain was willing to concede; and Britain's whole concept of what bound the British Empire together would need to undergo far-reaching change before she

[9] Beaslai *Michael Collins* I p. 158

would recognize an Irish Republic. At best she might grant a lesser form of independent government, for which the new formula made no allowance.

The leadership of the reconstituted movement was now a vital issue, of which the I.R.B. at least intended there should be no doubtful outcome. De Valera had already shown himself able to draw the support of differing elements. At a time when men still spoke of a further rising, any chance of a moderate controlling the movement was to be avoided at all costs. It was therefore imperative that Griffith should no longer be President of Sinn Fein, a view also held by many non-I.R.B. republicans.[10] Michael Collins was foremost among the I.R.B. men who now took steps to ensure not only de Valera's election to the Presidency of Sinn Fein, but also that of an executive committee pledged to Republicanism. Where the Presidency was concerned this manipulating was unnecessary. Griffith's horror of a split was such that he was willing to hand over, with a gracious tribute to de Valera, the organization he had built up with his own toil throughout the years.

The election of the Executive revealed how moved the delegates had been by Griffith's gesture. His supporters topped the list of the elected. Joe McGrath, one of the tellers, has recalled that Collins got in only on the second count, at 4 a.m. next day.

The Convention provided opportunities for the gathering together of Sinn Feiners, many of whom now met for the first time, while others had not seen each other since the Rising. Ernest Blythe, indeed, chatted desperately for ten minutes to an uniden-

---

[10] Griffith had left the I.R.B. in 1910, though without acrimony on either side, when their policies became more definitely divergent. (Padraig Colum *Arthur Griffith* (Dublin 1959) p. 123). His views on the I.R.B.'s part in the growth of the national tradition, expressed at the time of O'Donovan Rossa's funeral in 1915 are informative:

'When Fenianism attempted armed and open war with the British Empire, the British Empire was able to defeat it . . . but the spirit of Fenianism, which was the spirit of Young Ireland, which was the spirit of Ancient Ireland, it could not defeat. Fenianism had recalled Irishmen to their manhood. . . . So long as the spirit of Fenianism diffused itself through the body politic, Ireland marched on a hundred paths of political, social, industrial, and educational effort to National Regeneration.' *O'Donovan Rossa Memorial Booklet* (Dublin 1915)

tified acquaintance who turned out to be Eoin MacNeill without his beard. The deliberations over, the delegates returned to their own Sinn Fein clubs. The new Constitution had been approved and the political arm of the national movement united. Its first aim was the contesting of every seat at the next general election. The sooner it had its own constituent assembly divorced from British control the sooner it could put its programme for economic and independent growth into practice.

If the Sinn Fein Ard Fheis only increased Michael's disgust at what appeared to him a highly undesirable preponderance of the cautious-minded in the political field, the Volunteer Convention which immediately followed it was more satisfactory. It was held in secret, and attended by several hundred delegates. De Valera was elected President of the Volunteers as well as of Sinn Fein: unity of leadership had been attained, though neither wing of the movement was in any way controlled by the other.

Irish-Ireland was, in this manner, brought into line for battle. The British had little time to think of Ireland. Their eyes were on the muddy horror of Passchendaele, on a staggering Italy, on the food shortage, and Zeppelin raids at home.

The Convention that Lloyd George had thrown out as a drag anchor against Ireland's rapidly increasing drift towards separatism continued its laborious proceedings. The Castle authorities pressed on no less desperately to regain control of Ireland by arrests, prohibitions and raids. Ireland, of whatever persuasion, settled down grimly to a changed, if traditional, way of life.

CHAPTER SIX

Resurgence

(1918)

I

On the surface Collins was little changed from the young fire-brand the London-Irish had known in pre-Rising times. Beneath the gasconading exterior, however, a very different man had developed. Though he had not calmed down – he never really did calm down – the energies of which that manner was the overflow had become more effectively channelled. The restlessness of frustrated directive ability had been replaced by the drive of one who has too much to do and revels in getting it done notwithstanding. The man who had listened eagerly to Hyde Park orators now hurried about Ireland making his own Sunday afternoon speeches, to more constructive purpose.

He knew that the revolution that hesitates is lost. Only by decisive strokes could the ground of popular support be held and used for further advance. Such an advance must, however, be steady and methodical. No isolated act of defiance would avail unless the whole country was geared to support such resistance.

He had been given the task of drafting a new Volunteer Constitution, as Director of Organization. Yet, for all his growing influence, he was still a comparatively unknown quantity to the men who had formed the spearhead of the Volunteers since 1913. When, in March 1918, both Collins and Richard Mulcahy were suggested for the post of Chief of Staff, even the far from cautious Dick McKee, Commandant of the Dublin Brigade, showed some relief when the choice did not fall on Collins. All felt his dynamism. Only when he had proved himself fully capable of controlling it would complete trust follow.

He was not long in gaining it. Most of his Volunteer work at this time was done in a small, backstairs room in Cullenswood House, where the boys of St Enda's had heard Padraig Pearse tell of Finn and his earlier company of young warriors of Ireland.

Here Collins planned the integration of the widely-scattered bands of men who drilled and sorted themselves into formal companies under his direction.

The need for arms was ever-present. Tom Clarke had maintained, with good reason, that there were arms enough in Ireland already. In some parts of the country attempts were now made to put these into Volunteer hands. The bulk of them remained untapped, locked away in R.I.C. barracks. The Big House arsenal of sporting rifles and shotguns was deemed an easier source of supply, and the most antique weapons were not disregarded by Volunteers eager to possess some kind of arms.

Such attempts were no part of official Volunteer policy, however, and injunctions that they must cease were publicly issued by the Volunteer Executive. The proper opponent for the Army of the Irish Republic must be the armed forces sent to oppose it, not private individuals, whatever their sympathies.

Any war was, as yet, visualized only as a defence against aggression. The soft hat and the trench coat did, nonetheless, mark a decisive change in the Volunteers, as yet perhaps not fully comprehended by the men themselves. More and more the Volunteer uniform was becoming an emblem, a display of defiance. For the vital backroom work in country barns where meagre arms were apportioned and instruction given in their use, uniforms were as out of place as a flag amid camouflage.

After the reorganization of the G.H.Q. Staff, Collins became Adjutant-General. His reputation for interference in others' work should not be overemphasized. M. W. O'Reilly, for instance, Director of Training until late in 1918, found Collins always ready to let him get on with his own job in his own way. Collins had the leader's gift of knowing that the way to win confidence is to show it.

His primary concern was integration of Volunteer work. He co-operated to the full with those whose difficult and often dangerous work was bound up with his own; at the same time he was probing hitherto unexplored methods of countering the enemy. Eamonn Duggan, officially Director of Intelligence, was a colleague who soon found that such probing included the whole of his territory.

Robert Barton, the former British officer, whose contact with his prisoners after the Rising had brought him over to their side, came to know Collins in these days. He recognized that a quality of aloneness gave Collins his strength. Already, when Barton met him, he was the focus for information. 'See Mick about it' was the general advice to those coming up from the country. Where communication is underground nothing travels faster than appreciation of those skilled in secrecy.

The British network of local R.I.C. observers, District Inspectors and the detective or G division of the Dublin Metropolitan Police was operating with increasing intensity. Collins scowled at the quietly circulating G-men as he went about Dublin, and began to give their presence a serious attention they were not used to getting from his openly derisive colleagues. The commonsense that had recognized the British electoral machine as a two-handled weapon now saw British Intelligence as a system whose very strength might be turned upon its own weakness.

Where the R.I.C. was concerned, circumstances favoured him. Low pay, slow promotion and service where they had no local ties were grievances aggravated by the increasingly unpopular anti-nationalist nature of their work. As for the intelligence machine in Dublin Castle itself, Collins had no need to make the first move. It had come in fact as early as March 1917 from a young detective named Eamon (Ned) Broy, for whom the Rising had recalled his own family roots in the nationalist tradition.

Broy was employed at Detective Headquarters, typing out the reports sent in daily on the movements of Sinn Feiners up and down the country. Now he slipped in an extra carbon and kept Sinn Fein informed not only of how far their activities lay under the microscope but also of such projected British moves as came to his knowledge. Though he did not know it, it all found its way into the methodical hands of Michael Collins.

There were other detectives who were coming to look upon their work as a national betrayal and who were now getting in touch with the movement; Joe Kavanagh was one; and James MacNamara who, immersed in a newspaper, hung about constantly opposite Sinn Fein Headquarters, noting movements and preparing to ensure that those notes benefitted only those upon whom he kept benevolent watch.

As yet Collins had nothing that could have been termed an

Intelligence Service. A handful of Volunteers, among them a dark, sleek-haired young man, Liam Tobin, Intelligence Officer to the Dublin Brigade, came and went with information. Yet already his nose was on every trail and anyone hearing of something afoot was liable to find that Collins was there before him.

He had a sixth sense that could spot trouble a mile off. Mrs Kathleen Clarke remembers making out a list of names for him which he would not accept until someone else had copied it. 'The way you write a "K", he told her, 'would lead anyone finding this straight back to you'.

With the reabsorption of the released prisoners into community life the National Aid Association no longer needed a paid staff, and it now ceased to employ Collins, leaving 32 Bachelor's Walk to him and, later, to his assistant, Tom Cullen, who used it for Volunteer work.

Politics engaged his attention only where he saw they could be of practical advantage. He took a macabre interest in the health of Nationalist M.P.s, and the vaguest hint that one might be ailing, let alone mortally ill, was enough to set him flogging likely Sinn Fein candidates into the constituency. Swift MacNeill was rumoured to be dying : Collins dispatched Fionan Lynch to Waterford. Lynch, however, was out of gaol under the 'Cat and Mouse' Act, which released men on hunger-strike to hale them in again later. Collins, his ear as usual to the ground, sent word that the hunt was on once more, and Lynch slipped unobtrusively away on a bicycle, as instructed, and so escaped for the time being. Swift MacNeill failed to die to expectation and years afterwards lectured the would-be candidate for his seat on Constitutional Law.

Lloyd George's Convention had ended. It had failed because 'its object was to secure a compromise at a time when the atmosphere of compromise had passed from Irish affairs'.[1] Its passing meant nothing to Sinn Fein. The general amnesty that had marked its opening had been followed by unremitting arrests, censorship, suppression of newsprint, and military control in certain areas.

On 2 April Michael was arrested. After months of weekend

[1] Nicholas Mansergh *The Irish Free State: Its Government and Politics* (London 1934) p. 21

speechmaking throughout Leinster and Munster he had at last earned the customary distinction of 'making a speech calculated to cause disaffection' at Legga, near Granard.

He was coming out of his Bachelor's Walk office when a group of G-men pounced upon him. Hitherto he had escaped the constant supervision which had been the lot of his colleagues. Joe McGrath, crossing O'Connell Bridge, saw a crowd gathered, in the centre of which, wildly resisting, he soon discerned Collins.

McGrath pushed his way in and persuaded the police to fall back while he reasoned with their recalcitrant prisoner. Pointing out that Collins was outnumbered and might as well give in, he then suggested that he should walk with him to the police station while the G-men followed. In this somewhat unconventional fashion the whole troop set off for College Street station. Collins was duly brought to Longford and thence to Sligo Gaol.

'Sligo Jail,
Wednesday 10th Apl '18

My dear Hannie,

In again but I suppose you'll have heard something about it 'ere this. They arrested me in Dublin yesterday week after coming back from the south. Sad! Sad!! Sad!!!

I was brought up at Longford this day week formally charged and remanded to the Assizes which will be in July I understand. Before me therefore is the prospect of prolonged holiday and of course July will only be the real commencement of it. Can't be helped. . . .

Being on remand here I have hardly anyone to talk to. Three of my fellow remands went off for trial today so for the present I am all alone. Reading and writing a good deal. Doing Irish language & Irish History mostly. Of course the Language part won't be very effective as I have no help.

Perhaps you could send me on a few of the better class novels – in very cheap editions. You know the kind I mean, the readable things that suit yourself for instance.

Up to the time of writing I haven't seen today's papers but I'm very anxious to know what Lloyd George has done about Conscription for this country. If he goes for it – well he's ended. . . .

Fondest love
Michael'

He also began to keep a diary. 'It was awful when I looked
at it some months afterwards but I was highly pleased with it
at the time', he wrote in later years.[2] His mental grasp was
expanding rapidly. Mr W. T. Cosgrave says of him : 'I never
knew a man develop so quickly and so profoundly in such a
short number of years.'

Lloyd George had been pressed too long and too insistently
by Henry Wilson and other military advisers. On 9 April he had
introduced his Man-Power Bill to enable him to extend conscription to Ireland. On 16 April it became law.

Conscription brought extreme protest from the Irish Party
which at last faced what Sinn Fein had for so long preached,
that self-determination was for the taking and would never be
given for the asking. The Party withdrew from Westminster; in
doing so it handed its claim to speak for nationalist Ireland to
Sinn Fein, never to regain it.

The time for passive resistance was over. All Sinn Feiners imprisoned in lieu of bail now gave it and returned to take part
in more emphatic forms of protest. Michael was among them.

The prospect of putting enforced idleness behind him was
like an invigorating draught. 'You can read for yourself that I'm
in good form – in fact too good, maybe', he wrote on 20 April,
announcing his departure to Hannie. He was not, however, under
any illusion about the future, and added, ominously, 'How long
I am left my comparative freedom remains to be seen.'

This was, as it happened, to be his last experience of imprisonment. He cast it behind him and returned to Dublin. 'The Conscription proposals are to my liking as I think they will end well
for Ireland', he wrote. He knew that nothing could be more
calculated to close all ranks within Ireland than this proclamation
of coercion from without. Britain had blundered again.

I I

180,000 Irishmen had already volunteered for war service. By
the end of the war 49,000 of these would have fallen in battle.
The Government's announcement that it needed more men from

[2] Letter to Mrs Llewelyn Davies dated 13 May 1921

Ireland might justifiably have met with the retort: Take your garrisons if you wish.

Lloyd George announced a Home Rule measure to go hand in hand with conscription: rejection of the one would mean enforcement of the other. Ireland was, however, quite simply, tired of being pushed around. The conscription threat was an even more potent move than the Easter executions to provide common cause for Irish nationalist interests; more potent, indeed, than any other single factor in the whole history of Anglo-Irish relations.

If Lloyd George had looked to conscription to solve any possibility of further rebellion while the war lasted he must now have had second thoughts. Revolt was endemic in the Irish air. Voluntary recruitment for the British forces dropped like a barometer before a storm.

Men flocked instead to join the Volunteers. An ugly pressure was building up and the British Government reacted hastily. The Executive, civil and military in Dublin Castle was withdrawn as being either too sympathetic to Irish interests or too ineffectual to withstand open defiance. Lord French, the new Lord-Lieutenant, moved into the Viceregal Lodge.

Nominally the Lord-Lieutenant was a political figurehead: it was the Chief-Secretaryship, also a political post, that carried the power of decision over Irish affairs. However, as a Cabinet position, it required its holder to be absent from Ireland for prolonged periods, leaving the conduct of affairs to the Under-Secretary, and an advisory vacuum, if he so desired, for the Lord-Lieutenant.

Lord French was not the man to take easily to the rôle of figurehead, nor can it have been intended that a man of such military mind should do so. Significantly, he too had a seat in the Cabinet – the only occasion on which both Viceroy and Chief-Secretary held this position.

American opinion continued to carry much weight in government circles, and American opinion was showing itself hostile to Irish Conscription. The German offensive on the Western Front allowed no margin for anti-British counsels among the Allies. Some means must be found of discrediting those in Ireland, particularly Sinn Fein, who opposed conscription. Ideally, it should also provide an excuse for removing the leaders of the growing movement.

Providentially for the British administration, Germany, on her own initiative and seeking closer contact with Sinn Fein, deposited an Irishman in the Casement tradition, collapsible boat and all, off the west coast of Ireland where he was duly arrested. Some Volunteer officers had been advised of Joseph Dowling's proposed mission; the Sinn Fein Executive had not.[3] Nevertheless, this evidence of a German Plot sufficed Dublin Castle.

> Oh, write it up above your hearth
> And troll it out to sun and moon :
> To all true Irishmen on earth
> Arrest and death come late or soon.

As the Master of the King's Musick had intransigently written, so the forces of His Majesty's Government now acted : not altogether as successfully as they would have liked. Methodically the Castle prepared a list of those it intended to arrest. Methodically Ned Broy copied it and sent it to Sinn Fein, where Collins received it.

On the night of Friday 17 May, Collins attended a meeting of the Sinn Fein Executive, and gave warning of impending arrest to those on the list. He had done the same at a meeting of the Volunteer Executive earlier that evening. Nevertheless, by the end of the following day over seventy of the Sinn Fein leaders were gone, including de Valera and Arthur Griffith. The Volunteer Executive had proved, by comparison, elusive. But the British coup was not to achieve what the authorities had intended. The 'German Plot' round-up had removed, not the motive force of Sinn Fein, but its moderating influences. Moreover, the Government's inability to produce any evidence to support its allegations aggravated instead of allaying American distrust of its handling of Ireland.

Nationalist affairs in Ireland were now grasped in the main by two men. Harry Boland took over the direction of Sinn Fein; Michael Collins concentrated on the Volunteers. The watchword for neither man was moderation. The removal of so many of their fellow-workers, while it left serious gaps, gave

[3] Macardle *The Irish Republic* pp. 253–4

them a clear field in which to develop their own administrative qualities. It cannot be too strongly emphasized that had either fallen into British hands on the night of 17 May subsequent events in Ireland would undoubtedly have been materially altered.

In Harry Boland Collins now found the man who was to be his closest companion in the days when, for all his sociability, his growing command of the movement was to mean an essential solitariness. Each now flung himself into his work, undeterred that both, like most of their associates who were still free, were now on the run. Collins in particular accepted the constant need to evade arrest almost as a necessary component of the air he breathed. Concealment of caution seemed, indeed, more vital than caution itself. It was a case of Chesterton's 'if you didn't seem to be hiding no one hunted you out'. The years in London aided him, and he moved through Dublin with the sense of anonymity the metropolis had given him. The countryman in a city has a constant expectation of being noticed. Collins went about as one who would be surprised if he were.

He allowed no encroachment upon what was, essentially, a routine office existence. Nor did he allow restriction of his social life. Generally with Harry Boland, sometimes alone, he would go off for an evening or weekend to Granard. The hotel there was owned by the Kiernan family, with whom he had first become friendly in the days of the Longford election.

The relaxed atmosphere of the small country town suited him. He joined the house parties which gathered at the country home rented by the family a few miles out of Granard. The local police were friendly and, in days of increased tension, a scout would be posted. Occasionally Michael took part in a game of tennis, though usually, after a few over-vigorous strokes he would get bored and wander off to seek out the most stimulating mind in the company, or to take long walks by the lake or across fields with one or more of the Kiernan girls. For a few hours the countryman would take in the familiar scents, the homeless man pretend to be at home. Then he would return, reinvigorated, to the work that kept him a stranger to both.

Some glimpses of the overwhelming amount of sheer routine correspondence required for the task of strengthening Volunteer resistance remain for us.[4] Innumerable affiliation forms listing the positions of every company in every battalion in every brigade in every county; their distance and direction from the nearest town; the names and addresses of their officers (many of these filled in only to be followed by a brief 'In Jail'). Transfer forms for men on the move, often as the result of enemy pressure. Inventories of arms and equipment, these last revealing simply and awfully the extent of Ireland's arsenal in the face of British military strength, deployed though that strength was on other fronts.

'No. of men on roll : 32. Relied on : 32. 6 revolvers and ammunition. No bayonets or pikes. 12 bicycles.' '59 men on roll. 2 Lee-Enfield rifles, 40 rounds of ammunition, 3 revolvers, 1 automatic.' Stretchers, bandages, signalling equipment, explosives. . . . Michael Collins, Director of Organization, pieced together the details of his country's resistance. Companies were regrouped, ammunition redistributed, training instructors dispatched.

It could all have been part of an efficient, impersonal machine. If it had, such letters would not still exist like that sent by Collins to Alderman Tom Kelly, then assisting with the secretarial work of Sinn Fein. A Volunteer officer was on the run and starving; he had appealed for help in a note to Collins (who, like him, had no paid job, though there is no mention of it here) : Collins would take the liberty of suggesting that £20 be sent at once....[5]

Nor was his humanity only a matter of basic necessities, or the response to appeals. He went to endless trouble to provide those in prison with whatever his thoughtfulness considered they would most welcome. 'I know you don't smoke', he wrote to Mrs Clarke, sending her a gift in Holloway, 'but I remember your saying you liked candies.'

Collins was weaving the strands of his Intelligence net, turning that certain eye for the right man on the cheerful and resilient Tom Cullen, the more serious Liam Tobin and, above all, that youthful and dedicated figure, Joe O'Reilly. Joe O'Reilly was

[4] Microfilm copies of the originals in the Ministry of Defence Archives are in the National Library of Ireland. Quotation from them is made here with the kind permission of the Minister for Defence, Ireland.
[5] Letter dated 25 August 1918. Brother W. P. Allen's Papers

more than an Intelligence officer, more than an aide-de-camp. He combined the rôles of Sancho Panza, guardian angel and whipping-boy. He played David to Collins's Saul, singing *The Foggy Dew* and other patriotic airs as required, submitted to being hectored and bullied by him, wept, fled from his rage, and came back to continue his devoted slavery.

Collins was also developing that extraordinary system, so vast in its dimensions that its details have never been fully put together, so simple in its operation that men and women up and down the country took part in it undetected under the most implacable attempts to penetrate it: his communications network. By it men in prison received detailed plans from outside as efficiently as if Collins had merely to pass the information from his left hand to his right. Volunteer officers up country dispatched details of projected operations to Headquarters under the noses of those employed to discover them, and received sanction or instruction by return while the Castle agents were still wondering how their own secret communications had unaccountably fallen into enemy hands.

These underground workers soon learnt that anything done for Michael Collins was done for Ireland and he had no time to thank them on Ireland's behalf for doing it. They also learnt that he asked nothing of them that he would not do himself. Occasionally, very occasionally, someone would demur at being exploited in this way, usually at risk of job or life itself. Collins, told of such a case, would pass no judgement. The person concerned would merely find that the calls on his or her co-operation had ceased. If Collins gave no vicarious thanks, he wasted no time in blame.

Besides the 'German Plot' internees there were several sentenced prisoners, most of them in Ireland. Austin Stack, Fionan Lynch, and Ernest Blythe were among those in Belfast. Most of Collins's letters to Belfast were addressed to Stack as their senior officer; many of them have been preserved and provide a valuable insight into Collins's view of developments throughout the latter half of 1918 and in the following year.[6]

[6] Quotation from these letters is made with the kind permission of the Trustees of the National Library of Ireland, and of the Kilmainham Restoration Committee, in whose hands they now variously rest.

Stack is remembered by his contemporaries as a kindly, companionable man, but not one whose capabilities matched the great responsibilities placed upon him. In prison he was a resourceful and brave leader, and gained a reputation as such. On the basis of this prison leadership he was later given high authority in the administrative sphere, for which greatly different qualities were required. It would be unjust to overlook Stack's tenacity of purpose and courage in resisting often appallingly brutal prison conditions. These in turn were responsible for the breakdown in health which was to make a cheerful man an embittered and suspicious one.

Collins himself was in large part responsible for building Stack up into an exaggeration of the man he was. Many men, faced with an apparent over-estimation of themselves by Collins, discovered that they did indeed possess latent qualities which no one else had ever suspected in them, and broadened and bore fruit accordingly. Stack was one of the few who did not. It was a blunder on Collins's part which was to have serious repercussions politically and bring heartbreak to himself.

Several reasons probably lie behind this singling out of Stack by Collins. He knew that Sean MacDiarmada had placed confidence in him at the time of the Rising, though circumstances had then outmatched him. They had worked together in the industrious and optimistic atmosphere of 6 Harcourt Street. Stack had been a renowned footballer – in 1904 he had captained Kerry to win the All-Ireland Final – and Collins admired physical prowess. Again Stack, some years his senior, with his legal training, his ability to discourse on such subjects as European freedom movements, must have attracted Collins, still relentlessly educating himself, as honey does a fly.

There were never any half-measures with Collins. No man ever had a better friend: few were capable of returning friendship in such abundance. Collins's letters to Stack bubble over with warmth of feeling. He addresses him as 'Amico' and 'old son'; Stack's photograph is beside him as he writes; when he cannot get the exact cut of tobacco Stack favours, he writes to Hannie to search London for it. He offers a choice of books, from Burke on Froude to *Robinson Crusoe* in Irish.

He constantly asked Stack's opinion, giving the impression

that he relied upon it. Those imprisoned with Stack, judging him at such tellingly close quarters, sometimes wondered why.

Collins always took an active interest in the movement's propaganda work. The *Irish World*, edited by Denis McCullough, owed much to his efforts. He solicited contributions from every quarter and was constantly in and out of the editorial offices; nevertheless, the attentions of the Censor hampered the paper's effectiveness, and he saw the need for a secret production. In August a long-cherished scheme was realized: *An t-Oglach*, a periodical designed to help knit the Volunteers into an effective force, came into being. Collins himself contributed many articles to it, laying down a sound structure for organization, national and local. 'Forget the Company of the regular army', he warned. It is the key to the whole concept of the Volunteers in the years which followed.

The disadvantages against which *An t-Oglach*'s editor, Piaras Beaslai, and those concerned in bringing it out laboured, are referred to constantly by Collins in his letters to Stack. Indeed, any activity at all was increasingly hampered by constant raids and the need to keep in touch with colleagues whose whereabouts were invariably uncertain. 'I feel sorry sometimes Austin that I missed them on the 17th [May]', he wrote in mid-August. 'One could have a rest sometimes or even a fight'. In November: 'It's very hard to find anybody in this town at the moment' and: 'H[arcourt] St is a damned bad place to leave anything at present – worse than damned'.

Harcourt Street, or those offices in No. 6 devoted to Sinn Fein's political concerns, received little attention from Collins during these months, though he continued his work there on the Committee of the Irish Republican Prisoners' Dependents Fund. He was exasperated by the predominance of what he considered the 'moderates', against whom the leavening of men of Boland's mind worked heavily. His was the disgust of the extremist who wants to sweep ahead. There is no recklessness to be discerned anywhere in his letters to Stack, however; no urging of action for action's sake.

'The S.F. organization lacks direction at the present moment', he wrote to Stack on 19 August. 'The men who ought to be directing things are too lax and spend little or no time at No.

6.' Of a meeting of the Ard Chomhairle (it was, naturally, only a substitute Executive at this time) : 'the attendance was poor & most of the things lacked any great force'. In October, with the Sinn Fein Ard Fheis ahead, with its policy decisions to be taken at a time when conscription seemed imminent, he wrote : 'I wish to God there were more of the people out whom one could discuss things with & in whom confidence could be reposed'. But by and large he left Boland to keep Stack and the others informed of Sinn Fein activities and concentrated on Volunteer concerns.

The start of a new Parliamentary session on 15 October was generallly expected to mark the announcement that conscription for Ireland would no longer be deferred. The Volunteers waited for what would be, for them, a declaration of war. Lloyd George, however, had prudently decided to await the outcome of the changing situation on the Western Front.

Collins was in bed with a crippling attack of pleurisy. 'I'm fed up today', he admitted to Stack on 12 October. 'It's the first time for 8 years I've felt it necessary to stay in bed. . . . Of course I'll be alright tomorrow but I'm very very impatient'.

He was, indeed, an appalling patient. His letters are more reasonable than his behaviour. For all the gratitude he showed to those who ministered to him when he was too weak to stand they might have been staging some sinister plot to keep him from work. He staggered back after a couple of days though for some time he found it difficult to keep going with anything like his old *élan*. 'I make an effort to ignore my ailments', he wrote engagingly to Stack a fortnight later. He forbore to add that he was likely to murder anyone who did not similarly ignore them.

Peace came in Europe. The celebration of it, in Dublin at least, occasioned encounters of a far from peaceable nature between representatives of the Crown forces and Sinn Fein. Collins summed it up succinctly to Stack :

'As a result of various encounters there were 125 cases of wounded soldiers treated at the Dublin Hospitals that night. . . . Before morning 3 soldiers and 1 officer had ceased to need any attention and one other died the following day. A policeman too was in a very precarious condition up to a few days ago when I ceased to take any further interest in him. He was unlikely to recover. We had a staff meeting so I wasn't in any of it. . . .'

Peace brought no lessening of the tension in Ireland. By the end of 1918, in that year alone over 1,000 Irishmen had been arrested, 91 deportation orders and 973 sentences had been passed; one man had died in prison. Twelve newspapers had been suppressed, over eighty bayonet and baton charges had been made in which five men had died, and innumerable meetings had been proclaimed. On visiting Ireland towards the end of the year G. K. Chesterton noted:

'My first general and visual impression of the green island was that it was not green but brown; that it was positively brown with khaki. . . . I knew, of course, that we had a garrison in Dublin, but . . . I had no notion that it had been considered necessary to occupy the country in such force, or with so much parade of force. And the first thought that flashed through my mind found words in the single sentence: "How useful these men would have been in the breach at St Quentin." '[7]

No doubt there had been Irishmen in their stead at St Quentin, as there had been at Suvla Bay and in the Dardanelles. 'Home Rule when the war is over' was the promise for which they had fought and died in their thousands. Home Rule remained, unimplemented, on the Statute Book as their memorial now that the fighting was done.

Those who had joined the Volunteers simply to evade conscription now dropped out. A useful number remained and Collins, no longer needing to ask whether all the men on the Company rolls could be relied on, pressed forward with his plans for Divisional groupings to tighten control between Headquarters and the areas of greatest Volunteer concentration: Cork, Kerry, Limerick, and Tipperary. Conscription was a thing of the past; he was under no illusion that 'the brown island' would not remain that colour to active purpose.

Sinn Fein was now intent on the General Election. Michael remained unrepentantly averse to things political, despite his

[7] G. K. Chesterton *Irish Impressions* (London 1919) p. 69

own candidature for South Cork. His part in the proceedings was to ensure that those nominated by Sinn Fein would be men of strong Republican outlook, ready for forceful action. His methods of obtaining 'suitable' candidates were, to put it mildly, decisive. All those nominated were supposed to sign their assent. For some in prison this presented difficulties. Collins obligingly signed for them without, in all cases, troubling them by notification that he had done so. The first that Fionan Lynch, for instance, knew of his candidature was the congratulations he received on being elected unopposed for South Kerry.

The turmoil of politics, Collins wrote to Hannie, 'leaves me almost unmoved'. Nevertheless he went to Cork and delivered an uncompromising speech. He was one of the twenty-five Sinn Fein candidates returned unopposed.

Sinn Fein had to campaign as an illegal organization. Nevertheless it swept all but the Unionist areas of the country. The Nationalist Party, whose leader, John Dillon, had lost to de Valera, retained six seats.

The election of 1918 ended the era brought in by the Act of Union. As that Act had marked the political shackling of Ireland to Britain, so the Sinn Fein refusal to go to Westminster now marked their separation. Britain's inability to accept that, though the Act of Union remained unrepealed, this separation was a fact and not merely a threat, accounts for the period of bloodshed and bitterness that followed.

The departure from Westminster lost the Irish an advantage no other geographically separate country in the Empire, before or since, has ever had, the power to have a voice in Britain's own affairs. Such a privilege is a poor substitute, however, for the right to govern one's own country.

The vast majority of the Irish people were by no means dedicated Republicans. They had voted for Sinn Fein, not because of any radical change to separatist thinking, but because it was the party of resolute opposition to British domination. Father Michael O'Flanagan, Vice-President of Sinn Fein, saw clearly enough: 'The people have voted Sinn Fein. What we have to do now is to explain to them what Sinn Fein is.' With the people's mandate to form an independent National Assembly, Sinn Fein now had the only platform needed to make that explanation.

CHAPTER SEVEN

Sinn Fein

(1919)

I

Sinn Fein had won seventy-three seats, returning sixty-nine candidates.[1] Of these, thirty-five were in prison,[2] three had been deported and six were on the run. It was nevertheless proposed to call an assembly of all Irish M.P.s, though it was a foregone conclusion that the twenty-six Unionist and six Nationalist members would not attend.

Those of the newly-elected who were on the run could now count on receiving even more attention from the British authorities than heretofore. A preliminary private meeting of Sinn Fein members was called for 7 January 1919. Michael, in West Cork on Volunteer business, came up by train to Dublin, narrowly avoiding detection. The warrant for his arrest, in force since the 'German Plot' round-up, had in fact been withdrawn, an immunity which was to last exactly four weeks.

At the meeting of 7 January the twenty-four representatives present took the following oath :

> 'I hereby pledge myself to work for the establishment of an Independent Irish Republic; that I will accept nothing less than complete separation from England in settlement of Ireland's claims; and that I will abstain from attending the English Parliament.'[3]

At a further meeting on 14 January declarations were produced for the first session of the first Dail Eireann, which was to be held in public on 21 January. Collins himself was 'very much

---

[1] De Valera, Griffith, Eoin MacNeill, and Liam Mellowes had each been returned in two constituencies.

[2] Count Plunkett was released in time for the first meeting of the newly-elected representatives on 7 January 1919

[3] National Library of Ireland MS 8469

against' any such assembly while so many members remained in prison.[4] Possibly he felt that the few free to attend were not representative enough of the whole body to achieve any useful purpose in meeting. He was also against the socialist tone of the 'Democratic Programme' prepared for the opening session's approval, and attempted to have it suppressed, but without final success.[5]

Dail Eireann saw its national authority unequivocally. Its 'Declaration of Independence' at the opening of its first session reflects Mirabeau's answer to the King's officer in the French National Assembly of June 1789: 'We are assembled here by the will of the nation, and we will not leave except by force.'

The forces which were to defend the nation were not specifically invoked in the day's proceedings. The right of the Volunteers to take up arms on Ireland's behalf was implied in the recognition that the Irish Republic had been proclaimed in 1916 'by the Irish Republican Army acting on behalf of the Irish people'; the necessity for them to do so was implicit in the undertaking 'to make the declaration effective by every means at our command'.

Collins became Minister of Home Affairs in the Dail Cabinet, of which Brugha was elected Acting President. Michael had not been at the historic first meeting of the Dail. Instead, he was in England, making arrangements for the escape of de Valera from Lincoln gaol. Allowing for every eventuality, he asked Hannie to have money ready should it be needed. He approached a friend with a request to find him motor cars. Asked why he wanted them he replied casually: 'Oh, I'm going to rescue de Valera.' A few weeks before he had boasted of a plan to organize the Irish race throughout the world. This latest attempt to impress was treated with amused disbelief, as no doubt Collins himself intended it should. In the event, taxis were used as being less awkward to engage and dismiss. On 3 February de Valera duly left Lincoln, under Collins's personal supervision.

The newly-assembled House of Commons heard of this disconcerting departure next day. Leaving de Valera to follow when the hue and cry at the ports should have died down, Collins returned to Ireland.

[4] Letter to Austin Stack dated 15 January 1919
[5] O'Hegarty *Ireland Under the Union* p. 727

His own freedom was again precarious. On 6 February at Longford application was made for forfeiture of the bail given on his release from Sligo Gaol the previous April.[6] On St Patrick's Day he wrote in exasperation to Stack : 'I believe they're on my track again. I'm sick of it.' Nevertheless he admitted no impediment to his movements. He had an instinct for safety. Gearoid O'Sullivan introduced him to Mrs Leigh Doyle; when she offered to show Michael the back way out of her house in Rathgar as a precaution O'Sullivan replied : 'That fellow will find it soon enough if he wants it.'

All Irish prisoners interned in England were now released, mainly as a face-saving gesture. De Valera was now deemed free of pursuit and returned quietly to Dublin.

Other events took place in March to boost Sinn Fein morale. Robert Barton, arrested in February for a pithy speech concerning renewed ill-treatment of prisoners in Mountjoy, had himself been imprisoned there. He now decided to leave, aided from without by Michael, and took an unprecedented departure over the twenty-foot wall one moonlit night. Collins described this further escape to Stack as 'a faggot to keep the pot boiling'.

The pot, indeed was boiling over. On 29 March there was a mass break-out from Mountjoy, gleefully celebrated by the ballad-makers of Dublin :

J. J. Walsh and Pierce Beasley the trick did quite easily,
Some pro-German devil a ladder did throw;
Then some twenty Sinn Feiners like acrobat trainers
Scaled the wall and got free all Alive, Alive O.[7]

With de Valera's return to Ireland and the release or escape of most of the Sinn Fein deputies, a second session of Dail Eireann was convened early in April 1919. As expected, Eamon de Valera was elected President (*Priomh-Aire*, literally First Minister) of Dail Eireann. Collins became Minister of Finance.

Many of the Cabinet appointments were of propaganda rather than constructive value. Michael, indeed, commented grimly that, in the view of most of the Cabinet's friends, 'our appointments simply ensure the hanging that was only probable had we re-

[6] National Museum of Ireland
[7] From a printed copy in the possession of Mr Robert Barton

mained merely members of the Dail'. Nevertheless he added : 'At
any rate we may not be despondent in all the circumstances.
Whether we achieve our object or whether we fail gloriously a
mark has been made that can never be effaced.'[8]

The proceedings of this small group of men and women must
arouse our admiration. Confronted by the enormous parliamentary and civil machine of the British administration, they conducted their work in orderly and unemotional fashion with only
a propensity for meeting in private to suggest that they were in
any way threatened by disruption. Early in the following year,
General Sir Nevil Macready was able to keep a copy of Griffith's
The Resurrection of Hungary on his desk and mark in it the
dates on which the measures proposed in it were carried out.[9]

Michael, with his old awareness of living in history, described
something of his feelings at this setting up of a native government
in a letter to his sister Lena (Sister M. Celestine) in an English
convent, written on 13 April 1919 :

> 'The week which has passed has been a busy one for us –
> perhaps it has been an historical one for very often we are
> actors in events that have very much more meaning and con-
> sequence than we realise. At any rate – permanent or not,
> consequence-full or not – last week did, I feel, mark the incep-
> tion of something new. The elected representatives of the
> people have definitely turned their backs on the old order
> and the developments are sure to be interesting. Generally the
> situation is working out to the satisfaction of Ireland – that
> is in Foreign countries. At home we go from success to success
> in our own guerilla way. . . .'[10]

I I

The Peace Conference's deliberations had begun in Versailles
in the new year. One of Sinn Fein's aims was to secure Irish
representation in its councils as a small nation, seeking independence. President Wilson visited London shortly after the Armis-

[8] Letter to Mrs Mary Powell dated 24 April 1919
[9] Sir Nevil Macready *Annals of an Active Life* (London 1924) II p. 430
[10] From a copy in the National Library of Ireland, with the kind permission of Fr P. Kiely, owner of the original, and Sister M. Celestine

tice. Collins was one of four men sent over to try to obtain an interview with him and submit Ireland's claim. Collins, included for his quick grasp of essentials rather than for his delicacy in word-handling, made a characteristic suggestion over the phrasing of a particular sentence: 'Leave it out altogether'. He was no less summary about the likelihood of Wilson's receiving them. 'If necessary, we can buccaneer him!' President Wilson, however, with half a world asking his intercession, had no time for interviews and went on to Paris.

This meeting of the Irishmen had been in the Kensington home of Mr Crompton Llewelyn Davies, Solicitor-General to the British Post Office and an authority on taxation and land values who had aided Lloyd George considerably in his land reforms of 1910. His wife was the daughter of a former Nationalist M.P., James O'Connor, imprisoned for some years in the Fenian days. Both were to give active support to Sinn Fein, and in particular to Michael Collins, in the years which followed.

Mrs Davies's first impressions of Collins were of a rather pale, heavily-built young man who smoked incessantly and was given to bombastic utterances. Like most other people she was soon to recognize not only the determination behind his words but the ability to convert the determination into action.

President Wilson's championship of 'small nations' had been the beacon-light of Irish aspirations. Yet from the start the admission to Versailles of Ireland's own representatives was improbable. The issue at the Peace Conference was, in effect, the recognition of Ireland's right to call herself a Republic or anything else she might prefer as against Britain's claim to speak for her; but President Wilson's hands were tied on far broader issues than any declaration already made by Ireland unilaterally.

At home his cherished scheme for a League of Nations might fail were the Democrats to lose their traditional command of the Irish-American vote. Yet he badly needed Britain's friendship in Europe; she equally was heavily indebted to Washington for the War Loans. Wilson's inbred antipathy to the Catholic Irish, and Lloyd George's need to hold together a coalition whose right wing veered strongly towards Belfast, found mutual relief in the solution which decreed that only claims for representation at Versailles unanimously approved by the Committee of Four should be allowed. America would not embarrass Britain by pressing Ireland's case.

Irish-Americans did what they could, and succeeded in sending a delegation to Ireland, with British permission, to judge conditions there for themselves. On 9 May a public session of Dail Eireann was held to welcome them. The previous month Dublin Castle had raided a similar session in a vain attempt to arrest wanted members. Now, inopportunely, it tried again. Collins described what occurred in a letter to Stack two days later:

'After the Dail meeting at the Mansion House on Friday a few of us had a very interesting experience. No doubt you will have seen the cryptic reference that Mr B[arton] & Mr C[ollins] were present throughout the entire proceedings. They were, also Mr K. [Ted Kelly, a Volunteer on the run, who held up a detective at gunpoint to get in.] Well at about 5 o'clock the enemy came along with 3 motor lorries, small armoured car machine guns probably 200 or 250 troops. They surrounded the building with great attention to every military detail. They entered the Mansion House and searched it with great care and thoroughness but they got nobody inside. The wanted ones codded them again.'

The wanted ones were, in fact, up a long ladder and into a neighbouring building. The troops remained in position until the Americans returned for a civic reception that evening, when they were thoroughly searched; a performance that must have answered in no uncertain manner the question of one of them earlier in the day when, addressing the Dail, he asked if he were too optimistic in hoping that his and their aspirations were about to come to 'a beautiful realization'. Collins, having descended once more, appeared at the reception in Volunteer uniform.[11]

The American delegates achieved little of what they had purposed. President Wilson made the remark to them that was to be frequently quoted thereafter, on the tragedy of small nations which looked to his words as giving them a hope he was unable to realize. Nationalities were coming to him which he had not known existed when he made his declaration that every nation had a right to self-determination.

[11] See Frank O'Connor *The Big Fellow* (Dublin and London 1965) p. 50

Ireland's tragedy was not that President Wilson was unaware
of her claims; it was rather that he knew them too well, and had
taken care to side-step them in time.

The Treaty of Versailles was signed on 28 June 1919, and was
marked by 'peace celebrations'. In Dublin the celebration, in
Collins's words, was 'protected by fixed bayonets all along Cork
Hill Dame Street & College Green. The loyalists were well in
evidence but the populace, where it congregated on the line of
march at all, greeted the performance in silence'.[12]

De Valera, seeing the United States as a valuable field for
recruitment of support, particularly with a Presidential election
approaching in which the Irish-American vote would be a strong
bargaining counter, had announced his intention of going there.
Harry Boland was accordingly smuggled over to New York at
the beginning of May 1919 in great secrecy to prepare for his
arrival.

Without his support at Sinn Fein headquarters Collins became
increasingly antagonistic to the 'moderate' influences on the Executive. 'I am only an onlooker at the Standing Cttee now', he
wrote to Stack on 11 May. Boland's nominee for his position as
joint honorary secretary was set aside and this evoked a stormy
complaint from Collins on 17 May :

'The position is intolerable – the policy now seems to be to
squeeze out any one who is tainted with strong fighting ideas
or I should say I suppose ideas of the utility of fighting. Of
course any of the Dail Ministers are not eligible for the Stan.
Cttee and only $\frac{1}{3}$ of the entire number may be members of
the Dail. The result is that there is a Standing Committee of
malcontents, and their first act is to appoint a pacifist secretary
and announce the absence of H. B[oland]. Our own people
give away in a moment what the Detective Division has been
unable to find out in five weeks.'

'We have too many of the bargaining type already [he wrote
in similar vein next day]. I am not so sure that our movement
or part of it at any rate is fully alive to the developing situation. It seems to me that official S. F. is inclined to be ever less
militant and ever more political & theoretical. . . . There is I

[12] Letter to Austin Stack dated 20 July 1919

suppose the effect of the tendency of all Revolutionary movements to divide themselves up into their component parts. Now
the moral force department have probably been affected by
English propaganda. . . . It's rather pitiful and at times somewhat disheartening. At the moment I'm awfully fed up, yet 'tis
in vain etc——'

He had personal reason for his hostility to Sinn Fein – or at
least to the little group who were already snapping at his heels.
There was nothing of great issue, just a continual murmur of
criticism of Collins who took so much on himself, Collins who
wanted to run everything, Collins the 'Big Fellow'. It was the
jealousy of smaller men and Collins, who knew no jealousy, was
hurt and irritated.

'I'm fed up,' he told Stack again on 6 June. 'Things are not
going very smoothly – although perhaps that's too strong an expression. All sorts of miserable little undercurrents are working
and the effect is anything but good.'

About this time Michael suffered the first of the attacks of
acute pain which were to dog him intermittently thereafter. They
are referred to lightly by him as 'stomach trouble, not really
serious but enough to prevent one doing anything more than just
the routine things'.[13] He carried on mechanically until they
passed. Since his attack of pleurisy he was also highly susceptible
to colds. Undoubtedly these things were a symptom of the sheer
hard physical and mental labour which he was now, more than
ever before, shouldering against constant harassing by the British
authorities.

Lawlessness, in the eyes of the British Government, was the
threat against which it must pursue its relentless course. It is
instructive to turn once more to the views of a historian of revolution : 'A revolution is not a period of anarchy. . . . There is not
less government during a revolution, there is more government. . . . The reality of revolutionary government is quite
unaffected by an obsolescent fiction about its legality.'[14]

Dail Eireann supplied effective proof of its 'reality' at its fourth
session, held privately in June 1919. Land agitation demanded

[13] Letter to Austin Stack dated 1 July 1919
[14] Edwards *The Natural History of Revolution* pp. 107–9

that some controlling machinery be set up, and the Dail therefore decreed the establishment of National Arbitration Courts.

In the absence of de Valera, Arthur Griffith became Acting
President of the Dail. In the course of this session the prospectus
for a Loan for home subscription was approved. Michael Collins,
as Minister for Finance, knew only too well that if the Government of the Irish Republic was to function it would need money.

The launching of the Dail Loan was not to be confined to Ireland. The secret channels of the I.R.B., under Collins's direction,
had quietly taken de Valera from Ireland and brought him on the
Celtic to New York towards the middle of June.

III

Irish-America was dominated in 1919 by two men: John Devoy
and Judge Daniel F. Cohalan. Devoy's name had been linked
with Fenianism since its inception. With Davitt he had founded
the Land League;[15] with Parnell they had both devised the 'New
Departure' which embraced separatism through physical force.
Undeterred by failure to achieve independence by these methods
in Ireland, Devoy worked actively towards the same end in the
States. As Editor of the *Gaelic American* Devoy, obstinate, advanced in years, deaf, yet still possessed of the purposeful tenacity
that had set him on the pinnacle of Tom Clarke's esteem, was the
uncompromising spokesman of the Gael in America.

Judge Cohalan, born in New York State of Cork parents, was
a close friend of Devoy. Such support in the Senate as Ireland's
case had won was due mainly to his efforts. Cohalan was, however, American-Irish rather than Irish-American. Proud and
ambitious, he had already incurred the deep enmity of President
Wilson who, no less autocratic, had allowed this personal antagonism to bear on his judgement of Irish affairs. Other men also,
inside Irish-American circles, were at work to discredit Cohalan
who, it may be said, seems to have been constantly prepared to
submit to personal rebuffs in the interests of Irish-American unity.

Into this undercurrent of factional unrest emissaries from Ire-

[15] Charles Callan Tansill *America and the Fight for Irish Freedom
1866–1922* (New York 1957) p. 51

land were inevitably drawn. The situation was aggravated by differences over policy. Dr Patrick McCartan, Dail Eireann's representative in the United States, was allied to those who favoured nothing less than a claim to recognition of an Irish Republic. Devoy and Cohalan, however, deemed it advisable to plead only for recognition of the right to Self-Determination which, in their view, was far more likely to succeed both in the United States legislature and in capitals abroad. Harry Boland was also drawn into anti-Cohalan circles.

There was thus, when de Valera came upon the American scene, an established, though as yet unrevealed, rift in Irish-American ranks. It was a rift into which de Valera was, unfortunately, to be drawn. It has been remarked that his manifest ability to unite the different forces of Sinn Fein was entirely lacking in his American visit. The answer can only be that American issues are resolved by Americans alone. De Valera was powerless to erase the dividing line between Irish and American fields of interest, and his reliance on advisers partisan in what was, after all, an American quarrel aggravated differences which were not his to solve. His personality, more elevated than those of Cohalan and Devoy, and as strongly individual, was to add another dimension to embittered relations.

In Ireland de Valera was the undisputed leader in those nationalist circles that no longer followed the Irish Party. His reception in America was not calculated to remind him that Irish-America had its own organizations and leaders to whom he was a guest and not a dictator of policy. He was fêted in city after city and subjected to an intensive atmosphere of near-hysterical adulation which seemed aimed as much at his person as at his position. His position, indeed, despite his protests, was translated by his American public from that of President of Dail Eireann to President of the Irish Republic.

De Valera's own view was that he was in America solely to advance Irish interests. It was for Ireland, represented by himself, to say how those interests would best be served. This was not, however, the view of Devoy and Cohalan. The resulting clashes undoubtedly arose largely through the failure of de Valera's advisers to guide him on matters of American procedure, of which they themselves may well have been ignorant.

The bond-certificate drive launched by de Valera proved overwhelmingly successful. On 20 July Collins was able to write to Stack: 'The situation in America is hopeful. The President is getting tremendous receptions and the Press in its entirety has thrown itself open to the Irish propaganda. . . . Money is coming in well – really well not a mere addition of noughts. Yet our hope is here and must be here. The job will be to prevent eyes turning to Paris or New York as a substitute for London.'

As yet there was no inkling in Ireland of any incipient quarrel between de Valera and the Irish-American leaders. This would be made apparent, both at home and in the United States, only in the following year.

IV

'Collins never went into a job without knowing all about it', is Mr W. T. Cosgrave's comment. He undertook the organization of the Dail Loan with a clear insight into the obstacles confronting him. He was a wanted man; his accounting system would be liable to raids and destruction; any money collected might be seized; collection itself would be hazardous, advertisement subject to suppression; those who had money to lend would, even supposing they were Republican supporters, be chary of risking considerable sums in such an enterprise.

Griffith himself had doubted whether such a loan would bring in the required resources. The most Sinn Fein had ever been able to raise was a few thousand pounds. Collins replied confidently that they would get £250,000. A close associate recalls that Griffith looked at Collins thereafter with new respect. He had begun to realize that the bellicose young man, so critical of Sinn Fein, had a sound head after all.

Much of Collins's Loan activity was carried on in his office at No. 6 Harcourt Street. A martinet for office decorum, he frowned on relaxation during working hours, permitted no swearing in front of the ladies, and held Desmond FitzGerald's head under a tap to teach him to recognize one, when FitzGerald politely refused admittance to a stranger who turned out to be Michael's cousin, Nancy O'Brien. He also saw that the ladies got their lunch at the proper time. He himself had no time to eat. If lunch were brought in he often ate it cold a couple of hours later, or wolfed down a few sandwiches fetched by the faithful Joe O'Reilly.

He was tireless night and day. He worked as if he were on military manœuvres. 'Unless you had business with him you couldn't get near him,' remarks that most indefatigable of General Secretaries, Mr Padraig O'Keeffe. Anyone wishing to get near Collins would, indeed, first have to run the gauntlet of Mr O'Keeffe. Fixed by that gentleman's keen blue eyes the would-be waster of Collins's time – Ireland's time! – would, if he were wise, retreat. Mr O'Keeffe did not share Collins's views about swearing in the office.

An attempt to advertise the Loan met with the instant suppression of all papers which carried it. The Castle authorities had so far agreed to countenance the assembling of the Dail; they were not, however, going to watch it take over their own functions.

Collins found an alternative means of advertisement. A film was made, showing Bond Certificates being issued to a group of Sinn Fein leaders. Two copies of it were printed and taken to the cinemas by forceful young men who ensured its showing, making a quick departure before the police could arrive.[16]

Michael determined to inaugurate the Loan in his own constituency. It was his first visit home since his brief trip in January and he made the most of it. The children adored him; he was a natural companion of the young, as of the very old. He could also be decidedly avuncular, as his nephews Sean and Michael Powell discovered when playing with a toy boat by the River Lee. Unable to swim himself, Collins distrusted deep water, and when they refused to stop their game he tossed the boat far out of reach into the current. He was, in all things, a man to be obeyed.

He duly attended the Loan inauguration meeting in Dunmanway, despite the increased risk of capture whenever he travelled in country areas. As usual, Providence looked after him. He had arranged to go first to Clonakilty. Word of this leaked through: a posse awaited him at Clonakilty station. After leaving Cork he fell asleep, missed the junction, and was carried safely to Dunmanway. 'I had no excitement', he wrote to Hannie. In Dunman-

[16] *Evening Herald* 6 November 1965

way he opened the Loan with the first instalment (£25) of his own contribution; a large enough sum, for it represented nearly a month's means of livelihood.

Collins's Finance Committee sought to establish a gold reserve. Small amounts of gold were collected all over the country, but getting these safely to Dublin was a hazardous undertaking, the risk of discovery in raids ever present. Batt O'Connor has described how the bulk of it was concealed in the foundations of his Donnybrook home in a baby's coffin. Other hoards were built into walls and floors in various houses, Maurice Collins's shop, for instance, and the cellar of Kirwan's, also in Parnell Street.

Throughout the constituencies contributions were collected generally by the Deputies and their assistants tramping the country, making door-to-door calls. Money came usually in small amounts. Joe McGrath, for one, would wait patiently while it was fetched, as often as not, out of an old sock hidden under the owner's bed. The Irish people distrusted banks : the Loan organizers hardly less. Where the money could not be changed into gold it was deposited in the name of prominent Sinn Fein sympathizers in various branches of different banks.

Lists of subscribers were obviously of vital interest to the British authorities. On 12 September No. 6 Harcourt Street was raided. Collins sat on the roof until the visitors departed, when he descended again to his office and continued his work. There was elation among those of his associates who were not yet used to his prowess in evasive action.

'When I heard about the raid on No. 6 I expected to [be] able [to use] about you a phrase that you yourself used when you heard that I had got caught', runs a badly damaged letter to Collins from Sean McGrath in London. Collins's reply was laconic : 'I am very glad that you were saved the necessity of using that impious expression. I fear you were an optimist.'[17]

Some of the difficulties encountered in carrying out the Loan work and how they were met are to be found in the correspondence between Collins in Dublin and Terence MacSwiney in his constituency of mid-Cork.[18] On 2 October MacSwiney, sending

[17] National Library of Ireland: Ministry of Defence Archives
[18] All extracts from these letters which follow are quoted by kind permission of the Deputy Keeper of Records, Public Record Office of Ireland

details of his local organization, commented: 'The police are causing us *much* trouble', and, in a note written the same day from Macroom: 'Anything may happen us here – I had a narrow shave yesterday – armed police held me up & searched bag – got nothing. But they probably had instructions to lift me – if any excuse.'

On 21 October he wrote again to Collins:

'We need 5,000 more *copies of the Prospectus*. This will enable us to work the *whole* constituency. We need them *at once*, as we are about to begin the house to house canvass. . . . Our reliance is almost entirely on Volunteers for distribution of literature & canvassing. Their mobilization lines are being well worked accordingly. . . .

'As ordinary press advertising & Posters were out of the question we had to rely on making distribution of special printed matter effective. . . . A particular night was selected for the distribution, the Volunteers were mobilized & the distribution was carried on simultaneously throughout the whole Constituency – another safeguard against raids! Though the police raided the Constituency in all directions they got nothing worth speaking of – & the distribution was a complete success.'

Collins interested himself in the design of the projected Bonds. He possessed an old Fenian Bond and hoped to get something similar produced. Although at least two designs were submitted the Bonds were never actually printed. Instead, official signed receipts in green, gold, and black were issued, printed secretly by Colm O Lochlainn.

Despite the precaution of taking another office at 76 Harcourt Street, complete with secret cupboards, Collins could not carry on his Loan work unmolested for long. In November this office, too, was raided. Collins escaped once more, swinging down through the skylight of the Standard Hotel nearby – he cracked a rib on the rail as he cleared the stair-well – and proceeded down to the street to join an interested crowd watching the raid. All the other men on the office staff were arrested. In Diarmuid O'Hegarty's absence Collins took over payment of the Dail salaries. It may be remarked that when O'Hegarty returned he regained this job but not his secretary. Staff problems were not for Collins!

Keeping accounts in these conditions must have been a nightmare. As Minister of Finance Collins had charge of far more than the Loan money. A typical note of his to the Dail's Accountant, Daithi O'Donaghue, gives some indication of the innumerable small amounts which might come in from any source for various purposes at any time, all liable to instant seizure by the British, whose aim was to crush the Loan.

20 Dec 1919

'D.O.'D.   All for the Self Determination Fund
£37.6.6.   per W. T. Cosgrave

Loan
£10   Gold.   E. D. Ryan
                        Cashel

All gold in envelope ⎫
You need not count it ⎬   *M.C.*
as I've done that   ⎪
£2   Mde Gonne. ⎭

Please be in today 1 to 2 if you can. A man who I think has some money is meeting me at that time.

M.C.

£65 Gold   From Manchester per
£235 Cheque.   P. O'Donaghue   Manchester
                This has to go to Suspense.'[19]

By the end of the year Collins was regarding the Loan results with mixed satisfaction and exasperation. On the one hand there was the country district of which he wrote feelingly to Austin Stack: 'If you saw the bloody pack down there & their casual indefinite meaningless purposeless way of carrying on——' On the other hand there was Terence MacSwiney who had calculated that if the eighty constituencies of Ireland were to raise the Loan total of £250,000 among them mid-Cork had better make up what the North-East of Ulster undoubtedly would not.

[19] Brother Allen's Papers

'I am writing this line to confirm the safe receipt of £4,035', Collins wrote to him on 19 December, making no attempt to hide his pride in the men and women of Cork. 'May I say that this amount is twice as great as any amount received up to the present from any Constituency. I need hardly say that I think this most creditable, and certainly Mid Cork, in its working, must have presented difficulties that very few other Constituencies presented.'

V

On leaving England in July 1919 Field-Marshal Smuts declared : 'Unless the Irish question is settled on the great principles which form the basis of this Empire, this Empire must cease to exist.'[20] Settlement, in the eyes of the British Government, first required subjection.

The Dail, which had not met in public since May, was giving further evidence of its determination to run the country. It appointed consuls, produced propaganda material which it dispatched to foreign newspaper correspondents, set up numerous committees to enquire into every aspect of national life, and established a Land Bank.

On 12 September 1919 the Dail was declared 'a dangerous association' and was suppressed. Everything else suppressible, Sinn Fein, the Volunteers, the Gaelic League, Cumann na mBan, and the national Press were also proclaimed.

Ireland responded. Britain had, in Irish eyes, declared war. With the suppression of the Dail all mention of it was to vanish from the Press for nearly two years. The 'dangerous associates' continued, however, to meet in secret. The Dail had held firmly to a policy of 'civil disobedience' which was in fact one of obedience to the Dail itself. Forcibly driven underground it now turned all its powers, civil and military, upon its aggressor. The combat in arms, long seen by Collins as the only contest capable of solving the Anglo-Irish struggle, was now at hand.

It did not begin immediately. A country does not swing overnight from defence to attack, even when the way has been paved

[20] Quoted in H. Duncan Hall *The British Commonwealth of Nations* (London 1920) p. 325

by an increasing number of scuffles with police, occasionally fatal and, in some cases, deliberately provoked by the defending forces; by inflammatory speeches, gaol breaks, sporadic bursts of gunfire, and the singing of seditious songs.

'The Irish', declared Lloyd George about this time to Lord Riddell, 'are a curious people. Whenever you try to help them, they turn and rend you.'

On 22 December he introduced his 'Better Government of Ireland' Bill. It was partition again, with two separate Irish Parliaments and Westminster in ultimate authority. Arthur Griffith declared, 'There is nothing for Irishmen to discuss in the English Premier's proposals. They are not intended to be operative. They are made in order to affect and mislead opinion in America.'[21]

Erskine Childers saw Lloyd George's new Bill as 'this heroic defiance of the weak by the strong'.[22] Ireland indeed, as has been aptly pointed out by her historians, was not interested in Better Government. All she wanted was to govern herself.

[21] The *Irish Bulletin* 23 December 1919
[22] Ibid. 4 March 1920

CHAPTER EIGHT

The Irish Volunteers

(1919)

I

'I think in long strides', Collins once wrote. It was this ability to grasp essentials in perspective that made him what Lord Rosebery once described as 'that most formidable of all men of action, the practical visionary'. His vision was of Ireland free; yet somehow, inevitably, spies and informers had always infiltrated the freedom movements to destroy them from within. This much was well known. Collins looked further. Spies and informers are effective only where machinery exists to use what they have to sell. Collins now concentrated on rendering that machinery in Ireland not only useless to the British but also profitable to Sinn Fein.

The young detective, Ned Broy, had been sending information to Sinn Fein since 1917. Now, in January 1919, he met Collins for the first time. When Collins came into the room it was as if an electric current had suddenly been switched on. The thought came to Broy instantly : 'We're going to win. We have a man at last !' The meeting was to prove one of the most effective of any Collins had had. On 7 April 1919 Broy arranged to bring him into detective headquarters. Collins spent the evening as usual meeting contacts at Vaughan's Hotel. He asked Sean Nunan to wait and, when the others had gone, suggested they should go for a walk. It was 12.30 a.m., an odd hour, Nunan considered, for walking. They found Broy waiting in the D.M.P. Station in Brunswick Street. When they left three hours later the procedure and extent of the police Intelligence network lay within Collins's grasp.

He constructed his own organization on two planes, civil and military. On the civil side he recruited men and women in the post offices and railways of Ireland and Britain. In every prison in Ireland warders worked for him. Commercial travellers made good intelligence agents, their work enabling them to move about unsuspected. Later, in curfew times, they could often obtain passes, a valuable consideration. Collins drew what he called his 'Q' Division from among the sailors and dockworkers who manned ports throughout Europe and in America.

Hundreds of those who worked for him never met him and never knew if those who worked beside them were also part of his organization. They were unpaid, anonymous, efficient workers for Ireland who scorned danger, and the full extent of their service can only be guessed, for only Collins ever knew it. For him alone all the jig-saw pieces fitted into a coherent whole. To keep it so was the only answer to the informer.

Although he was not officially designated Director of Intelligence until June 1919 Collins was also making sure that all information passing through Volunteer hands found its way to him. He was, indeed, beginning to see the necessity of co-ordinating all Volunteer work lest serious cross-play of endeavour should develop.

In Intelligence work, as in their activities generally, the Volunteers were pitted against the R.I.C. rather than against the military, whose conventional combat training left their intelligence system floundering when faced by guerilla warfare.

The eyes and ears of the entire Collins network was the I.R.B. He was ultimately to become President of the I.R.B. Supreme Council, a position which made him Head of the Irish Republic in the eyes of the organization. In practice the Brotherhood no less than Collins himself recognized the Dail as the lawful government of Ireland. By his position in the I.R.B., however, Collins was ideally placed to perfect his Intelligence by the support of its members, whether they worked through the Volunteers or, like Sam Maguire in London and Neil Kerr on the shipping routes, in civil positions.

Many members of the R.I.C. protested strongly against their rôle as a political strong-arm force. They demanded the status of unarmed policemen with normal functions, and many resigned when their plea was unsuccessful. Others stayed on to work for Collins in difficult and dangerous conditions.

Collins now launched a campaign against his most insidious enemies, the G Division of the D.M.P. These men were also devoting less time to crime detection and more and more to political work. Sinn Fein leaders were followed ceaselessly; arrests were almost invariably the result of G-man activity. On 9 April Collins's warnings that these political actions must cease were pressed home by a raid on one G-man's house and the tying up of another in the street.

'Mick is very well & very hearty', wrote Robert Barton.[1] 'A tower of strength & by no means the wild extremist he is supposed to be. The only extreme things about him are daring & determination.'

These were undoubtedly qualities he shared with his G.H.Q. colleagues. Through the nature of his work in Organization and Intelligence Collins also gained exceptional opportunities to use them.

The offices of the G.H.Q. Staff of the I.R.A. were scattered all over the city. Collins in Bachelor's Walk or Cullenswood House, Gearoid O'Sullivan in Eustace Street. The names and professions described on the doors were calculated to bewilder rather than to guide. One acquaintance of O'Sullivan and O'Hegarty was as taken aback as they were when he came face to face with them in the office of 'George Doyle, Insurance Agent'. Numerous young men rode up on bicycles to University College where Richard Mulcahy was engaged in studies which would have astounded the Medical Faculty. It would be more enlightening to say that the G.H.Q. offices were wherever its members happened to be.

Those having business with them would come unobtrusively to the small pubs frequented by the I.R.A. Staff, Devlin's, or Kirwan's, or Vaughan's (designated Joint Nos. 1–3 respectively) and go as casually as they had come. Hunted, never stopping for long in one place but going their deliberate ways about Dublin, usually on bicycles, these men studied no manuals for the waging of war. In the words of one of them: 'Manuals wouldn't have told us what window to climb out of in a raid. We didn't even know where we'd sleep that night.' They were men of similar background, guided by a spirit of common dedication. Each shouldered the work that came to him in that spirit in which recognition of the need for co-operation was dominant.

In its construction the Irish Volunteer body, which during this year became known generally as the Irish Republican Army or

[1] Letter to Mrs Llewelyn Davies dated 13 June 1919

I.R.A., appears on paper like any other national defence force. The brigades were under the direction of G.H.Q. Staff in Dublin, each having its own local headquarters and staffs. There the resemblance to a regular, home-based army ends. In the country brigades each Volunteer followed his own occupation, drilling and receiving military instruction at evening or weekend meetings. Even where instructors were available arms all too often were not. Battalion and brigade staffs met with difficulty, often converging from far-flung villages in their area where every movement was open to R.I.C. suspicion. 'Headquarters' might be a cottage, farmhouse, or back room in a pub and changed as circumstances compelled.

Collins had his own methods of recruiting officers. He wanted Sean MacEoin to lead the 1st Battalion, the Longford Brigade. MacEoin, the blacksmith of Ballinalee, was supporting his widowed mother and family, and feared it could not be done. Collins insisted. A wrestling match resolved the argument and Collins won. It was the start of a notable friendship.

It should be stressed that no offensive action was contemplated in official quarters while the political sphere of action provided by the Dail was allowed to function.

Troops, armoured cars, tanks, lorries, and all the paraphernalia of war continued to pour into Dublin. The R.I.C., well over 9,000 strong, stock-piled their arms in town and village barracks. Provided the Volunteers could be prevented from obtaining the means to confront this militant array, it might well be supposed that the British would easily enough control the situation. The overwhelming advantage in arms which they possessed was, however, outweighed by three primary disadvantages: the need to operate on their opponents' home ground, the spirit of the Irish people which every coercive act only served to unite more strongly against them, and Collins's Intelligence system.

II

Michael was fast becoming a badly-wanted man, although the Castle's agents' renewed search for him made little difference to his way of life. He might curse the G-men profusely for making his work more difficult : at no time did he regard himself as a man 'on the run'. His companions might don stage moustaches or clerical garb. Collins disguised himself in normality. It was the one camouflage that British agents, raiding monasteries for impostors, watching for the cautious, the evasive, never questioned.

Collins met brigade officers at Vaughan's, men from the country areas in Upper Abbey Street, sailors down in Shanahan's pub, detectives at Tomas Gay's house. This in addition to his financial work in Harcourt Street. He slept with a revolver under his pillow, sharing a room and often a bed with Harry Boland or Piaras Beaslai or Gearoid O'Sullivan. Two men in a raid fought better than one. He carried no gun as he bicycled swiftly from one appointment to another. There would be arms at hand at his destination if they were needed; if he were held up in the streets his most effective weapon was bluff and a disarming cheerfulness. Documents were carried, for the most part, by Joe O'Reilly or by unobtrusive young men and women going about the city. Collins carried only his small black appointments diary. When he needed to carry other written information he put it in a single sheet of paper in his socks, scorning the bulky padding worn by some of his colleagues.

Though he came and went openly, only one man always knew where he was and hid it from everyone else. 'My nice lad', Collins wrote of Joe O'Reilly; yet, obsessed by the need to be forever working at top speed, he would almost kick O'Reilly from the room to hurry him on a mission.

If he had less time for social life than others, work and not fear of pursuit made him curtail it. He would drop into a party : the guests would hear his laugh upon the stairs and feel a breeze as the door was flung open and he bounded in. For half an hour the room would be animated with his overcharged vitality, then he would be gone again, leaving a feeling of having been winded on the company, which would only slowly regain its normality, still conscious of the desolate air of the flattened cushions where he had hurled himself.

Any of his family could always be sure of a welcome, no matter how fierce the pressure of the hunt. In the summer of 1919 his sister, Katie Sheridan, came up by train from Mayo wearing a brown gabardine coat, a fact that the touts waiting to betray Michael Collins into Castle hands quickly conveyed to Dublin. It would be easy to identify her there, and only a matter of time before she led them to Collins. The train was delayed at Athlone. Katie had been ill; a friend who saw her there was struck by her wan appearance and insisted that the gabardine coat be changed for her own fur one. The train reached Dublin at midnight. The platform was surrounded by military; the passengers were ordered to keep their seats. Word was passed that Michael Collins's sister was among them.

Among the few people waiting on the platform Katie was horrified to see not only Joe O'Reilly, but Michael himself. She sank back, ill with fright, but Michael saw her and pushed forward. He angrily asked a porter the cause of the delay. The news that his own capture was imminent enraged him further. He stalked up to a British officer. That damned Collins again! This was his third hold-up that day on that blackguard's account. Here, moreover, was a lady who was ill. What possible use could there be in detaining her? The officer agreed that she certainly looked ill. Since her description in no way tallied with that of Collins's sister. . . . Michael courteously handed her out and O'Reilly escorted her from the station. Michael, still muttering imprecations followed them out.

His love for children was manifest wherever he went. Probably those he saw most at this time were Batt O'Connor's. Their home was for a long time his headquarters, working, eating or sleeping. The five children adored him. They lavished attention on his old Raleigh bicycle, which nonetheless clanked alarmingly as he sped about on it. They gave up inviting other children home. In all the months of war, when his life might depend on a proud boast that they so much as knew him, they kept silent. They helped with cooking, shopping, and housework, since neither maid nor tradesman now came to the house. In return Michael never missed playing with them each day. It might be an elaborate game in the evening; he might have time only to hear their prayers. By no excuse of work or war or weariness did he ever disappoint them.

'Children are good for him', observed someone shrewdly when another complained of his preoccupation with them when delay might mean disaster. In a world of bloodshed and brutality in which he had so often to give the word for men to die it may well have been that but for the children who came for brief moments into his life his mind would have lost its assurance that Pearse's 'things bright and green, things young and happy' would, after all, remain when the horrors had passed.

In this year of 1919 Collins finally shouldered his way to the forefront as a leader of men. That is not to say that his was as yet a name, as de Valera's was, behind which Ireland rallied. De Valera was the shibboleth; the necessary personification of the tricolour, Easter Week, and the declaration of the Republic. Collins was that more down-to-earth figure, the man who expounded no vision, devised no formula, but got to work and saw that others did the same. The name of Michael Collins meant probably little or nothing to the Volunteer in a remote company. To his brigade commandant, running the gamut of the Castle network to go to Dublin to look for arms, arrange for a military training adviser, or discuss how to weld scattered units into a fighting entity, Collins was all-important.

There are two kinds of leader : one appeals to a nation's idealism, the other to the individual's everyday necessities. The one stands apart from the people that he may the more clearly be seen; a personage rather than a person. This was the leadership required by those who had pledged their lives to the Irish Republic in all its symbolism : to fill that rôle they had chosen de Valera.

It was a rôle for which his own nature had cast him. He was the ascetic, the tall, remote figure, un-Irish in appearance, who could yet claim to speak for Ireland. Perhaps most of all his Spanish name mantled him in mystery, giving added romanticism to his pronouncements.

In Michael Collins Ireland was to find that other type of leader whose pre-eminence lies not in any difference from the people but in identification with them. Such leaders are found with their men in battle, sharing equally in danger and revelry. Collins found his creed in Yeats's *Oisin*. He too preferred to cast his lot with his friends and 'dwell in the house of the Fenians, be they in flames or at feast'.

Collins lived life to the full, though not to excess. Most of his rendezvous took place in bars where numbers of men coming and going would arouse no comment. Since the man without a drink would be suspect he was always to be found with a small sherry or port by him, though he often left it scarcely tasted. He favoured brandy with curaçao, an occasional whiskey.

He had good reason for not developing a drinking habit, knowing only too well that he could not afford to be anything but cold sober. He was anxious to instil the same awareness into his fellow-workers and was particularly concerned that anyone falling into enemy hands should beware the friendly warder, only too willing to slip in a bottle. 'It is bad enough outside but when it occurs inside it is much worse', he wrote to a priest who had warned him of one such case. Informers, as the authorities knew, are more often made than born.

He had little time for women, and his blunt ways annoyed many. One hostess who had offered her house as the venue for a meeting waited in delighted anticipation for her first glimpse of the legendary Big Fellow. Opening the door at his knock she was almost thrust aside, greeted with a peremptory 'Which room?', and found herself clutching his hat while her guest showed himself up, taking the stairs four at a time.

A man who rejoiced in his own strength, of mind as of body, he could show ruthless self-control. In these early years of hard work and danger he was a heavy smoker. Suddenly he stopped. He explained to his sister Katie : 'I was becoming a slave to cigarettes : I'll be a slave to nothing.'

His influence on others was incalculable. He radiated his own self-confidence to others, so that they not only attempted the hitherto impossible but did it. He had most truly that misjudged attribute of being all things to all men. He had to be. He dealt with seamen, statesmen, soldiers, and priests, going perhaps in a matter of minutes from men of better education than himself to men of no education at all, from men who would risk their lives for him to those who needed convincing before they would venture a shilling in Ireland's support.

His changes of mood were as spectacular and unpredictable as the play of the Northern Lights. An ugly scowl at a hint of blame, a hearty laugh that relieved tension. Embarrassed to the point of surliness by sympathy for himself, another's tragedy easily moved him to passionate tears. All his emotions were extreme and he made no attempt to hide them. Maintaining a defiant pride in what he termed his 'real tempers' he was equally unashamed of his tears.

His reaction to military feats often took the form of a generous impulse to show his delight. Unfortunately, like so many of his actions, it laid him open to misunderstanding. On one occasion, when George Plunkett and others had featured in a successful fight, he offered them ten pounds with which to celebrate. Plunkett recoiled in outraged pride. Such an incident may well have been the basis of many another man's bitter antagonism to Collins, who remained hurt and bewildered. He knew he had blundered time and again on people's susceptibilities; he never learnt to side-step in time. He showed his feelings in actions rather than words, and too often the action smashed through what the circumspect word he could not find would have smoothed.

For his lads, carrying out his orders without question simply because they were Mick Collin's orders, there would be the slap on the back, the word of praise. The words they soon forgot; the slap on the back was the seal of comradeship and to earn it they would have died for him.

Collins has been aptly likened to Danton. *L'audace et toujours l'audace* is the shout of youth. Collins was a young man leading young men. Few of his fellow-leaders in Dail or Army were many years older. One of the exceptions was Cathal Brugha. It is a striking sign of how youth-dominated the movement was that a man in his mid-forties, who in a British Cabinet would probably have been conceded years by his colleagues, had been active in the struggle when Collins and his peers were scarcely boys out of school.

No man was ever more ready to cry *l'audace!* than Cathal Brugha. Yet it must soon have become apparent to him that it was Collins's utterance of it that commanded attention rather than his own. Collins had ordered the deaths of over-zealous G-men and the G-men died; Brugha advocated the systematic dispatch of the entire British Cabinet and his colleagues started up in protest, Collins foremost amongst them. Brugha's war was to the uttermost. He did not reflect as Collins did, and as Collins did not forbear to point out, that a Cabinet inevitably replaces itself; a G-man's knowledge died with him, and his successors became increasingly reluctant to search it out afresh.

Above all, as he was to become aware of Collins treading upon his heels, Brugha was to distrust the younger man's control of the I.R.B. He knew its power and its hidden resources; and, as Minister for Defence, he distrusted it profoundly as a dangerous challenge, not only to his own authority, but to the authority of the Dail.[2]

Brugha was a slave to Ireland. Hard as he worked, however, his position was in any case one that laid itself open to interference. Other Dail Ministers worked full-time at their departmental jobs and drew salaries accordingly. Brugha continued in his occupation as a director of Lalor's ecclesiastical candlemakers. He ran the Department of Defence from his business office and forewent his ministerial salary. Much of the work inevitably fell on the shoulders of the Chief of Staff, Mulcahy, who was, when all is said and done, better suited to deal with it.

In the evenings, the office work – the work of all his offices – done, Collins held his interviews. Those whom he wished to see knew where to find him. Otherwise a blank stare from Christy Harte, the porter at Vaughan's, or from Liam Devlin, or Jim Kirwan at the other 'Joints' would be as effective as a locked door in shielding the quarry from unwelcome intruders. Because he trusted them, men and women of every kind gave him their protection. For many of them it was all they had to give.

III

'It looks as if peace conditions were going to be no less thrilling than those prevailing in war time', Michael wrote to Hannie on 23 August 1919. 'For the moment (apart from American Exchange) things are settled enough but I am looking forward to the winter for significant happenings – perhaps not in England

[2] Collins himself was publicly to deny that the I.R.B. sought in any way to undermine the authority of the Dail. In a written reply to an American correspondent he declared: 'One body only has the right and authority to speak for the Irish people . . . DAIL EIREANN. That is the Government of Ireland, and to it all national organizations within Ireland give allegiance. . . .' – c. March 1921. Collins Papers.

but certainly in many places and so far as we ourselves are concerned in America I think.'

In these early days of de Valera's mission to the United States Collins's hopes of its outcome were threefold. Firstly he looked for the success of the External Loan drive; secondly he hoped that the Irish-American vote in this pre-election year would make both Republicans and Democrats alive to Ireland's claims and bring pressure to bear on Britain; and thirdly he believed that large numbers of Irish-Americans would show their loyalty by returning to fight for Ireland. Only the first of these was to be realized. Meanwhile, in Ireland itself, the country was rapidly being carried from the defensive into open war.

There developed at the same time an awareness that it must be fought along guerilla lines, in which the advantage would always be with the I.R.A. so long as a small body of men could choose their own battle-site, could remain mobile and avoid encirclement, and could strike swiftly and retire secretly. Guerilla warfare favours the home side over an extended period. Its serious disadvantage for the I.R.A. was lack of arms, the decisive factor that was to make the struggle both prolonged and desperate.

Shortly after the suppression of the Dail Collins issued orders to all brigade commandants that monthly reports of all activities were to be submitted. This would not only enable G.H.Q. to build up a comprehensive picture of the progress of operations throughout the country, but would also spur the less active to greater effort.

From rudimentary and unpromising beginnings the I.R.A. would forge itself, with training and the tempering processes of practical warfare, to become the highly-integrated spearhead of the national intent. For these men, small farmers, shop assistants, students for the professions, were of the stock of the Wild Geese, who had leavened the great European armies in three centuries of fluctuation in the balance of power. Among the finest mercenaries the world had known, they had attended the fall of monarchies and the rise of Empires. The history of Europe is in no inconsiderable part the history of Irishmen in exile who 'left their bones at Fontenoy and up in the Pyrenees', as Collins so often and proudly called upon their descendants to remember. That the Fighting Race had indeed not died out had been witnessed more recently in Flanders and the bloody conflict of Suvla Bay. Small wonder that, once such a people adapted this formidable heritage to the exigencies of guerilla warfare, it should bring the Crown forces in Ireland to a hold.

Yet even the most go-ahead areas faced difficulties peculiar to guerilla formations. One dispatch ran apologetically :

'You must excuse me for not going to see you on the 1st of the month. I expect you are aware that I was to be arrested on the 1st ins. for a fine which was imposed on me for breaking up, in the last strike in Mountjoy. . . . If you still wish to see me you can drop me a note & I will be able to go up to the city on last train on Sat. night or Sat. week if not arrested in the meantime.'[3]

Another commandant, asked for news of one officer, could only admit to having difficulty in discovering his whereabouts, he having been on the run for nearly two years.

On occasion Collins acted as a buffer between brigades and G.H.Q. in the extraordinary conditions of volunteer service. A peremptory demand to know why no Brigade Council meeting had been held in one area in September was met by an explanation that it had proved impossible for its members to attend during the harvesting period. The commandant himself had had to work overtime in his civilian job nearly every night that month. Collins replied, somewhat dubiously, 'I think the explanation is all right'.

He was not always so sympathetic. 'I would ask you whether something could not be done to put life into the Companies of — Brigade. Quite clearly the Officers are not doing their work, and such being the case, it is hard to expect activity on the part of the men.'

Reports unsigned or written in pencil, slackness in the holding of company parades, or in the taking of action against offenders by their superior officers roused his wrath. 'I return herewith the Battalion Report Forms as these are for your own information. They appear to be in an extremely slovenly form.'

[3] National Library of Ireland: Ministry of Defence Archives, from which source all the quotations from correspondence between Collins and the I.R.A. brigades which follow are taken.

Though he knew well enough that to many of his correspondents pen and ink were more terrifying than a revolver Collins insisted on a high standard of neatness and businesslike method in all dispatches. His own surviving ones, many of them bearing evidence of having been worn about the feet or buried in damp places, are meticulously concise, every item being separately paragraphed and numbered. The answer was required to be similarly tabulated.

He was concerned also with the question of organizing Volunteer units in England, and wrote in October to Sean McGrath in London suggesting that he band the London-Irish together for this purpose.

Collins's Volunteer correspondence must have been staggering in its volume and variety. While most of what remains of it deals with routine matters of reports, forms, information on projected journeys, payment of subscriptions to *An t-Oglach* and the like, now and then a glimpse is afforded of how greatly these men relied on him to get them over any problem, great or small, personal or otherwise. Some of their requests are unexpected, as, for instance, an enquiry for 'a decent chap who knows the liquor business, bottling etc. You might get somebody to make enquiries if such a person is to be had. He would need to be a T.T.' Or again : 'My absence for a few days will be due to my marriage. Don't faint. . . . Would it be in order for me to get married in uniform? If you think so I will require the loan of your uniform & slacks. It is the only one I know would suit me.'

In all Collins's letters to brigade officers there is a simplicity, an unpretentious realization that these men were human beings, each coping with problems of local environment. Though he demanded a high standard of discipline it was no part of his philosophy to insist on regimentation at the expense of local enterprise. He preferred to give each commandant a free hand, so long as his operations lay within the broad terms of national policy.

His own plans were meticulously conceived. Robert Barton, bored with being on the run since his escape months before, would wander to the shed in Cullenswood garden of an evening, and add his flair for plotting to that of Collins. The two became close comrades in daring designs.

In August 1919 Cathal Brugha, as Minister for Defence, put forward a motion which was approved by the Dail that all its members and, in addition, the entire body of the Irish Volunteers should take an oath of allegiance to the Irish Republic and the Dail. Hitherto the Volunteers had been subject only to their own Executive. By taking this oath they would acknowledge the Dail's right, and specifically that of the Minister for Defence, to control their actions. It was considered desirable that the elected government of the people should accept responsibility for what was done by the Army.

Theoretically the oath should have enabled the Dail to refute any suggestion by the British that I.R.A. operations were mere acts of terrorism by lawless bands, to be stamped out before the Dail's claims to legislate for the Irish people could be considered. In fact it is probable that this linking of the two arms of the movement was a proximate cause of the suppression of the Dail three weeks later. The British continued to insist to the last that Sinn Fein and the 'moderates' in the Dail, that is, those deputies who were not Volunteers, were being coerced into condoning the 'gangster activities' of the 'extremists' or I.R.A. leaders.

Collins was opposed to the Volunteers taking the oath. He saw the thin edge of the wedge of political manœuvring in it and did not need Alderman Tom Kelly's reminder to the Dail of how the Volunteers of 1782 had fared at the hands of the politicians. He was well aware too of Brugha's propensity for seeing the hand of the I.R.B. in Volunteer affairs. The friction that ensued between the two men was to increase henceforth. Long before the motion came before the Dail, however, Collins had given way. De Valera, President of the Volunteer Executive, favoured its acceptance. In the debate on the motion Collins uttered no word, and the oath was administered the following year throughout the Volunteer body. Collins himself accompanied Dick McKee in visiting the various companies of the Dublin Brigade for this purpose. This was, incidentally, the first and last occasion in the course of the war on which many of the rank and file caught a glimpse of him.

In practice the I.R.A. continued to act as an autonomous body, subject only to the decisions of their G.H.Q. with which Brugha was, of course, closely associated. Certain areas, reacting strongly under British pressure, began to apply their own pressure on Dublin to be allowed to take the offensive.

All over the country action against the R.I.C. was assuming a pattern rather than occurring spasmodically as hitherto. It was action fully approved by Collins. With the suppression of the Dail many of his colleagues who had advocated political rather than military action realized as he had done from the first that force would, in the end, prove the only effective answer to force.

Collins himself was now driven to take the action anticipated in his warning to G-men the previous April to abandon their political activities. The more assiduous among them were not, clearly, to be discouraged by mere threats. On 30 July Detective-Sergeant Smith was shot down in a Dublin street.

There was no elation for Collins in his killing, though the G-man had been a particularly injurious thorn in the nationalist flesh for years. He regretted the necessity for such action: he never shrank from it, or sought to disguise his acceptance of the necessity in either delight or deprecation.

Collins was already picking certain men from the Dublin Brigade – later to be known as The Squad or, ultimately, The Twelve Apostles – to undertake with Dail Cabinet sanction the highly dangerous task of eliminating those whose knowledge would otherwise soon have nullified the work so far achieved, as had happened to every freedom movement in Ireland in the past. Collins knew that if he did not strike now, and unerringly, he and his fellow-workers would themselves be struck down.

Eventually the Squad was to operate on a full-time, salaried basis, the striking arm of Collins's Intelligence. No member of the Squad was ever, under any circumstances, permitted to shoot even a known spy without authority, except in self-defence. From the first Collins stressed the importance of remembering that an indiscriminate bullet might eliminate, not an enemy, but a vital link with enemy intentions.[4]

[4] In a written account of the formation of the Squad Major-General Paddy Daly has stated that eight men – Daly himself, Joe Leonard, Ben Barrett, Sean Doyle, Tom Keogh, Jim Slattery, Vincent Byrne, and Mick McDonnell – were called to a meeting early in September 1919 by Collins and Mulcahy, at which the Squad was formed, only the first four named

The hostile G-men were not left in ignorance of the new dispensation for long. The raid on No. 6 Harcourt Street on 12 September has already been mentioned. The indefatigable Detective Constable Daniel Hoey knew his prey. He had pounced on Sean MacDiarmada in 1916. Now he had come for Collins. Collins, however, was not to be found and the raiding party had to be content with Ernest Blythe and Padraig O'Keeffe. O'Keeffe saw that Collins had escaped and, with ominous intuition of what lay in store for the man who had so consistently ignored Collins's warnings, turned to the G-man: 'You're for it tonight, Hoey'.

That night Hoey was dead, shot down outside Detective Headquarters. Ironically, though he had been first on the list of the condemned, he died from a bullet fired in self-defence by Mick McDonnell. Greek had met Greek by the way and read death in each other's eyes.

In the ensuing months more G-men died. They did so for specific, never general, actions. It was customary for them to sign the reports of their activities submitted to Broy for typing. Each one, in effect, had signed his own indictment and death warrant.

Collins was expanding his Intelligence. Having absorbed the methods used by its British counterpart he now set about making full use of his information. He had filing systems for photographs, newspaper cuttings, and the mass of apparently trivial information collected in every quarter by his agents. He obtained keys to the cipher codes of the police, military, and Castle. He tapped the communication channels and perfected his own, so that vital information could be sent quickly to the area concerned.

Charles James Fox once remarked: 'I would make the people of Ireland the garrison of Ireland.' Collins proceeded to do just

being then selected. Comdt Vincent Byrne, in a statement to the author, can recall attending no such meeting, and points out that it would have been strange to announce what was afoot to eight men and then select only four of them. His impression is that Smith was shot by ordinary Volunteers chosen in the main from the 2nd Battn, Dublin Brigade, and that two 'unofficial' squads of four men each, under Daly and McDonnell respectively, carried out the shooting of the G-man, Barton, in November 1919 under authority from Collins, the Squad proper being formed in March 1920, when Comdt Byrne himself and Jim Slattery both left their civil employment to join it in a full-time capacity.

that. Under him men and women all over the country, no matter how obscure their way of life, held the land for Sinn Fein.

The British were becoming increasingly alert to Collins's importance. He was driven afresh from his old haunt at Miss Mac-Carthy's, whither he had ventured to return. His offices too were becoming dangerous. When both finance offices in Harcourt Street became constantly subject to enemy action he hunted round for new quarters. For a few weeks he used a room over Mrs O'Keeffe's confectionery shop in Camden Street, moving to 22 Mary Street in the new year. Throughout November and December the hunt intensified. Michael wrote of 'living in such a turmoil . . . that it's not at all easy to be clear on all matters at all times'. 'Impending raids made my situation precarious', he explained when a letter to Hannie, early in December, had been left unfinished the night before. 'The amount of attention They are *trying* to pay me is really extraordinary but however I manage to keep clear and as active as ever. No doubt though an end will come to that sometime but however it's well to be carrying the long day.'

He would not admit to despair or discouragement. 'You are inclined to be too despondent', he rebuked one commandant, and added his favourite quotation from Wolfe Tone: 'It is in vain for soldiers to complain.'[5]

An unsuccessful attempt to ambush Lord French took place on the eve of the introduction of the Better Government of Ireland Bill. Lloyd George remarked to Lord Riddell: 'It [Ireland] is a most unfortunate country. Something awkward always occurs at critical moments in her history.'[6]

For a growing preponderance of Irishmen the 'something awkward' was England herself. Her renewed policy of coercion, if carried to its conclusion, must leave Ireland an embittered shambles to threaten the fabric of the entire British Empire. Yet Britain firmly believed that to abandon that policy could only have the same result.

Not only Ireland but the concept of the Empire was at stake. For both sides the stake was the highest the idealism of either

[5] National Library of Ireland: Ministry of Defence Archives
[6] Lord Riddell *Intimate Diary of the Peace Conference and After 1918–23* (London 1933) p. 153

could aspire to; both, as the final tragedy, believed they could win. In the passion of those days neither was able to see that the only solution was compromise and a time for adjustment from the unnatural bigotry of war to the more co-operative reasonings of peace.

CHAPTER NINE

The Black and Tans

(January – June 1920)

I

The new year, 1920, opened in the mood which was to mark it as the Year of Terror. Martial law was declared in parts of the country, and for the first time the I.R.A. captured an R.I.C. barracks with its store of arms.

This action marked the change in I.R.A. policy decided upon the previous October in talks between G.H.Q. and brigade leaders which followed the suppression of Dail Eireann. As the 1916 Rising had been a symptom of changes to come, this conflict reflected a change now established.

In January, too, the British Administration lost control of the local government of nearly the whole of Ireland. The Government vacillated. It had increased the power of the military, but hesitated to hand over to it the hitherto purely civil province of trial and sentence. It finally allowed large-scale arrests and deportations but failed to ensure immediate trials. By mid-February Irish gaols were overcrowded, and those in England were filling up. The division of authority, civil and military, which was to bedevil the British campaign in Ireland throughout its course had become apparent.

Amid the unending succession of raids and arrests Collins pursued his task of getting at the direction behind them. The striking was too accurate for his liking. The margin of time between Broy, Kavanagh, or MacNamara's warnings and the raids themselves was becoming uncomfortably narrow, and this despite the G-men's growing lack of enthusiasm for their political duties. Their reluctance was so apparent, indeed, that a new Assistant Commissioner of Police, an efficient Belfast man, William Redmond, was appointed to ginger up the flagging spirits of the D.M.P. He arrived early in January.

Intelligence was soon after him. Collins reported to a G.H.Q.

meeting: 'That man Redmond will get us all if we don't get him first.' The Squad went daily about the streets, instructed by their colleagues of the Intelligence Department, so that they might know and use their opportunity when it came.

It came, but only just, on a windy January afternoon as dusk closed in. Joe Dolan was waiting as usual to mark Redmond's exit from the Castle. On this day of all days he came early, to Dolan's dismay. For three weeks they had waited, marking the route he would take to the Standard Hotel. They had established times as methodically as men planning a military operation, as indeed this was. Now, as Redmond emerged smartly through the heavy gates, the Squad, timing their arrival to a nicety of apparent casualness, were not yet in their places.

Redmond paused, turned, and walked back into the Castle. He did not delay long, but it was enough for the Squad to saunter into the positions Collins himself had appointed. Paddy Daly was somewhat aggrieved; his place was at the end of the route, just below the Standard Hotel. He asked Collins sarcastically if he were to wait for the Stop Press editions. Collins replied, prophetically, that the man in the goal often gets as much of the ball as the rest of the team.[1] When Redmond started out again he walked rapidly, escorted at a distance by the Squad. There were too many people about to risk firing, however, and he had almost gained his hotel when Daly stepped towards him. Redmond went down, shot dead at two yards range.

A succession of spies followed, each man hunting for Collins, each to be hunted down himself by Collins's men. The G-men, too, at last remained quiescent. The D.M.P. had become 'a mere cypher so far as the preservation of law and order was concerned'.[2] Outside Dublin the R.I.C. was a depleted and demoralized force.

As the odds shortened slightly in favour of Sinn Fein, the British made vigorous moves. On Redmond's death the Castle offered a reward of £10,000 for evidence leading to convictions for the deaths of fourteen D.M.P. and R.I.C. men. On the same

[1] National Library of Ireland; Daly's account is quoted here with the kind permission of Eoin Neeson
[2] Macready *Annals of an Active Life* p. 438

day, 25 January, a putative offer was made of £10,000 for 'the body, dead or alive, of Michael Collins'. If no such offer was in fact made, all Ireland and every British agent therein believed that it had, and that it would be honoured.

On 23 February the Dublin metropolitan district was placed under curfew between midnight and 5 a.m., hours which were to lengthen as the months passed. The ordinary Dubliner, friend, foe, or indifferent observer of the struggle between Crown and Republic, was to learn that from now on, willy nilly, his everyday life was part of the conflict.

As the streets emptied, the military and police barracks alone came to life. Armoured cars, tanks, and lorries roared through darkened streets, to draw up in a blaze of searchlights before whatever house was first on the list for the night's operations. Loud knockings would follow, doors would be opened at gunpoint, and men and women herded downstairs while peremptory men with bayonets searched for wanted persons and rifled drawers for suspicious documents.

March 1920 saw Britain's Irish policy in all its chameleon-like colours. Lloyd George was endeavouring to blend the age-long alternatives of conquest and pacification into a workable mixture. On the one hand there was the 'Better Government of Ireland' Bill under debate at Westminster. It was known in Ireland simply as the 'Partition Bill', and nobody pretended that it presented a satisfactory solution. At most Lloyd George must have hoped all parties would make the best of a bad job; at worst he could point out to world opinion that he had tried to please everyone and the onus of the consequences of rejection could not fairly be placed on him.

C.P. Scott, that sanest of commentators on Anglo-Irish affairs, remarked that 'the present Bill has no relation to the needs of the situation. . . . Its effect, one fears, will not be to make a solution easier, but to make it harder by creating a fresh and powerful obstacle'.[3]

Early in March Dublin Castle struck at the Dail Loan, ordering disclosure of bank records. Mr Alan Bell, a Resident Magistrate who had performed a similar service for them in Land

[3] J. L. Hammond *C. P. Scott of the Manchester Guardian* (London 1934) p. 273

League days, was empowered to dig out recalcitrant managers. Collins scowled. This was money, most of it, from the poor of the land, entrusted to him so that he could carry out the promise of a better deal for them in the future. He did not intend to see it follow the £400,000,000 in overtaxation which, at his conservative estimate, had been extracted from Ireland since the Act of Union.[4] His scowl boded ill for Mr Bell.

Republican holders of public office were, naturally, marked men. The new Lord Mayor of Cork was Tomas MacCurtain, whom Collins esteemed highly. He wrote to Terence MacSwiney on 25 February: 'Somebody told me that Tomas was not very well. I hope there is nothing serious the matter with him.' His words were to have grim irony little more than three weeks later when MacCurtain was shot dead in his home. The district had that night been cleared by police patrols. The jury brought a verdict of wilful murder against the R.I.C., though Lord French contended that MacCurtain had, in fact, fallen victim to Sinn Fein colleagues who had, allegedly, recently condemned him as lacking in extremism.

Had the British known of Collins's earlier note about MacCurtain's ill-health one wonders what sinister intention they might not have claimed to discover in it. His comments after his death they would have found less equivocal: 'I have not very much heart in what I am doing today thinking of poor Tomas', he wrote to MacSwiney on 22 March. 'It is surely the most appalling thing that has been done yet.'

On 9 April he contributed ten guineas to the memorial fund for the Lord Mayor, whose office had now been assumed by MacSwiney.

'It is to be hoped that this Fund will rapidly run to very large dimensions', Collins wrote, expressing regret that he could not send more himself. 'Every subscriber who gives his or her contribution gives proof that he or she knows that the late Lord Mayor of Cork died for Ireland, and signifies belief that he was murdered by the agents of England. This memorial is in no way a private matter. It is fully a national one, and it is more than

[4] Sir Anthony MacDonnell had reported to the Primrose Commission in 1912 that at that time Ireland had been overtaxed by over £300,000,000. Macardle *The Irish Republic* p. 890

that – it is the answer of our people to the enemy people who are slandering our dead comrade.'

General Sir Nevil Macready, son of the famous actor, was appointed Commander-in-Chief of the British forces in Ireland in March. Until now Commissioner of the Metropolitan Police in London, there was little doubt that he would use a firm hand in carrying out the British Government's policy. It is to his credit that, in the months that followed, the military forces earned a reputation among the Irish for strict soldierly conduct, despite the disheartenment of what the troops themselves felt to be lack of Government support. Except in the martial law areas the army was to remain in the frustrating position of being able to take no action save at the request of the police who, infinitely less co-ordinated, were to become notoriously more undisciplined.

In London Sir Henry Wilson found it imperative to 'urge with all my force the necessity for doubling the police and not employing the military'.[5] The Cabinet which Sir Henry had labelled 'absolutely apathetic' listened to his urgings, and advertisements in certain sections of the British Press sought recruits for 'a rough and dangerous task'. Men who had survived the roughness and danger of trench warfare to return to the less honoured conditions of bleak unemployment at home flooded to join up.

The Irish belief that the prisons had been opened to provide recruits to the Black and Tans (they were so nicknamed after a famous Co. Limerick pack of hounds because of their scratch uniform), is undoubtedly unfounded; it is also undoubtedly true that large numbers of those accepted lost little time, once in Ireland, in qualifying for prison terms. These men were, with a good proportion of exceptions who, inevitably, never reached the headlines, the sediment of a heavily-populated country whom war and postwar conditions had caused to sink still further. The Cabinet, presumably, must have known what type of man would be likely to enlist. Nevertheless, the new recruits were being sent to Ireland to restore law and order; that they should further disrupt it cannot have been envisaged.

It was hoped that the injection of such large quantities of ex-soldiery into the R.I.C. would better enable it to cope with

[5] Major-General Sir C. E. Callwell K.C.B. *Field-Marshal Sir Henry Wilson Bart., G.C.B., D.S.O.: His Life and Diaries* (London 1927) II, p.222

the conditions now prevailing in Ireland. Not unnaturally, however, the Black and Tans were completely at sea when it came to guerilla fighting. Besides, they had had enough of discipline in France. They were there to 'make Ireland a hell for rebels to live in'. If they made it a hell for everyone else, it was no concern of men whose future was not bound up with that of Ireland. They were, indeed, to incur the abhorrence of Unionists no less than Sinn Feiners. The Unionists were as anxious to solve the Irish Problem as the Government, and twice as eager to do so by peaceful methods. 'We have got to live there' was their simple argument.

In April Irish prisoners in Mountjoy and Wormwood Scrubs went on hunger-strike, arousing national protest. Collins had little time for hunger-strikes, since they produced little except popular sympathy. He once turned on a man who had remarked on the 'luck' of another in evading arrest, as if luck alone were required. 'Any fool can go to gaol and be a hero', snapped Collins. 'All you need do is go to the door, shout, "Up the rebels!" and you'll be in Mountjoy in five minutes. It takes a good man to keep out of it, and he's the only man I need.' Laurels, in Collins's opinion, were not to be won simply to have something to rest upon.

To ensure that there should be fewer inactive 'heroes', at the end of February Collins sent out an armed guard who waylaid the Castle mail as it left the sorting office and brought back the day's official correspondence. Intensive raiding failed to bring any of it to light. It was the first of a series of similar coups.

Collins had his own correspondence to send, as well as all the G.H.Q. Staff mail. All dispatches for the south were cleared at Kingsbridge Station by Sean O'Connell, employed there as a clerk. Certain guards on the trains would hand them over to contacts at the appropriate stations down the line. In Naas, for instance, they were collected with the surrendered tickets. One of the least of the I.R.A.'s worries was expenditure on postage.

On Easter Saturday, 3 April, at the time when the Castle nervously expected the annual, non-eventuating repetition of insurrection, raids of a new nature took place. While troops were moved into Dublin, trains searched, and main roads cordoned and barricaded, the Volunteers slipped quietly out and, in an operation as popular as it was strategic, burnt income-tax offices up and down the country, tidying up the work already begun by also burning more than three hundred vacated police barracks.

The British applauded the 'bravado' of those who burnt buildings safely emptied. There was more behind the operation than a show of pointless daring, however. It was a planned demonstration that the Volunteers were an integrated force, not sporadically animated groups. Nor was it anticipated that the barracks would be needed again; any British ideas to the contrary had now been effectively thwarted. Furthermore, the problem of how to prevent the collection of taxes by the usurping power to the detriment of the Dail had been solved at a stroke.

By mid-March Mr Alan Bell had already extracted a considerable sum from the Munster and Leinster Bank, believed to belong to Sinn Fein. He was shot dead on his way into Dublin one morning. It is possible that there was more behind his death than his activities in seizing the Loan funds. Collins is said to have regarded him as being high in the British Intelligence in Ireland. A Secret Service officer who spent a lengthy, if harmless, stay at Vaughan's Hotel at that time was remarked to have shown no consternation at any shooting except that of Bell, which evidently shook him considerably.[6]

The Loan was saved. Collins turned his energies upon its consolidation to such good effect that, speaking his mind to Terence MacSwiney on 29 May 1920 about one Loan organizer who was not pulling his weight, he was able to write: 'I was feeling very strongly on the matter for a long time, but I must admit that I am somewhat softened now owing to the success of the entire venture. You know that were it not for that I should be out probably with a scalping knife.'

As equipment for war and the motley and all unpredictable tribe of the Black and Tans poured into Ireland, the Volunteers, too, were strengthening their position. The country was now truly at war.

With the collapse of the old R.I.C. the need for a new force to keep civil law and order became pressing. The Dail, striving to make its shadow administration a reality, had no police force to assume those duties, which devolved instead upon local Volun-

[6] Piaras Beaslai, in the *Irish Independent*, 28 May 1957

teer bodies. In all their activities the military and political forces of Sinn Fein, supported from conviction or prudence by growing numbers of the Irish people, aimed directly at the overthrow of the British administration in Ireland. Devised as retaliatory measures, they provoked further repression that increased as the grim campaign of terror and counter-terror wore on. Only in two spheres could Sinn Fein show a clear advantage : in Intelligence, and in propaganda.

Circumstances favoured Sinn Fein. It is easier to denounce the intruder in one's house than for him to justify his presence there, particularly if that justification is based merely on squatter's rights, however immemorial they may be to him. Nothing is immemorial to the Irishman, and Sinn Fein used all the indictments of history to support its claim to be the victim of aggression, stretching back to the very year when the long British squat had commenced.

It concentrated on capturing foreign support at which, despite Press censorship at home and the need for secrecy rather than publicity of the Dail's meetings, it was to exceed by far the efforts of Castle and Unionist propagandists alike. In that fecund year of 1919, Sinn Fein had also acquired the talents and allegiance of Erskine Childers.

No sudden convert to Irish separatism, Childers's beliefs had rather evolved along clearly deducible lines. Unionist influences had predominated in his early life, as they had in that of his cousin, Robert Barton, with whose Co. Wicklow family he had been largely brought up. He had become a Home Ruler, yet even when *Asgard* had sailed into Howth he had not reached the decision that the interests of Britain and Ireland demanded an absolute rejection of the claims of one or the other. When war broke out he joined up. As he was later to testify, he had no hatred of England, only of her imperialism, which conflicted increasingly with his deepening loyalty to Irish nationalism. Meanwhile he fought imperialism in another guise in the Mediterranean. He served with distinction as an Intelligence Officer in aerial reconnaissance and earned the D.S.O. before he was recalled from France. His position as uncommitted nationalist had suddenly become useful. Lloyd George needed such a man as secretary to his Irish Convention.

It was the Convention that finally convinced Childers that Britain was incapable of solving anything to Ireland's advantage. He became a Republican. In 1919 he announced to the Press that Separatism was the only answer, and came to live in Dublin.

His house in Waterloo Road became a meeting place for Republicans. Among them, inevitably, was Michael Collins. Collins was quickly aware of Childers's capacity. Undoubtedly he admired his literary talents; the old predilection for the company of the man of learning drew him to the spare, courteous, austere figure, even if he was at times irritated by the pedantic attention to minutiae that was reminiscent of de Valera. At the same time he cannot have failed to detect the quietly self-deprecating humour which had given much of its delight to *The Riddle of the Sands*.

Collins was soon making full use of the new convert, though as a rule he distrusted such people, in contrast to Griffith who tended to welcome them, often to his later discomfort. Griffith, indeed, seems at this time to have been as pleased as Collins by Childers's propaganda work.

Collins's enthusiasm for putting Childers to work was entirely shared by Childers himself. Yet one incident concerning Childers reveals a fault in Collins. Unlike de Valera, who was later to keep an inimical cabinet in working order, Collins would fling men who simply could not pull together into joint harness and leave them to get on with it. Collins complained that Sean MacEoin's dispatches were scrappy. MacEoin replied, with dignity and point, 'I undertook to fight for you : I never undertook to write for you!' He agreed however to accept Collins's choice of a super-adjutant to do the writing for him, and was forthwith introduced to Childers. A more incongruous pair of collaborators would be hard to imagine. The big young blacksmith with his genius for ground-fighting, and the scholarly, coldly-mannered Childers. The association lasted one week.

Gaiety is the natural antidote to despair. Men constantly facing death gave each other an amicable *nom de guerre*: 'Fergus' for the soft-voiced, lion-hearted McKee who, despite the problems of Brigade and G.H.Q. work, yet had time to greet each of his men in passing; 'George' for Gearoid O'Sullivan, Collins's shadow, hiding his gentleness under such ruthless directives as 'recruits to the R.I.C. are to be made unfit for carrying out the duties of the R.I.C.' – a formula surely echoed rather than originated by him. More characteristic is his agonized 'For God's sake, don't get this pinched' to the improvident enquirer for yet another new covering address in Dublin.[7] 'Mick' or 'The Big Fella', half-mocking, half-reverential, was for Collins himself, now a near-mythical figure to British and Irish alike.

The British forces, searching for arms and documents and men, thought that in the capture of these lay the restoration of the old order in Ireland. They should have sought instead the guiding spirit of unity and resistance that now ran abroad despite the curfew. Revolutions do not sweep a population instantly. It is the big gun of its opponents that a revolution's leaders must resort to a certain measure of cajolery and downright intimidation before, with time and the reiteration of the new doctrine, their movement gathers enough momentum to attract nation-wide allegiance. The British foresaw the momentum even as they committed the supreme error of employing the methods that set it in motion.

II

Never unnecessarily reckless, Collins avoided hold-ups so long as avoidance would not cause suspicion. Otherwise he bluffed his way serenely out of cordons. The officer in charge would find a young man on a bicycle at his elbow, explaining with a disarming grin that this would make him late for his job at the Castle just once too often; if they could possibly search him quickly. . . . The officer, glad of a civil word in an unpopular task, as often as not would wave him on with an exchange of pleasantries, possibly the only man to get such a thing from Collins that morning. For a man possessing all the charm in the world, Collins used remarkably little of it wastefully.

The secret of his safety lay as much in his trust of others as in his refusal to act like a man seeking safety. He never bothered to destroy the contents of the wastepaper basket after a meeting at Batt O'Connor's; Mrs O'Connor knew he relied on her to do so, and she pounced on it the moment he left the room. He

[7] National Library of Ireland: Ministry of Defence Archives

looked neither to right nor left as he went from the house; yet, knowing his disregard of danger, his men made it their care to see that he was never first away.

He scarcely went near the Intelligence office in Crow Street, where the 'Irish Products Coy' made a singularly unproductive showing for the quantities of paper work done there. Nor did the Squad see him in the Abbey Street office of 'Morland's, Cabinet Makers'. He met his men in Vaughan's after dusk if he needed to; otherwise he delegated his authority so effectively that the least man in any department controlled by him felt he was working under Collins's eye.

The offer of £10,000 that had baited the trap more heavily than ever against him endowed him in the minds of the forces who sought him with the qualities of a super-beast, who had so begun to haunt their strained nerves that they habitually dashed into houses on raiding missions with cries of 'Where's Michael Collins?' His was the figure down the side street, the footfall heard round the next corner, the hand waiting to strike them down, regardless of whether they were out on duty or trying to find brief relaxation about the town. They hunted him with the intensity of the foredoomed.

Now he found a new hiding-place. An aunt of Gearoid O'Sullivan, Mrs O'Donovan, kept dairies in Mespil Road and Rathgar, and had already been of service to Sinn Fein, supporting the Loan and supplying the proper food for men recently released on hunger-strike. Collins needed further trustworthy account holders for depositing Loan money, and made his own way to her house in Rathgar. It struck him at once that here was an ideal shelter, a widow whose visiting West Cork relations' accents would blend well with his own, whose young family promised the security he always sensed when surrounded by children. Hitherto he had never remained under one roof for more than a few nights. As if he foresaw that this house would never be discovered in all the months of pursuit and terror ahead he settled down.

Probably only Gearoid and Joe O'Reilly knew of his new sanctuary. He relaxed, throwing the smaller children in the air, listening sympathetically to the older ones. When they had birthdays he never bought them toys, but always books. He quoted poetry constantly, capping Mrs O'Donovan's contributions, usually ending with a triumphant 'The Sixth Book!' – a reference to the classic and comprehensive reader they had both used in their National Schooldays.

The one maid never knew who it was who had joined the family, referring to him, ironically enough, as 'The Big Fellow', and to Gearoid as 'The Little Fellow'. Only the children knew his name, and never told it. As with the O'Connor children his safety was their constant care. He would stroll with them across St Stephen's Green. 'I wish he wouldn't!' exclaimed one of the smallest, fearful that someone might ask her his identity. They little realized the protection they afforded him.

The dairies provided an ideal cover for goods in transit. Pistols came in butter boxes, rifles in egg cases. One day a porter at Kingsbridge rang up to report some boxes that had arrived broken open. He was going off duty and could not trust his successor. The eldest boy, no more than twelve, whipped up the pony and dashed down to the station in the cart. 'At least we'll have a pony that died for Ireland!' he told his sister Eileen, who sped in search of Gearoid O'Sullivan by the simple, if breathless, method of running up and down every office stair in Eustace Street where she knew he worked. She found him, to his dismay. The 'butter' was gone overnight from the stable where they had hidden it.

The secrecy in which Michael had so successfully wrapped himself could not last for ever. After a few months there was a knock at the door. It was only Tom Cullen, but Collins rose up in fury and went from the house. Thereafter he slept there infrequently. If Cullen had discovered his hiding-place, others might also.

He used the house instead for meetings every Sunday. 'See you at the usual time' was his only notification that he would be there. The 'usual time' meant any time, and any number for lunch. Scouts waited down the road. Soon there would come Mulcahy, Rory O'Connor, Dick McKee, Neil Kerr, sometimes Kevin O'Higgins, or men up from the country, Tom Hales or Liam Deasy. They lunched alone, though their talks went on regardless of the children who served the meal. As always Collins trusted completely or not at all.

The work over, he allowed himself time to play. He romped with the children and dragged the others into it too, cheering uproariously when little Tadgh bumped Kevin O'Higgins so forcibly on the nose that it bled. With their world dominated by the ruthless deeds of war he liked to see his friends against the normal background of womenfolk and family. He deplored the custom that took men out to drink in pubs while the women stayed at home. Drink, to Collins, should be the occasion of sociability, not its deterrent.

Everywhere he made brief homes for himself, never practising the circumspection of a visitor, which only a man with his own four walls for retreat can sustain. He became for an hour, a night, a week, a member of the family whose life he shared. His very demands ensured that they treated him as such. He wrestled, swore at Joe O'Reilly without ceremony, or asked his colleagues in for working lunches. No one resented it. Into the houses of those who would have done he did not go.

His Intelligence system reached into every nook and cranny of the land. It profited by the fact that no Secret Service Branch of the R.I.C. now existed. It bedevilled British military communications. 'Please treat this as "Very Secret" and do not divulge it to anyone except as may be absolutely necessary and this under a bond of secrecy', runs a captured British memorandum.[8]

Other waylaid documents must have raised a few Volunteer eyebrows at British punctilio. Those members of the military sent to requisition houses in Cork, for instance, were directed :

> 'The Officer commandeering the building will politely express his regret at having to put the occupiers to inconvenience but will firmly make it quite clear that he must have the house. . . .
>
> 'Officers & Other Ranks will doubtless, in some cases, be received with abuse & rudeness : the only way to deal with such persons is to treat them with cold politeness.'[9]

This subtle advance on the methods of eviction used against their fathers was, one fears, lost upon families thus 'put to the inconvenience' of being thrust from their homes, to make what shift they could for shelter.

Again, on 25 June 1920, Major-General Boyd was found to

[8] National Library of Ireland: Ministry of Defence Archives
[9] National Library of Ireland: Ministry of Defence Archives

be pondering whether an armed man running away could justifiably be shot as a potential armed assailant. When, a week later, the British Command decided that he could, its opposite body in the I.R.A. doubtless felt that at least this cleared up any misconceptions.

The refusal to recognize men out of uniform as soldiers was understandable in an army steeped in orthodox military tradition. To the end the British Government, while admitting that 'a state of war' existed, refused to recognize that Britain and Ireland were *at* war. To have declared war would have admitted Ireland's claim to be a separate state; to have called it civil war would have invoked a phrase no one really accepted.

To Ireland's advantage, then, the British Army remained an army in virtual reserve. On the other hand the I.R.A. suffered considerably when its members became 'civilian, arms-carrying prisoners', and liable, not to prisoner-of-war treatment, but to death on charges of murder.

How to treat its prisoners was a further problem that exercised the British Command. If the I.R.A. were not an army, what was it? British compromise triumphantly designated it 'the opposing side', whose members, when captured, were to be treated 'with courtesy'.

Even here the trouble was not over, and a lieutenant-colonel in Cork wrote feelingly of an officer who, acting under a misconception of how a truckful of civilian, arms-carrying prisoners was to be treated, ran into an ambush in which several of them escaped. The officer had, it appeared, interpreted 'courteous treatment' to mean that they should be allowed to shout and sing rebel songs. 'It was largely owing to this that his party was ambushed.'[10] One presumes by civilians, carrying arms.

If there is any advantage to be found in the garrisoning of one's country by the forces of another, the Irish were, in one respect, fortunate. The British Army, by and large, behaved in a civilized fashion. It was more than could be said for the Black and Tans, whose awfulness fully compensated the Army's restraint in the scales upon which nations weigh each other.

The I.R.A. by contrast was a highly disciplined force. The Volunteers were neither the Galahads nor the Torquemadas that

[10] National Library of Ireland: Ministry of Defence Archives

their protagonists and opponents then and since have attempted to make of them. They were young men faced with a situation in which the awareness of a national past rent with violence and glorified in song and, significantly, in prayer, struggled with the subservience to the landowning classes that had been their lot for generations. This subordination conflicted with the urge to repossess the land for their own race. Most of them were chivalrous and high-minded. A few showed a callous indifference to life that was almost medieval in its peasant fatalism. Violence begets violence and undoubtedly, by the end, deeds were done in cold blood that would scarcely have been contemplated in the hot anger of personal conscience in the first days of taking up arms.

III

The British Government was taking a hard look at Dublin Castle. Macready, within forty-eight hours of setting foot in Ireland had proclaimed himself 'fairly astonished at the chaos that prevailed'. Lord French had confided to Lord Riddell that the administration was 'as bad as it can be. . . . There is no proper control. It is impossible to make a satisfactory alteration under existing conditions.'[11] As far back as 1885 Joseph Chamberlain had called for the reform of 'the absurd and irritating anachronism known as Dublin Castle'.

In April Sir Hamar Greenwood was appointed Chief Secretary, a position that had changed hands frequently of late. Sir John Anderson was brought over, nominally as Joint Under-Secretary, in fact entirely to take over the effective administration. Mr A. W. Cope was appointed his assistant. General Tudor was made Police Advisor, to co-ordinate police and military operations against the I.R.A. On his recommendation Brigadier-General Ormonde Winter took over Castle Intelligence.

The new Executive's policy was a matter for long and largely unsatisfactory discussion. Lord French, feeling the inherent paradox of his rôle of active figurehead, urged the Cabinet to place Ireland under complete martial law. He was supported in effect by General Tudor who, however, seems to have envisaged putting

[11] Riddell *Intimate Diary* p. 147

vigorous measures into force without actually declaring martial
law. The Chief Secretary and General Macready also preferred
to try intensified military operations under the existing civil law,
though Macready, to the end, pressed vainly for a unified control
of both military and police.

Sir Henry Wilson preferred to shoot all the Irish leaders by
roster. The Government, uncertain, fidgetted from one foot to
the other. The public would not stand for martial law; there was
a shortage of troops. The Government sent vast quantities of
transport material into Ireland to strengthen the troops already
there, while withholding a mandate to use that strength fully.

The Castle was addicted to promoting the image of a Sinn
Fein rent by schism, the victim of the 'extremist' element represented by Collins, which would undoubtedly liquidate the
moderates unless the Castle came to the rescue. This casting of
itself in the rôle of St George failed to impress, largely owing to
an unfortunate propensity on the part of the Castle for devouring
the Sinn Fein maiden itself when the I.R.A. dragon refused to
do so.

To preserve the semblance of civil administration in Ireland
and to relieve the demand for military backing, Churchill suggested that the R.I.C. should be further strengthened by the
recruitment of a force of ex-officers. These auxiliaries were to be
drafted into police barracks all over Ireland and take charge
of the Black and Tans, already showing their mettle. Eventually
it was decided to maintain them as a separate force.

The Auxiliaries made no pretence of playing at being policemen. They were a military force, though they never came under
the British Military Command. Only one division, the 'F' Division, took its orders from Dublin Castle. The rest operated
throughout the country, centred on strategic towns in their own
barracks. They were, on the whole, better disciplined than the
Tans, though this depended on their local commanders. They
were also tougher and capable of a far higher degree of organized
hell-making than the slap-happy Tans. They included Dublin in
their field of operations.

By the end of June all prospect of resolving the situation by
negotiation seemed remote. Lord French had declared, in answer
to Lloyd George's desire to meet 'some authority who can repre-

sent Sinn Fein and "deliver the goods" ', 'I do not believe that
any such authority will ever be found.'[12] Lloyd George had discovered that the Irish people were impossible in their present
mood. Sir Henry Wilson was 'very unhappy about Ireland'.
General Macready was becoming more convinced than ever that
the only solution lay in giving the military a free hand, an
operation which, he was later to admit, would, while effective,
have left the solution of the Irish Question as far off as ever.[18]
Sir Horace Plunkett summed up the administration of Ireland
as 'government by the dissent of the governed'.

The British Courts in Ireland had now ceased to function:
there were Republican Courts instead. Justice in the wide variety
of civil and criminal cases heard by them was not only done
but was seen to be done, to the surprise and approbation of many
Unionists, whose increasing patronage of the Republican Courts,
in lieu, admittedly, of any other means of redress, provided what
was undoubtedly Sinn Fein's strongest argument for Dail
Eireann's ability to govern the country soberly and well.

At the end of June the Dail held a one-day private session,
the first of the year. It was a confident, determined, and as
Collins himself wrote, a constructive day's work. He was one of
those who ran the great risk of attending.

At this session Collins announced the forthcoming closure of
the Dail Loan Issue. He did so in a bare, formally worded motion.
In a letter written the following day, however, he permitted
himself a restrained satisfaction: 'It may be mentioned that the
Loan total is just £290,000, so that I got the money in spite of
all the hindrances and difficulties.'[14] It was left for Griffith to
describe the achievement of what Collins had set out to do in
the face of such odds as 'one of the most extraordinary feats in
the country's history'.

[12] French *Life of Sir John French* p. 367
[18] Macready *Annals of an Active Life* II, p. 444
[14] Letter to Mrs Llewelyn Davies dated 30 June 1920

CHAPTER TEN

The Changing Order

(July – September 1920)

I

Rumours of dissension in the United States between President de Valera and the Irish-American leaders had reached Ireland early in 1920. In February de Valera's controversial interview with the *Westminster Gazette* had appeared to favour Britain's application of her own Monroe Doctrine to Ireland, acknowledging her independence but debarring her from entering into any treaty that might compromise British security.

De Valera had been a convinced Republican since before Easter Week. He hoped by his suggestion to induce Britain to start negotiations which might end in a satisfactory settlement. Britain, however, ignored him, and his opponents in America saw his speech as selling the Irish Republic. His blunt reactions to this adverse criticism led to an open quarrel with Cohalan and Devoy.

The Dail Ministry knew little of what was really afoot in America. They were bound by loyalty to de Valera, in American opposition to whom they saw a failure to back Ireland's own declared policy and a personal rejection of Ireland's elected leader.

The growing breach, until now largely that between the personalities of de Valera and Judge Cohalan, was now lifted into the field of American party politics. Divided counsels at the Republican Party Convention in June 1920 resulted in failure to achieve any resolution on Ireland at all. The Democratic Convention was now under no pressure to woo Irish-American votes. This had a vital bearing on events in Ireland. Since American statesmen of both parties had refused to make Ireland a live issue the British Government saw no need to temper its policy to American opinion.

Constructive work was nevertheless being done in America. De Valera, aided by Harry Boland and Sean Nunan, continued

149

to tour the States raising money for the Irish Bond Drive, James O'Mara doing the bulk of the organization for this work. Amounts running into thousands of pounds were constantly remitted to Collins. A Committee set up to investigate atrocities in Ireland was to have a far-reaching effect on world opinion about Britain's Irish policy.

Despite the flow of money from the States Collins felt that, in terms of more comprehensive aid, America had let Ireland down. He had held a lively hope that de Valera's mission might produce not merely cash but men and arms. Despite quite considerable active support for Ireland, America at no point had a decisive bearing on the Anglo-Irish struggle. Lord Mountjoy had once been able to say : 'We have lost America through the Irish'. Hamar Greenwood would never tell Westminster : 'We have lost Ireland through the Americans'.

II

In the two-handed policy of coercion and cajolery favoured by the Government towards Ireland, Sir Hamar Greenwood's job was to be that of exerting the stronger arm. 'No happier choice could have been made', observed one of his supporters, and Sinn Fein was inclined to agree as it noted his consistently spirited defence of the Black and Tans. Sir Hamar was to become probably the most hated man on the Irish scene. How far he earned this distinction is hard to judge. He took responsibility for the Government's policy and presumably had a not inconsiderable part in its formulation. Yet the Black and Tan excesses were condoned rather than authorized; and there is evidence that, towards the end at least, he was prevented from being more openly conciliatory by Lloyd George, who preferred to keep his 'strong man' type-cast. It is clear that Sir Hamar, a Canadian, had no personal vindictiveness for the Southern Irish. He had accepted his job and did it without fear or favour, if with a certain self-righteousness.[1]

[1] C. P. Scott of the *Manchester Guardian* met Greenwood for the first time in December 1921 and wrote of him in his diary: 'a dreadful person, vulgar and soapy like the worst type of Methodist preacher only less sincere.' (British Museum: Add MS 50906)

The new Under-Secretary, whose job it was both to advise his Chief and to follow his instructions, was Sir John Anderson. His personal estimation of the Government's vacillations was not a high one; yet he had come to Ireland to restore law and order, and was determined to do so. He was as grimly against the lawlessness and disorder displayed by the Crown forces as he was against Sinn Fein's campaign of violence and worked resolutely against both. His preference was for a solution by negotiation.

Of his subordinates, Mr Alfred W. Cope was to prove one of the most spectacular Castle-dwellers Dublin had known. From a more everyday background than most of his colleagues, excitable and hypersensitive, he was genuinely devoted to the task of winning peace in Ireland. Lloyd George had first discovered his unconventional talent for cryptic enterprise in, of all unlikely places, the Ministry of Pensions. Between Cope and Lloyd George, indeed, there existed a close bond, based on a common addiction to the cloak-and-dagger. Here was the second string to the Government's bow. While Macready was sent to hammer home the lesson of superior force in the hopes of achieving peace by subjection, Cope's job was to burrow underground and find that person or persons of whose existence Lord French despaired, who could talk for Sinn Fein, and negotiate a settlement.

Sharing Mr Cope's functions was Mr Mark Sturgis, who also provided a much-needed closer liaison with the Viceregal Lodge. His particular interest in these pages lies in the diary which he kept during his sojourn in the Castle. Apart from chronicling the events of those guerilla times in a manner detached though not unsympathetic, he reveals not only much of the mind of the Castle Executive, but also something of the behind-scenes activities of the Cabinet.

This revitalized, more liberal administration in Dublin Castle reflects all too clearly the inevitable curse laid upon Britain's dealings with Ireland throughout her history. It came several decades too late. Better government could no longer satisfy Ireland. The new régime was received, not with optimism, but with hand grenades.

Shut away in the stronghold of the Castle they were safe enough. It was the military and Auxiliaries who tore about in lorries, truculent in the face of the fear, contempt, and hostility of the Dublin populace, to whom Aungier Street was now known as the Dardanelles, so many times had grenades been hurled from doorways and the street raked with bullets from unseen guns as they passed. 'Patrolling the streets at night was sheer hell', one British officer has told the author. 'You padded round corners in the darkness with a revolver wondering if you might not meet one of Michael Collins's men doing the same thing. It was the Irishmen's country, and as far as I was concerned they were welcome to it.'

Nor was it only the Crown forces who felt the hand of the I.R.A. Where the British held back from declaring martial law, the I.R.A. had, in effect if not by Dail promulgation, done so instead. Men suspected of British loyalist activities were tried by secret courts-martial and, if convicted, shot, their bodies being found in easily observable places with the legend : 'Tried and executed by the I.R.A. Spies and informers beware' pinned to them. More and more R.I.C. men, including Black and Tans, were shot. In time of revolution it is not so much the leaders of the opposing régime who are eliminated as their supporters, whose willingness to carry out their policy will alone render it effective.

Michael Collins, more perhaps than any other, had a horror of killing that could not be justified as vital to the interests of the freedom movement. Paddy Daly, of the Squad, has related how an R.I.C. Superintendent, accompanying a military search party to his house after the Rising, had struck down his small crippled daughter for calling him a traitor. The British soldiers had thrown the policeman out of the house in protest. Now, in 1920, Collins sent for Daly, who found him in a towering rage. He had heard a rumour that Daly was planning to shoot the Superintendent, still living in the district. Though Daly claimed he had no such intention Collins warned him that the man who had revenge in his heart was not fit to be a Volunteer.[2]

For an insight into the British Executive in Ireland's view of the situation in the latter part of July 1920 we may turn to Sturgis's diary. He had not been in Ireland ten days before he noted : 'I have always been, and am, a convinced Unionist but I don't believe that you can *force* a country to have what's good for it if it is wrongheadedly and obstinately against it. If the

[2] From Daly's account already quoted

great majority of these South Irishmen insist on "Self Government" sooner or later they must have it.'

The inability of the Government to make up its mind on a clear policy was particularly worrying to the Executive, which quickly concluded that the only solution would be an offer of Dominion Home Rule, which might unite the moderate elements of all parties in Ireland in a body strong enough to overrule the 'extremists'. As yet, no offer as far-reaching as Dominion Home Rule appeared to be forthcoming. Lloyd George continued, in Sir Henry Wilson's phrase, 'to be satisfied that a counter-murder association was the best answer to Sinn Fein murders'.[3] Sinn Fein, Sir Henry noted, was 'steadily getting the upper hand'.[4]

No one arm of the British administration had authority over another. 'The more I see of it', wrote Sturgis, 'the more convinced I am that if it is war we must have a virtual Dictator – to be obeyed by everybody, military, police, civil service, etc. As it is we are a great sprawling, jealous hydra-headed monster spending much of its time using one of its heads to abuse one or other of the others by minute, letter, telegram, and good hard word of mouth.'

The coercion end of the see-saw was uppermost in the summer of 1920. Curfew was imposed in Cork between 10 p.m. and 5 a.m. Desmond Ryan, visiting the area, observed 'an intenser terror by day and night than in Dublin . . . the fight fiercer here than in any other part of Ireland'.[5]

It was impossible to enforce curfew in the country areas. The Crown forces concentrated on the towns and the city itself. Every householder was required to place a list on his door of those sleeping within. Raids and gunfire became a commonplace. Cork waited, with grim fortitude, for worse things to come.

In Dublin systematic cordoning of the city took place. The Auxiliaries, paid twice as much as the Tans, quickly showed that they intended to earn their pay. They were perhaps better aware of why they had been sent to Ireland, if the half-dozen new recruits to the Tan ranks encountered by Liam O'Briain on the Holyhead train are typical of that force. These told him that they were going to protect Ireland from the Chicago and New York-

---

[3] Callwell *Sir Henry Wilson* II, p. 251
[4] Ibid p. 255
[5] Ryan *Remembering Sion* pp. 274–5

controlled gangsters who were terrorizing the country. So much for American influence on British policy.

To the men and women who knew him, as much as to the British themselves, it seemed that Michael Collins was invincible. He would cycle along Parnell Street, hat down, in a fierce pre-occupation that ignored stray groups of Auxiliaries. At Maurice Collins's he would go straight through to the kitchen. He cared not at all that the shop was being raided perhaps five times a day. One of the family would stand at the door and announce the arrival of the next raiding party. Collins would take the news of their approach casually. 'Haven't they plenty of room?'

Had he hesitated, lurked in one place, sooner or later they must have caught him. He cycled through the Terror, counting gold brought to him in this or that house, appearing punctually, leaving with dispatch but not haste. He dropped into his Mary Street office in the afternoons to sign letters, showing only a jocund interest in the two Crossley tenders filled with Auxies which habitually pulled up outside twice daily for medical supplies from the chemist's shop opposite. He used an upstairs room of a firm which smoked hams in the basement. No one in the office asked any questions when the big, lithe figure bounded up the stairs, followed shortly afterwards by Rory O'Connor or Gearoid O'Sullivan or anyone else having business with him.

Though they never came after office hours, someone must have drawn the Castle's attention to the building, for one night it was raided. A British officer ran down to the basement, opened the door, and was met by a blast of the blinding, pungent smoke given off by the oakchips and turf used in smoking the green hams. He staggered out choking. 'If Michael Collins is in there he can damn well stay there!' was his comment.

Collins knew that a protective wave of prayer and well-wishing went with him. He might grumble that he needed a camel to carry all the objects of devotion showered upon him. He was nevertheless sustained by such a display of love. He hid his feelings awkwardly, flinging himself the more into the commonplace of living dangerously. 'There were men ready to die for him, and I didn't blame them', Mrs Clarke remembers. 'He took all the same chances in the fight that any man did, and he never looked to get an easy way out, though others took the easier road.'

Despite his passion for being always spick and span – 'The neatest man I ever met', Mrs Batt O'Connor called him – his restless movements always made him appear ruffled. The restlessness was entirely physical. He was mentally concentrated all the time. Taking in details of clothes, manner, or surroundings at a glance, he nevertheless gave the impression that he noticed nothing. Whatever he saw he remembered. No matter what the time, day or night, fresh or after long hours of gruelling work, his brain seemed tireless, his spirits capable of inexhaustible ebullience.

It was no use anyone's expecting him to suit his mood to theirs. He sat at breakfast on one occasion in Mrs Leigh Doyle's house in Carlow with Gearoid O'Sullivan and Desmond Fitz-Gerald. FitzGerald had embarked upon one of his interminable, exquisitely-told reminiscences, poking fun at himself. Collins chimed in with witty comment at every opportunity. O'Sullivan sat silent, afflicted by the sense, not confined to Irishmen alone, that such repartee ill befits the early hours of the day. When he could bear it no longer he laid down his knife and fork. 'Oscar Wilde', he remarked, 'points out that only dull people are brilliant at breakfast.' Collins stared at him with interest. 'Well, thank God for the dull people!' he exclaimed, and turned back to FitzGerald.

The Dail Loan closed officially at the end of July 1920, although a great deal of promised money still remained to be collected. On 31 July Collins wrote to Terence MacSwiney: 'At the time of writing the entire total exceeds £355,500'. Ten days earlier he had written: 'At this closing stage I would mention that I am of opinion the prompt response in Mid Cork was the greatest factor in making the Loan a success. . . . Mid Cork, and West Limerick made a headline at a time when it was badly needed. The promptness and the faith which that promptness showed, deserve well of Ireland.'

MacSwiney was now concerned with publicizing the work of the Republican Courts. He arranged for foreign Press representatives to see them in action. 'The justice of their decrees is acknowledged', he wrote, 'and their judgements are enforced where English writs have ceased to run.'

In July the Southern Unionists Association made it clear that they preferred to contemplate Dominion Home Rule, which would, in effect, sanction the constructive work undertaken by Dail Eireann, rather than support the Government's coercion policy in which they had recently been invited to co-operate. This stand was in marked contrast to that of their fellow-Unionists in Ulster. The savagery in this part of Ireland boded ill for any move the Government might make towards conciliation in the South.

The situation was tense. The I.R.A. campaign intensified in the face of violence from the hostile populace in the North-East and the Crown forces in the South. The first of the full-time active service groups who were to change the I.R.A. from partially-operational units into regular flying columns began to function in East Limerick. Yet, despite the gathering impetus of the Terror on both sides, life for the ordinary citizen was not noticeably disrupted. There was the curfew, of course. Yet race meetings went on as usual. No Irishman, whatever his political views, and no Englishman garrisoned in Ireland, could countenance disruption of this basic tradition of life there. It is noteworthy that many of the *pourparlers* for peace were conducted on the racecourse.

Beneath the strange mixture of normality and sudden violence there was a unity of purpose such as Ireland had never known. Sinn Fein was heavily outnumbered in men and guns – Collins himself estimated that not more than 3,000 men able to secure arms had served in the Volunteers throughout the whole country, and of these only a fraction were on a full-time basis – but the people were behind them.

The two worlds of Ireland, the purposeful and the unnoticing, were clearly seen by one young woman who would stand at the window of her room in the heart of Dublin where she hid intelligence papers and cheques for thousands of pounds for Michael Collins. Looking out she would see people strolling out to play tennis who cared nothing for the new order that was struggling for life. Collins, she felt, hunted relentlessly in the name of peace, lived in greater service to Ireland than any of these casual inheritors of summer Society, for whose protection the Black and Tans had been loosed upon the country.

III

Most of Collins's friends recognized in his boyish manner, half-bullying, wholly good-natured, the depths of an incredible loyalty. How anyone might conceivably change towards himself Collins, incapable of rancour, could never understand.

A man like Robert Brennan, who had worked with him ungrudging of his abilities yet never liking him personally could handle him well enough, without animosity. 'What the hell do you know about Finance?' Collins demanded, but the reply, 'More than you do about manners', brought him, penitently enough, to heel. There were others, however, less impervious to his rough edges – the impatience that lashed slower men, the tactlessness that wounded deeply where he had only intended to ginger into greater efficiency. Austin Stack was one of them.

While Stack was in prison Collins had made it clear to him over and over again that he, of all men, was most missed in the work being done. 'No, you're not rated one bit too highly', he insisted in one letter, an ominous pointer that Stack himself, from self-knowledge as much as modesty, may have made some attempt to refuse the crown of laurels being pressed upon him by the over-enthusiastic Collins. Collins had rescued Stack, a sick man, from Strangeways; while he was being nursed back to health, he was equally expectant of great things from him. 'Stack can be our Attorney General', he exclaimed to Robert Barton.

He was not, of course, the only one responsible for placing Stack in a position beyond him. Stack and Brugha shared lodgings for some time after Stack's escape; Brugha's confidence in him was apparent when he appointed him Deputy Chief of Staff at the end of 1919, a position which seems to have rested lightly enough upon him : he never pretended otherwise. Brugha now evidently imparted his own growing resentment of Collins to Stack, who became increasingly Brugha's ally against him.

Collins soon discovered his error. He was already ruffling up Brugha, who, he complained, never used a typewriter. Although he treated him with a not unaffectionate respect, he paid bare attention to his position as Minister of Defence; he was not going to have Brugha tangling up his intelligence lines merely to keep him happy. Stack was on firm ground in work involving legal procedures, such as the establishment of the Republican Courts. He was less happy in other spheres. The day came when Collins blurted out, witheringly but without malice, 'Everyone knows, Austin, your Department is a bloody joke'. He never ran a man down behind his back; he never thought twice before doing so to his face. Almost certainly he at once forgot the incident. But Stack had been defending himself stoutly against others' complaints on this occasion. Perhaps he had looked for Collins's support: he never forgave him. Thereafter he referred to Collins as 'Mickeen' to show his diminution in his own eyes. Any motion proposed by Collins was instantly opposed by Stack, till even Brugha regarded him with a rueful wonder.

Part of the trouble was, as it had always been, Collins's inarticulateness. He could write easily enough to Stack in prison : 'You've had a bad time for the past three years.' To Stack, weakened in constitution and undermined in temper by those years, he was unable to speak his sympathy. His own lack of words exasperated him. 'Is it not a pity we cannot transmit our words to paper as quickly as we can say them', he wrote, 'and sometimes is it not a pity we cannot say them as quickly as we can think?' He knew he often appeared ungrateful, and admitted despairingly : 'The worst of it is that I'm inclined to console myself – Pharisee like I fear – that it's all right so long as I don't forget. It is not really tho'.'[6]

Yet it was not indifference that now led to an open quarrel with Brugha. Collins wanted to pay the men engaged in making explosives sixpence an hour more than the Union rates. Brugha said the thing was contrary to principle. Collins retorted that the men were on the run and needed the money. The delay on this occasion while they argued led to their near-arrest.

Collins was still avidly pursuing the world of education and culture. Part of this determination stemmed from his wish to overcome his natural shyness in such company. 'I think I was and am the worst', he confessed, and quoted Shaw's dictum on shyness : 'Next to poverty it is the worst of all the vices.'

Even at the height of the Terror he continued to make swift

[6] Letter to Mrs Llewelyn Davies dated 13 May 1921

breaks away from the anxieties of Dublin to snatch a few hours in Granard. He travelled by backroads, with scouts at various outposts to warn of Black and Tan activity. Outside the city he was less cognisant of where danger might lie, and took precautions accordingly. Whenever he got the chance he would lose himself in reading or a visit to the theatre: *Hedda Gabler,* the latest Shaw, or such writers as Victor Hugo, Chesterton, and Swinburne, all three, incidentally, men who had at one time or another viewed Irish nationalism with a sympathetic eye.

Miss MacCarthy's house was now too closely watched for him to risk sleeping there. More than ever he was a man having no home, for now, more than ever, his homes were legion. He would spend a night in one house, return, or go elsewhere again. Like all the hunted he had his own trusted refuges: the O'Keeffes, the Maurice Collinses, the Batt O'Connors. Often he came to houses where the husband was himself on the run and dared not sleep at home. The wives remained, adjusting the family routine to his presence, if necessary dismissing what help in the house they had to ensure secrecy. Hospitable women with nerves of steel and, above all, reticence: these stood behind the fighting men all over Ireland. In the cities, where a knock at the door could be a hunted man or a raiding party, and in country farmhouses where a dozen exhausted and hungry men might come in after nightfall, the women received them, tended their wounds where a doctor or a hospital might mean discovery; moved the children into one bed to make room for them and, if the house were raided and the men had time to escape, moved the children again so that a warm but empty bed would tell no tales. They faced interrogation and the ransacking of their homes, rose before dawn to cook and launder for their extra guests, and brought up young and usually large families as if life were normal. Their spirited fortitude was the answer to the British propagandists who claimed that Sinn Fein held the land by terrorism.

The confusion into which his Intelligence Department was throwing the enemy gave Collins moments of glee which made up for the dangers and hardships. At the end of August the British Military Flying Corps office safe was unaccountably left unlocked. Next morning papers giving details of the Castle courier service in Ireland and of the stationing of guards in

Dublin had vanished. In their place was a message – 'Many thanks, will call again – I.R.A.'[7]

Castle Intelligence under Ormonde Winter prepared to strike back. Sturgis noted : 'The gay Ormonde's scheme to photograph the entire population of Ireland back and front is maturing !' The most wanted man of them all was, however, noticeably camera-shy. Only one photograph of Collins, taken at the April 1919 Dail meeting and showing him scowling in the singularly unpleasant fashion his legendary malevolence required, was available for the scrutiny of his adversaries. Collins produced a copy of it to Desmond FitzGerald. 'There are seven assassins over here at present on my account', he remarked. 'We have them all located.'

Many of the D.M.P. men knew him well enough. Whether for reasons of sympathy or personal safety they remained mute witnesses of his passings to and fro. Mrs Leigh Doyle, walking with him over O'Connell Bridge, saw a policeman salute him and smile. It was a situation which Collins, with his eye for the comic, labelled in his usual way as 'a queer thingeen !'

At the beginning of August 1920 the Restoration of Order in Ireland Act, known more simply as the 'Coercion Act' was announced. This measure, a sop to the advocates of martial law, gave increased powers to the military arm under Macready. Sinn Fein answered this move with increased rather than lessened guerilla warfare. Less violently, if no less positively, the Castle Executive itself deplored the new Act. There were threats of resignation. Mark Sturgis wrote in disgust : 'The Irish aren't fit to govern themselves; of course they aren't, but I'm damned if the English are either – or even the Welsh !'[8]

The Irish were hardly being allowed a chance to prove their ability or otherwise to govern themselves. On 1 July there were forty-seven Sinn Fein elected representatives in gaol. On 12 August Terence MacSwiney, Lord Mayor of Cork and T.D. for Mid Cork,[9] was arrested.

MacSwiney went immediately on hunger-strike in protest

[7] Sturgis Diaries, 30 August 1920
[8] Sturgis Diaries, 3 August 1920
[9] *Teachta Dala* (Member of Dail Eireann)

against 'the incessant arrest of public representatives',[10] as ten untried prisoners in Cork Gaol had done the previous day. On 17 August he was deported by destroyer to Brixton Prison.

Though Collins himself had never favoured the hunger-strike as a weapon there had been close ties of comradeship between him and Terry MacSwiney. It was hard to think of MacSwiney, the resourceful toiler, lying in long-drawn-out and painful inaction. He eased his mind by casting about for effective methods of reprisal should his friend's gesture meet with no response from the British authorities.

The Government had other problems. Winter was approaching with its more favourable conditions for Sinn Fein. Macready had hoped that an all-out drive under the new regulations would bring him victory. Now he felt paralysed, his only alternatives a weakly-spread-out force unable to control local I.R.A. activities, or a concentration of battalions that must abandon whole areas to the I.R.A. Yet the Chief Secretary's suggestion that special constables from the 'loyalist North' be enrolled was met with opposition from both Sir John Anderson and Macready himself, who saw in such a move civil war contrived by the Government.

Ulster, or more properly its north-east portion, was now a centre of active controversy. Since July over 5,000 Catholic workers had been driven from their homes and jobs, not, for once, for ostensibly sectarian reasons but avowedly in a move against Sinn Fein. Dail Eireann now proposed economic sanctions against Belfast. Known as the 'Belfast Boycott' this was aimed at the promoters of the Orange campaign who largely controlled the commercial interests of the North.

Collins was at pains, in a Press interview later, to point out that the issue was not one of Southern jealousy of the Belfast trading position, but a protest against the political and religious victimization of a minority. He saw the boycott as 'something in the nature of a war blockade'.[11]

The Castle Executive was faced not only with the problem of hunger-strikes but also with that of reprisals. Macready in particular was torn between maintaining discipline and taking the heart out of his troops. The Government believed that reprisals,

[10] Macardle *The Irish Republic* p. 383
[11] Collins Papers

while unofficial, would alone be effective in checking the I.R.A.
and keeping up police morale.

Black and Tan excesses had been encouraged rather than
otherwise by the publication of the new police paper, the *Weekly
Summary*. The incitements to violence this contained were castigated by Collins's old acquaintance of London days, Robert
Lynd. Writing in the *Daily News* he protested that they 'had
their natural result in making the Black and Tans feel towards
their Irish "enemies" as men feel towards wild beasts'.[12] Macready, eyeing the Tans coldly enough, urged the authorities to
change their motley uniform as quickly as possible for one that
could not be mistaken for that of the Army.

On 20 September the American Consul in Dublin, Mr
Dumont, wrote to the Secretary of State: 'The Black and Tans
of today dominate and terrorise. . . . When all is said and done,
and without regard to old quarrels between the Irish and Great
Britain, the British Government is responsible for the present
condition of affairs in Ireland'.[13]

With reprisals and growing concern over the hunger-strikers,
Sturgis could only write bleakly as August ended: 'The prospects of peace seem much worse than a month ago'.

It was of the utmost importance to Collins to show a firm
hand, particularly in the light of recent British attacks. Reprisals
were figuring large in his plans as September wore to a close.
Ten men lay, progressively weakening, in Cork Gaol. Yet it was
upon the solitary figure of the Lord Mayor of Cork in Brixton
Prison that the eyes of the world were now fixed. Lloyd George
made anxious enquiries of the Castle Executive as to the possible
outcome were MacSwiney released. The reply was not encouraging. Only a certainty that peace would result would justify such
a move, and this was impossible.

Collins was not prepared to offer surrender in exchange for
MacSwiney's life: such a course would be entirely contrary to
the principles for which his friend lay dying. He would offer war
instead. The Squad was called out to shoot half a dozen active
G-men as they left the Castle. Friendly detectives were in the

[12] Quoted in Edgar Holt *Protest in Arms* (London 1960) pp. 216–17
[13] Quoted in Charles Callan Tansill *America and the Fight for Irish
Freedom: 1866–1922* (New York 1957) p. 407.

party, however, and the signal to disperse was given. For Sunday after Sunday they waited, running an almost insane risk, before they were finally called off.

Death was becoming a commonplace, the bitter round of reprisal and counter-reprisal kept up mainly between the I.R.A. and the police, with civilians often caught helplessly between the two. It was evident to all who hoped for a solution by other than violent means that the time had come to seek a settlement by negotiation.

The Government still clung to the old formula of divide and rule. Not for nothing had Sir John Anderson, early in September, ordered General Boyd, commanding the Dublin area, on no account to touch the moderates, led by Arthur Griffith, but to continue to harry Michael Collins and those others generally referred to as 'gunmen'.

Arthur Griffith, however, was not prepared to be a catspaw of the British. He was undoubtedy under pressure from his own moderate wing of Sinn Fein to seek some terms whereby a truce could be arranged, pending discussion of peace. Yet Collins for one must have been urgent in pressing the contrary view, that a truce under conditions imposed by Britain would inevitably be construed as a renunciation of the right to independence. Any peace settlement that followed would be based on this vital British advantage.

Recognition of Dail Eireann was, he knew well, the king-pin of the political aspect of the struggle; its achievement must not, however, be won at the price of military surrender, or a Pyrrhic victory would be the result. It was not to those who cried 'Enough!' that Britain would concede large issues, but to those who stood their ground and answered force with force.

CHAPTER ELEVEN

A Hell to Live In

(October – December 1920)

I

Guerilla warfare was proving its effectiveness against forces based on pivotal positions. The pattern of attacks on police barracks by Volunteer groups quickly mobilized from neighbouring farms or villages was changing. Equipped with Crossley tenders, the Black and Tans and Auxiliaries were striking out across wider areas, radiating from their headquarters in each district. Whatever route they took, however, inevitably began and terminated at one of these bases. The Volunteers were now forming regular flying columns, consisting of a few men on full-time active service, not usually more than thirty in number at the most. Almost impossible to hem in, excelling in flanking and feinting movements, these small bands of men succeeded by reconnaisance, ambush, and sudden attacks on enemy positions in keeping 50,000 troops and 15,000 armed police in full-time deployment against them.

Dublin, for all its raids and its curfew, had not as yet known the intensive terror of smaller, more vulnerable towns. Apart from isolated scuffles over arms the military had hitherto been unmolested within the Dublin district, and Auxiliaries came and went easily enough. They were allowed to do so advisedly. The I.R.A. leaders realized the importance of free access to Dublin, from where they directed the overall campaign.

Increasing military raids, however, now called for answering pressure by the I.R.A. In these days Dublin at last became a battlefield. It also proved that guerilla warfare need not lack the chivalry of more traditional engagements.

Sean Treacy, the great Tipperary fighter, cornered one night in a Dublin house with his comrade Dan Breen, escaped only after five British troops had been shot down. Two days later – 'a hell of a day' Dick McKee was to call it – despite intensive raids and echoes of ricochetting bullets in the streets, Treacy attended the funeral of the dead officers. Without doubt he did so in a spirit of respect for fellow soldiers fallen in battle. A quiet, deeply devout man, in whose presence men forbore to swear, Treacy personified the ideal Volunteer, particularly for a realistic lover of the ideal like Collins. Swift upon the trigger, indifferent to danger, untouched by hatred, he neither romanticized war nor treated it cynically, but fought a clean, hard fight.

Later that same day he was himself hunted down and shot dead in a Dublin street. The British in their turn were to show respect in death to a fearless fighter, saluting his body as it passed, in crowded procession, to burial in Tipperary.

The eyes of the world turned more intently upon the Anglo-Irish confrontation as October wore on. On 25 October, after seventy-four days without food, Terence MacSwiney died in Brixton Prison.

This was to be one of those events which are indelibly stamped upon the calendar of a nation's history. A prominent Irishman had gone deliberately to death to emphasize his country's right also to go its chosen way. To many Irishmen the Republic was no longer merely an ideal to strive for, but a faith made irreducible by sacrifice.

MacSwiney's death brought to the British public also a new concept of Irish affairs. Hitherto the ordinary British citizen had regarded Sinn Fein as a few terrorists with guns, attempting to foist impossible demands on their more sober-minded countrymen. The Government, wishing to show a world now extremely interested in its Irish policy that no state of war existed, allowed MacSwiney's body to pass through the streets of London on its way to burial in Ireland.

The citizens of London who turned out in curiosity to see the cortège pass by were left strangely moved and thoughtful. The Government might continue to inveigh against 'irresponsible gunmen'; to many Englishmen such words would henceforth conjure up a memory of proud, soldierly young men in uniform round a tricolour-shrouded coffin which thousands followed in procession through London, capital of the Empire.

Collins respected the heroism of his friend's death; but whereas the nation mourned its hero, Collins writhed at a loss which that nation could ill-afford.

Next to Collins himself, dead or alive, Castle Intelligence sought to capture the Dail funds, the life-blood of the Republican movement. Sturgis's diary reports:

'Tuesday 26th October
—came in this evening in a chestnut moustache and wig, trench coat, flannel trousers and bowler hat – looking *the* most complete swine I ever saw – he had been pinching M.C.'s 'war chest' from the Munster and Leinster Bank – quite illegally I expect – brought in about £4,000. £15,000 more to come.'

A comparison of Loan Statements bears witness to this coup. Those dated up to 21 October 1920 show deposits with the Munster and Leinster Bank of £10,000. That of 12 November 1920 places this amount briefly to 'D.R. (Enemy)'.[1] The bulk of the Loan money remained undisclosed. Sturgis might well remark to his diary that 'The Bank's transactions as disclosed in commandeered stuff are casual to the point of Conspiracy!' The final Loan total, subscribed by over 135,000 people, reached the figure of £378,858.[2]

Although a race to annihilation rather than peace remained the apparent aim of those embroiled in the struggle, exploratory moves towards negotiation were taking place. On 6 October, in *The Times*, Brigadier-General George Cockerill, C.B., M.P., urged a truce and a meeting, to amount to an international conference, between plenipotentiaries of both nations to seek the best peace possible. Less public moves were afoot, but these lay very much beneath the surface. It was to be almost a year before Ireland's case would be brought to the conference table.

II

Within a week of MacSwiney's death Ireland was to have another martyr. Eighteen-year-old Kevin Barry, captured in a Dublin street-battle, was sentenced to hang. The old question of whether

[1] Collins Papers
[2] Macardle *The Irish Republic* p. 986

he was an accessory to murder or a prisoner-of-war took secondary place in shocked Irish minds. His reputation as a particularly fine youth, and his youth itself, gave hope that the sentence would be remitted. His reported torture and proud refusal to betray his leaders added anguish to the hope.

'What can they do for you now?' it is said was the contemptuous question.

'Nothing: but I can die for them', is the answer still remembered in Ireland.

Doing nothing was not, however, Michael Collins's way. He set about devising a way of rescuing Kevin Barry. Had he not magicked twenty men at a stroke out of Mountjoy before? He worked feverishly, lost to all other considerations. Time was running out, and he did not share the belief that a reprieve would be granted.

His intense, painful ability to enter into the victim's mind placed him under intolerable strain. Little habits in his friends, scarcely noticed at other times, assumed enormous proportions. Diarmuid O'Hegarty, for instance, would work, a cigarette drooping from his mouth, the ash falling where it would. Without warning, Michael struck the cigarette away with an oath. The gentle O'Hegarty protested in amazement. Later, Michael would apologize. Now he was all but unbalanced with worry.

Months later he was able to voice something of what then obsessed him. In the old Fenian days men had gone to prison, and frequently death, unsupported by a word from those who directed the national movement. 'I determined it would not be so in our day', he said. 'I determined that we would accept responsibility for what we believed was necessary. No more lonely scaffolds in our time.'

Kevin Barry's case was discussed by members of the Castle Executive and the Lord Lieutenant on the morning of Sunday 31 October. Lord French reminded them soberly that a life was at stake, and the proceedings were grave and thorough. There was little doubt of the outcome, however. Some would have preferred to have Barry shot as a rebel under martial law as a cleaner and more fitting way to carry out the policy of no compromise, than hanged as a murderer under so-called civil government; the prevailing view was that to show clemency would be to encourage violence.[3]

Barry went, erect and smiling, to die. It was Collins who, haggard and in utter despair, all plans for rescue in vain, sat out the long night's watch in Vaughan's, waiting for the dawn, staring at nothing. Once he gave an exclamation of pity. For the rest he was silent, enduring the agony of those who give orders for which those who obey them die.

After Barry's death young men flocked in hundreds to join the I.R.A. 'The doves of peace', as Albert Camus once wrote, 'do not perch on gallows.'

In a renewed effort to round up Sinn Feiners before winter checked such operations, General Macready now set up concentration camps at Ballykinlar and on the Curragh in which thousands were to be interned. At the same time Macready himself was involved in the initial stages of a new round of abortive peace moves. As always they were doomed because they were not conducted, on the Irish side, by those behind the war campaign. Arthur Griffith, when approached, stated plainly that what Sturgis calls 'the untrustworthy wobbliness of Lloyd George' was a major bar to any settlement. The Irish people might be longing desperately for peace, but it was a longing that the British, and not the I.R.A., would allow them to enjoy it.

Michael was now faced with the most serious threat to his Intelligence he had yet encountered. He had long ago accounted for all the G-men who mattered; the remainder confined themselves strictly to investigating petty crime or co-operated actively with him. It had long been realized that plans formulated within the Castle itself were known to Collins almost before they were mooted. A new element in British Intelligence was obviously called for.

What was to be known later as the 'Cairo Gang' was sent over to Dublin. British officers with Secret Service training, their single purpose was to track down and destroy Collins and his Intelligence lieutenants.

It was not long before Collins, aided by the Dublin Brigade, had dossiers on all of them. Dick McKee and his Vice-Brigadier, Peadar Clancy, undertook, of stark necessity, the elimination of

[3] Sturgis Diaries, 31 October 1920

the group before it could eliminate them. It became clear that the action could not be carried out too soon. But the group's dossiers were complete enough, even for Collins. Of thirty-five men, including many not of, but associated with, the Cairo Gang, fifteen had been exempted as having insufficient evidence against them. Twenty remained, and G.H.Q. gave its sanction for their execution.

The date fixed was Sunday 21 November 1920. Curfew hour came on the Saturday night. Collins, McKee, Clancy, Brugha, Mulcahy, and the rest were in the smokeroom at Vaughan's. Sean Kavanagh, one of those who made unscheduled visits there that evening, had arrived after curfew. Christy Harte, the porter, told him that 'Mr C. and other gentlemen' were in the smokeroom, and showed him into a small pantry under the stairs. Here he found Piaras Beaslai and Sean O'Connell, and a stranger, Conor Clune, a young Clareman who had come to Dublin to meet Beaslai because of his interest in Irish.

The four chatted. Out in the hall Christy Harte watched suspiciously as a hotel guest made a telephone call, then went out, despite the curfew. Ten minutes later he returned. Harte went rapidly upstairs. The meeting broke up instantly.

The first the small group under the stairs knew of trouble brewing was a commotion in the hall. O'Connell stuck his head out and said, 'It's the Tans'. They were not unduly alarmed. Two minutes earlier Dick McKee had collected his bicycle from the back, glanced in to say goodnight, and gone out. The party upstairs, apparently, had all made a safe getaway. Beaslai and O'Connell faded gently out of the back door. Kavanagh, having nothing incriminating on him, decided to stay where he was, despite being on the run. Clune was very nervous, and Kavanagh tried to calm him.

Before long an Auxiliary noticed them and brought them into the dining-room, with others, for questioning. Kavanagh was able to convince his interrogator that he was a bona fide guest : he had a toothbrush in his pocket. Conor Clune was next in line. 'This damned fellow hasn't even a toothbrush', his searcher growled. Clune was still palpably nervous and he was ordered to one side. The man whose movements had first alerted Harte's mistrust was also held.

Dick McKee, with Peadar Clancy, had gone to a friend's house in Gloucester Street. In the early hours of the morning a group of Auxiliaries came. McKee sprang from his bed and busied himself at the fireplace. The two men were ordered to dress quickly, then taken to Dublin Castle. Among the ashes in the grate lay the list of the British Intelligence men whose deaths McKee and Clancy had arranged for a few hours later.

Morning came, wintry but fine. As the bells rang for nine o'clock Mass people hurried, singly or in little groups, to church. No less purposefully, singly or in little groups, young men in trench coats and black hats made their way also to their destinations in the city.

They were apprehensive. The men they sought were practised marksmen. The only element in their favour was surprise. On the hour they knocked. Landladies, maids, a small boy, opened doors to their revolvers. Some of the young men stood guard; others went swiftly up the stairs. There followed a rapid succession of shots, screams, the sound of running feet, and shouting; more shots. The young men, most of them as white and shaken as the listeners downstairs, hurried away, stuffing hastily gathered papers into their pockets.

Ten British officers, some of the Cairo Gang, others regular Intelligence officers, had been killed and four wounded, one of whom died later. There were three or four tragic errors of identity; Several of the group escaped. Of the Volunteers who took part in the operation, some would never recover completely from the nerve-shattering work of that morning.

Dublin Castle was at breakfast when the first news reached it. Dave Neligan, a detective now working for Collins, was told: 'The British Secret Service has been wiped out'. Writing in his diary late that night Mark Sturgis noted that those killed had been 'Military officers – mostly either those who have been employed in Courts Martial or Secret Service men'. Ormonde Winter, Head of Castle Intelligence, he found 'distinctly nervy and overwrought'.

'It has been a day of black murder. What they hope to gain by it God alone knows', he added. The simple answer was, their lives; and through them, Irish freedom.

Collins heard of the killings soon after nine. No less shaken than those who had acted on his orders, he shouted at O'Reilly. His first thought was for his men's safety, his second for that of the people flocking into Dublin for the afternoon's G.A.A. Football Challenge match. Beneath all lay the lurking fear : where were McKee and Clancy?

When they told him he must have known it was all over. The imagination that saw too clearly the horror of the morning raced now to the Castle and the inquisitors whose eyes would also see only blood that day. After the first numbing shock, however, he sprang into action. MacNamara, the G-man, believed two men had just been sent from the Castle to the Bridewell. Neligan was ordered to search it. Even that intrepid man was appalled. Into the Bridewell he went, however, bluffing his way from cell to cell, pretending to the sergeant on duty, who knew him to be a policeman, that he was looking for a cousin. McKee and Clancy were not there.

Collins had relapsed into stupefied brooding. As with Kevin Barry three weeks before, now he could only wait. Sean Kavanagh had just seen the man 'arrested' in Vaughan's the previous night walking free; he reported this to Collins who hardly seemed aware of his presence.

McKee and Clancy were still in the Castle. With about twenty other prisoners they spent the day in the guardroom, being taken out for intermittent interrogation. Here was quartered the notorious 'F' Division of the Auxiliaries. As the day wore on their prisoners watched in apprehension as, in hysterical reaction to the carnage, at the extent of which only McKee and Clancy themselves could guess, they grew increasingly drunk and took to wild firing practice, intermingled with violent threats.

Beyond the guardroom the Castle was in uproar. Intelligence officers – or their remnant – were crowding the gates with their families and possessions, their value as 'plants' among the ordinary citizens gone. Jostling them came the touts and spies whose little back-street lives had suddenly lost their comfortable anonymity. Michael Collins, they felt in their panic, knew all about that whispered word, that discreet passing of money in a dingy pub.

British reactions generally reflected horror at what appeared to be wanton and unprovoked murder of defenceless officers. The Prime Minister, however, using one of his unofficial links with

Sinn Fein negotiators, sent a message to 'ask Griffith for God's sake to keep his head, and not to break off the slender link that had been established. Tragic as the events in Dublin were, they were of no importance. These men were soldiers, and took a soldier's risk.'[4]

Collins had realized belatedly that the football crowds might well be suspected of containing Volunteers come up to Dublin to take part in the morning's shootings. But the crowds had gathered and the match could not be called off.

Lorry-loads of Auxiliaries from Beggar's Bush tore up to Croke Park in the afternoon. According to Sturgis's diary entry of that night, it had been arranged some time previously to surround the football ground with military, after which police would move in, order the crowd out of the exits by megaphone, and search all the men on the assumption that large numbers of wanted Volunteers from both Dublin and Tipperary would be among them, complete with arms.

In the event, the police moved in early. Generals Tudor and Boyd reported that three men on the grandstand fired first, in the air, while Sinn Feiners at the gates opened fire on the Auxiliaries, stampeding the crowds. Commanding officers, however, are seldom eye-witnesses. There was no doubt of the outcome. The Auxiliaries fired wildly with rifles and machine guns, raking the ground for ten minutes. Fourteen men and women died, hundreds were trampled in the panic-stricken rush to the gates. A Tipperary player in his coloured shirt lay dead; a small boy died in his mother's arms.

Michael had lunched as usual at Mrs O'Donovan's, crossing the tension-filled city to do so. Though the place where Dick McKee had sat the previous week was empty, he concealed all emotion. He was waiting for word from MacNamara who, in a last, desperate attempt to find a chance of rescue, went down into the Auxiliaries' canteen adjoining the guardroom. He found them 'drunk and thirsting for vengeance'.[5]

Beside himself, and reckless of danger, Collins went off in the evening to Parnell Square. Dick O'Hegarty saw him there. At

[4] *Irish Times* 16 November 1965
[5] Charles Dalton *With the Dublin Brigade (1917–1921)* (London 1929) p. 114

Collins's request he went to Vaughan's, and established that, as suspected, the British were still inside. Collins was unarmed. 'You're out of your mind to be here', O'Hegarty urged him, and Collins turned away.

That night most of the prisoners in the Castle were taken to Beggar's Bush. Only McKee and Clancy remained in the guard-room with the nervous young Clareman, Conor Clune, suspected of travelling to Dublin to take part in the Secret Service killings. Why a man who knew little or nothing of Dublin should have been picked for such work, requiring an intimate knowledge of houses and short-cuts, was not, presumably, one of the questions put to him.

Early on Monday morning the end came. Its only witnesses were the Auxiliaries themselves. 'Shot whilst attempting to escape' was the official report. It is not inconceivable that the three had made a desperate bid for freedom, or at least for a swift death. From what they had attempted to escape will probably never be known. They had been identified; McKee's position in the Dublin Brigade was known; their part in the previous day's killings could be deduced. Such a chance to extract a betrayal of Collins, Mulcahy, and Brugha was not one to be lightly lost by Auxiliaries aflame for reprisal. That night a doctor examining the bodies found bayonet thrusts, one of which had penetrated McKee's liver, and multiple abrasions as well as bullet wounds.

As for Clune, he may well have died merely to prevent his giving evidence of what he had seen. McKee, the beloved Brigadier, and the gay-hearted Clancy went to their deaths in the same silence that enshrouds the true manner of it.

Collins was at a wedding breakfast. He hid all sign that the fate of his friends, still unknown, had engulfed his thoughts for upwards of twenty-four hours, and appeared in all his careless normality. He believed them dead. In his grief he had undergone a shock so deep as to cause detachment from reality. When the wedding photographs were taken he allowed himself to appear in one, though he retained sufficient presence of mind to half-turn his head away.

That night when the bodies of McKee and Clancy were handed over, Collins overrode all protests and went to the Pro-Cathedral to watch in grim silence while doctors examined what

remained of his friends, and to help dress them in Volunteer
uniform. On the morning of the funeral he was at the Requiem
Mass, and was one of those who carried out the coffins.

He cared nothing for the men waiting for a chance to identify
and seize him. For days he appeared to care nothing for anything
at all, but moved recklessly about Dublin. For the first time he
seemed to regard his own death and that of the rest of his friends
as inevitable. 'We shall be fortunate if we get a clean death,
like poor Sean Treacy', he said. And again, 'It would be nice if
we could all live to be old men'.

The old fighting instinct at last forced its way once more to the
fore. A few months later he wrote : 'What one feels so furious
about is the feeling of impotence – the feeling of the justness of
a retribution that it is impossible to visit them with.'

Only a couple of weeks later the informer who had betrayed
McKee and Clancy was visited with his retribution. Yet enough
was enough. Sean Kavanagh again sought out Collins to tell him
that the informer of Vaughan's Hotel had returned there.
Michael scowled. 'We'll do nothing. We know about him. We
don't want anything messy.'

III

The echoes of Bloody Sunday sounded long after. Among those
arrested in the aftermath of panic was Arthur Griffith. Macready
claimed that this move had a calming effect on police and troops.
It had the opposite effect on Lloyd George, whose 'slender link'
in the moves for peace was thereby dangerously weakened.

Griffith appointed Collins his reluctant successor as Acting
President. Collins was in the Dail Cabinet, not as a politician, but
because he was a practical financial man who revelled in constructive work. Nevertheless, he did as Griffith asked. He was
probably the one man who knew as much of the peace moves
then afoot.

Though the I.R.A. in Dublin was lying low – Collins was one
of the few who were out and about as usual – elsewhere it was
waging war in earnest. On 28 November, fifteen Liverpool ware-
houses went up in flames. On the same day the historic Kil-

michael ambush took place. On that bleak afternoon in the deserted countryside, Tom Barry's men were flung into battle so effectively that of the eighteen Auxiliaries who had set out in convoy from Macroom not one survived.

Collins rejoiced, gay as a schoolboy. These were the men of Cork, *his* county, proving to Britain that Ireland was not beaten yet, not by a long chalk.

Large areas of the country were now under martial law. At the same time the most far-reaching peace moves to date began. Neither approach was to prove conclusive. The Irish people, desperately anxious for peace, had an even more basic need, which comes to all societies in revolution : the need to rally behind a leader.

At this moment of national crisis, de Valera, after an absence of eighteen months, prepared to return home. The intensified activity on both the war and peace fronts continued throughout the weeks of December preceding his return.

In Cork martial law was celebrated by the destruction of the city by fire. Auxiliaries, Black and Tans, and some soldiers roamed the streets throughout the curfew hours. The fire brigade was obstructed and looting was rampant.

Sir Hamar Greenwood subsequently made the hopeful suggestion that the irresponsible citizens of 'Rebel Cork' had burnt their own city from pure fecklessness. The less circumspect Auxies swaggered about with burnt corks in their glengarries in lieu of battle honours. Despite desultory talk in administrative circles of disbanding the whole inglorious lot, when it came to reprisals, it was widely felt, those that were unauthorized brought better results than those officially sanctioned.

The search for Collins was unrelenting. Mark Sturgis from time to time noted its progress with something of the camaraderie the hunter may feel for the hunted.

'Thursday 4th November. Tudor tells me they have caught at Longford a man they *think* is Michael Collins and have ciphered for a strong body to come from Dublin to identify him. Sounds too good to be true.

'Friday 5th November. They have *not* caught Michael Collins at Longford.'

On another occasion: 'M.C. has, I hear, grown a beard. He is the idol of the young men'. In mid-December: 'The C.S's [Greenwood's] permission given this evening for the courteous searching of two monasteries in one of which it is hoped, on what seems good information, to catch the elusive Michael. This search is to take place tonight.' 'But', he added next day, 'no sign of Michael.'

A few days later he recorded a report that 'Michael is often disguised as a priest with a remarkably high collar', adding shrewdly enough, 'I don't incline to believe these disguise stories'. Probably nearer the mark comes another report, on 22 December, ' — said that several of the most wanted men were walking about the City almost daily. . . . Michael Collins he only saw once in his life but is certain he saw him two days ago in Dame Street undisguised'.

Michael himself summed up the constant, abortive harrying of himself and Ireland generally in a defiant note to Hannie written on the same day: 'Times get worse and worse here, or better and better according to one's way of looking at things'. The extent of the Terror was the measure of his success.

The latest gropings after peace in which he had been involved had come to nothing, partly because of both sides' suspicion of any open negotiation, partly because Lloyd George doubted that any secret emissary from Griffith had the support of Collins and the I.R.A.

A promising mediator now appeared in Archbishop Clune of Perth, Australia, an uncle of the murdered Conor Clune. Influential Irishmen in London had asked him to see the Prime Minister. At Lloyd George's behest the Archbishop went to Dublin, where he saw not only Griffith in Mountjoy, but Collins himself. This meeting took place on 4 December, at Miss Gavan Duffy's school on St Stephen's Green.

'I wonder', wrote Sturgis, 'how it is that the Archbishop sees Collins apparently without difficulty in Dublin and our intelligence fails to find him after weeks of search – but Dublin is a terrible warren of a place.'

Collins was, as always, supremely master of his own movements. In close touch with Griffith by letter, he now drew up a formula for a truce: 'If it is understood that the acts of violence (attacks, counter attacks, reprisals, arrests, pursuits) are called off on both sides, we are agreeable to issue the necessary instructions on our side, it being understood that the entire Dail shall be free to meet, and that its peaceful activities be not interfered with.'

Dr Clune returned to London confident that the I.R.A. would obey any Dail decision over negotiations. But Lloyd George could count on no such support from his own militarists, who remained adamant for war. On 10 December he announced to the Commons that 'the extremists must first be broken up'. Further attempts by the Archbishop to negotiate a truce failed. The British terms hardened to the handing over of arms. Griffith could only point out that this was not truce, but surrender. There could be no surrender.

Dr Clune might well protest that no sooner had he negotiated agreement with Sinn Fein than the British shifted their ground. The talks were patently at an end. He and Michael Collins, meeting on 18 December, both came to this conclusion. Sturgis wrote in his diary: 'I can't help being uneasy that we are not taking a *big* enough view of the position – not only the future of the Irish is at stake but the future relations of two countries which must ever live side by side and there is so much talk as if we had nothing to do but to beat an enemy.'

Martial law was proving no less abortive than the peace talks. 'Government by Black and Tans' continued unchecked. Lloyd George now tried legislation. On 23 December 1920 the Government of Ireland Act was passed. Ireland was to be sawn in two against the will of the majority of her people, with two half-powered parliaments, one in Belfast grudgingly accepted by the minority whose interests it was designed to protect, and one in Dublin where a duly elected assembly was already functioning as best it could under impossible conditions. The most that could be said for the Act was that it partially repealed the Act of Union, which the Southern Irish had always regarded as unconstitutional in any case.

Lloyd George himself, unsuspected by the Irish, hoped that Partition would provide an ultimate solution. Those able to regard it dispassionately admitted that it cleared one major obstacle from the path to settlement, since without it the Ulstermen would have remained irreconcilable to any recognition of a Dublin legislature. Sinn Fein, however, could hardly be expected to see Partition in this light. 'This plunderous and impossible Act', Collins termed it.[6]

Less than a week after he had sat down with Dr Clune Michael had the closest escape from capture that he was to experience. It was Christmas Eve. Knowing the virtual isolation into which his presence plunged Batt O'Connor's children he had improvised an 'election' in their houses to decide who was the most handsome of the numerous men on the run who called there that evening. Now he determined to observe his own festivities. He summoned a few friends to dine with him in the Gresham, hotbed of British agents. Outrageously, he sent an invitation to Dave Neligan, working for him in the Castle. 'And ask him is it safe', he added as an afterthought to the horrified messenger. When Neligan politely declined to join him in presumptive suicide Collins chuckled. 'Dave's getting windy', he said. Whether out of bravado in the face of his taunts or from a refusal to see him go off into the jaws of Death alone, Gearoid O'Sullivan, Rory O'Connor, and Tom Cullen agreed to accompany him.

Even Collins in this boisterous mood had not overlooked all precautions. The private room that should have been reserved for them was not available, however, and they had to make do with a table in the crowded public dining-room. Inevitably, the Auxiliaries pounced. Michael, desperately affable, was escorted to the cloakroom and compared with his 'official' photograph, probably more copies of which were distributed about Dublin at this time than of the King himself. Prepared to sell his life dearly, he was about to spring for the Auxie's gun when his enemy suddenly turned on his heel and called off the search.

For the first and last time in recorded history Collins proceeded to get drunk. Furthermore, he led his equally unsteady companions, the tremendous upsurge of relief gone to their heads as much as the gulps of neat whiskey, on to Vaughan's, then about the most dangerous spot in town even for men with their wits about them. Tom Cullen, fortunately, had kept some of his. Curfew was at hand. He herded them down Parnell Square to

[6] In a written answer to a Press question, 22 January 1921 – Collins Papers

Devlin's and ran to find a car. Piaras Beaslai turned up at this juncture to find Michael and Rory O'Connor 'sitting on the ground embracing one another and Gearoid half-lying on a chair'.[7]

The car appeared and the highly-elated trio were shepherded into it. They had recovered sufficiently to be able to make the length of the road to Mrs O'Donovan's, though they were still very excited. Michael, his hair still wildly dishevelled where the Auxie had run his fingers through it, fell to wondering what would have been the effect of his capture. 'Rory, what would you have told the country lads?' O'Connor seized a knife and drew it dramatically across his throat. 'I wouldn't have been here to tell anything', he declared emotionally. Content with this evidence of his friend's fervent regard, Michael allowed himself to be gently led away to bed.

He had been up early that morning. 'This will be a proud day for you to remember', he had told young Eileen O'Donovan. She had watched, puzzled, as he set off into the half-dark of the December morning. Later she knew what he had meant. His destination had been a house in a Dublin Square. In it he was to meet de Valera who, with Michael to make the arrangements for his safe voyage, had returned that morning from the United States.

[7] *Irish Independent* 28 August 1963

CHAPTER TWELVE

The Terror Ends

(January – July 1921)

I

De Valera's return, if unproclaimed, was not unexpected. The Castle was instructed on Monday 20 December that, in the event of his landing in Ireland, he was to be regarded as a political rather than a military problem, and that no step to arrest him was to be taken without reference to London. Having proclaimed the Government's 'double policy' Lloyd George intended to drive with an even rein.

Since the differences between de Valera and the American leaders had first become apparent the Dail Cabinet had consistently stood by its leader. Whatever the rights or wrongs of the transatlantic storm its first duty was to maintain its own solidarity and the position of the Republic at home.[1]

Michael was unfeignedly glad to see de Valera back. In the past he had viewed with misgivings the return of old colleagues from the States. Americanisms crept into conversation, outlooks altered, it seemed, with the clothes they brought home. His reactions were symptomatic of his constant fear that the focal point of the fight might be allowed to drift away from Ireland, where its direction could be properly controlled. De Valera, he noted, seemed to have developed no such alarming notions. Writing of another recent repatriot to Father P. J. Doyle of Naas on 29 January 1921, Collins observed : 'I hope America has not had

[1] Collins himself had come to comprehend something of the differences in outlook that had caused the split. In a written reply to a question from an American press correspondent he said: 'Ireland itself is the pulse and all organizations outside of Ireland and all effort on behalf of Ireland in foreign countries must be directed by and subject to home considerations. It must be borne in mind that our organizations abroad have to work in accordance with the allowances granted or the restrictions imposed, as the case may be, by the laws of the particular country in which the organization operates.' – c. March 1921. Collins Papers

the usual effect on him. There is only one person whom I have come across yet, upon whom America has had no effect – that is, the President.'[2]

De Valera's protracted stay in America had inevitably affected his comprehension of the way the winds blew in Ireland. One of his earliest actions was to ask Collins to go to the States, as the first step in a unilateral slackening-off of the military campaign.

It was a suggestion supported by Brugha and Stack. Both were active in the physical force party; in view of the bitter enmity they had now openly combined to show for Collins, it must be assumed that their backing for Collins's removal from the scene of action was inspired chiefly by personal resentment. It is unnecessary to assume that de Valera had a similar motive. Since the coercion end of the British 'double policy' was aimed at the I.R.A. militant, it seemed to him advisable that the campaign of reprisal and counter-reprisal should be eased off and an atmosphere more conducive to negotiation allowed to develop. [See, however, the account of his position in Longford – O'Neill, pp. 117–8.]

He found no further support for his suggestion. 'One good battle a month' was how one I.R.A. leader disgustedly summed it up; or as a historian of revolutions puts it: 'The moderate reformers in time of revolution always try to govern the army by political instead of military methods. The results are uniformly and universally disastrous.'[3]

Collins firmly refused to leave Ireland, or to allow political possibilities to outweigh military realities. The British claimed to be putting down disaffection rather than waging a war in Ireland; yet, in the areas where there was little disaffection, the Crown forces acted no less repressively than in those where force answered force. The outcome of the Clune talks had given Collins all the proof necessary that to slacken the I.R.A. campaign now might indeed lead to speedy peace talks – on Britain's terms. To meet the growing number of raids, arrests, and street hold-ups Collins had, indeed, now recruited his own full-time 'auxiliaries' to the Squad, known as the Active Service Unit.

De Valera must have quickly observed the stresses within his

[2] Collins Papers
[3] Edwards *The Natural History of Revolution* p. 146

Cabinet. Cathal Brugha indeed, while at loggerheads with Collins on account of authority allegedly overreached, was no less quick to hound de Valera himself when he seemed prone to admit any suggestion of compromise into discussion. Austin Stack had become, if anything, more bitterly opposed to Collins than Brugha himself. Answering an admiring comment about Collins by Padraig O'Keeffe, Stack hissed : 'He's only a polished clerk' – an odd phrase. The spectre of former comradeship must have stood very close at his elbow, killed, in his eyes, by Collins himself.

Collins was not only deeply hurt; he felt a mounting unease at a situation which might split the Cabinet on a vital issue. De Valera, however, was clearly on his guard against such an outcome and Collins himself, while admitting the bitter personal antagonisms against him, hardly believed that such considerations would outweigh those of the country's good.

Quantities of Collins's papers were seized in a New Year's raid. These were, in the main, old Intelligence documents. Sturgis remarks that he personally delivered to Lord French from amongst them two letters 'dated last March and August respectively. . . . H.E. had never seen either before – also a complete copy of the Viceregal list of private switch telephone numbers with names. . . . This a bit out of date'.

Lord French took a remarkably philosophical view of the author of this diversion of his postbag, who had also been responsible for his attempted assassination. He was willing to admit, at least in private, that Ireland was at war. He 'said he always saw a strong likeness between this war and South Africa; that all we now say of Michael Collins they said then of Smuts, "and look at him now".'[4]

The hunt for Michael seemed now to be concentrated on every house in and near Dublin. Even that safe lair, Mrs O'Donovan's, was raided, albeit by mistake. They more nearly stumbled upon him at Linda Kearns's nurses' home in Gardiner Row. Michael was dining there, and the raid came too suddenly for him to get away. He promptly disappeared, with his plate, under the table, where the cloth concealed him from the raiders, who left empty-handed.

The constant strain of the chase, however much he shrugged

Sturgis Diaries 3 February 1921

it off, coupled with his superhuman burden of work, was having its effect. Bouts of stomach pain left him white and drawn. He would be unable to eat, submitting with a lack of protest that in itself indicated that he was unwell to that last of all degradations, a bowl of curds and whey.

One of those arrested at this time was Rory O'Connor. Mistaken at first for Michael Collins, a common fate, he was subjected to considerable ill-treatment and put in the Curragh internment camp, where he developed tuberculosis. At this time he was still devoted to Collins, observing of the breach between Brugha and Collins that, 'Mick was the only man one could go to and rely on to get anything done'.

The raid in which Collins's documents had been seized resulted in the arrest of Ned Broy. His removal had little effect on Collins's Intelligence network, since the British had some time since withdrawn their detective operations to the Castle itself. But Collins was not the man to be complacent on that account. Broy was his friend, and Collins did not lightly lose his friends. He sent for MacNamara and Neligan in a fury of haste and, by well-chosen threats to other D.M.P. men, saw to it in no uncertain fashion that no charges were preferred against Broy.

The friendly G-men were still able for a time to keep Collins informed of projected British moves. But MacNamara was suddenly dismissed early in 1921. Joe Kavanagh, the first to have enlisted for Collins, had died. Neligan remained, and retained his usefulness by getting himself sworn into the Secret Service. The panic of Bloody Sunday had subsided, and the Castle relied on the Secret Service men to live outside its walls. Neligan lived in Dun Laoghaire under the guise of an insurance agent, and had contacts with both Collins and the Castle. The day came when these met simultaneously on his doorstep. Neligan introduced them laconically, and discussed insurance in a manner to inspire a surprised admiration in both, an emotion which they were equally at pains to conceal from each other.

The war was entering a new phase. The Crown forces numbered about 60,000 troops and 15,000 Auxiliaries and Black and Tans in addition to the regular R.I.C., supported by more than a hundred armoured cars and numerous armoured lorries. Calls for larger I.R.A. units, which came mainly from the southern brigade officers, now led to its reorganization into divisions. While the Crown forces still had the upper hand in the towns, the I.R.A. could now claim to be in charge in the country districts.

'Ireland defends herself against the bully', wrote Michael Collins, 'and she looks forward to the time when she can resume her proper national activities and work out her own problems and her own destiny without interference from outside. Ireland wants peace, but she will not surrender. England wants peace but she insists on surrender.'[5]

'Magnanimity in politics is not seldom the truest wisdom', Burke had written. While not in the mood to offer magnanimity as a peace solution, the British Government was still interested enough in a negotiated settlement to turn aside from the 'surrender' demand upon which the Clune talks had foundered and explore other avenues.

Lloyd George now announced that the Clune talks had failed because all his Irish advisers had said that truce without the surrender of arms was impossible. 'This', wrote Sturgis sardonically, 'is contrary to my recollection.'

Collins remained convinced that the British objective was to isolate Sinn Fein in the public mind from the I.R.A. 'Many a time I have pointed this out to the propaganda Dept', he wrote, 'but I fear they did not grasp it & it is too commonly thought that it is a question of "impossibilists" of "extremists" of "murder gangers" or whatever other names English spokesmen wish to use.'

The efforts of the Castle peacemakers, while commendable, were invariably fruitless. Sinn Fein, rightly, would not place any confidence in their credentials while Lloyd George continued to give his most attentive ear to the militarists. Nor can the Castle have been blind to the fact that each negotiator, initially welcomed by Lloyd George, had been shown the door in favour of another just when his attempts seemed likely to succeed by committing the British to the only terms acceptable to Sinn Fein.

The Prime Minister's attitude is, perhaps, best explained by a later entry in the Sturgis Diaries on 11 May 1921, which followed a conversation between Sturgis and Miss Frances

[5] In a written answer to questions from the *Boston American* under letter dated 22 January 1921 – Collins Papers

Stevenson, Lloyd George's personal secretary (later his wife):
'Miss Stevenson . . . admitted what I have long thought must
be so – that all the high fallutin reasons against L.G. making a
definite offer might not weigh quite so heavy if he didn't hope in
his inmost heart that Southern Ireland might still be persuaded
to work his Act without any additions whatever.'

II

Increased I.R.A. activity during February and March was particularly apparent in the south-west. For Collins it was Cork all
the way. When a county whose lack of national spirit had earned
Michael's soubriquet of 'the lousy county' suddenly bestirred
itself, he wrote with guarded satisfaction: 'they seem to be getting
a little of the Cork humour'. When a Cork Volunteer, a light-
hearted lad of eighteen, was shot, Collins broke down. He had
et him, once, some months before. His death struck him as
snarply as if he had personified all that was best of Ireland.

He continued to rejoice at any success in his home county, and
was highly delighted at a *Daily Sketch* report that he had died
of wounds received when, mounted on a white horse, he had
reputedly led a column into battle not far from his home. It
was a delight only outweighed by his admiration for Tom Barry
who had extricated his entire column scatheless from an awkward
position.

A day or two earlier, in the first week of February, he had
been deeply saddened by the death of Johnny's wife, who left
eight children, the youngest only a baby. His family provided
the one reality he could cling to amid realities only too divorced
from the things he cared about. On 5 March he wrote:

'My Dear Sister Mary Celestine
'Only today I got your very nice letter written at Xmas, but
even so it is better to get it now than not at all. It is good and
pleasant and hopeful to know that one is thought of and
prayed for although one may deserve neither – I suppose
Providence has its own ways for fixing things. . . .
'We are losing many splendid men – many fine noble friends.
I hope someone will be left to pay due tribute to their deeds

and their memories – but only one tribute can repay them – the freedom of this land and in God's good time that will rest with us.

'Yes indeed the English papers have been giving me plenty of notoriety – a notoriety one would gladly be rid of but they must make a scapegoat. *Daily Sketch* had a gorgeous thing once upon a time – "Mike" the super hater, dour, hard, no ray of humour, no trace of human feeling – oh lovely! The white horse story was an exaggeration. I have not ridden a white horse since I rode "Gipsy" and used her mane as a bridle.

'Goodbye for a while and may God love you always.

'Micheal'[6]

He was too hard pressed to write regularly to his family. In any case, as he wrote to his sister, Mary Powell, on 24 March 1921 : 'You know it is through no lack of feeling nor indeed through any lack of thought for you but those to whom I write are doomed to have trouble brought upon them. As one of the great English officers said recently on a raid – "Anyone who is a friend of that man is bound to suffer".'

He was at this time much concerned for Robert Barton, who had now been in Portland Prison, under increasingly appalling conditions, for almost a year. 'Please give him my fondest love – tell him I am constantly thinking of him and that he is no end of a loss to us', he wrote on 11 February to Barton's sister.

The imprisonment which he felt most keenly occurred early in March. Sean MacEoin had already won a name for intrepid fighting marked by an almost reckless humanity for the enemy wounded that was reminiscent of Botha on Spion Kop. This was to earn him Oliver St John Gogarty's salute as 'a Bayard among blacksmiths', and Collins's undisguised love as a man to rank with Ireland's most legendary heroes.

It also brought him to the attention of Cathal Brugha. Brugha had again raised his old solution to all Ireland's difficulties, the systematic assassination of the British Cabinet. 'You'll get none of my men for that', Collins had growled, and Brugha replied, 'That's all right, Mr Collins. I want none of *your* men. I'll get men of my own.'[7] The finding of men willing to carry out his purpose was not altogether easy. Joseph Sweeney for one emerged from an interview with Brugha to confront Mulcahy with an astounded : 'The thing's completely amoral'.

Sean MacEoin also received a summons to meet Brugha. One of the most wanted men in Ireland, he came up from Longford and, though knowing little of Dublin, managed to find his way undetected to Brugha's office. If Brugha had a fanatical determination, he was also scrupulous not to let it bear upon the personal conscience of others. He gave no commands; rather he sought volunteers to do his work. MacEoin, however, saw the I.R.A. as an army whose function was to carry out the policy of the Dail Government, to which it had sworn allegiance. He agreed to go to London, of which he had even less knowledge than of Dublin. Brugha thereupon ordered him not to return to Longford but to remain in the city for two days, after which he would take up duty under the direct orders of Brugha himself.

MacEoin emerged into the Dublin streets and ran into Collins, whose consternation on seeing him was peremptorily and wrathfully expressed. He packed him off to Mulcahy who, no less horrified, cancelled Brugha's orders and told him to get home at once. MacEoin, reflecting no doubt with relief, that a soldier obeys his last order rather than his first, left the Chief of Staff to sort matters out himself with the Minister of Defence, and caught the next train home. He was arrested at Mullingar, attempted to escape, and was seriously wounded. Brought back to Dublin, he was taken under heavy guard to hospital.

Collins's remarks to Brugha when this news came through are unrecorded : no doubt they did little to patch up the rift between them. He now strained every sinew to rescue MacEoin. 'Get a permit to see him', he ordered Miss Brigid Lyons.[8] By the time she was allowed to see him MacEoin had been moved to Mountjoy. Lying huddled in his hospital bed, he gave her the impression of a caged and wounded lion. In the room with him were an

---

[7] Desmond FitzGerald Papers, quoted in Colum *Arthur Griffith* p. 223

[8] A niece of Joseph McGuinness, Miss Lyons had fought in Dublin in the Rising. Later to become Dr Lyons-Thornton, she was commissioned in the Army Medical Services of the National Army in 1922, thus earning the distinction of being the only woman to serve in the Army.

Auxiliary, a warder, a sergeant, and a deputy-governor. There was a sentry over the inner door of the prison.

While Miss Lyons continued her visits, Collins devised several plans by which MacEoin might be rescued. Despite their failure, he continued to work feverishly to save his friend.

He was coming under new attack from Cathal Brugha, this time over the Purchases of Arms accounts. Brugha complained that the total cost of arms coming into the country did not tally with the amounts released for their purchase. He would not allow that, with the purchase of arms in the hands of a wide assortment of sailors, businessmen with connections abroad, and occasional contacts willing to see what they might be able to pick up, it was impossible to strike any normal balance. Yet 'A' Account in London, showing particulars of goods and prices for the period February–December 1920, is scrupulously detailed. The total of the account for these months, including taxis for the transport of arms to Liverpool, a trunk with straps, packing cases, and storage was £1,055 3s. 3½d.[9] Had every agent been as punctilious Collins would have had little to answer for.

Guerilla war had a queer unreality. The death of Archbishop Walsh of Dublin in April was marked by the chaplain's receiving telegrams of condolence simultaneously from the respective Chiefs of Staff, Macready and Mulcahy. Winter was reported furious at Sir John Anderson's insistence that there should be no attempt to arrest any Sinn Fein leaders who might appear in the funeral procession. The possible capture of even Michael Collins on such an occasion would be outweighed by public outrage at such a move.[10]

This breathing-space was not appreciated by Collins. 'I have had some severe hunting', he wrote. 'Closer and closer it has been, but yet they have not had the ultimate success. . . . Things have been harder than anybody knows.'

He had just taken a blow that struck him where he was most vulnerable. The systematic destruction of houses in reprisal for I.R.A. activity was in full swing in the martial law areas. According to Macready this type of 'official punishment' included the notification, in writing, with reasons, of the owners of the houses to be destroyed, and time to remove valuables. Only Brigade

[9] Public Record Office of Ireland   [10] Sturgis Diaries, 14 April 1921

Commanders could authorize such destruction. Further, 'explosives were used to destroy houses. They were never burnt as a punishment'.[11]

On 16 April Woodfield was burnt. John Collins was attending a County Council meeting in Cork. The women of the house opened the door to two officers of the Essex Regiment, one of whom was Major Percival.[12] These announced that they had orders to burn the house. The children's bedclothes might be removed, but nothing else.

Apart from a threatening note the previous month this was the only notification the Collins family had received. The troops broke the windows with their rifles and forced at bayonet point a number of young men of the neighbourhood, whom they had brought as hostages, to pile hay inside the house, and to sprinkle it with petrol. The house and outbuildings were then set on fire. Only the building in which Michael had been born and which was now used as an outhouse was left standing.

The eight children and two women watched while the various articles they had attempted to save were thrown back into the flames : the baby's cradle, made years before by Michael's father for his own children; milk pails, a new separator. On the whole the soldiers had little heart for their work. Their captain spoke gently to the children who, having so recently lost their mother, were now losing their home. Two soldiers waited until Major Percival's back was turned and rescued the sewing machine. Others, however, having stacked their rifles, forced one of the little boys to hand over a small trinket box he had saved. The detachment then moved on to burn three other houses in the neighbourhood.

John Collins was taken from the train at a stop outside Clonakilty by Black and Tans who feared a hostile crowd in the town, and was informed that his home had been burnt. Next morning he was taken to Cork Prison and thence to internment on Spike Island. Sam's Cross remembered an old prophecy, such as blow out of nowhere across the remote countryside of Ireland and

[11] Macready *Annals of an Active Life* II, p. 523
[12] Later Lieut.-General A. E. Percival, C.B., D.S.O., O.B.E., M.C., to whom was to fall the task of defending Singapore against impossible odds in the Second World War. He surrendered to the Japanese with 85,000 troops.

leave half a memory behind, that early in the 20th century there would be no Collinses left at Woodfield.

Michael heard the news in a black rage of impotence. In his most desolate moments he had always known that Woodfield remained. It symbolized all that Ireland was fighting for, the sane things of home and family and toil in the fields that would give its harvest in due season. To his bleakness was added the knowledge that Johnny, looked up to since childhood, was in the hands of the enemy. 'They knew where they could hurt me most', he told a friend. He had no doubt that Woodfield was destroyed in retaliation against himself.

It was not in him to be vindictive. On 13 June he wrote : 'The thing I *shall* never forgive the English for is saying I had no sense of humour'. He invariably discounted any suggestion that he was inspired by hatred for them as a people. He would hunt the individual campaigners in England's national policy if need be to the death. To hate human beings on principle because of the accident of race would have shown a bigotry of which he was incapable.

Further moves towards peace were afoot. Lloyd George was reported to be 'in a much more yielding mood'.[13] Anderson met Sir James Craig in London, and Craig declared himself willing to meet any Sinn Fein leaders wherever they chose, indicating as Anderson reported later that he was prepared 'to help de Valera to attack the Government' to get anything short of a Republic which would not detract from Ulster's position under the Government of Ireland Act. Craig also saw an amnesty as imperative before agreement could be sought.

Lord Derby made a covert but ineffectual attempt to bring peace by visiting Dublin as the emissary of the Government. His somewhat theatrical disguise was immediately penetrated by the Irish, who treated him more with amusement than as a serious negotiator, though he did have a meeting with de Valera.[14]

The Sinn Fein leaders remained determined that only direct

[13] Sturgis Diaries, 27 March 1921

[14] Lord Derby, unaware that his coat, with his name in it, had been found by a maid in his hotel room, was convinced that his identity had been discovered when, staying with a friend in his country house, he asked a gardener the name of an apple tree. The man told him, in all innocence, that it was a Lord Derby. – Sturgis Diaries

negotiation between Dail and Government, without conditions, could be contemplated. Any other emissaries they regarded as splinter-groups, encouraged by Lloyd George in order to weaken Irish unity and get her to modify her demands.

III

The Government of Ireland Act came into force in April 1921. Sinn Fein had decided to use the machinery it provided to get a new mandate from the Irish people for Dail Eireann to remain the elected assembly of the Irish Republic. This would strengthen Sinn Fein's hand should negotiations with Britain for a settlement finally be undertaken.

Collins was one of those nominated to stand for a Northern Parliamentary constituency as well as being returned unopposed for a seat in the South. Electioneering still had no appeal for him. On 13 May, in a letter to Mrs Davies, he wrote of being 'engaged in scrawling out – slowly and painfully & with many a heavy heart beat a kind of election address for Armagh. . . . It's not good for I had not the time to give it and it is surprising how long it takes to do properly a thing of this sort.'

This electoral address was duly carried to his constituents in South Armagh. It was a plea for unity, for a fight 'against the privileges of the few, against the partition of our country, against religious and political intolerance. . . . Ireland has room for all her people.'[15]

The election results were declared on 1 June. In the South the only seats not held, uncontested, by Sinn Fein, were those of Trinity College. In North-East Ulster Sir James Craig's party won forty seats, and Sinn Fein and the Nationalists six each. Michael was returned for South Armagh with over 12,000 votes. With his usual schoolboy elation he wrote on 2 June: 'Think of it. I am member for *Portydown*.'

Much of his energy was being directed towards the rescue of Sean MacEoin. He perfected a daring plan, involving the seizure of an armoured car. I.R.A. men, posing as British officers, drove into Mountjoy itself, but the alarm was raised, and they were

[15] *Irish Independent* 21 May 1921

forced to flee for their lives. Collins, despite his bitter disappointment, did not accept defeat. That afternoon Miss Brigid Lyons was brought a note by Joe O'Reilly:

'14/5/21

A Chara Dhil

I have a heavy heart now. We just failed to get him. A slight alteration somewhere or other.

Try the visit anyway. No doubt they'll give you the devil's own searching now. . . .

We have had very hard luck with Sean, yet there must be something good somewhere. It's only to start again now.

Do chara go buan.

Micheal.'

Undeterred, Collins continued to plan. Seeing a photograph of his friend, taken in prison, he exclaimed: 'Look at the fiery energy rushing from him!' It was clear that there were no lengths to which he would not go to save him.

MacEoin was, however, brought to trial on 14 June 1921. His speech from the dock was a profession of the whole I.R.A. position. He was no murderer, he said, but an officer of the Irish Republican Army, who had taken up arms in defence of his native land. Defence of one's native land had ever been the privilege of the people of all nations. He craved neither mercy nor favour; as an officer of the Irish Army he merely claimed the same right at their hands as they would have received at his had the fortunes of war reversed the position.

The sentence of the Court was death, with no recommendation to mercy. Despite the unheard-of appearance of Auxiliaries as defence witnesses and a plea for clemency from the family of the man for whose shooting he had been tried, MacEoin was returned to Mountjoy to await his execution.

While he had been planning MacEoin's rescue, Collins was concerned with what was to be the most spectacular operation of the whole campaign. As a pre-election gesture, symbolic of the Irish determination to end British rule, and for the more practical purpose of dislocating British civil administration, the Custom House in Dublin was burnt on 25 May. The Dail Ministry authorized the action as a 'military necessity'. Indeed, the crippling paucity of arms made destruction by fire the most effective weapon now available to Sinn Fein.

Since his Mespil Road office had been raided in April, Collins had worked chiefly at 22 Mary Street. The day after the burning of the Custom House he was lunching with Gearoid O'Sullivan when he suddenly announced that he was not going back as was his habit. Something was wrong there, he felt. Later he found that his sixth sense had not misled him. The office had indeed been raided.

Brigadier-General Winter reported gleefully to the Castle that he had 'cleared out' Collins's 'new headquarter office' (it had been in use for almost eighteen months). Collins himself reported the result of the raid in somewhat different terms: 'They have run me close – brushed shoulders with me in fact. They raided a place where I was – at least according to their information. Well I ought to have been there at that precise moment. They depended too much on my punctuality. . . . They missed me and missed practically everything else also.'

There was no slackening of the hunt for him. Yet another of his offices, at 29 Mary Street, had now fallen to the enemy. He continued to use his old office at Bachelor's Walk for a short time, took up quarters once more with the Batt O'Connors, and rented a private house at 17 Harcourt Terrace, which he used constantly until after the Truce. This house was ideally situated, being surrounded by the houses of those whose loyalty to the Crown was unquestioned. Michael may well have reflected that the quietest spot is behind the enemy lines.

So many raids of such a well-informed nature had brought him an uneasy conviction that he was being betrayed by someone near to him. Almost certainly he knew who that person was. He took no retaliatory action, then or afterwards. On 9 June he wrote: 'The chase I think has not been less hot. In fact I have moved among them for several days. They have got several items of information. They got them by torture and extraction. Well they are welcome to them. They'll make the fight harder & still more unequal but there is the greater reward consequently.'

He remained emphatic on one point: he was not on the run. 'I have (or think I have)', he wrote, 'a fair knowledge of the mental attitude of the others, and he is on the run who feels he is on the run. I have avoided that feeling. Others have not – It is these who make themselves remarkable by their actions and movements.'[16] On another occasion he wrote : 'If people "on the run" didn't attract attention there would be fewer on the run and more work done.'

He was now planning a boycott of the British-controlled Post Office Savings Bank and allied places of deposit. He estimated that over £15,000,000 of Irish money was being made available by these to the enemy, and intended to ensure that the Irish people transferred their money to Republican banks and savings schemes.[17]

Living a precarious existence in which death might come to him at any moment, as it had to so many of his friends, Michael revealed a thoughtfulness of outlook in the letters which he wrote at this time. Writing late at night in houses that might be raided at any time, he would move restlessly from recent events to other matters that occupied his mind, ranging widely, often to be interrupted only by the sinking of the candle by which he wrote.

Destruction of things of beauty, buildings, or works of art filled him with anger. Only a belief that the burning of the Custom House would bring great advantage had led him to contemplate such an act. Referring to some pointless deed of vandalism he wrote : 'Just imagine destroying all that pleasure and glory in a world where these things are passing rapidly enough of their own accord.'

Religion was a matter to which he returned frequently. Sending a message to a nun he wrote : 'Tell her I am really & truly a pagan but that I have sort of surrendered and am accepting my captivity with philosophy'. His faith was more deeply rooted than his words admitted. A couple of weeks later he was recalling :

'Once I had a Prayer Book given to me when I was very young. It was however for a grownup. It used always happen that I had read all the "Prayers at Mass" by about the time the Altar boys were racing madly through the "Confiteor". Then I turned over the leaves of my little book looking for the stories and after a time I found they were not only stories but

[16] Letter to Mrs Llewelyn Davies dated 24 June 1921
[17] Memoranda dated 6 and 7 June 1921 – Collins Papers

that they sometimes had a lot in them and I have always remembered them in some strange sub-conscious way. They arise in queer ways too – sometimes to confront one sometimes even to comfort.'

His favourite saint was St Paul. 'I know him fairly well', he wrote, observing that he carried a relic of that apostle of many perils in his pocket. It was no mere sharing of tribulation that attracted him to the saint, however. 'You see he had the divine saving grace of not having been always good', he wrote.

Thoughts of another Michael aroused a strange interest in him at this time. This was Michael Davies, a nephew of Crompton Llewelyn Davies and one of the family for the amusement of whom, or perhaps through whom, James Barrie had created Peter Pan. Collins had always been a lover of Peter Pan; the eternal boy in himself was fascinated, perhaps even a little envious of him. The drowning of Michael Davies at Oxford at the beginning of a promising life struck Collins with an odd poignancy. 'If I had known the dead Peter Pan I'm sure he'd have been a friend of mine', he wrote to Mrs Davies. With more of superstition than reason he felt that the boy's name in some way had a significance. Since even Peter Pan could die, a strange presentiment that his own life might be as vulnerable seems to have been brought home to him.

Not all his reflections were as sombre. When he saw that a Cork firm was supporting Sinn Fein's 'Buy Irish' campaign by including some remarkably flavoured soft drinks among its farm products he observed: '—& Co are in my child's eye as people who sold "Sheep Dip" and their cordials must be just the same. Clove Cordial=Converted Sheep Dip.'

The Parliamentary elections were followed by an outbreak of rioting in Belfast, with several fatalities. By the irony of officialdom it was at this time of bitter passions in Belfast and of increased hunting of himself in Dublin that Collins, as a member of the Northern Parliament, received an invitation from the Chancellor and Senate of Queen's University, Belfast, requesting the honour of his presence at the forthcoming graduation ceremony.[18]

[18] Collins Papers

Mr Cope's indefatigable efforts to bring peace to Ireland had resulted, early in May, in a meeting between Sir James Craig and de Valera in Dublin. This was regarded as at least a promising start to further discussions. While Lloyd George welcomed the meeting between the two leaders, both he and his Cabinet believed strongly that any move towards a cease-fire must come from Sinn Fein, not the British Government.

Collins, it seems, was only too correct in assuming that only a move on the scale of burning the Custom House could keep Sinn Fein in a position to negotiate at all. Yet, apart from bluff on Sinn Fein's part, another factor weighed against the British Government's swinging to all-out war : the increasingly vociferous opposition in Britain itself to such a move. The strongest government could not ignore such widespread protests for ever; and Lloyd George's Coalition was far too diverse to be able to speak with a strong and single voice.

On 15 May Cope had returned from Craig in Belfast, bringing de Valera an 'agenda' of how far Ulster was prepared to go. The Republic was not mentioned, and Sinn Fein remained silent. De Valera's private stand was, however, less uncompromising, though he never departed from Ireland's claim to independent nationhood.

Tom Casement, Roger Casement's brother, was hopeful that Field-Marshal Smuts, Prime Minister of South Africa and his close friend, might use his influence on Ireland's behalf at the Imperial Conference then being held in London. An extract from Casement's diary for 14 June 1921 reads : 'Talk in evening with de Valera. During our talk I told him that Smuts could not stand for an Irish Republic, as he was Prime Minister of a Dominion, de Valera frankly told me that a Republic was out of the question. All he wanted was a Treaty between two nations. I saw that point and told him that I would put it before Smuts.'[19]

Field-Marshal Smuts was dining at Windsor, where the King was anxiously concerned lest his projected opening of the Belfast Parliament later that month should be construed as a deliberate affront by the Southern Irish. Smuts suggested that His Majesty's speech should be a call of peace to all Irishmen. The suggestion

[19] National Library of Ireland MS 10723

Michael Collins at
Christmas 1916, after his
release from Frongoch
where he had been
imprisoned following the
Easter Rising.

One of the company
mobilisation orders issued to
the Irish Volunteers prior to
the Easter Rising of 1916.
(*National Musuem of
Ireland*)

IRISH VOLUNTEERS.   COMPANY MOBILISATION ORDER.
DUBLIN BRIGADE.

The......B......Coy.,......4th......Batt., will mobilise ~~today~~ at the hour . on Sunday 23

of......Y...... m. Emerald Square

Point of Mobilisation......Emerald Square

Full Service Equipment to be worn, including overcoat, haversack, water-
bottle, canteen.

Rations for......8......hours to be carried.

ARMS AND FULL SUPPLY OF AMMUNITION TO BE CARRIED.

Cycle Scouts to be mounted, and ALL men having cycles or motor cycles to'
bring them.

......P. Egan......

Captain or Officer Commanding.

Dated this......23......day of......4 month......, 191.6.

Collins as Minister for Finance in the Dail government. (*Public Record Office*)

Members of the first Dail outside the Mansion House, 21 January 1919. The three central figures in the front row are (*left to right*) Count Plunkett (with beard), Cathal Brugha and Sean T. O'Kelly. Kevin O'Higgins is second from the left in the middle row, Robert Barton — one of the signatories of the Treaty — is to his right and slightly above him while Richard Mulcahy is above and to the right of Barton.

The first meeting of Dail Eireann in the Round Room of the Mansion House, 21 Janaury 1919. (*National Library of Ireland*)

Arthur Griffith.

Michael Collins (*left*)
and Harry Boland (*right*) at
Croke Park, 1921.
(*Cashman Collection, RTE*)

Members of the Black and Tans.

Wedding party, 22 November 1920, the morning after 'Bloody Sunday'. Collins stands, second from the left at the back, between Mrs O'Donovan and Gearoid O'Sullivan, his head half turned away from the camera. Sean Hyde (*centre back*) was one of Collins's staff officers in command of the previous day's operation. Beside him is Dennis Lynch from whose safe house in the grounds of the Dublin Whiskey Distillery beside Croke Park Collins and the bridegroom, Michael O'Brien, had made their perilous journey. (*The O'Brien family*)

Collins photographed in full army uniform at Arthur Griffith's graveside.

Collins and General Richard Mulcahy marching in Arthur Griffith's funeral procession. (*Murtagh Collection, RTE*)

O'Connell Street during the Civil War. Much of the physical fabric of Dublin's main thoroughfare was destroyed in the fighting. (*National Library of Ireland*)

Following the Treaty, troops of the provisional government of the Irish Free State replaced the British Army. This photograph captures one of the change-overs as the British (*left*) march out and a contingent of the National Army marches in. (*Cashman Collection, RTE*)

Sean Collins, stunned and in mourning, beside his brother's coffin.

bore fruit, and both the King and Lloyd George agreed to the text for a speech on these conciliatory lines.

Such a personal appeal from the King would be hard for British or, indeed, Commonwealth opinion to ignore. Impasse had in any case been reached. As a letter quoted in the Lords declared: 'We live in Ireland under two Governments, and neither is powerful enough to protect us from the other.'

On 22 June the King delivered his speech in Belfast. In it he appealed to all Irishmen to pause, to stretch out the hand of forbearance and conciliation, to forgive and forget, and to join in making for the land they loved a new era of peace, contentment, and goodwill.

The next step was patently with Lloyd George. The King urged him quickly to avail himself of the atmosphere of tolerance which had resulted from his speech. Collins himself was no less hopeful. Characteristically, if fancifully, he saw the means of reaching an understanding by what a later age would call Cultural Relations. Sir James Barrie had developed a strong interest in an Irish settlement. Michael wrote to Mrs Davies on 24 June: 'I'm glad you saw J. M. Barrie. I wonder who on the enemy side appreciates & loves Peter Pan. Shall we find a bridge that way?'

Mr Cope saw a more immediate solution. He presented himself at a Cabinet meeting in Downing Street. Unless the Government made a definite offer of peace the more hopeful atmosphere would be lost for ever. His desperate and impassioned sincerity convinced even the most reluctant, and his determination finally carried the day.[20] Although the Cabinet refused to make any offer of terms, Cope returned triumphantly to Ireland next day, bearing a personal letter from the Prime Minister to de Valera. This invited a meeting in London between them and the Ulster leaders to see whether a way to peace could be found.

Sinn Fein was still not prepared to trust Lloyd George who, it felt, intended to appear, not as a warring party, but as an arbitrator between North and South, as two dissidents under Crown surveillance.

Collins, dubious about Lloyd George's sincerity, and seeing in this invitation a move 'to put us in the wrong' nevertheless

[20] Sturgis Diaries, 25 June 1921

admitted : 'The position has gone completely beyond resting on any one individual or even a group.'

Lloyd George had, after all, decided that the time had come to change horses. His Government of Ireland Act was patently not going to work. Since war *à outrance* would not be tolerated by either King or country, the only alternative was peace, if possible with Ulster supporting Britain in the rôle of referee.

De Valera was equally determined. His reply to Lloyd George stressed that London and not Belfast was the seat of Sinn Fein's adversaries. He called a meeting of representative Unionists in Dublin, including Sir James Craig. But Craig had a parliament behind him now, and no longer sought the expedience of common cause with the South which had inspired him in pre-election days. De Valera's efforts to face Lloyd George with an All-Irish front had a bleak enough prospect.

Yet, with peace moves now official and open, it was clear that a truce to hostilities could be only a matter of time.

PART THREE

The Day Came So Strenuous

CHAPTER THIRTEEN

Truce

I

Truce was signed on 9 July 1921. Ominously, there were differences in its terms as published by either side. Writing to Mrs Davies on 10 July Michael pointed this out :

> ' . . . on our side (1) the use of arms is not prohibited and (2) military training is to take place just as it is in their Army. . . . It is only the first move. Now we are going to be really tested. The days ahead are going to be the truly trying ones and we can only face them with set faces and hearts full of hope and confidence. It would be very dreadful if we did anything wrong. It would be very excellent to have the advice of all friends *now*.'

Truce was to take effect from noon on Monday 11 July. On 8 July the *Freeman's Journal* reported that a British Government spokesman had denied that any reward had ever been offered for the death or capture of the Hon. Member for South Cork.

The Hon. Member in question pasted the cutting on a piece of paper and wrote beneath it :

> 'Tudor offered £4,000 to any of his men who'd bring me in dead. Even up to 12.30 tomorrow I'm sure the offer will be honoured.'

Peace had a dreamlike quality, remote from the political position. 'After the Truce, the Republic' was the confident prediction. In the reaction from the nightmare years of bloodshed it was hard to remember that the British had not been beaten, particularly for the young Volunteers, fêted in their native villages.

The longer heads among them welcomed the Truce, not as a cessation of war, but as a much-needed respite in which to prepare for its resumption. Many assumed that the Truce would soon be over. Seventy-two hours' notice of termination of the cease-fire by either side had been arranged.

Violence was not over. The Truce had been ushered in by rioting in Belfast. Fifteen people were killed and hundreds of Catholics driven from their homes and jobs. As Collins is said to have remarked grimly, Truce had broken out.

For those who took a long look at the situation, Ireland's position was as delicate as ever. No country would move against Britain in supporting the Irish Republican claim. Yet recognition of a sort could now be said to have come from Britain herself. In instructing her Military Command in Ireland to negotiate a cease-fire with representatives of the Army of Dail Eireann, Britain had tacitly admitted that the Dail itself had an existence. Lloyd George was at pains in all his ensuing correspondence to insist that no Republic could be recognized. Unfortunately for Ireland, external recognition of nations does not come by tacit and, moreover, loudly disavowed admission.

Talks between Lloyd George, de Valera, and Craig were arranged to begin in London on 14 July. Craig was the most strongly placed. Both Britain and Southern Ireland needed his concurrence if each was to hold its desired position. Craig, however, preferred not to be wooed. In London on 11 July he announced to Sturgis: 'Tell Cope I'm going to sit on Ulster like a rock, we are content with what we have got – let the P.M. and Sinn Fein settle this and if possible leave us out.'

De Valera and his party left for London on 12 July. An unexpected well-wisher who now comes briefly upon the stage with something of the whimsicality of one of his own characters is Sir James Barrie. If the bridge to unite the British and Irish peoples was not to be Peter Pan, why should it not be his creator? Barrie dreamed of an agreement to be signed by Lloyd George, with whom he was on friendly terms, Craig, and de Valera in his own room, with its glimpse away down-river of the Houses of Parliament. Michael passed his invitation to de Valera but, even had the idea been practicable, the party had already arranged to stay elsewhere. 'Barrie is very charmingly simple', wrote Michael, wistfully enough. He was a simple-hearted man himself, and would have liked to see the matter of Ireland so happily settled.

The conference between Lloyd George and de Valera was scarcely portentous of agreement. De Valera harked back to Cromwell [Churchill], leaving Lloyd George 'white and exhausted'. As Craig had observed to Sturgis: 'Lloyd George would always rather make a bad bargain in five minutes than a good one in five hours. I warned him to give them lots of rope.'

Having said which, Craig bowed himself and Ulster out. De Valera might protest, Lloyd George washed his hands of the whole matter of All-Ireland. It was plain, or it should have been, that Craig had won. Southern Ireland's refusal to accept that the North wanted, not Irish unity on certain terms, but Partition at any price, was to give her every move in negotiation an air of unreality. Each step taken by the South was made to purchase an essential unity that had already been sold.

The Truce had not lessened Michael's instinct for anonymity. Hostilities might recommence at any time. On 23 July he wrote of:

' . . . quite a good thing that happened last night. We were at the Mansion Ho[use] and as everyone, I mean those who were celebrities left he [de Valera] was cheered again & again. I made a bet that I'd go out unrecognized. *Out I goes* and not a look or token of recognition. I was awfully pleased – just to know I was right & there were dozens there who knew me & would have gone mad over it but I was down the steps & through the crowd with Messenger Boy rapidity (I exclude Telegraph Messenger boys).'

He now determined to go to Cork, revisit what remained of Woodfield, and, if possible, see Johnny, still on Spike Island. His going was deliberately open.

In a letter to Mrs Davies dated 23 July he wrote:

'Yes indeed I did go to Cork and I was very glad I did go & I took very good care *they* knew I was there. But I don't believe a single one of their agents laid eyes knowingly on me. That was my intention and I think I carried it out successfully. The little people are not doing too badly if one makes certain allowances. There are many pathetic incidents, and it was simply heart-breaking in the morning early to see two little lads of 12 and 9 respectively looking after the morning work connected with farms. The little boy of 12 is really prematurely old. Outwardly he laughs a great deal and merrily but he knows what he has lost and he feels the burden of everything. . . . They did not give me a permit to see my brother – that would have shown the human thing too clearly, and they couldn't do that – *could* they?'

Despite his reluctance, the pre-truce circumspection began to be dispelled. Unwillingly, he began to let himself be photographed at the weddings which were a feature of the Truce, though he lurked in the background, head down. It was all too likely that the methods of escape, the aliases, would be needed again.

It was probably in these early days of the Truce that he met Sir William Darling, then one of the most effective of the Dublin Castle propagandists.[1] A collision occurred at Newry between a police car and that in which Collins and others were travelling. With them, but unaware of Collins's identity, was 'a high official' (Mr Cope?). Darling picked up the group in another car and proceeded to Dublin. He and one of the Irishmen sat in front. The stranger, having correctly guessed Darling's identity, said 'quite simply and very agreeably', 'I am Michael Collins'. They reached a hotel. The 'high official' hurried upstairs with the other two men. Darling and Collins chatted below. That it was indeed Collins is supported by the subjects discussed: von Lettow-Vorbeck on guerilla warfare in Africa; Whitman's *Leaves of Grass* which both quoted amicably; and, a matter for amusing consequences, Chesterton's *The Napoleon of Notting Hill*, a book which Darling concluded that Collins was almost fanatically attached to.

The Napoleon of Notting Hill anecdote was all that emerged from the night's adventure, but it travelled far. Lord Riddell heard it when he met Sir John Anderson on the road to Inverness in September: 'He told me that the only book Michael Collins reads

[1] Darling, recounting the episode in his autobiography *So It Looks to Me* (London 1952, pp. 211–13), sets it in the pre-truce period. Obvious doubts arise from this suggestion. A reference to a relevant memorandum of Sir Wm. Darling (2–3 Aug. n.d.) among the Tudor Papers by H. Senior (Irish Historical Studies, XII, p. 280) would appear to argue that the later chronology here given it is the correct one.

is *The Napoleon of Notting Hill*, by Chesterton. Very much to
the point, I thought.'[2] Nor did it stop there. *John O' London's*
on 1 October 1921 commented sardonically on the report. Collins
read it and wrote in amusement : 'I wonder who has given me
away? Not that it is my favourite novel but I did enjoy it tre-
mendously. 'Twas so absurd. The elders of Notting Hill fighting !'

The Truce was quickly used by the I.R.A. for intensive training. These courses provided more than their obvious objective of
preparation for further battle. They maintained the discipline
which would otherwise have slackened as the weeks of relaxation
lengthened.

One of the I.R.A.'s most serious problems was the liaison
agreed with the British for preventing breaches of the Truce. As
the terms of this were interpreted differently on both sides it was
impossible to avoid a good deal of mutual recrimination, and the
trigger-happy attitude of a few irresponsible men aggravated the
continual exchange of grievances.

As with the Volunteers in the anti-conscription period, many
fair-weather soldiers now flocked to join local units; 'Truciliers',
as they became known, whose chief aim was to cash in on the
laudation accorded those who had served in time of war. More
commendably there came, too, boys just old enough to be
accepted, anxious not to lose all chance of emulating their older
brothers.

At the time of the Truce more than thirty Dail deputies were
in prison or interned. The British agreed to release these to allow
a full meeting of the Dail. The only exception was to be Sean
MacEoin, convicted of murder. Collins drafted a furious protest.
De Valera wrote threatening an end to negotiation. 'Commandant MacEoin typifies in his person everything that we have
been fighting for.' He was released on 8 August.

The bulk of the prisoners and over 4,000 men in internment
camps remained there. The kidnapped Lord Bandon, the only
prisoner in I.R.A. hands at the beginning of the Truce, had been
promptly released.

Collins's thoughts turned to Ned Broy, in solitary confinement
in Arbour Hill, for whom the outlook must well have appeared
bleak. He was, after all, liable to prosecution on charges of

[2] Riddell *Intimate Diary* p. 320

treasonable activities while a member of the D.M.P. Collins pressed Cope through an intermediary. It was a risky business, since his interest hardly supported Broy's claim of innocence. Cope, however, for whom the Truce was largely the result of his own efforts, was more than willing to be obliging, and Broy was duly released – and dismissed from the Police Force.[3] Since it was not a point he cared to argue, he went. Allegiance requires no formal contract : he asked Collins's leave before going away, until such time as he should be needed again.

De Valera sent his Cabinet's formal rejection of the British proposals for a settlement to Lloyd George on 10 August. 'We cannot admit', he wrote, 'the right of the British Government to mutilate our country, either in its own interest or at the call of any section of our population.' Solely as a means to secure national unity, however, they would be prepared to negotiate 'a certain treaty of free association with the British Commonwealth group, as with a partial league of nations'.

The doctrine of External Association had been formally advanced for the first time. To de Valera it saved the essential Republic. Far from refusing to advance beyond Cromwell, he had leaped several years ahead of the evolutionary processes of the Commonwealth which were even then becoming apparent to those who cared to ponder them. He was dealing, however, not with political scientists, but with politicians, and neither Craig nor Lloyd George would look whither he pointed.

The Second Dail met in public session on 16 and 17 August. Out of its deliberations the Irish people, weary of war, and even less doctrinaire Republicans than their leaders, were offered the alternatives of a Republic or total war, alternatives which they accepted with an extraordinarily courageous readiness, and no apparent wish to query whether there could, after all, be any other way out.

Collins himself clearly believed that, sooner or later, negotiations for a settlement would begin, rather than the resumption of war. He also foresaw that Ulster, far from being the rock upon which all hope of such negotiations must founder, might prove

---

[3] Later, as Colonel Broy, he was to become Commissioner of the Garda Siochana.

the means of settlement. On 22 August he recalled : 'Lloyd Geo. mentioned the unity of Ireland and later made reference to the position of Ulster being inviolable'. What was now needed was a formula that would embody the points 'That the N.E. corner stands equally in the way of Irish Unity (& hence settlement from the Irish side) and of settlement from the point of view of Lloyd Geo. himself.'

He had used the British Intelligence machine to catch its own masters : he could not foresee that Lloyd George, 'the Welsh Wizard', might magick the illusion of Irish Unity out of Craig's intransigence itself.

For the present it was essential that Ireland establish freedom of position before agreeing to meet Britain in conference. This was to be the keynote of the long and exhaustive exchanges, by letter and telegram, which now took place between de Valera and Lloyd George.

Michael was, if anything, busier than he had been before the Truce. He was quite plainly tired out; but Intelligence work had to continue. Cabinet and Dail sessions also took up much time; financial and army work and all the trappings of truce filled his days. When he could snatch a moment he sought, as always, country places. During these long summer days he might be encountered wandering along the small tracks about the summit of Howth, flanked by bracken, high above the blue tranquillity of Dublin Bay with no sound about him but the cries of soaring seagulls. Once he was found lying on his stomach, gazing in absorption at a flower as if he had never expected to see one again.

He had never lost his deliberate, rather rolling walk, that of a man bred to tramp country ways. 'I suppose it is an indication of where my proper place really is', he commented in one letter. 'Yet I sometimes think I am adaptable.'

He still made time for his friends. He romped anew with Harry Boland, now back from the States, and insisted that the Leigh Doyles take him picnicking in the Devil's Glen at Rathdrum. He and four-year-old Brendan both fell in the river. Brendan's clothes were hung out to dry; Michael, more trammelled by convention, spent the day in trousers stuffed with the Sunday papers, practising revolver marksmanship with his comrades.

Even at picnics the possibility of renewed warfare was not far from their minds.

Other people's homes, other people's children – these were the substance of which he had hitherto built his life. For a man to whom home and children held all that was best in life, it was not enough. He was approaching his thirty-first birthday. Now that so many of his friends were marrying before the uneasy truce could end and the dark days return, Michael, too, had no wish to let the chance of happiness slip by.

During July he had been several times to Granard. In Horse Show week Kitty Kiernan had come up to Dublin and he had escorted her about during that traditionally gay time which no anxiety for the future could mar for those who jostled in the Show Grounds by day and danced to the memory of the curfew late into the night. When she returned to Granard there was little doubt that it was she he intended to marry.

Here was a girl of his own people, brought up in the Irish way of life. Other women stimulated his intellect, his ambition to better himself; with Kitty there was no need to adapt his countryman's walk. If there were books to be read, it was he who introduced them to her. To her he was to confide his darkest moments as well as those of happiness.

The Dail met again in public session on the 26th. A new Ministry was elected under the renewed presidency of de Valera, those within the Cabinet being Arthur Griffith, Austin Stack, Cathal Brugha, W. T. Cosgrave, Robert Barton, and Collins himself, still as Minister of Finance.

After the Dail meetings Collins embarked on a strenuous tour of army inspections, on which political work crowded inescapably. He wrote on 31 August to Mrs Davies from Wicklow:

'I was up at 5 a.m. Sunday morning and the next time I took off my clothes was at 4.30 a.m. on Tuesday morning. . . . I was on the road again at 7.30 that morning. This will show you what the peaceful restfulness of the Truce is.'

The Most Rev. Dr Fogarty, Bishop of Killaloe, one of the trustees of the Dail National Funds, to whose cheerful advice and unfailing comfort Collins had paid tribute in the Dail wrote to him on 30 August:

'Dear Mr Collins,

. . . I am very uneasy about the shape things are taking these days in the Papers. Of course I know nothing except through the papers, and there may be some policy not visible in them. But a war of devastation without the good will of the people behind it would be a ruinous disaster and it looks at least in the papers as if things were drifting that way. Apart from Partition, which may be remedied in whole or *in part*, the people feel that there is in the British proposals something very substantial to negotiate & work upon.

With my fervent prayers for guidance to all who have to decide on the momentous issues now awaiting us,

I am,
Yours sincerely,
X. M. Fogarty,
Bishop of Killaloe'[4]

To this letter Collins replied on 1 September 1921 : '. . . May I assure you that we too are keenly alive to our responsibilities at the present moment. I can only repeat Your Lordship's wish and hope that we shall not act in a manner that will give the enemy gain or advantage.'[4]

I I

In his letter to Mrs Davies of 31 August Collins had written : 'They have asked me to go north to Armagh for a meeting on Sunday. A rally for Ireland! I must do it although I hate a Public Meeting like I hate a plague. . . . I'm going to endeavour making such an appeal to them as will make them rock to their foundations – at least I'm going to try.'

He wrote to Kitty : 'Are you betting that the Ulster Specials will have a pot at me?'

The beginning of September 1921 certainly seemed an unpromising time for a man of Collins's reputation to go wooing the populace of Armagh. Renewed violence had broken out in Belfast in the last days of August and newspaper correspondents noted Collins's intention to speak at Armagh on Sunday 4 September with general foreboding.

[4] Collins Papers

The uneasiness was not confined to the newsmen. Collins himself on 2 September, in the midst of discussions with 'men from the North' – he had rushed back to his office from Carlow at six o'clock that morning – dashed off an unhappy note: 'This damned meeting is making me feel nervous already. I should more gladly look forward to an ambush but perhaps I'd have that also. The Unity of Ireland is going to be my main idea I think.'

He left for the North on the Sunday morning, to rumours that ambushes were indeed being laid for him by Orangemen. Nevertheless, he reached Armagh unmolested, accompanied by Harry Boland. The city went wild. The *Irish Independent* declared that 'the attendance from Armagh alone in the College grounds went into several thousands, but the contingents from country districts exceeded anything ever seen in the city'. The *Morning Post* noted less enthusiastically that men bared their heads when Collins rose to speak.

Whatever the crowds had expected from the forceful young man who had sprung on to the platform 'to rock them to their foundations', they got a speech that brought them out in wave after wave of cheering. Much of it was a down-to-earth argument of figures to show that the North-East had not progressed under British rule, but decayed more slowly under it than the rest of Ireland. Freedom, he declared, was coming, bringing with it an era of prosperity and development. Were these Ulster counties really going to deprive themselves of the benefit of economic association with the new Ireland?

His words were not directed solely at the Nationalists. He appealed to the Orangemen 'to join with us, as Irishmen to come into the Irish nation . . . to come in and take their share in the government of their own country'.[5]

The Orangemen did, indeed, ambush him after this, but it was with stones which proved ineffective.

Agreement upon the terms for negotiation between Britain and Ireland seemed, if anything, more remote. Once again it was the King who stepped in to plead for moderation from the militants now grouped about Lloyd George, on holiday at Gairloch, and a conference on more liberal terms was offered.

[5] *Morning Post* 5 September 1921

His Majesty, indeed, throughout the days of trouble, displayed a keenly sympathetic concern for the Irish for which he has not, perhaps, been held in sufficient remembrance. His interest in their political aspirations went beyond mere exigencies of office, and he held an affection for the Irish people which had nothing to do with politics. As little to do with politics, and proof that the affection was not misplaced, was the kindly piety of villagers on the south coast of Ireland when, it is recorded, they set candles in their windows on the night of the King's death to light him home.[6]

De Valera now felt that delegates to a conference might be appointed. The Dail Cabinet accordingly met to discuss nominations. There had hitherto been no doubt in his colleagues' minds that de Valera himself would lead any delegation to meet the British. Now, however, he announced his intention of remaining in Dublin.

The most important reason for this decision, since put forward by de Valera himself, was that should External Association be agreed upon, he would be in a better position to win acceptance from Dail and Army for such a new departure than if he were one of those who had negotiated such an agreement. Failing agreement, however, a breakdown would come better through Arthur Griffith, whom he proposed should lead the delegates in his stead, since Griffith was a known moderate, and de Valera himself was already being represented as an intransigent.[7]

If this argument was, in fact, put forward by de Valera at that time, Griffith, Collins, and Cosgrave voted against his decision, and it was approved only by de Valera's use of his casting vote.[8]

Griffith accepted his nomination as chairman of the delegation. De Valera then proposed that Collins should also go. Collins protested strongly. This, he felt, was a job for politicians, and he was none. He pleaded that his whole reputation as an extremist would make him far more effective kept menacingly in the background as a counter to unacceptable British proposals. De Valera, however, argued that Collins would elicit better terms by his

[6] Geraldine Cummins *Dr E. OE. Somerville* (London 1952) p. 100
[7] Frank Gallagher *The Anglo-Irish Treaty* (London 1965) p. 74n
[8] Frank Pakenham *Peace by Ordeal* (London 1962) p. 96

supposedly intransigent presence at the conference table – a reasoning that makes his own proposal that, as a reputed extremist, he himself should stay at home, look a trifle odd.

How widely Collins's reputation as a diehard held with the British leaders may have been overestimated by both de Valera and Collins himself. Dublin Castle, at least, believed by now that he stood with the 'moderates'. In any event, preconceptions must go by the board in the intimacy of serious discussion; de Valera can scarcely have believed that Collins would prove as inflexible as he was reputed.

The selection of Collins certainly suggests that de Valera, mindful of his influence with the Volunteers, foresaw that that influence would be needed in winning the Army's acceptance of any settlement. There can be as little doubt that he expected any settlement to be based on External Association, in effect the Republic joined with, not isolated from the Commonwealth.

Collins, in great distress of mind, finally agreed to accept nomination, but only 'as a soldier obeying his captain's order'. T. M. Healy records that 'I had warned Collins not to go unless de Valera also went, but he was too unselfish and unsuspecting to refuse'.[9] Yet Collins's misery may well have arisen mainly because his inclusion in the delegation would leave de Valera with Brugha and Stack as his chief advisers in Dublin. His first words to Barton on the latter's return in July had shown desperate worry over what he implied was jealousy on Brugha's part; there was by now for all to perceive 'an atmosphere of cold embattled reserve on both sides'.[10]

Brugha had adamantly refused to negotiate; it is notable that, in Barton's recollection, Collins suggested Stack as a member of the team. Apart from his legal training, a matter of some importance in the selection of both delegations, Collins may well have reflected that Stack's inclusion might modify Brugha's attitude. Stack, however, emphatically refused to go. A modest man, he had no pretensions to be a negotiator.

Apart from any fears of a Cabinet split Collins was under no illusion as to the chances of wresting a Republic from the British; the task of wresting anything, he felt, was for subtler minds.

[9] T. M. Healy *Letters and Leaders of my Day* (London 1928) II, p. 644
[10] Robert Barton to the author

The remaining delegates were selected. Robert Barton was chosen for his knowledge of economics, and because his cognizance of the circles in which the British statesmen moved was considered likely to be useful. Eamonn Duggan, picked by Collins, was a solicitor closely associated with Sinn Fein affairs. Sturgis describes him, not unfairly, as 'a pleasant little man with no obvious appearance of distinction'. George Gavan Duffy, a kindly, highly sensitive man, had been Irish representative in Paris and, later, Rome. His prolonged absence on the Continent had removed him from the sphere of developments at home, as had lengthy imprisonment in England for Robert Barton. Both, therefore, might be expected to approach negotiations in a different spirit from the other three, who had been closely involved in all the *pourparlers* of the months leading up to the Truce.

Erskine Childers was selected as principal secretary. He seemed pre-eminently qualified to be so. Arthur Griffith, however, was openly hostile to the appointment, and one must ponder how far subsequent events arose from this dislike, how far his mistrust was justified by them. John Chartres, Fionan Lynch, and Diarmuid O'Hegarty were to act as assistant secretaries.

These nominations were given the Dail's approval at a private meeting on 14 September. Mrs Clarke recalls of Collins's final acceptance of his appointment: 'He laughed. He took everything with a laugh. But he certainly didn't want to go.'

De Valera's reply to Lloyd George's Gairloch proposals had thrown any conference once more into jeopardy. Collins for one was against the wording of the letter, which was to be taken to Lloyd George by Harry Boland and Joe McGrath. Before they left Collins growled to McGrath: 'You might as well stay where you are. Make sure you make your way back.'

Yet again the King was to counsel conciliation to his Prime Minister. The deadlock reached at Gairloch was finally resolved when, on 29 September, Lloyd George issued a fresh invitation to de Valera for a conference in London on 11 October, 'where we can meet your delegates as spokesmen of the people whom you represent with a view to ascertaining how the association of Ireland with the community of nations known as the British Empire may best be reconciled with Irish national aspirations'.

De Valera accepted.

Collins chose his own staff for London. The rest of the delegates were to stay at 22 Hans Place; Collins alone elected to make his headquarters at the other house put at their disposal, 15 Cadogan Gardens. In Robert Barton's opinion the reasons for Collins's decision were : 'He wanted the personal privacy and freedom of his own establishment; he wished to meet his intelligence officers and others privately; he wished to avoid social ties; the whole set-up at Hans Place was distasteful to him; I think that he always believed that the negotiations would break down and that his security might depend upon a rapid and unobtrusive get-away.'[11]

In London Collins would need someone to handle secret papers and act as his general factotum. Ned Broy received a summons to Dublin. 'You're coming with me', Collins told him.

Each delegate received his credentials from de Valera. These appointed them 'as Envoys Plenipotentiary from the elected Government of the Republic of Ireland to negotiate and conclude on behalf of Ireland, with the representatives of His Majesty George V, a treaty or treaties of settlement, association and accommodation between Ireland and the community of nations known as the British Commonwealth'.

Any agreement reached by them would be submitted to the Dail for ratification. They were also given written instructions which, while their plenary powers were recognized, stated that any final decision must be submitted to the Cabinet in Dublin before any treaty might be signed.

As much argument was later to hinge on these credentials and instructions as on the Treaty itself. Did the instructions subtract from the plenipotentiary status and if so, were the instructions valid? If they were not acceptable to the plenipotentiaries, why had they not objected to them when they were first handed them?[12] Did the fact that the credentials were never officially accepted by Lloyd George alter the whole standing of the pleni-

[11] Robert Barton to the author

[12] Griffith's biographer states that since they had received their plenipotentiary status from the Dail, the Ministry could not instruct them but only make recommendations to them; that 'it was as recommendations that Arthur Griffith received the paper that Eamon de Valera handed him'. Colum *Arthur Griffith* p. 279

potentiaries, since Lloyd George, had he accepted them, could have been held by inference to have accepted them as those of representatives of the Republic? In fact, he merely waved them aside, as it should have been obvious he would do. To have pressed them upon him would inevitably have caused the breakdown of negotiations before they had begun.

In fact, the whole of the negotiations was founded upon implicit agreement to disregard all points of status – and the Irish credentials were one – upon which the talks might founder.

The delegates also took with them 'Draft Treaty A', containing the proposals, some in the barest form, which the Dail Cabinet was willing to negotiate upon.

One point was clear to Collins. The status they were being sent to London to negotiate for was not the status for which they had been fighting. He knew as well as de Valera that for many of those who had fought, the Republic alone could meet their national aspirations. His own ideals were theirs. He had sworn allegiance to the Republic. The falseness of his position was plain enough in that he was going, in the eyes of these men, to negotiate on behalf of the Republic; whereas in fact he was being sent to make proposals, as embodied in Draft Treaty A, in which the Republic was not so much as mentioned, so far was its recognition patently out of the question.

He made what provision he could. Immediately before his departure for London he conferred with Liam Lynch and other I.R.B. officers in the South. He gave a warning for the first time that a successful outcome of the negotiations might depend upon some modification of the full Republican demand.[13]

The other delegates, with their staffs, left for London on Saturday 8 October 1921. Collins would join them on the Monday morning. On that Saturday he became engaged to Kitty Kiernan.

For the first time in long days the weariness that he now admitted fell away from him. 'I had at last a good refreshing night's rest', he wrote to her next day, 'and I did more today in 2 or 3 hours than I have been able to do in three *times the time* for many weeks.'

It was the evening of Sunday 9 October, and he was about

[13]Florence O'Donoghue *No Other Law* (Dublin 1954) p. 192

to cross to England. He wrote: 'This will be about the last act of mine before going away on the big venture. I am leaving in about half an hour's time and this must therefore be my last farewell to you for a few days. Goodness knows I have a heavy heart this minute but there is work to be done and I must not complain.'

CHAPTER FOURTEEN

London

(October 1921)

I

Euston seethed with a vast crowd of Irish who had turned out to give the delegation a vociferous welcome; but if Irish London rejoiced at the arrival of the men who had come, many believed, to take formal seizin of the Republic, others did not. That night, on the pavement outside the house in Hans Place, were whitewashed the words: *Collins the murderer.*

Collins himself, with Ned Broy and Emmet Dalton, slipped across unobserved, arriving on the morning of Monday 10 October. Writing to Kitty he noted: 'This presence of the home staff makes the place feel less strange which is an immense advantage.'

These letters to Kitty, which he sent every day, were to be written at odd moments carved out of long hours of work. Though they contain no details of the negotiations, they graphically reflect his moods as the battle fought out in Downing Street ran its course.

Collins can scarcely have hoped to preserve his anonymity for long. The evening papers carried the triumphant results of an interview explaining 'in Collins's own words' how he had successfully evaded discovery on his arrival. He commented to Kitty: 'What do you think of the enclosed? Writing all bosh. I never said any of those things. Just a few remarks. Newspaper men are Inventions of the Devil.'

It was the morning of 11 October, the day on which negotiations were to begin. 'Of all the times in God's World', his letter ran, 'do you know when I'm writing this? Almost 4 o'clock in the morning. . . . Later also during this same day I have to go to Downing Street. . . .'

The sense of compulsion remained. In that dark dawn of an autumn morning while the rest of the house slept he may well have asked himself which of the paths he had trodden had brought him to this. Woodfield; the years of clerkship here in London; the subsequent years, shorter in number but infinitely longer in experience and responsibility spent in the pitting of wits against armed force and in the aggrandisement of a national exchequer from nothing but his own will working upon that of his people – what of all this had prepared him to go now to Downing Street, the hub of the Empire, to bargain for Ireland with the most brilliant team of statesmen Britain could have mustered in decades?

To the very end he would protest, rightly, that he had no qualifications for such a task. Yet one qualification he did have which outweighed any skill in diplomacy. Through him there ran, deep and well-defined, a love of Ireland, its people, and their way of life. Because his belief in these things was the fibre of his own life, he would bring to the conference table an instinct for their preservation as deep as the instinct for his own survival. No wiles of statecraft would avail against his blunt expression of that instinct, which he summarized early in the negotiations : 'The extent to which the British clear out of Ireland is the extent to which we shall be free.'

It was the practical man's way of going about a task. Its advantages in wresting the utmost in concession were unarguable; its danger lay in its disregard for the idealists, since all that his hard bargaining could achieve must, in the end, depend upon their acceptance that this was the utmost then to be got; that to accept a part was not to obliterate all chance of ultimately gaining the whole.

On this first morning, as on every subsequent one throughout the negotiations, he slipped out to eight o'clock Mass at Brompton Oratory. On the eve of his departure a priest he knew had written to him : 'I know *you* have "much religion left after the demoralizing things of warfare". . . . You know you have not alone Ireland's temporal destiny, but her spiritual one as well in your hands. That is a dreadful responsibility remember.'[1]

The British delegation was, indeed, a formidable marshalling. Lloyd George led, as his principals, Austen Chamberlain, to whom the Unionists would clearly look for support; Lord Birkenhead, the prosecutor of Roger Casement, whose name was

[1] Collins Papers

closely linked with that of Carson and whose birthday on 12 July could only appear as an Act of God; and Winston Churchill, most noted in Irish eyes for his imperialist's bellicosity. Of the remainder of the team, Sir Gordon Hewart and Sir Laming Worthington-Evans were little known; Sir Hamar Greenwood only too well so.

Collins's views of the Englishmen must, at this initial stage, have been influenced by the brief studies of them he had requested from Crompton Llewelyn Davies. Those of the four principals were as follows:

'*Lloyd George* : Fickle, holding lightly to persons and prin-ciples, but has a charm which wins people. . . . He sees in a flash the essentials of a situation for immediate political pur-poses. . . . He is fertile in expedients, adroit, tireless, energetic, and daring in ways which would be reckless apart from his uncanny intuition. . . . Skilled in political strategy, he acts swiftly in emergency, but is ready to do so because he has reviewed all possible moves in the back of his mind, and has previously manœuvred for position. He is careful to keep alternative avenues open. . . . He would like to go down to history under big names : The Man Who Won the War; The Man who re-conquered Ireland; or The Man who made peace between England and Ireland. If he can be captured by the glamour of the last of these titles, much can be wrung from him. He alone has the energy and persuasive force to carry through such a task. And as head of a Coalition government he is free from the difficulties which have prevented any party hitherto from making peace. . . . In Conference he is master of all the arts. . . . Above all, he likes success. If he decides upon his new rôle, he will pay a big price, and will carry others with him in paying the price, to secure it.

Lord Birkenhead : Loyal to the facts. . . . Ready to face an actual situation and face it bluntly. . . . If convinced that peace is required for England will see that it must be real peace. An incredibly quick worker, and a heavier weight than he lets it commonly be supposed. Does not object to be reputed thick-skinned and supercilious, but personal relations may be pleasant enough with him.

Chamberlain : Trustworthy. Old-fashioned in his loyalty to his friends and his principles. More concerned to master a question and act rightly upon it than with mere personal and party interests. . . .

Churchill : The "dark horse" of English politics. Too adventurous and independent for the ordinary party ties and labels. . . . Can hammer out an argument thin, and has an intellectual thoroughness which is very rare in a politician. . . . In spite of his reputed "militarism" and dictatorial air, has more real idea of freedom and care for it than other politicians, and a better understanding of its political framework, and more real regard for the future of England and the British Empire as based on freedom. Can look ahead to necessary and desirable developments.'[2]

Robert Barton recalls of these early stages in negotiation that 'the atmosphere was strained and formal. The English studied Griffith as the Rebel Vice-President but I should say that their interest concentrated upon Collins as the man who had done most to thwart them in the physical force campaign. At that date it must have been unusual for a man with £10,000 on his head to sit at the Downing Street Cabinet table.'[3]

Lloyd George's initial view of Collins was handsome enough : 'undoubtedly a considerable person' he described him to Lord Riddell during that first week.[4] As time went on his opinion would change.

There was little compatibility between the two. Both had the shrewd native wit of their people, but what in Collins came out in a forthright relish of a close bargain ran through Lloyd George's veins with all the sinuosity of an illicit still, and with results no less potent of disaster for those who tasted them. Lloyd George came to despise Collins; Collins distrusted Lloyd George from start to finish.

The reactions of Cope and Macready to their first meetings with Collins in these days are as diverse as their own sympathies. Sturgis heard from Cope on Saturday 15 October : '. . . Michael Collins is showing frankness and considerable reasonableness.'

[2] Llewelyn Davies Papers
[3] Robert Barton to the author
[4] Riddell *Intimate Diary* p. 329

Macready found that 'Collins was a great disappointment, flippantly trying to get out of corners by poor jokes in bad taste'.

Collins's true *métier* lay in personal discussion for which the sub-committees offered better scope than the more formal plenary sessions, and he was appointed to all of them, a tribute from his colleagues to his wide-ranging abilities.

Sunday 16 October was his birthday; his thirty-first, though he wrote of it to Kitty as his thirtieth. Perhaps it was that not unpronounced touch of vanity in him, perhaps Peter Pan still asserted his influence.

His thoughts that afternoon turned to Granard, and he dwelt on its rivers, the lakes whose still waters he loved, and the low, wooded hills of Longford and Westmeath with their embattled history. He recalled how he had stood in the early morning on the Mote of Granard and 'looked out across the Inny to Derryvaragh over Kinale & Sheelin (& thought of Fergus O'Farrell) to Mount Nugent and turning westward saw Cairnhill where the beacons were lighted to announce to the men of Longford that the French had landed in Killala'.

The delegation had decided as a matter of policy not to allow themselves to be drawn into social occasions which might be used by the British. Collins in particular, with his London background, could have renewed old ties with a host of Irish friends. He had determined before he left Ireland, however, that the success of their mission might depend largely on his leading as quiet a life as possible, and he sought out only a few old and tried friends. Always, of course, there was Hannie, a comforting presence in the background. Mrs Duggan too was in London with her husband for much of the time, always ready to welcome him.

He did take Kevin O'Higgins's bride to Bourne & Hollingsworth to buy her a hat, a promise made, it seems, at the height of the Terror and never discharged. O'Higgins himself declined to accompany them further than the shop doors on such a frivolous enterprise.

One new friend whom he did allow himself to meet was Sir James Barrie. Here, he felt, was a fine man whose sincerity could not be doubted. Barrie, for his part, could not wait to telephone the Davieses, who had introduced them. 'He has completely charmed me', he declared. 'He is blazing with intelligence.'

They were to meet more than once afterwards. In later days Barrie confided to Hannie that he had intended writing his own impressions of Michael. Something in the West Cork background had eluded him, however – perhaps the weaver's cottage in Kirriemuir and the Woodfield farmhouse had too much in common for one also so deep-rooted to view in all their dimensions – and the tribute was never paid.

Work pressed unceasingly upon Michael. He was as certain as ever of his unsuitability as a match for men like Lloyd George, Chamberlain, Birkenhead. The fear gnawed at him constantly that he might fail, by inexperience, to wrest from the British what a more accomplished diplomatist might have contrived.

This dread preyed on his mind, making him moody and short-tempered. After a small family party he wrote miserably to Kitty : 'Yes it was a lovely party, but I was unpleasant as I have really too many things to carry at the present moment. It is not right for me to inflict myself on people.'

Even when they tried to reassure him that they understood the cause for these moods, he thought they were dissembling, humouring him like a fractious patient. 'I don't like Gramophone effects. I like the people to say what they themselves think and mean', he wrote stormily, in fierce reaction from Whitehall meetings at which he could say neither what he thought nor meant with perfect frankness.

He withdrew into himself. 'Trouble everywhere', he wrote on 19 October to Kitty. 'My own fault. . . . Last night I escaped from all my people and went for a drive alone. Rather funny – the great M.C. in lonely splendour. I am lonely actually. . . .'

Ironically, he was finding himself very, very popular. The English had discovered that the hatchet-faced, murderous thug of past propaganda was a handsome, cheerfully debonair young Irishman with magnetic appeal. Stories of his escapes were rife; as he had once written to Hannie of the worship accorded 'popular idols' : 'The English people are so demonstrative and excitable. In comparison to the Irish on these occasions it certainly *is* so.'

The insincerity of public adulation from those who a short

time before would have rejoiced as readily to hear of his death only heightened his affection for those who had been his friends when it was less fashionable to be so. Hearing that a man who had stood by him in those days had just joined the Carmelite order, he wrote to him :

'I would like you to know that you are one of the people whom I always think of for you were one of my friends when I had not so many friends as I appear to have now. You will understand very well that I don't quite know what to say in a case like yours, but you will also understand that although I may be lacking in the vocal part of it, I wish you every happiness in your life that God can bestow.'[5]

Running through his letters to Kitty appear flashes of that steady philosophy which had supported him in other times of test : 'Life has to take in the serious things as well as the light things and even though we may like sunshine always it is not practical nor indeed – and remember this – is it desirable.'

Again, speaking of love : 'If it can't last through misfortune and trouble and difficulty and unpleasantness and age then it is no use. In riches & beauty & pleasures it is so easy to be quite all right. That is no test though.'

Hitherto his visits to Brompton Oratory had been secret. Only when a waiter expressed anxiety at these early morning disappearances did Ned Broy quietly follow him. Collins's rage at being discovered abated when Broy, with the fierceness of love, demanded : 'If you were missing and captured could I say it was no business of mine?' Michael, unconcerned about possible risks to himself, nevertheless renounced something of his loneliness thereafter, and Broy went with him each morning.

II

For the first fortnight the negotiations were productive of little, and there was a general sense of frustration on the British side. The Irishmen were grimly determined to fight every corner. Three fundamental issues lay ahead : allegiance to the Crown

[5] Collins Papers

as head of the Empire; the partition of Ulster; and British retention of naval bases in Ireland.

Before serious discussion had been entered upon, a storm broke ominously over the wording of telegrams between the Pope and the King, and another from de Valera who used the occasion to reiterate Ireland's inalienable independence. It was another case of the implicit disregard of status which de Valera was unable to see as an expedient of diplomatic etiquette, but only as a challenge to Ireland's claims. Lloyd George seized this opportunity to parry the Irishmen's delaying tactics, and he demanded a straight answer on Allegiance.

Collins crossed to Ireland for the weekend. Despite the secrecy surrounding the negotiations, Saturday's papers carried rumours of crisis. Mark Sturgis noted darkly : 'Collins was seen this morning talking to Mulcahy in the hall of the Gresham and words portending war have been reported to me.'

Collins's purpose in returning to Dublin was probably to discuss the Truce situation with G.H.Q. Staff. Certainly the visits he paid home throughout the negotiations were largely taken up with meetings with I.R.A. leaders. While the plenipotentiaries were negotiating for peace their hands would be considerably strengthened if the British knew that Ireland was prepared for war.

The telegram crisis must have supported his fears, which were also those of Griffith, that de Valera was being influenced by the 'no concession' members of the Cabinet left at home. Significantly, he informed de Valera that the delegation wished him to hold himself in readiness to cross to London if required.

There was a more subtle cause for depression. Collins had left London where the atmosphere was becoming weighted more and more with the inevitability of some sort of compromise; where every discussion centred on how far both sides might make concession; and where the Republic was never mentioned, the British stating their whole argument in Dominion terms.

In Dublin those to whom he spoke thought in terms only of the Republic with, at best, some nebulous link with the Empire to placate British sentiment. That British sentiment was backed by a position of military superiority was not a prevailing consideration. Too many Republicans were claiming that the British had called for a truce because they were beaten. Collins knew too well that they had done so because they had been, to a certain extent, bluffed to a hold, and because public opinion in Britain had sickened of coercion. With every day that the British could point to further efforts to find a peaceful settlement, this latter advantage was deserting the Irish. He was ready to resume the fight, if necessary. He also knew that, despite the vast improvement in the I.R.A.'s arsenal in the past weeks of truce, it would certainly be a fight against impossible odds, and fatal for himself.

He remained a convinced Republican. He was, however, becoming increasingly dubious whether the practical difference between the Republic and Dominion status as he conceived it in all its ultimate possibilities was worth asking the Irish people to make further sacrifice for.

He could not explain this new conviction – as yet it was less conviction than a dawning realization – to men whose principles were irrevocably pledged to the Republic. He could only ask himself whether he could honourably carry on in London, knowing full well that neither he nor any man in Ireland could bring back the Republic.

He returned to England on Sunday night, 23 October. The next day the Irish proposals would be presented to the British. His letter written on the boat to Kitty shows he was in the depths of homesickness; lonely and far from all that he felt really mattered.

Allegiance to the Crown was, for the Irish, translatable only in terms of External Association. Griffith's manner of presenting this did at least leave the matter open. The British were encouraged rather than otherwise to believe that the ghost of the Irish Republic might yet be well and truly laid. The Irish, on the other hand, may well have congratulated themselves that the British might, after all, accept G. K. Chesterton's recent dictum that the separation of Ireland from England was 'a condition to be assumed, not a conclusion to be avoided'.[6]

Lloyd George was determined to reach a settlement. He now turned to the age-old stratagem of divide and rule. A casual 'conversation' at which Griffith and Collins joined him and Chamberlain marked the point at which the delegations ceased – though

[6] Chesterton *Irish Impressions* p. 155

no one at Hans Place or in Dublin realized it – to meet in plenary session again.

There are two principal reasons why Lloyd George acted thus. The first was that, like Collins, he found individual discussion more satisfactory than the more formal deliberations of a group.[7] The second reason lay in the composition of the Irish delegation.

Marked differences among the five Irish plenipotentiaries must already have appeared. These may be summed up by saying that whereas Griffith and Collins were prepared to contemplate alternatives to the full Irish demand once they had wrung the utmost in concession from the British, Barton and Gavan Duffy were not. Duggan from the first had shown himself willing to follow Collins's judgement. His liaison work in Ireland in any case kept him from figuring largely in the London developments.

Lloyd George had a third reason for desiring to include only the principals in conference – Erskine Childers. Griffith and Collins may well have been no less relieved to confer without secretaries present. Griffith was personally antagonistic to Childers. Collins, while he still regarded him as a friend, was becoming increasingly annoyed by his hair-splitting preoccupation with what Collins's practical mind regarded as non-essentials. Both were uneasy in the belief that Childers was supplementing Griffith's own daily reports to de Valera with 'watch-dog' submissions of his own. Lloyd George looked on Childers as a fanatical convert to Republicanism and believed that he exerted an influence on de Valera that would overrule all chance of settlement.

Some measure of responsibility for the personal stresses which developed as a result of the new departure must rest with Collins. He cannot, of course, be blamed for the psychological differences of the Irish team which have already been noted. In handling these differences he acted, however, with some unwisdom. If Barton and Gavan Duffy were to be cut out of conference, they might at least have remained more fully in their leaders' confidence. Collins seems never to have had much in common with Gavan Duffy; perhaps he suspected the 'legal trimming' he had always mistrusted in lawyers, though Gavan Duffy's sincerity

[7] Sir Geoffrey Shakespeare *Let candles be brought in* (London 1949) p. 82

in probing the minutiae of the issues involved cannot be questioned: it was for this that he had been sent over. Barton, on the other hand, had been Collins's comrade under the admittedly vastly different circumstances of war. One can sympathize with Barton's growing feeling that developments were afoot of which neither he nor Gavan Duffy were fully informed.

The close friendship between Barton and his cousin, Erskine Childers, may account in part for Collins's close-mindedness. Chiefly it arose from the habit, the cause of so much antagonism in the past, of dealing with a problem in his own way. Now, since he and Griffith worked well together, he set aside those whom he felt hindered their progress. It played straight into Lloyd George's hands. How much it may have affected later events can only be a matter for regretful conjecture.

The British now stated, inevitably, that 'on the Crown they must fight'. De Valera warned Griffith that the only alternative to allegiance to the Crown was war. His instruction that this must be stated as soon as possible nearly put an end to the conference. Were the plenipotentiaries to become puppets? Collins, indeed, was so furious that only Griffith's persuasion kept him from quitting and going home.[8] We may guess that Collins was less jealous of their powers than dismayed that the President was not fully in sympathy with their approach – a dismay which de Valera's reiterated refusal to come to London cannot have alleviated, suggestive though it was of his confidence in themselves.

Indeed, the situation as it now stood could hardly have been more paradoxical. The delegates might discuss association with the Crown without exceeding their instructions. Any decision must, however, be referred to Dublin, where, in de Valera's words, 'all were at one' that any settlement which recognized the Crown must be rejected in favour, if necessary, of war.

Yet the British had made it clear that there could be no settlement without recognition of the Crown. One can only conclude that the Irish still hoped for such modification of the British terms that, while Ulster sentiment would still feel securely 'linked' to the Crown, the rest of Ireland would not feel that it demanded allegiance.

The Irish negotiations were to be debated in the Commons on

[8] Gallagher *The Anglo-Irish Treaty* p. 98

Monday 31 October, and Lloyd George knew well that the outcome would depend on his statement that definite progress was being made. A written statement of the terms on which negotiation might continue was now given and demanded by the British.

Lloyd George, hypersensitive as always to Press opinion, telegraphed to C. P. Scott of the *Manchester Guardian* to discuss the situation with him. They met on 28 October at that most horrible of all schemes ever devised by Lloyd George, a 'political breakfast'. Scott recorded the Prime Minister's views in his diary next day.[9]

The Tories, Lloyd George said, were 'restive', the Sinn Feiners 'very difficult'. He had, he told Scott, 'had great difficulty in bringing them to the point. He would talk to Griffith and find him quite reasonable. Then he went away and came back after consultation with quite another story.' Erskine Childers was, he thought, 'the villain of the piece', always seeking to counter every approach to concession.

Lloyd George then reviewed his own position. 'He was determined if it were possible to put the negotiation through and secure peace. . . . He now regarded himself in the light of a *judge*. If Sinn Fein refused the minimum concessions he regarded as necessary he would fight them; if the Tories refused to accept them when conceded he would fight them. The moment he got the essential concessions from Sinn Fein then he would deal with Ulster. He could say Sinn Fein had made concessions and now it is your turn to help.'[10]

Before he left, Scott suggested that it might be useful if he were to see Griffith and Collins himself. Lloyd George agreed and Scott accordingly arranged to see Collins that afternoon at Cadogan Gardens.

It was a meeting of great possibilities. The *Manchester Guardian* had been an effective champion of Ireland against coercion, the most sympathetic viewer of Irish aspirations, if not of Irish methods of achieving them. Here, surely, was one Englishman whom Collins could trust.

[9] British Museum: Add MS 50906
[10] C. P. Scott notes at this point that he had been told that T. M. Healy had reported Carson as advising this course, Carson himself being prepared to support it

Collins, however, was never at his best at a first meeting when he felt socially divided. Coupled with his defensive fear of 'doing anything wrong' may have been the knowledge that Scott had been earlier that day with Lloyd George. Fortunately Mr Scott was a patient man. He had, indeed, to wait for more than two hours, Collins having been held up at Hans Place, presumably in conference over the terms of an answer to the British memorandum.

'Collins [Scott records] turned up in immense force at Cadogan Gardens, turned everybody, including an unhappy typist, out of the room with a sweep of his arms and settled down to talk for an hour and a quarter. The telephone rang at intervals when he sprang upon it fiercely as an enemy and yelled a challenge that might have split the instrument. Then FitzGerald would appear and he relapsed into gloomy silence till the interruption was over. In spite of these mannerisms I found him a straightforward and quite agreeable savage.'

On the question of Allegiance, obviously the crux of the interview, Scott could make no progress.

'At last I had to point out that if he had come to negotiate on the principle of claiming everything and conceding nothing he might have spared himself the trouble of coming and might just as well pack up at once. Then he became more moderate and evolved a constructive policy of his own. Why not have a linking of constitutions, each country swearing allegiance to its own constitution. But where I asked would the King come in? "Oh! We'll find room for the King", he said.'

This was hardly what Scott was looking for. He recalled past statesmen who had taken up the Irish question; of them all, only Lloyd George was in a position to 'deliver the goods', and deserved some help from the Irish themselves.

Collins remained unimpressed. He knew nothing, he said, of British politics. He had only to think of Ireland. Scott persisted. 'You have got to think of our politics if you want to get anything done.' Collins could hardly have been more insouciant in the face of this unpalatable truth. Then there came a change of tone. All the same, he did not want war; he wanted peace. But one could not sell the honour of one's country.

At the end there came a real cry from the heart. Perhaps here, after all, was an Englishman who might understand why this whole question of allegiance was so difficult. 'Ireland *was* a nation. Every Irishman felt it in himself. It was not a theory. "It was there".'

'Surely', he told Scott as they parted, 'it would be a discredit to us all if after coming together in conference we did not manage to agree.'

Collins in these days was showing marked nervous depression. He had telegraphed Kitty to join him for a few days, but there was, after all, little she or anyone else could do. On the surface he was as full of life as ever. There was a dinner party at Hannie's on 27 October, with Arthur Griffith and the Duggans, followed by a visit to the *Beggar's Opera,* Griffith's favourite. There had been a reception for the delegates at the Albert Hall, on Wednesday 26 October, arranged by the Irish-Ireland societies in London, and attended, so it seemed, by every Irishman in Britain. Michael, spying a crony of former days at the front of the press, bounded to seize him by the hair, shaking him vigorously with a cry of 'You here, you old devil!'

Beneath it all the strain remained. Pressure of work occupied time he would otherwise have spent with Kitty. He had, indeed, warned her so, and delegated Tom Cullen and Gearoid O'Sullivan to look after her, a thoughtful gesture which she could hardly appreciate.

It would always be thus. In the conflict of devotion the claims of Ireland would always take precedence of any other. The necessity for such a conflict caused him intense anguish, since it made those he loved unhappy. Yet he would have sacrificed everything for Ireland, and made no secret of it.

Collins's suggested 'union of constitutions' was not at all what Lloyd George wanted. He had two days in which to extract an unequivocal statement on Allegiance from the Irish to put before a hostile Commons.

Scott was with him at Chequers when the Irish proposals arrived. 'Lloyd George was a good deal excited. It was better than he had feared. On the naval question there was no concession, but on the question of allegiance "a considerable advance" – not enough, Lloyd George said, "but it was enough to go on with" – there would be no breakdown.'

The 'considerable advance' is hard to discern in the Irish document. 'Unimpaired unity' remained the precondition of an extremely qualified nod to the Crown as head of the Empire with which an Ireland 'secured in absolute and unfettered possession of all legislative and executive authority' would be associated, and even this the delegates were no more than 'prepared to recommend'.

'Enough to go on with' Lloyd George had called it. But the censure motion in the Commons still threatened – to his advantage. He prepared to extract his 'essential concessions' from Sinn Fein.

He invited Griffith and Collins to a private discussion at Churchill's house in Sussex Gardens on the evening of 30 October. By now he was prepared to take 'divide and rule' yet further. He had already dismissed Collins to Scott as 'an uneducated rather stupid man'. Collins was relegated to a downstairs room with his host and Lord Birkenhead. Lloyd George bade Griffith come up higher, and they adjourned accordingly for private conversation.

The evening was to be something of a turning-point for Collins. Probably for the first time, in the informal atmosphere so different from that of the conference room, he saw these two as men rather than statesmen. Between him and Birkenhead there was soon to be a very real friendship, based, at first glance, upon strange disparities. What could draw together the young I.R.A. leader, dedicated to Irish independence, with a self-confessed suspicion of legal men and a complete lack of sophistication, and the Lord Chancellor of England, the most brilliant advocate of his day, polished, urbane, the 'Galloper Smith' of the great Covenanting days?

Here was, in fact, more than the mere attraction of opposites: the man of rugged action for the other of lightning riposte; the fresh young man without finesse for one to whom the ways of the world were well-tried indeed. Similarities lay beneath. Both men possessed deep humanity; and an extraordinary capacity for loyalty to friends surpassed only by a love of country which was willing to abandon old tenets at personal sacrifice when they believed their country required it.

It was surely Collins's own single-mindedness which made him acknowledge Birkenhead's 'true to the facts' quality. 'We have not enough of that quality in Ireland', he told a friend regretfully. There was also that in Collins which could not but delight in contemplating a man who, by his own efforts, had not only risen from middle-class obscurity to walk at will along the highest paths in the land, but could also retain an independence that held lightly to what he found there. For his part, Birkenhead must have been struck by the younger man's quickness to grasp the roots of a problem, his ability to look with new eyes upon old matters. Perhaps, too, he was moved to find a willingness to trust where, thus far, there had been nothing but suspicion.

Upstairs with Griffith, Lloyd George had come straight to the point. The Irish memorandum was not couched in terms clear enough for him to face the diehards with it. If Griffith, he said, would give him personal assurances on the three fundamental issues of Crown, Empire, and naval facilities he himself would (the words are those reported by Griffith to de Valera) 'go out to smite the diehards and would fight on the Ulster matter to secure essential unity'.

Neither Lloyd George nor Griffith wanted a breakdown. Personal assurances from Griffith which would help Lloyd George to secure essential unity could hardly bind the whole Irish delegation in conference. Griffith may well have felt that he was, if anything, building a bridge of gold for a flying enemy. He promised his personal assurances. Their terms evidently satisfied Lloyd George.

'I really feel', he remarked to Geoffrey Shakespeare, then one of his secretaries, as they drove home afterwards, 'there is a chance of pulling something off.'[11]

Did he speak merely of the next day's debate? If so, his optimism was more than justified. The vote of censure was defeated by a crushing majority. It is unlikely, however, that Lloyd George had not intended a deeper meaning to his remark.

[11]Shakespeare *Let candles be brought in* p. 83

CHAPTER FIFTEEN

The Treaty

I

On the surface the Irish delegates' personal relations were cordial enough, if the menu of a dinner attended by them on 10 November is any indication. It included:

'Soup: Peace "Thick"; Publicity "Clear"
Fish: Hans Plaice; Coduggan Steaks
Entrees: Economic Cutlets (Reparation Gravy)
    Minced Ulster (North East Sauce)
Joint: Roast Beef of Old England
    Aide-Memoire of Potatoes (Delegates' solution)
    Formula of Beans (No solution)'[1]

There was now a deep understanding between Griffith and Collins which was not dependent on any stratagem of Lloyd George. Griffith placed a confidence in Collins that was coupled with a strong sense of gratitude for his support. Collins recognized Griffith's real statesmanship. Perhaps he saw, too, his weariness. Certainly he himself shouldered more and more of the work, while continuing to rely upon Griffith to decide the tactics of discussion.

Reared in the Fenian tradition Collins had hitherto taken the Republican symbols for granted. But Griffith's own conception of Sinn Fein cared little for forms and symbols. His sole aim had always been to establish Irish national self-sufficiency. Now Collins too was coming to accept, unsuspected by his colleagues, that this integrity was dependent, not upon the symbol of Republic or Crown, but upon the opportunities afforded Ireland to develop her own economic and social life.

It was, moreover, through no seeking of his own that Collins had been sent over as the 'big stick' of Republican demands. On

[1] Brother Allen's Papers

the question of allegiance he remained adamant. On 'recognition' of the Crown and the whole concept of its rôle in the Commonwealth he was being introduced to new ideas.

Colonel Josiah Wedgwood M.P., interviewed for Collins's benefit, expounded his own ideas on the future of the British Commonwealth. The member states would become rather a League of Free Nations; as Wedgwood put it 'the bond being that there would be no bond'. Into this association of autonomous communities, linked for mutual benefit, he hoped that not only the existing members of the British Commonwealth, but also other nations, notably the United States, might be drawn. Allegiance to the British Crown must then patently cease to be the link that joined them, and any undertaking concerning the Crown made now must, within a measurable time, lose all relevance.

There had also been submitted to Collins another memorandum which touched, not on unguaranteed possibilities of Commonwealth development, but on definite facts which showed that development was already taking place in a way that opened up new visions in world politics.

It also pointed out that British failure to concede Ireland's independence in the same degree as that of any other Commonwealth state would be regarded by those states as prejudicial to their own position.[2]

Here then was a new view of the Association into which Ireland was being asked to enter. Not the least of its attractions was the realization that such a concept held out great hopes of Irish unity. Collins jotted down in broad outline the basis of a memorandum on the subject on 18 November.[3] These notes end with the observation: 'There are no precedents for this present situation, but this will be a precedent for perhaps many a new situation.'[4]

It was a precedent which was, indeed, to result in the Statute of Westminster ten years later. The tragedy for Ireland in 1921 was that neither the British nor the Irish people had, as yet, seen the new vision.

[2] Collins Papers
[3] The final memorandum was presented to the British delegates on 25 November 1921
[4] Collins Papers

Griffith's 'personal assurances' about the Irish proposals had, at the insistence of the other delegates, been submitted in writing by him as head of the delegation. Armed with this document Lloyd George, who was to meet Craig on 5 November, had declared himself ready to resign rather than continue the Irish war. By 8 November, when the Ulster Cabinet had met in London, it was clear that Ulster would remain immovable, no matter what Griffith promised.

Lloyd George was in a quandary. Sinn Fein had tied all concessions to essential unity. But 'essential unity' now seemed as impossible as renewed force against the South, which he had declared his readiness to resign rather than contemplate.

The Prime Minister, however, did not intend to resign. He had not lost his old skill in keeping alternative avenues open. By the weekend he had secured from Griffith a document promising that he, personally, would not repudiate the suggestion of a Boundary Commission (the inference was substantial gains for the South) in lieu of an All-Ireland Parliament should Ulster, inevitably, opt out of one. To Griffith, reporting the discussion to de Valera, this was no more than a 'tactical manœuvre', and a British proposal at that, to put the onus on Ulster for any breakdown during Lloyd George's immediate discussions with the Northern Cabinet. To Chamberlain, setting forth for Liverpool the following week to rally Unionist support for the negotiations, it was no mere manœuvre, but a firm undertaking to allow Ulster to opt out of any settlement, subject only to the findings of a Boundary Commission (not necessarily involving significant changes in area).[5] It did not occur to Chamberlain that it was a conditional document, any more than it ever occurred to Griffith that Chamberlain or anyone else on the British side believed it to be anything else.

Collins was once more in Dublin. These weekend visits home had their compensations, crowded though they were by work, innumerable meetings, and the incessant strain of balancing the two political atmospheres of London and Dublin in his mind. He had written from London to Kitty on 8 November (he had managed to get away briefly to Granard):

[5] See Pakenham's definitive exposition of this manœuvre, as of the whole course of the negotiations, in *Peace by Ordeal*

'The weekend (notwithstanding my own unpleasantness) did me a great deal of good. The constant & changing fresh air was a great tonic. Yesterday morning's journey back was lovely. Very cold, but I didn't really feel that. Practically the whole way I was lost in admiration of the view. The various colourings of the leaves were beautiful in the extreme and as we came in view of Lough Owel the sun – which seemed to have caught all the waters as if in a saucer – shone brilliantly on the lake and transformed it into a glimmering silver. Really I never thought things looked so lovely. I wonder why? Perhaps it was that I was happy.'

Country ways, country people, took his mind off depressing days in London. Odd thoughts spring inconsequentially from the pages of his letters. 'Granard market is held on an ill-chosen date. Monday – how could anyone be in proper mood or manner for buying and selling on a Monday morning?'

And what Ulsterman could not read with pleasure: 'What the hosts of Enniskillen require is quart measures. Glasses as they are at present are not nearly large enough to enable them give proper demonstration of their hospitality.'

On 12 November Collins met Mark Sturgis, now in charge of liaison duties, which had been transferred from military to civil hands. Sturgis wrote next day:

'There is more of truth and less of malicious humour in Macready's description of Collins than I expected . . . and he is certainly as Macready says much too quick to make jokes of everything and often bad ones. But he is undoubtedly quick to understand and I should imagine is twice the man if he is up against you than he is when his obvious object is to be agreeable. Strong, brave and quite ruthless.'

They spoke of the growing unrest marking the long weeks of truce. Sturgis continues:

'He was equally frank when he spoke of the stupid things sections of his people had done and were quite capable of doing now unless firmly handled, and it was at that stage that my opinion of him as a big force began to improve. I certainly thought more of him at the end of the interview than the beginning. He was quick to see and to admit the growing difficulties of a jerry-built truce and made no sort of attempt to score or make points against me.'

Collins had been exploring the financial aspects of any settlement. Early in the negotiations he had written angrily to J. J. Walsh: 'The enemy attitude is to extract the last penny from us, and a penny after that as well'. His hope now was that Britain's rumoured preparation for renewed war against Ireland should the negotiations break down might sway the Washington Disarmament Conference to refuse any remission of the British War Debt. On 15 November the Second External Dail Loan was decreed. On the same day he heard from Mr James Douglas, then in New York, whom he had asked to seek an answer to a question of primary importance: whether American financial support would be forthcoming for Ireland should she fail to reach a settlement with Britain. Mr Douglas advised:

'. . . There is plenty of money here to be lent to Ireland, if there is peace but I am afraid the big men will not take [*sic*] loan otherwise. O'Mara has a big job to raise his bond drive – I am trying to help him behind the scenes but it is no easy matter. . . .'[6]

Should negotiations break down, therefore, and renewed warfare result, Ireland must stand alone. It was a prospect that was to have an immense bearing on Collins's attitude to the negotiations.

On that day, too, the British handed the Irishmen their draft proposals for a Treaty. These avoided inimical phraseology. There was no mention of Crown, Oath, or Allegiance. Nevertheless they provided no loophole for escape from the Empire. Small wonder, then, that Collins should write to Kitty of being 'in a ferment of haste and worry'.

The National Unionist Association conference at Liverpool took place the next day. Not Chamberlain only, but Birkenhead helped to ensure that this stronghold of Ulster Unionism would support the continuation of negotiations. Birkenhead had come to believe that the Irish delegates were men who, once pledged to an agreement, would keep it even with their lives. For himself,

[6] Collins Papers

he 'believed in the settlement more than he had ever believed in anything'.[7]

Both Birkenhead and Collins, in their widely different fashions, had arrived almost together at the view that their deepest loyalties would be enhanced, not betrayed, by co-operation. It had not been an easy transition. The way ahead would be littered with charges of treachery and trimming to expediency. Yet now, for the first time, the negotiations become exciting. They are no longer mere arguments to find a way out of impasse; for on each side of the conference table there are men, the one who came in defiance, the other who came 'rather bored', who now see the hopeful possibility of a new way to peace.

The Irish delegation's original plan to avoid all social contact in London had now seen a certain change. As far as accepting British hospitality went, this was observed to the end. Collins and Griffith, however, now relaxed the ban for meetings on neutral or pro-Irish ground. They have been adversely criticized for doing so; but to those who believe that the understanding of differences is the best way to solve them this meeting of the enemy on informal ground must rather seem a brave foray.

Sir John Lavery, the Irish-born painter, was then working on the portraits of the delegates. Collins wrote to Kitty on 16 November: 'By the way I sat today for my portrait – my interesting life! Absolute torture as I was expected to keep still and this you know is a thing I cannot do. . . . Sir John Lavery is painting me.'

In Sir John's recollection: 'Collins was a patient sitter, but I noticed that he liked to sit facing the door. He was always on the alert.'[8]

Lady Lavery, his beautiful American wife, had long been a sympathizer with the Irish cause, and at last brought British and Irish together at her dinner-table. The informality of Lavery's studio, where their gatherings frequently took place, speeded an end to mistrust. Suspicions that their hostess was a British spy were soon dispelled, at least for Griffith and Collins. The British may indeed have made what use they could of her influence. It was soon apparent enough, however, that the warmly romantic

[7] Stanley Salvidge *Salvidge of Liverpool* (London 1934) p. 204
[8] Sir John Lavery *The Life of a Painter* (London 1940) pp. 214–15

glow in which Lady Lavery observed Michael Collins cleared her of any deliberate connivance in possible British schemes.

In all Collins's friendships with women of sophistication a mutual attraction between gun and drawing-room was apparent. As always, however, Collins while admiring beauty and temperament, remained blind to the fascination he exercized.

Other London hostesses able to 'capture' Collins viewed his lack of formality with mixed alarm and delight. He was visiting Mrs Parry, Casement's cousin, when she remembered that she was due elsewhere. Collins bounded forth to find her a cab, and in a remarkably short time one stood at the door. As he drove off the cabby remarked with awe: 'That's a forcible butler you've got, Ma'am!'

Before the new Irish proposals were handed to the British, further trouble broke out in Belfast. The way matters were moving in Ulster emerges in an interview C. P. Scott had some days later, on 3 December, with Lloyd George. Scott records:

> 'I said Ulster was now the danger spot. The Ulster Government was not fit to govern. They were purging the old constabulary ([Lloyd] George had not heard of this) and making it a purely sectarian force, levying also large numbers of violent Orange partisans, had uttered no word of protest on the expulsion of nearly 10,000 men from the shipyards, and were in fact preparing for civil war. [Lloyd] George had no word to say in defence. He merely remarked that he had been a good deal surprised at the sort of man who had come over to represent the Northern Government, of whom, however, Craig was the best.'[9]

Against this background of insuperable antagonism in the North-East, the Irish handed their draft proposals to the British on 22 November 'upon the assumption that the essential unity of Ireland is maintained'.

Lloyd George declared vehemently that they offered no hope of a settlement. Deadlock seemed inevitable but, as neither side wanted a breakdown, further discussion was arranged for the following day.

De Valera's tactics in sending Collins to London as the 'no

[9] British Museum: Add MS 50906

compromise' advocate had failed. Collins, the 'desperate extremist' was now the chief cause for British optimism. In concentrating on Collins, the one delegate who might control the I.R.A., they might yet have been forced into making concession instead of, as hitherto, demanding it, had not the bargaining strength so vital to the Irish position been vitiated by the fact that the decisions of the Dublin Cabinet depended ultimately on Brugha and Stack, who would never make a stand in support of Collins at the point where he believed the ultimate concession by the British had been made.

Collins's fears on this score may well lie behind his writing to Kitty on 15 November : 'If one broods over a thing one is very likely to give it an importance it doesn't deserve and a doubt cultivated is apt to flourish exceedingly'. Certainly, he was shortly to find himself, like De La Rey at Vereeniging, answering diehard demands to fight to the bitter end with a grave, 'Has not the bitter end come?' but with the knowledge that Brugha was no De Wet, to yield to the counsel of brave but far-sighted men prepared to compromise.

Collins, Griffith, and de Valera all knew that something less than the isolated Republic must be accepted; de Valera differed from the other two only in his belief of what that 'something less' entailed. To Collins and Griffith External Association would not provide the basis of settlement; they were prepared to explore other paths consistent with essential unity. Tragically, they did not realize that for de Valera External Association was, on principle, the only permissible way out.

It was now, on the very day on which further discussion of the Irish proposals was to begin, that the arms raid on Windsor Barracks took place. British militarists laid it squarely at Collins's door; others since have seen Brugha's hand in it. In fact, it would be hard to tell which of the two heard of the coup with the greater fury. Yet, indirectly, the old quarrel between them had set the scene for it.

This had recently been exacerbated by an argument with the British over levies. In pre-Truce times the I.R.A. in some areas had resorted to levies on the population, based as equitably as possible, to maintain the basic needs of their forces, which the Truce had not lessened. The British, while they harassed Collins

with allegations that levies violated the Truce agreement, raised
no objection to mere 'collections' of money. The Dail Ministry of
Defence gave orders accordingly.

It had been done purely to pour oil on troubled waters, and
in no way admitted any British right to raise such objections. For
Liam Lynch, O/C the 1st Southern Division, I.R.A., however,
the order presented a problem. On 10 November he wrote to
Mulcahy, the Chief of Staff. Did this new order mean that the
Ministry of Defence, in declaring levies illegal, was repudiating
brigade officers' actions in the past?

Mulcahy, well aware that Lynch's concern was for the satisfaction of his officers, passed this query to Cathal Brugha, with a
request that, in the circumstances, approval of past levies be
granted. Brugha replied:

> 'We cannot approve as having been regular what we never
> sanctioned. On the other hand we fully appreciate the circum-
> stances that induced the local Commanders to make the levies.
> If the local Officers send us a full list of the monies received
> and the manner of its expenditure we will credit the sub-
> scribers with having contributed to the National Exchequer
> and take the sums into account as a set-off in calculating the
> amount due from them in the case of future taxation, or re-
> funding the amount as may be decided.'[10]

Mulcahy, before rewarding Liam Lynch's services to his
country with such a demand, wrote to Collins for his comments
as Minister of Finance. Collins's reply was to the point:

> 'It has never been suggested, so far as I know, that any
> Levies should be incorporated into the National Funds and
> should be charged consequently upon future National finances.
> It is a proposition which would be wholly impracticable so
> far as the o/cs. are concerned. It seems to me that it would
> have been a very simple matter to have issued the necessary
> endorsement to the O/C. 1st Southern.
>
> 'You will readily understand that the matter raises a tre-
> mendous question so far as the liability for levies by the
> Government goes. You would have an idea of the amount

[10] National Library of Ireland: Ministry of Defence Archives

levied or collected by semi-levy (it would be very hard to differentiate); probably it runs into very many thousands.'[11]

Once again Brugha had been set at naught by Collins. It was one more bitter pill which it was not in him to swallow.

The I.R.A. was still short of arms. Early in November Brugha had sent two men, Michael Hogan and Ned Lynch,[12] to London to buy arms. Their chief instructions were to keep away from Collins and Sam Maguire. Brugha was not having any I.R.B. meddling in his arrangements.

The two men spent a week in London, during which they bought between them one ·32 revolver and a Parabellum at very high prices. Lynch was gloomily contemplating their failure when a message arrived. 'The Big Fellow wants to see you. He's surprised you haven't called on him yet.' Lynch, the former London-Irishman, went. He had no intention of revealing his business, but Collins, the Director of Intelligence, did not ask it. So Lynch was over buying arms, with money apparently no object. On whose orders? When he was told he said curtly : 'If this Treaty isn't signed you'll have more guns than men to use them. Things are being made difficult for us over here – don't make them more so.' They shook hands and parted.

Ironically, at this point arms came tumbling to hand. Lynch met a couple of Irish Guardsmen in a pub, one of them a Sergeant Roche. By the end of the evening patriotism was running very high indeed. If the Treaty was not signed, it was declared, the Irish Guards would have a say in it. On a foggy night a van with Hogan, Lynch, Roche, and a couple of others set off for Windsor.

The haul was considerable. Packing it all up, Lynch and Hogan pelted each other gleefully with saw-dust. Next stop, Woolwich Arsenal. They had done good work for Ireland.

The news of the raid broke ominously upon the negotiations. Roche, captured as he and Lynch made for Dublin, held out long enough for the rest to get away, then admitted that the I.R.A. was behind the raid.

In British eyes, the I.R.A. was Michael Collins. There were

[11] National Library of Ireland: Ministry of Defence Archives

[12] The account of what followed is based on an interview with the late Ned Lynch

furious accusations. Broy, who had supposed Collins knew of the raid, was appalled at the fury with which he ordered Hogan to be sent for. Hogan, however, preferred to face a British court.

In Dublin a bewildered Lynch met Brugha's wrath. Part of his rage arose from the discovery that Lynch had seen Collins after all. Mainly he was concerned about possible repercussions on the negotiations. It has been alleged that he engineered the Windsor raid to discredit Collins. Whatever his personal vindictiveness for Collins, Brugha was a minister of the government which had sent him to represent it in London: he was incapable of such chicanery.

I I

The two days which followed the presentation of the latest Irish proposals were spent in a tussle over the Crown and Allegiance. 'We have been at it in most serious fashion all today', wrote Collins on 24 November. Some advance on defence, trade, and finance had been made, and settlement on these seemed probable. On the main questions of Allegiance and Ulster the gulf yawned as widely as before.

Concessions were to be made on both sides within the next few days. The end was clearly at hand. The question of the exact definition of the rôle of the Crown remained. Both sides saw each other's view as insuperable: both awaited concession.

Craig was to be sent the final British proposals on Tuesday 6 December. The Irish were to take them to Dublin for informal discussion in Cabinet the weekend before.

At the Cabinet meeting Michael would face the hostility which he had felt to be insidiously brewing behind his back. His letters to Kitty show his longing to escape the undercurrents of hypocrisy that had made him the scapegoat of Ireland's hopeless position, and the self-searchings of depression. On 30 November he wrote:

'I am not demonstrative (except in showing my temper sometimes) and I hate demonstrative indications of feeling – I mean before people. They stand somehow in my mind for a kind of insincerity. . . . It really means that I'm on the side

of those who do things not on the side of those who say
things. . . .

'I'm in a very troubled state of mind this morning. Troubled
about many things. . . . Little wrongs I may have done people
never cease coming back to my mind. This is a side that
perhaps you could not regard as being there, but it is there.'

Next day, however, he cast aside his sombre thoughts:

'Please don't think of my cold. With very occasional exceptions there "ain't no such thing". Above all don't think of
remedies – they're no good to me as I always forget to use
them or as for instance during the past two or three years the
remedy was always somewhere else. Many a time the estimable
qualities of Thermogen Wool have been dilated upon to me
but I have always withstood the lure. In this present instance
however I assure you that it's not necessary and you wouldn't
in such circumstances subject me to it would you? . . .

'Whatever other faults I may have the fault of wishing for
personal comfort is not among them. And indeed this is no
tribute to myself for I rather enjoy the state that people would
regard as non-comfortable therefore its absence is pleasing
enough to me.'

Griffith left for Dublin early on the Friday; Barton had already
gone. Collins and Childers spent the morning arguing finance
with British experts, whom Collins met alone, and in greater
strength, in the afternoon. By the end of the day, like a hero of
Irish legend, he had, if not compassed their slaughter, held them
at bay.

Nor did he come from battle without bearing away a trophy.
His next letter to Kitty carries the embossment of the Prime
Minister's crest on Downing Street notepaper. With Childers, his
sword-bearer in the fight, he sat down to dinner at Hans Place.
To them both came C. P. Scott.

Scott had lunched with Lloyd George, who had not been hopeful of settlement. Responsibility for failure, however, would rest
where it would suit him best, not on Ulster, but Sinn Fein. Without concession there must be coercion. The estimated number of
men required for a full-scale invasion was 200,000; he spoke of

a blockade instead. Scott shrewdly noted: 'The fact is he had evidently not in the least made up his mind what he would do.'[13]

The Prime Minister did not altogether despair of a peaceful solution, however. He begged Scott, whatever they did in the *Manchester Guardian*, not to encourage Sinn Fein to stand out on Allegiance. But Scott was less than acquiescent. He understood Sinn Fein were willing to accept a form of oath of their own. The form of oath seemed to him to matter very little. The real bond of union was moral and entirely different. He appealed to Lloyd George to 'get down to facts, to the actual things we wanted, and not to stand on phrases and pleas of legality'.

Scott saw Collins briefly alone, and then joined him and Childers at dinner. Both were in haste to catch the night train to Holyhead. Scott told Collins that he had come to do whatever was in his power to save the situation. He could hardly have pleaded the cause of peace with greater sympathy for Sinn Fein's position should failure come. 'I urged that in their reply S.F. should put their case in the best light for the British public stating quite strongly and definitely what they were prepared to accept. As e.g. common citizenship – so that Ll[oyd] G[eorge] might not be able to throw all the blame of any failure on them and exonerate Ulster.'

His efforts made little headway. Childers could not have been more uncompromising; Collins affirmed with emphasis that he expected a breakdown. They had gone to the utmost length they could.

Yet this apparent implacability was deceptive. Collins was, in reality, in an optimistic mood, as he revealed to a friend who saw him on the train that evening. His cheerful anticipation of defeat arose because he did not, despite his words, expect it. Certainly he believed that Sinn Fein could go no further on the present British proposals. Yet the adjustments already made on these had encouraged the belief that more might yet be won. Childers might shake his head with Gavan Duffy over the terms that they were taking to Dublin; Collins was not in the mood for quibbling over phraseology. His business was with realities: what naval facilities really entailed; whether full fiscal autonomy might not still be won, and, with it, American financial support.

In the frame of mind, therefore, of a pioneer who sees the promised land opening before his people, Collins set off from Euston. Though areas of that land remained to be cleared, he had every faith that firmness of purpose would overcome these in the end. The first thing was to take possession of the land. Above all, the way to the unity of Ireland, that great essential, still lay open.

The Cabinet meeting in Dublin lasted for six hours. It was the hurried manner in which it closed, leaving the various members with widely divergent impressions of what had been decided upon, that had catastrophic repercussions.

If the day's labours seemed only to have clarified how far from agreement those who had toiled over them were, some decisions were quickly reached. De Valera would not go over, as Barton had suggested, since Griffith had undertaken to bring the Treaty back unsigned for submission to the Dail. The delegates were to return immediately to London. They would tell Lloyd George that the oath of allegiance, if not amended, was unacceptable to the Cabinet; that they could not sign the document; that it was a matter for the Dail; and that they were prepared to face war if necessary. It was further decided that they should try to make Ulster the crux on which negotiation broke down. If they thought fit, they were empowered to meet Sir James Craig.

Time was short. The delegates hurried to return to London. Barton, Gavan Duffy, and Childers went one way, Griffith, Collins, and Duggan another. Six hours of going over their differences with a tooth-comb demanded a temporary respite for over-strained nerves.

The hurry to return has never been explained. The British were expecting them; to have telegraphed for a postponement would have been to admit indecision, a possible split in the Irish ranks, which must at all costs be avoided. Perhaps, after all, the Dail Cabinet felt that no further decision could be reached. Undoubtedly they believed that they were agreed on the course to be adopted. Had they, in fact, been so agreed it would have availed them little in the actual battle. All their calculations had reckoned without that great incalculable, Lloyd George.

III

Padraig Pearse once wrote that, in the choice between honour and advantage, woe would come to that man who chose advantage. Collins held Parnell's dictum to be self-evident: no man might set the bounds to the march of a nation. He himself was as ready to face death as Brugha was rather than concur in doing so. It was easy enough to choose honour above advantage; hard indeed at this time to know the difference. That Sunday morning at Cadogan Gardens he wrote grimly to Kitty: 'There's a job to be done and for the moment here's the place. And *that's that. . . .*'

He joined the other delegates at Hans Place, to find that what had seemed agreement in Dublin was now a matter for heated wrangling. The important point at issue was the exact wording by which de Valera had defined the King's position in the oath he would be willing to accept. The answer was, in effect, the difference between inclusion in the Empire and External Association. Which had the Cabinet agreed upon? It was clear enough which had been intended; British interpretation – and acceptance – might well hinge upon the answer.

There was further argument over whether they had been charged with presenting External Association yet again. Childers was adamant that they had, Collins that they had not. The British were expecting them at five o'clock. Griffith, Collins, and Duggan, faced with offering External Association once more despite all previous rejection by the British, refused to take the document to Downing Street. Those who wanted to break should present it.

Collins would still have argued over the oath. He was not prepared to return to Dublin and ask the people to face renewed war for External Association. The day before, Brugha had made a dig about the British having 'selected their men'. Those whom Brugha favoured could try for results for a change. He was in a towering temper.

Griffith agreed to go in the end, when Barton and Gavan Duffy prepared to go alone. He put up a splendid battle for External Association, again and again trying to force the break on Ulster. But, inevitably, the British rejected the Irish amendments. No Crown and Empire, therefore no settlement. All the Irishmen's anxious deliberations over the oath had, apparently, been for nothing. The British maintained that the fundamentals had, once again, been ignored.

The break came when Gavan Duffy, honestly enough, admitted: 'our difficulty is coming in with the Empire'. The British leapt to their feet. They would expect copies of the Irish proposals next day. These would be rejected, and Craig informed that negotiations were at an end. Then they parted.

Collins's absence from this meeting, in that it suggested schism in the Irish ranks, has been described as disastrous, and the Irish failure to combine as 'lamentable and fatal'.

Would Collins's presence have altered the British view of the proposals? It is doubtful indeed that they would have found them more acceptable had Collins been there than they had on previous occasions when a united Irish front had presented what the British claimed were the same proposals. Nevertheless, his absence had its effect. The Prime Minister, desperately seeking his customary last avenue of escape, was to decide that Collins's absence could only mean that he did not consider the Irish proposals final, and was, therefore, still available for further negotiation.

Lloyd George may well have rejoiced. Collins was the one man capable not merely of seeing no particular disadvantage in coming into the Empire, as Griffith did, but even a possible advantage. It was less than ten days since Collins had placed before the British his memorandum, described by Chamberlain as 'extraordinarily interesting though sometimes perverse and sometimes Utopian', on future Anglo-Irish relations.[14] It remained only to persuade Collins to meet him, alone if possible. From that evening onwards Lloyd George was to be after Collins like a bloodhound, through the medium of Arthur Griffith.

Collins refused to meet the Prime Minister. He felt that he had already argued all the points fully. Yet in the end he gave way. The next day, in a Minute of his part in the morning's proceedings, he wrote: 'This morning Mr Griffith came to me again

[14] 2nd Earl of Birkenhead *F.E.* (London 1959) p. 382

and suggested in his official capacity as Chairman of the Delegation that I should have the meeting with Mr Lloyd George as so
much depended on the Delegation at this vital time.'

The time suggested had been 9.15. Lloyd George was to see
the King at 10.00 and announce the end of the negotiations
before summoning the Cabinet. So much an eleventh-hour matter
was Collins's change of heart, however, that the interview did not
begin until 9.30. Once again Collins was acting like one under
orders. Yet if it was Griffith who 'suggested in his official capacity', it was surely for love of Griffith as a man that Collins
agreed to go to Downing Street that morning. If 'so much depended upon the Delegation' it was surely Griffith's long reliance
on Collins in particular of that delegation that made Collins
respond to the suggestion of the leader who felt he had no right to
command.

Lloyd George made it clear at once that the break, as matters
stood, was on the question of 'within or without' the Empire.
Not the basis, he was evidently confident, on which Collins would
want the negotiations to founder. He was therefore accommodat-
ing, in a vague way, about the oath. He would consider any form
the Irish wished.

Collins proceeded to detail his objections to the British proposals.[15] He was, he said, 'perfectly dissatisfied with the position
as regards the North-East'. Craig should be pressed for a letter
indicating either acceptance of conditions, which he must name,
or rejection. Lloyd George's reply was wily, and apparently re-
assuring. He remarked that Collins himself had pointed out previously that the North would be forced economically to come in.
Thus he implied, by offering Collins his own proposition, that
Ulster's status under the Treaty was immaterial. Sooner or later
she must come under the aegis of the South. Essential unity was
therefore, in the long run, inevitable.

Collins, ready at a pinch to treat the question of allegiance
on a long-term basis, was not, however, going to trifle with the
essential unity which was the key to all possible concessions.
Recent incidents had made the situation so serious that he was
anxious to secure a definite reply from Craig. With Collins's next

[15] Collins's minute of the interview is the basis for these details of what
occurred thereat – Collins Papers

remark comes the whole crux of the interview, one might say of the Treaty: 'I was as agreeable to a reply rejecting as accepting. In view of the former we would save Tyrone and Fermanagh, parts of Derry, Armagh and Down by the boundary commission.'

No one can doubt – or believe that Lloyd George doubted – that Collins was convinced, and was convinced that Lloyd George held the same view, that if the Treaty were signed the proposed Boundary Commission would not merely adjust the boundary line, but transfer to the South whole areas where nationalists predominated.

Collins, by not pressing for an assurance on this interpretation, gave Lloyd George the opportunity to avoid making any clear comment on it. The history of Northern Ireland ever since provides its own judgement on Lloyd George's silence.

A meeting with the Irish delegates was suggested for that afternoon at 2.00. If, Lloyd George said, those vital clauses, Empire and Crown, were accepted, he would be able to hold up any action until, if the delegates wished, the matter had been submitted to Dail Eireann and the country.

Collins was now clearly optimistic that essential unity was within the Irish grasp. The British, it seemed, had decided to back Sinn Fein against Ulster. Lloyd George was undoubtedly also optimistic. He had reopened the door slammed the night before.

The afternoon came. This time it was Barton who had to be persuaded to go with Griffith and Collins to meet the British. At three o'clock the last, bitter fight began.

The Irish, reasonably enough, demanded to know where Craig stood. How else could 'essential unity' be guaranteed? But Chamberlain and Birkenhead had risked their political futures in supporting Sinn Fein at Liverpool. Was it not on this very point that Griffith had promised 'not to let Lloyd George down'? Before anyone could argue that Craig had made no such promise to abide by the British proposals Lloyd George skipped on. There was little advance on trade, finance, or defence. The oath was another matter.

Crown and Empire, so vital to Lloyd George earlier in the day, seemed forgotten. Birkenhead produced a form of oath handed in by Collins that morning. Its author was, in fact,

Crompton Llewelyn Davies, upon whose legal judgement Collins had long relied. It is ironical that it should have been Childers' old friend who reconciled Crown and Constitution at probably the only point where, for a majority of both English and Irishmen, they could be reconciled. Birkenhead, after suggesting some small alterations, gave it his approval. In it the Irish would give their *allegiance* to the Constitution of Ireland, and be *faithful* to the King in virtue of Ireland's common citizenship with Britain and her adherence to and membership of the Commonwealth.

The British withdrew for a time. Left to themselves, the Irishmen appraised the situation. They must get back to Ulster. If an immediate answer on the Treaty was demanded they should break; in the last resort Griffith should require the views of the Commonwealth premiers.

When the British returned, however, Lloyd George was not with them. Churchill gave way a little on defence while they waited. At last Lloyd George entered, an envelope in his hand, a paper half-protruding from it.

It was, indeed, to be back to Ulster, but not on the Irishmen's terms. 'This insignificant scrap of paper', as Sir Geoffrey Shakespeare calls it, was the document 'seen and not objected to' by Arthur Griffith, which set aside essential unity if Ulster so required it, substituting for it a Boundary Commission.

Could Griffith have still broken on Ulster? Pakenham points out that 'there was no definite promise here that Griffith would assent to the terms mentioned *before* Craig had consented or had even replied'.[16]

Perhaps it was, after all, the knowledge that Chamberlain and Birkenhead had wagered their future on his word and now sat gravely and quietly across from him, more than the excited little Welshman whose blue eyes fixed so indignantly upon him, that counted most to Griffith at that moment.

'I have never let a man down in my whole life and I never will', said Griffith. With those courageous words the break on Ulster was lost to him.

Lloyd George, recounting the scene to C. P. Scott next day,

[16] Pakenham *Peace by Ordeal* p. 294

commented that Griffith had seemed a little surprised when the terms of the document were read. We may suppose that he was : where was their context of the British-proposed 'tactical manœuvre' against the Ulster Cabinet? Lloyd George had, he said, then spoken thus to Griffith :

> 'Knowing you to be the man you are, I am sure you communicated it [the document] afterwards to Mr Collins – he therefore is also a party to it. I have fulfilled my part of the bargain. I took the risk of breaking my party. You in Ireland often bring against us in England the charge of breach of faith. Now it is for you to show that Irishmen know how to keep faith.'[17]

Lloyd George had played his leading trump and won. Griffith was on his own now, committed to a pledge as the other delegates were not. It is certain from Collins's reactions that Griffith had never thought it relevant to mention the document to him. Collins had been in Dublin over the weekend when it was presented to Griffith and the manœuvre, though not the document, had, after all, been mentioned to de Valera at the time. Lloyd George played the rest of his hand swiftly. He slapped down the offer of full fiscal autonomy.

It was what Barton had set his heart on, placing the whole trade economy of Ireland in Irish hands. Before Collins's eyes there must have appeared once more the Promised Land in all its potential prosperity, a great tract of its unreclaimed area already cleared. And what pressures might not now be brought

[17] Scott writes: 'The words I have quoted stuck in my mind. I think they are almost exact.' Notably, he also records Lloyd George as saying to Griffith in reference to the document: 'You signed it.' There has never, however, been any evidence to prove whether or not Griffith had, in fact, signed. Lloyd George's whole account, as quoted by Scott, compresses and largely distorts the sequence of events. He omits all reference to the war ultimatum (Scott had repeatedly refused to countenance such a move), and makes the document – *'the terms on which Griffith would be prepared to settle'* – his last card. According to this account Lloyd George had already put the question of signature to the Irishmen individually – Collins had 'hesitated and declined' – before the document was produced and Griffith gave way, not merely on Ulster, but on the whole Treaty. British Museum: Add MS 50906

to bear on whatever would be left of Ulster by the Boundary Commission?

The offer was, of course, conditional. All the other terms of the Treaty must be accepted and signed. Sir James Craig was waiting for their answer. Now, tonight.

Griffith's position was, as we have seen, different from that of his colleagues now. They might still break on Ulster. He could break only on the Empire. This he had undertaken not to do. But that undertaking had been made when the way through Ulster still lay open.

For Griffith the Empire had never mattered; partition, however, mattered more than anything else in the world, excepting his own and Ireland's honour. He bowed to the ultimatum with a dignity which was to make Chamberlain say of him 'a braver man I have never met'.

Now Lloyd George turned to the other delegates. Valiantly Griffith tried to ward his attack from Collins and Barton. They had every right still to demand a reply from Craig. But Lloyd George saw triumph within his grasp. He played his last card: if they did not accept it would be war within three days. All of them were plenipotentiaries. He who refused to sign must bear the responsibility for that war, 'immediate and terrible', upon his country.

Sir Geoffrey Shakespeare has left us an idea of how Lloyd George must have imparted his ultimatum. ' "War" was a terrible word, with at least six r's at the end, and the reverberation of the r's and the fierce look on his face conjured up to his audience the horrors of war.'[18] For Robert Barton at that moment the Prime Minister possessed 'all the solemnity and the power of conviction that he alone of all men I ever met can impart by word and gesture – the vehicles by which one man oppresses and impresses the mind of another'.[19]

Yet did the Irishmen really need Lloyd George's histrionics to 'conjure up the horrors of war'? Failure to sign would mean resumption of a war whose terrors they already knew better than Lloyd George himself.

The Irishmen had till ten o'clock that night to make their

[18] Shakespeare *Let candles be brought in* p. 53
[19] *Dail Debate on the Treaty* p. 49

decision. In Churchill's words, 'Michael Collins rose looking as if he was going to shoot someone, preferably himself. In all my life I have never seen so much passion and suffering in restraint.'[20]

Next day at lunch Lloyd George, describing how for a time Arthur Griffith had stood alone, was to tell C. P. Scott: 'There you see the differences between physical and moral courage.' At dinner on that Monday night, while they awaited the return of the Irish delegates, he spoke in the same vein to Geoffrey Shakespeare of Michael Collins. ' "If only Michael Collins," he said, "has as much moral courage as he has physical courage, we shall get a settlement. But moral courage is a much higher quality than physical courage, and it is a quality that brave men often lack." '[21]

Though Lloyd George did not know it, Collins had already made his decision. We cannot tell how far he was affected by Lloyd George's accusation that by refusing to sign he might become the man who had preferred to see his people face war anew. Certainly, he did not believe that Lloyd George was bluffing. Yet, ultimatum apart, was he not already convinced that the Treaty in its actual terms and its implications offered all that Ireland could gain at that time, and that to refuse now would be to lose, under who knew what bitter and prolonged circumstances, the chance to make those terms the solid foundation of the full national claim? He must surely have thought of Sam's Cross, and asked himself which they would prefer: peace and the practical advantages of the Treaty; or adherence to Republican symbols coupled with further war which, as he of all men best knew, Irish arms unsupported by significant American aid could never win. With such a war would come the certainty of economic ruin that long years of unrest and devastation had already begun.

To sign the Treaty, moreover, would not commit either the Dail or the people of Sam's Cross to acceptance of it. Their choice would still be a free one. Collins was a man accustomed to make decisions. The choice rested, in the first instance, on him at this moment. And surely in choosing he must have been deeply moved by the sight of Arthur Griffith standing alone? As

[20] Winston Churchill *The World Crisis: The Aftermath* (London 1929) p. 306
[21] Shakespeare *Let candles be brought in* p. 89

he drove back to Hans Place with Griffith and Barton he made his decision. He would sign.

The agony of that choice cannot be minimized. He himself was certain that to sign the Treaty was not to abrogate the Republic, merely to further its ultimate recognition. But would those who had pledged their lives and honour no less resolutely to the Republic agree? What would happen to the Army? The future hung black and uncertain. Only the present concerned him now, less than two hours of it, limited by ultimatum.

Barton was overwhelmed by Collins's decision to sign. His reaction witnesses how far he had been excluded from Collins's mind during the past weeks. True, he must have seen Collins's memorandum on future Anglo-Irish relations. There was nothing in it to suggest, however, that Collins was contemplating Dominion status in any guise, or that he held any conviction other than that it might usefully put External Association in a more promising light.

Barton in his turn now stood alone. Duggan would follow his leaders, convinced that no better terms were to be got. Gavan Duffy, like Barton himself, was against signing, but, unlike Barton, he was not convinced that war was the alternative, and was therefore free of the horror of ultimatum.

The scene that ensued at Hans Place was tense and animated, Griffith enthusiastic, Collins more silent and morose.[22] They at any rate believed that unless all signed, war must follow swiftly. Upon Barton, responsibility for that war now lay. Of them all, his was perhaps the cruellest choice. Imprisoned away from Ireland during the bitterest period of the conflict, he had not experienced its horrors, could not judge the people's preparedness to face its renewal. Collins's decision was that of a man who knew the odds better than he. Against this he placed his oath to the Republic. For him at least, to sign the Treaty meant repudiating his word. Nor was he convinced that Britain had offered her final terms.

The intolerable trial of conscience went on for two hours, long past the time by which a decision was demanded. Who could think of reference back to Dublin now? Upon Barton's shoulders alone, it seemed, the future of Ireland was laid. At last he gave

[22] Robert Barton to the author

in, and with him Gavan Duffy. These two, of all, had the right to claim as they did later that they signed under duress. For the others the Treaty carried hope. For Barton and Gavan Duffy it was 'the lesser of two outrages' forced upon them.[23]

At 2.20 on the morning of Tuesday 6 December the Treaty was signed. The two men who had been drawn most closely to each other in putting their hands to the agreement that should bring peace between their countries made significant remarks as they did so. 'I have signed my own death warrant', said Collins to Birkenhead. 'And I may have signed my political death warrant', replied the Lord Chancellor, that man not yet fifty, for whom ambition and a brilliant career had thus far run hand in hand, but for whom neither now weighed in the scales against the conviction that right was being done.

Geoffrey Shakespeare, called in to receive the document for immediate transmission to Sir James Craig, remembers 'the tremendous excitement in the Cabinet Room when everyone seemed to be shaking hands with everyone else'.[24]

The presence in the background of two men should not be forgotten. Erskine Childers had spent the evening in the Inner Lobby at Downing Street in mental torment lest, despite all his selfless work, the Irish Republic might even now be signed away for ever. He had hidden his agony of mind by chatting with Geoffrey Shakespeare about *The Riddle of the Sands*, but there can have been little reflection of the dry and gentle humour of that tale of desperate enterprise in the slight, weary figure who waited, then hurried away to advise yet once again should it be asked of him during those bitter hours at Hans Place.

The other man who waited anxiously in the background was Alfred Cope, a shadowy figure indeed, for Sir Geoffrey Shakespeare cannot recall seeing him, though Sturgis reports that he was 'knocking about in No. 10 all night'. Though much of the credit for bringing Britain and Ireland to conference at all must go to Cope, it is perhaps fitting that even in the background on that last evening he was felt rather than seen. Cope's work was essentially a behind-scenes affair.

The three Irishmen who had signed the Treaty on that night

[23] *Dail Debate on the Treaty* p. 49
[24] Letter from Sir Geoffrey Shakespeare to the author, 14 April 1965

returned in silence. Robert Barton to his bed, Griffith to pace the floor and speak joyfully of the future. How Collins spent what remained of the night is unrevealed, except that he too went to bed at five o'clock, and was up again as usual to Mass three hours later.

'I don't know how things will go now', he wrote to Kitty, 'but with God's help we have brought peace to this land of ours – a peace which will end this old strife of ours for ever.'

Joe McGrath had crossed from Dublin during the night, and read of the settlement in the papers on the way from Euston. Going straight to Cadogan Gardens he found Michael alone at breakfast. 'Well?' Collins growled, 'are you satisfied?' 'It's good enough for me, for a start', said McGrath. 'That's exactly how I feel', said Collins.

One of his first actions was to demand, and secure, the release of all interned Irish prisoners. The Irish people must have proof that the Treaty really meant something.

We cannot leave these final scenes in London without a glance at the man without whose presence there would assuredly have been no Treaty. Lloyd George, over lunch that Tuesday with C. P. Scott, was 'jubilant'. 'To think,' he said, 'that we have succeeded at last in the task we have both worked at for more than thirty years.'

Irishmen who had lived under the Black and Tans and had faced his ultimatum would possibly have questioned the means which he had brought to the accomplishment of that task, and the spirit in which he had spoken of himself in the light of a judge in handling it. It is, unfortunately, the lot of oppressed peoples that they have no effective means of enquiring, 'Who made thee a judge over us?', nor of resisting the means with which the judgement is delivered, particularly if the means be 'immediate and terrible war'.

Undoubtedly Lloyd George deserves his full tribute for resisting strong pressures to discard the ways of peace for the renewed paths of coercion. In assessing his stand we may, however, ponder a remark made by Sir James Barrie. Referring to his regard for both Lloyd George and Michael Collins, he commented: 'I cannot help taking sides against my old friend. To the one I feel it is a game in politics; to the other it is life and death.'

CHAPTER SIXTEEN

The Questioning

I

Among the ancient sagas of Ireland are the 'Three Sorrows of Story-Telling'. They are tales of jealousy and treachery, of strife among former comrades, of battle and grief and death. The chronicler of the events that followed the Anglo-Irish Treaty of 1921 might well name them the Fourth Sorrow of Story-Telling. They have, however, one important difference from the tales of pre-history: in that unhappy period we find no treachery. Tragedy was to lie, not in men's failure to respond to the call of patriotism, but in their differences as to where its interests lay.

External reaction to the news of the Treaty was generally enthusiastic. Ulster's attitude was reported to the British Cabinet by Geoffrey Shakespeare: 'My impression is that Ulster would prefer a Cromwell, but, as one is not forthcoming, they will protest their loyalty and, making a virtue of necessity, accept the Treaty.'[1]

None of the safeguards prepared by de Valera had been destined to stand up to Lloyd George's skill in manipulation. Plenipotentiaries cannot be instructed, unless by a majority decision of the body by whom they are accredited, and the British Prime Minister had reaped to the full the advantage of the Irishmen's powers; powers which, as long as they refused to come within tangible range of agreement, he had ignored.

Nor could the delegates be fairly accused of having signed the same document which they had submitted to the Dail Cabinet. Nevertheless, despite fiscal autonomy and real advances on the oath and defence, Lloyd George's time limit showed that he knew well enough that the retention of the vital Empire clauses would imperil the Treaty's acceptance in Dublin.

There could be further analogy between one of the old Irish

[1] Shakespeare *Let candles be brought in* pp. 91–2

sagas, the First of the Sorrows of Story-Telling, and this twentieth-century episode. In that tale the Sons of Tuireann, having carried out seemingly impossible tasks in fulfilment of a bond, fall victim to a spell of forgetfulness and leave part of their undertaking unaccomplished. It has been suggested that Lloyd George, though he waved no wand, succeeded in so filling the Irishmen's minds with the need to save their country from war that, when they thought of Dublin at all, it was to recall with relief that ultimate freedom of choice still lay with the Dail.

De Valera did not see the text of the agreement until he read it summarized in the papers. Eamonn Duggan, crossing in haste from London, brought him a copy of the Treaty. But de Valera, about to preside at a lecture, had neither the time nor, one can guess, the heart, to glance through the full text of what he had already gleaned in its essentials.

The President cannot but have been puzzled and hurt by the apparent bad faith of the Dail's emissaries. The reactions of Brugha and Stack did nothing to minimize these feelings, and his first impulse was to repudiate the agreement. The quiet voice of Cosgrave and that of the still untried O'Higgins[2] were lifted against the heavier broadsides of those who could now justify their long distrust of Collins by declaring the Republic betrayed. Nevertheless, these moderate voices partially prevailed. The delegates were summoned home by telegram, not as traitors (the word was already in the air), but to discuss the Treaty in full Cabinet so that a decision could be laid before the Dail.

De Valera now declared his own inability to accept the agreement. Hitherto he had held an uncommitted course between the antagonists in his Cabinet. The time had come when he must stand with one or the other. He took up the position his principles dictated.

Collins set out for Dublin on the night of Wednesday 7 December. At Euston, news of the Treaty had brought out cheering crowds; but it was not public reaction in England that he needed to be reassured about.

When the boat berthed early on Thursday morning Tom

[2] At a Cabinet meeting attended by O'Higgins. Terence de Vere White *Kevin O'Higgins* (London 1948) p. 65

Cullen was first across the gangway. Michael seized him by the shoulders: 'Tom, what are our own fellows saying?' 'What is good enough for you is good enough for them', was the stout answer, though he knew as well as Collins that beyond that close little group a different answer was already to be heard.

Thus one of Ireland's plenipotentiaries came home. For Arthur Griffith, the architect of Sinn Fein and of the agreement that was to end seven centuries of strife, the return was as unceremonious. Only three people welcomed him off the boat.

The Cabinet meeting was held the same day. Both Griffith and Collins had returned still believing that, although Brugha and Stack would be bitterly opposed to the settlement, de Valera would share their own view, that while it fell short of the full national demand, there was enough in it to justify its acceptance rather than face renewed war.

This belief that the President, like themselves, thought in terms of degree rather than alternative is, perhaps, the true answer to why they signed without reference to Dublin. Had they, after all, been as worked upon by the mesmeric gifts of Lloyd George as has been suggested? For Barton and Gavan Duffy, certainly, that duress had been real enough. May it not rather be supposed that Griffith and Collins had decided that consultation with Dublin would be not only impracticable, but also unnecessary?

Lloyd George's ultimatum and his evasion of Griffith's specific plea for time to refer the matter to the Dail had left the delegates unable to fulfil precisely their undertaking to refer the Treaty to the Cabinet. Could they have resorted to the telephone? The one Cabinet member to whom in courtesy and by the practice of the negotiations they would have wished to refer was the President, and he was not in Dublin.

To locate him would have been complicated, discussion impractical. Was consultation in these circumstances still called for? External Association had been put once more to the British, and had been finally rejected. Could they justifiably assume that he would insist on breakdown, when the alternatives were that they should sign and recommend what they considered a not unrecommendable agreement or commit the country, unconsulted, to war?

Whatever their actual reasoning, Griffith and Collins certainly approached the Cabinet meeting of 8 December believing that they had acted as de Valera would have wished.[3]

They were quickly disillusioned. De Valera, Brugha, and Stack were unalterably against the Articles of Agreement being recommended to the Dail. Griffith and Collins were in favour, as much on the Treaty's own merits as in honour of their signatures. Barton alone of the three Cabinet delegates admitted to signature under duress and made it clear that he now felt bound to recommend the Treaty.

The Cabinet so far was equally divided. Fate seems to have looked ahead in fastening final responsibility on the unassuming but staunchly resolute shoulders of Cosgrave. He made his decision in favour of both delegates and Treaty.

Collins left the meeting in extreme distress of mind. He had not been prepared for a confrontation in the Dail of divided leaders, or to find himself ranged against de Valera, to whom his loyalty remained unchanged.

He now believed that the Treaty which he had expected de Valera's influence to carry against a vociferous opposition would be thrown out and further conflict in unequal arms with the British ensue. 'Poor Ireland', he said that night to a friend, 'back to the back rooms again'. Yet now the back rooms in which Ireland had put her trust lay bare to the enemy, her leaders unmasked.

Lost in self-doubt, he broke down and wept. If his Chief were against him, who would be for him? The days were beginning in which he must stand at the door of each of his friends, uncertain of them and of himself.

'My own brother will probably stand against me in Cork', he said bitterly on that first tormented day. Johnny's comment when they met for the first time since his release was certainly pithy. It concerned, however, not Michael's patriotism but his moustache, which it must be admitted lent him only an uneasy sheepishness. 'Next time you're shaving, don't overlook that thing

---

[3] Griffith's biographer tells us that on his return to Ireland Griffith 'was expecting objections to it (the Treaty), but he was reckoning on the President's support'. Desmond FitzGerald had to tell him, in the words he had himself heard from Austin Stack, 'He's dead against it now, anyway'. Colum *Arthur Griffith* p. 309

as well', was his elder brother's withering advice. Michael duly appeared at breakfast next morning clean-shaven.

Michael was, indeed, to enjoy one blessing that was denied to many. His family remained united in his support. Utterly dependent on the things of home, this was probably his greatest single consolation in the dark days ahead, when brothers up and down the land turned and went their separate ways.

The Irish people had greeted the terms of the Treaty with overwhelming relief, a reaction subsequently strengthened by the national Press. Stack for one was to complain that the newspapers gave the Treaty's supporters an advantage with which its opponents never caught up.

There was more than Press persuasion in it, of course. The evening before the Treaty was signed rumours of a breakdown had brought ugly shadows to the Dublin streets, as Auxiliaries re-emerged, revolver in hand, while men, formerly on the run, heard whispered warnings not to sleep in their own beds that night. Now the Auxiliaries would be going, and with them the British garrisons and the hated Castle administration, from Chief Secretary to interrogator's tout. The Crown was to remain : the Crown forces would not; and even the Crown's representative would sit in the Viceregal Lodge only because Irishmen had picked him for the job.

Perhaps the Treaty had been the result as much as the cause of the national attitude. Crane Brinton writes :

> 'It would seem to be an observable fact of human behaviour that large numbers of men can stand only so much interference with the routines and rituals of their daily existence. . . . Most men cannot long stand the strain of prolonged effort to live in accordance with very high ideals. . . . Thermidor comes as naturally to societies in revolution as an ebbing tide, as calm after a storm.'[4]

Nor can it be denied that many of the Irish people were indifferent to the Republic. They had wanted freedom, and had followed those who led towards it, without worrying unduly as to the form it should take. Also they were tired of war. They saw no reason why what had been a good fighting emblem should

[4] Crane Brinton *The Anatomy of Revolution* p. 224

be adhered to once it threatened instead to thwart the achievement of a reasonable peace. Relief that a decision had at last been taken was of no less importance. Griffith, for so long a national figure, provided a sound reassurance that what the Treaty said it meant. Above all, Michael Collins had accepted it. Even those who looked on him merely as the hero who had emerged from the long weeks of the legend-filled Truce were convinced that here was one fighting man whose aim was peace.

The Roman Catholic Church's support for the Treaty was another major factor in its acceptance by the people; and for the Southern Protestants, Arthur Griffith's promise, given early in the negotiations, that any settlement would not submerge their interests in those of Sinn Fein sufficed the majority of them. In settling down under the Treaty, which levelled their Ascendancy status for ever, many of them were to give active and often sacrificial service in helping to realize its promises.

Another small but significant group in the country, although separatist by conviction, was prepared, if reluctantly, to accept Collins's view of the Treaty as a stepping-stone to the fulfilment of the Republican demand.

Many separatists, however, were convinced that by accepting the Treaty all hope of gaining the full measure of Irish aspirations would be forfeit. Their argument was not that the Treaty gave Ireland so little, but that it gave so much. They realized too well that once the people settled down under it the whole impetus of national resurgence would be dissipated.

There was another group, and a potent one, for whom the terms of the Treaty were immaterial. Good or bad, they saw it as a dead letter on account of the oath. They had taken an oath to the Republic : the Treaty oath was not to the Republic. 'The scheme of things which the revolutionist believes in becomes sacred to him through the struggle to attain it.'[5] For these, if war was the only alternative to the Republic, they must face it, and those who sought to put that war from them were traitors.

Although the cleavage of the nation found the Treaty as its proximate cause we may, at this distance, see it less as an avoidable tragedy than as an inevitable after-effect of revolution. When

[5] Edwards *The Natural History of Revolution* p. 213

the pressures that mould widely divergent groups into a resistant whole are removed, they quickly revert to their normal courses.

Two groups whose attitude in the coming time would be vital were the Army and the I.R.B. A meeting of the Supreme Council of the I.R.B. was held on 10 December, when it was decided that the Treaty should be supported by the members of the Brotherhood, although those who were also Dail representatives were given freedom of action. It reveals how deeply the Treaty question went that many I.R.B. men could not in conscience follow the course laid down by their leaders.[6]

In the prevailing unrest in Ireland, the politicians' ability to control the Army was of the first magnitude. Ireland's crucial problem was that until now her method of advancing her political aims had been the physical force provided by her Army. The constitutional method of discussion among her elected representatives had been finally thrown over by the British in 1919 when the Dail was suppressed. The Army had thereafter, in fact if not in theory, been made not only the instrument but also to a large extent the arbiter of law and order. The Truce had brought back political affairs into constitutional and deliberative channels. That the resulting decisions should be deemed to be no concern of the Army was unthinkable. Both Dail and Army claimed the 1916 leaders as their own. It would be hard indeed for the politicians to deny the Army's interest in whether the Dail, in accepting or rejecting the Treaty, was upholding the principles enunciated in 1916.

Had the political leaders remained united, at least in abiding by the majority vote in the Dail, and quickly thereafter by that of the electorate, the problem of the Army would never have had the climate in which to develop. The lawlessness of the Truce period would also have been quickly suppressed. Calamitously, not only the signing of the Treaty, but the circumstances of that signing, were to raise questions of principle which would, as Brugha had foretold, in dividing the leaders, split the country from top to bottom, making the control of the Army by either side impossible, and aggravating the breakdown of law and order.

Both Collins and de Valera fully realized the Army's impor-

---

[6] See O'Donoghue *No Other Law* pp. 186 ff. for a detailed examination of the I.R.B. and the Treaty from the anti-Treaty view

tance. Collins, to whom the Army meant more than any other body, looked with foreboding upon the elements which had attached themselves to it since the Truce. For this reason, he told a friend, the Truce had been a mistake. Had the Treaty been signed under the war conditions of five months before by delegates negotiating under safe conduct, men who were now bellicose would have been down on their knees in thankfulness. 'The worst of it is', he added sombrely, 'so many feel they have arrears to make up.'

I I

The Dail debate on the Treaty began on 14 December.

Collins's manner was, as usual, striking. 'Michael Collins rose to his feet. In repose his eyes glimmer softly and with humour. When aroused they narrow – hard, intense and relentless. He speaks like this. One or two words. Then he pauses to think. His speech does not flow like a stream as it does in the case of Eamon de Valera. Yet not from one word is firmness absent.'[7]

The debate reveals Collins the man in the cloak of Collins the public figure. Throughout the long days of talk he would never wear it with complete assurance. When he spoke it was in 'a voice vibrant with the intensity of his feelings'. All those about him were his friends or, on a level personal rather than political, his enemies.

This sense of personal involvement had a real enough basis. He knew too well that the whole Treaty issue might be decided by the regard felt for himself by those who would vote on it. The unreasonableness of his position, which might make Ireland's future dependent on a hasty word of his own, weighed him down. Friendship itself seemed mortgaged to the Treaty, and the thought sickened him.

The proceedings of the next few days were not calculated to enlighten the public on how far the Treaty carried out the aims

[7] Padraig de Burca and John F. Boyle *Free State or Republic?* (Dublin 1922) p. 3. The author has used this invaluable eye-witness account of the public debates on the Treaty freely, as a corollary to the official Report on the Debates

of the Ministry. The rank and file of the Dail deputies them-selves had been of necessity left in the dark as to the course of the negotiations. It was finally agreed at the opening meeting that the Dail should go temporarily into private session (Collins was against this) to discuss questions on such conventionally reserved matters as the financial and military situation, and should reassemble thereafter in public to debate the motion of ratification of the Treaty.

It was at these private sessions that de Valera first brought forward what was to become known as Document No. 2, his proposals for an alternative to the Treaty. Though it was destined to remain an academic argument insofar as it never became an actual contender with the Treaty for ratification, its repercussions on the course of the Treaty issue were profound.

The proposals it contained were, broadly, those of the signed Articles of Agreement with the exception of the status clauses and that containing the oath. These were replaced by External Association. In putting forward Document No. 2 de Valera was undoubtedly making a sincere attempt, if a desperate one, to repeat what he had done in 1917 and prevent what seemed an inevitable split in the national movement. No one in the fore-front of that movement saw the Treaty as an ideal settlement. Therefore, to wreck national unity for it seemed an outcome to be avoided at all costs by substituting for its unacceptable proposals others which all could agree on.

De Valera, committed to the Irish Republic, though not to isolationism, stood by the ideals of those who would never settle down to the peaceful pursuit of Ireland's destiny while these remained unsatisfied, and was convinced that the proposals in his document reconciled their aspirations with the necessity of finding a *modus vivendi* with Britain.

De Valera, moreover, recognized the highly personal nature of Irish politics. Some, who failed in embittered days to recognize his high-mindedness, were to accuse him of having sent Collins to London with the intention of breaking him on the unachiev-able rock of the Republic. There is no need for us to look further than the explosive situation in a country where its leaders' per-sonalities have always commanded a far higher allegiance than political considerations. Any split that left de Valera and Collins ranged on opposing sides could only lead to a disastrous collision of loyalties throughout the country.

In bringing forward Document No. 2, therefore, de Valera was attempting not only to provide a policy unifying in itself but also to get back to the pre-Treaty position in which Collins had stood at his right hand as the stalwart but subordinate link between the military and political wings of Sinn Fein.

Document No. 2 was presented with a blind disregard of essentials which, from the outset, made judgement of it on its own merits extraneous to the very issues it was designed to solve.

Griffith, Collins, and Duggan had been convinced that neither renewed war – which they were offered – nor continued negotiation – which they were not offered – would bring them one iota nearer the realization of their full demands. Had they believed that the British might accept such terms as those of Document No. 2 in preference to those of the Treaty, they would not have agreed to the latter. They did not believe it. They knew that if the entire Irish nation marched with Document No. 2 to Downing Street, the British leaders would still refuse to consider it. The unity shown by Ireland was as nothing to the unity shown by the Empire.

It is also, surely, curious that de Valera, whose objections to the agreement signed by the British were partly based on his conviction that they would not honour it in a spirit to concede Ireland any advantage implicit in its terms, was nevertheless prepared to trust them to implement those of a document which they had not signed.

Document No. 2 was not, in fact, an alternative to the Treaty. It was a possible, but by no means certain, alternative to national disunity. The alternative to the Treaty was renewed war with Britain.

As far as Collins was concerned the Treaty bore his signature, and carried not only his word that he would recommend it, but his conviction that it was worth recommending. It was not what he wanted, but it was what he had been able to get, and against it proposals that were preferable but unobtainable had no meaning for him.

His letters to Kitty during the days of the private sessions reflect his anxieties. He was extremely doubtful that the Treaty would be approved. On 15 December he wrote: 'In a few days I may be free from everything and then we can see how the future goes. It's all a dreadful strain and it's telling a good deal on me.'

The closed sessions ended late on Saturday night 17 December, by which time Michael was 'very worn out indeed'. Since mid-September he had been shouldering inimical political issues; a political novice against brilliant men well-versed in statecraft; carrying on his own work, making decisions, undergoing pro-found emotional crises, and now defending himself to his friends.

The attitude of his friends mattered most. In America, initial praise for the Treaty had been followed by reaction against it among de Valera's followers when his rejection of it was made known. Foremost among them was Harry Boland. For Collins, inevitably, it was not only the Treaty Boland opposed, but himself.

On 18 December he wrote to Kitty: 'All this business is very very sad – Harry has come out strongly against us – I'm sorry for that, but I suppose that like many another episode in this business must be borne also. I haven't an idea of how it will all end but with God's help all right. In any event I shall be satis-fied.'

The British debate on the Treaty had started on the same day as the opening meeting of the Dail. Though Westminster accepted the Treaty, within the year it was to reject the men who had made it. Of all the issues of the time, that of the Irish Treaty drove the wedge finally through the Conservative Party and brought down the Coalition. 'It will not be a bad sort of finish', Birkenhead had said. Though he was to rise again to high political office there can be little doubt that his pledge of trust in Ireland's future as a responsible, self-governing nation was the chief stroke that cut short the most brilliant passage in a great and useful life, of which less than a decade then remained to him.

On Monday 19 December Dail Eireann reassembled in public session.

The proceedings began with an unexpected storm. De Valera wished Document No. 2 to be withdrawn. It had been put for-ward in a bid for unity. The attempt had failed, and he therefore wished its discussion at the private session to be treated as con-

fidential. Griffith and Collins took the view that the Irish people
were entitled to know that the alternative which those who
opposed the Treaty were offering was not the Republic.

Despite de Valera's request, Document No. 2 was to appear
again at intervals throughout the debate. Movingly, when de
Valera himself turned, with a despairing hope, to the vision he
had put from him of what he saw, not as 'a politicians' peace', but
real peace. Comically, when Kevin O'Higgins allowed it to pop
up like a player who habitually forgets that his part has been
cut out and has to be bundled unceremoniously off the stage.

It was after lunch when Michael Collins rose to speak. One
of his associates has commented that, when speaking in public,
Collins was capable of an impressive dignity of voice and manner.
John F. Boyle describes him as he spoke that day:

> 'He spoke passionately, eagerly, pervadingly. He had his
> manuscript before him. He rarely consulted it. He preferred
> to rely on his intuition – on the unfailing native power of the
> Irishman to move, rouse and convince his hearers.
>
> 'Now and again he felt his smooth chin. He tossed his thick
> black hair with his hands. He rummaged among his docu-
> ments. Like Mr de Valera, he stands now upright, now bent,
> now calm, and now quivering with emotion.
>
> 'On a previous occasion I said Michael Collins spoke slowly.
> He does – until he is aroused. Then the words come in a cease-
> less stream. . . . From beginning to end of his speech no
> responsibility was shirked. "I speak plainly", he said. He did.'[8]

He was quick to point out that he was not recommending the
Treaty for more than it was. In his opinion it gave freedom – in
the words of the draft which 'he rarely consulted' – 'Not the
ultimate freedom that all nations hope for and struggle for, but
freedom to achieve that end. . . . They [the British] have made
a greater concession than we. They have given up entirely their
age-long attempt to dominate us. They have admitted us as
friends in the nations of their community. We have to accept
or reject that friendship. They have given us the only recognition
we have ever secured as a nation.'[9]

[8] de Burca and Boyle *Free State or Republic?* pp. 13–14
[9] Collins Papers

Collins's words had a practical urgency: 'Do we think at all of what it means to look forward to the directing of the organization of the nation. . . ? Are we never going to stand on our own feet?'

Each point was made with assured firmness. In no uncertain terms he stood by his signature.

Hitherto there had been, amazingly, no mention of North-East Ulster. Collins did not evade it. Though the arrangement under the Treaty was not an ideal one, he said, it did make an effort to deal with the problem on lines of goodwill, and if their policy was, indeed, one of non-coercion, let somebody else get a better way out of it.

Humour was not lacking. A deputy had suggested that what could safely apply to Canada could not apply to Ireland: 'It seemed to me that he did not regard the delegation as being wholly without responsibility for the geographical propinquity of Ireland to Great Britain.'

There was, of course, much more. Most telling, perhaps, his point that their Gaelic civilization had been worn down less by British armed strength than by the peaceful encroachment of centuries. Griffith must have rejoiced that this young man in whom he had placed all his confidence had not overlooked his teaching. The Volunteers, such as Sean MacEoin, must also have responded to the assertion that once British armed force withdrew, Irish national liberties would be able to establish themselves.

In Collins these two great movements, political philosophy and physical force, came together. What de Valera had once united in a formula, Collins now united in his personal undertaking for action.

The speech of Erskine Childers which followed that of Collins makes depressing reading, for it carries all the weight of foreboding and none of the leaven of hope. Its opening, a spontaneous and generous tribute to Collins, is, indeed, one of the most heartening things about it. For all their differences, which led inevitably to where all words of mere comradeship had to cease, neither ever lost his respect for the other. Mrs Davies has written: '[Collins] recognized to the end of his life the courage, sincerity, willingness for self-sacrifice and, indeed, the noble-mindedness of Erskine Childers.' On this afternoon, however, Collins's feelings must have been more akin to despair, for he recognized what he had once highly esteemed, the ability of Childers to use the utmost of propagandist value in any argument in which he believed.

In the tail of the day Robert Barton got to his feet. His was a short speech, but a moving one. He was at pains to admit that he had, in his own eyes, broken his oath to the Republic – to him the most sacred bond on earth. Though the word 'duress' does not occur in his speech, it is inherent in every sentence of it. There was a price too high to pay for one's principles, he said in effect, the committal of one's fellow-man, unconsulted, to war. Having, on these terms, moved acceptance of the Treaty, he sat down and Collins quickly moved the adjournment.

The two met, as Barton remembers it, for the last time later that evening. They had all, said Collins, signed under the duress of their own conscience.

Collins wrote to Kitty next day:

> 'Yesterday was the worst day I ever spent in my life but thanks be to God it's over. The Treaty will almost certainly be beaten and then no one knows what will happen. The country is certainly quite clearly for it but that seems to be little good, as their voices are not heard. . . .'

Three more days of debate followed before the Dail adjourned for Christmas, the vote not yet taken. 'It is not hard to know how all my thoughts are fully occupied in this momentous hour', Collins wrote to Kitty, and, again, 'yesterday the day came so strenuous. . . .'

Not all, to his relief, measured the Treaty by their regard for Michael Collins. The day before the adjournment Mrs Clarke spoke quietly but resolutely against the agreement. Afterwards she sought out Collins to explain her belief that Tom Clarke himself could never have voted for it. 'I wouldn't want you to vote for it', was his earnest answer. 'All I ask is that, if it's passed, you give us the chance to work it.' It was his whole plea to those, friend and foe alike, who were divided from him on the issue.

His appearance in the lobbies rather than in the debating chamber chiefly struck his colleagues. 'Deadly serious, and the fun gone out of him', one of them describes him. Another noted a statesmanlike thoughtfulness unnoticed in the days before he went to London. For the first time, perhaps, he was weighed down by the thought that much of the youth of the country, the effective generation, was no longer solidly behind him. Desmond Ryan writes of seeing him 'with a weary and defiant face'.[10]

Michael spent Christmas at Sam's Cross. Whatever his doubts and anxieties, Sam's Cross, even with Woodfield gone, was able to dispel them for these few days. Here, at least, he need not doubt his welcome, as he sat in neighbours' farmhouses or reminisced in his cousin Jerry's Five Alls or in the small pub at the Pike near where he had first gone to school and listened in old James Santry's forge to tales of the Fenians. He needed little persuasion to render *Kelly and Burke and Shea* – or his version of it :

> Then here's to the Pike and Sam's Cross and the like
> Said Kelly and Burke and Shea!

he would declaim triumphantly, the crash of his fist on the table clattering the mugs of Clonakilty Wrastler.

Nor was it all talk of the past. 'There can be no standing alone for Ireland in the new world coming', he told Johnny. Aeroplanes, the new methods of communication, would open up what had hitherto been merely national affairs to a universal perspective, a perspective that must be accepted if nations were not to go under in a dangerous and obsolete isolationism.

They climbed together on Christmas morning to a nearby hilltop, *Carraig-a' radhairc*, the Rock of the View. When Johnny suggested it was time they went down to visit neighbours, Michael hung back, looking out across the fields and villages of South and West Cork to the sea. 'I've seen more of my own country this morning than I've ever seen in my whole life', he said quietly.

He returned to Dublin, his strength, like that of Antaeus, renewed by contact with his native earth. The Dail was to reassemble on 3 January. Collins, who had ever eschewed talk in favour of action, may well have pondered that phrase in his well-read copy of Walt Whitman, 'the never-ending audacity of elected persons'.

[10] Ryan *Remembering Sion* p. 279

He was still far from sanguine as to the outcome of the debate. His worry vented itself in unhappy outbursts, in which tears and violent language predominated, to the offence of some and the awkwardly-shown sympathy of others. That he knew he was being difficult only made matters worse.

The debate entered its last days. As the gulf widened, so too, in poignant fashion, did the deputies' desire to close it become evident. Collins now put forward his own solution for unity. It was what he had already begged privately of Mrs Clarke. Waving aside all cries of 'Order!' he leapt to his feet. They could not be weaker if they accepted the Treaty; if they rejected it England would be released from her bargain. If its opponents, who stood against it on principle, would only allow it to go through, without a division, would let the Provisional Government come into being, they could work out the Republican question afterwards.

But de Valera would have no part in assuming the rôle of a constitutional Opposition before the Treaty had been put to the vote and approved. Like Document No. 2, this attempt at unity was doomed, and lost in further speech-making. Faced with the now inescapable certainty that approval of the Treaty would sound the deathknell of the old unity, who can say that Michael, in his heart if not in his head, was not hoping that his fears that it would be thrown out might be justified?

'I would rather see it thrown out than passed by a very narrow majority', he told one friend. His sister Katie was in a Dublin hospital, and he went to see her. 'I have strained every nerve to get support for the Treaty', he told her, 'but I'm hoping now we'll be defeated at the division.' When she asked him in distressed surprise why this was so, he muttered: 'Either way there's going to be trouble.'

He must have been reflecting that a fight against the British with all advantage gone would be preferable to a fight against his own countrymen, for he added: 'If we're defeated I'll go down to Cork and join up as a private Volunteer.'

The end was reached at last. There had been many personal attacks on Collins. Quietly, Arthur Griffith made his affirmation of loyalty: 'Though I have not now, and never had, an ambition about either political affairs or history, if my name is to go down in history I want it associated with the name of Michael Collins.'[11]

'Arthur Griffith is Ireland', Collins had said of him once, in boyhood. Neither now had need to be ashamed of the other's epitaph on himself.

Griffith spoke without pretence. The Treaty was not an ideal thing; it could be better. But it had no more finality than they were the final generation on the face of the earth.

The time had come for the vote to be taken. De Valera made a last, desperate appeal: the Irish nation would judge what they had brought by the Treaty. For a moment he seemed to draw them back a hundred and twenty years to that other Irish Parliament which, in a building not far across the city whose people now gathered anxiously to hear their fate decided, had, in a vote like this, yoked their country to the Act of Union.

But it was not the voice of Grattan or Flood that rang through the chamber now in protest against such acceptance, but that of Michael Collins, strong and confident in the cause to which he had pledged himself: 'Let the Irish nation judge us now and for future years.'

The vote was taken. Sixty-four in support of the Treaty; fifty-seven against. As if, his work done, he had already handed on the torch to a younger generation impatient to hasten ahead, Arthur Griffith said no word. It was Collins who sprang up, assuring them that there was no kind of triumph in this result, begging for a joint committee, for unity in carrying the nation forward over the difficult transition from war to peace that came to all countries. Hand outstretched, he restated all his old love for de Valera, still his President. But de Valera, though he was plainly moved, had no time to respond. Mary MacSwiney, Terence MacSwiney's sister, was up and rallying any who would weaken to the cause of the true Republic.

Outside the news had been carried to the waiting crowds. Wave upon wave of cheering drowned any opposing cries while, inside the chamber, President de Valera had broken down and was weeping for the unity that was gone, while men and women in every part of the room wept with him.

[11] *Dail Debate on the Treaty* p. 335

CHAPTER SEVENTEEN

Provisional Government

(January – March 1922)

I

The bizarre dichotomy of government that was to ensue in Ireland was quickly seen when de Valera, having resigned as President of the Dail, stood for re-election as President of the Republic, on the clear understanding that, if successful, his executive would be drawn entirely from the minority, anti-Treaty party. The pro-Treaty majority might arrange their Provisional Government for which it provided as they wished. For its opponents such a government, while its work would not be obstructed, could only be seen as taking the place of the usurping Castle Executive.

One can hardly avoid sharing W. T. Cosgrave's bewilderment that constitutional practice should thus be interpreted as government of the majority by the minority.

Collins left no one in any doubt of his views. While his personal regard for de Valera was unchanged, such an impossible outcome, he said, would not be fair to de Valera himself. It was for the people, not the Dail, to elect a President of the Republic.

De Valera was defeated by two votes. One more step had been taken which marked what sober men could see was the inevitable forking of the road along which the nation had so far marched.

Michael wrote to Kitty that night : 'If you knew how the other side is "killing" me – God help me – we had to be at them again to-day. . . .' Next day he was 'running back to the University for more talk – talk – talk'. Yet after all there was not to be so very much more of it.

Collins proposed that Arthur Griffith be elected President of Dail Eireann. Soberly he warned of the difficulties facing all young governments. He believed that whether they liked it or not the world was entering a different era, and that there were better ways of adjusting difficulties between nations than by killing each other.

275

Once again he made his point that he was not asking the other side to commit themselves to what they could not approve. He concluded: 'I appeal to them for the sake of Ireland to let this motion go through, and give Ireland a chance.'

But the rift had gone too far. Before the vote was taken that made Arthur Griffith President of Dail Eireann, de Valera rose in protest and left the chamber. His supporters followed him, Robert Barton among them. The angry exchanges that marked their departure are significant only in that they reveal once again the horror with which both sides contemplated disunion.

'Every fool knoweth', said Sir Walter Raleigh, 'that hatreds are the cinders of affection.'

'The whole business was awful', wrote Michael to Kitty next day. '. . . Wishing to God I could be with you and had left it all. The tactics of the opposition were not very creditable at times but a great many things are allowable in positions like this.'

As important as the position taken up by the politicians was that of the Army. Cathal Brugha's last statement as Minister of Defence had been an explicit assurance that order would be maintained in the Army. Richard Mulcahy, the new Minister of Defence, was also at pains to make clear that the Army would remain the Army of the Republic.

Had the politicians succeeded in uniting, the dangerous split that was already threatening the Army would have been held in check. In the event, however, it was the Army which defeated the politicians' attempts to solve the country's predicament; not for lack of desire by the military leaders themselves to maintain unity in the Army, but because some of them attempted to do so by renouncing all civil control.

Collins, unlike some Volunteer deputies, saw with the eyes not only of a soldier but also of one with a firm grasp of political realities. He turned to practical means of reassuring the Army over the Treaty. He enquired whether the oath of allegiance must be taken by the Army or, if so, whether it might be administered in some mitigated form. He harassed the British authorities over the release not only of Irish internees but also of convicted prisoners – 'Don't forget Dowling!' runs a weary footnote to one of Cope's letters to the Colonial Office.[1]

[1] Public Record Office: CO 739/14

Collins announced his determination to see that the Constitution provided for in the Treaty would be one that had nothing in it inimical to the Republic. A strange undertaking, perhaps, but this was a Collins ready for any compromise to ensure unity, who had not yet embarked on the series of visits to London which were to face him afresh each time with British insistence that, in putting the Treaty into operation, nothing must be capable of equivocation.

De Valera's influence rather than opposition to Collins accounted for much of the anti-Treaty feeling, though all too often it was personal animosity, providing far too tempting an opportunity for those with old scores to pay off. Michael, whose clinging to old loyalties was to cause considerable unease among his less intense colleagues, faced his critics in misery and rage. Hearing some gossip about himself he flung his hat furiously across the room shouting, 'Anyone can talk of Michael Collins!' Another time he heard quietly that an erstwhile friend was slandering him. 'But it isn't the label they attach to me', he said. 'It is the label I attach to myself that makes me what I am.'

The Provisional Government was set up on 14 January 1922. It was clear that a distinction must be maintained between the two governments, that of Dail Eireann established in the name of the Republic, and the Provisional Government of the Irish Free State, set up under the Treaty to run until 6 December 1922 unless the people should reject it at the polls. Griffith therefore remained President of Dail Eireann and Collins became Chairman of the Provisional Government. While there were certain overlappings in the membership of the two Cabinets, it was significant that Mulcahy, Minister of Defence in the Dail, was not a member of the Provisional Government.

Two days later the Head of the Provisional Government took over Dublin Castle from the British Executive. His uncharacteristic lateness for the appointment arose neither from a desire to register 'a mark of disrespect' (Macready) nor, as the more romantic mind of Tim Healy would have it, because in magnanimous oblivion of seven centuries of British rule he had forgotten all about it. The complications of settling a railway strike and getting back from Granard where he had spent the weekend were the mundane reasons for his somewhat tardy arrival. It was a day of penetrating cold and, having fortified himself for the chilly grandeur of the occasion with hot tea at Mullingar station, he drove to the Castle without ceremony.

Sir Henry Robinson records fairly if stoically that there was nothing of the 'top-dog' about Collins as he met the civil servants about to come under his authority, and dispelled any reluctance on their part to shake hands 'stained with outrage and crime' as he 'grasped their hands with his iron grip and shook them warmly with the greatest bonhomie'.[2]

But if he received the reins of government soberly enough from Lord FitzAlan, the last Viceroy, his natural glee bubbled out once the solemnities were over. 'The Castle has fallen!' he announced to Griffith.

If ever men were entitled to a sense of achievement it was these two. The men of 1916 had roused the country from its sleep. The men and women who made the struggle in the years that followed had brought the British to acknowledge their nationhood; but it was the men who signed and accepted the Treaty, the only point at which right and power could then meet on terms at all approaching equality, who could claim to have shown the British Government and its armies out of Ireland.

Professor Crane Brinton has assessed the problems which generally faced what he terms 'the moderates' in taking over power from the old régime, ousted after revolutionary struggle:

'They were faced with the difficult task of reforming existing institutions, or making a new constitution, and taking care at the same time of the ordinary work of governing. . . . They found against them an increasingly strong and intransigent group of radicals and extremists who insisted that the moderates were trying to stop the revolution, that they had betrayed it, that they were as bad as the rulers of the old régime – indeed, much worse, since they were traitors as well as fools and scoundrels.'[3]

Revolutionary leaders who win power have the advantage that they are proven men of action, the disadvantage that they have

[2] Sir Henry Robinson *Memories Wise and Otherwise* (London 1923) pp. 325–6
[3] Brinton *The Anatomy of Revolution* p. 135

to contend with 'foreign invasion, domestic insurrection, and their own inexperience in government'.[4] With British troops in Ireland already preparing to depart, the threat of foreign invasion might seem to be giving place to an actual foreign evacuation. It was not least evident to those who aimed to defeat the Treaty position, however, that any failure to uphold it to Britain's satisfaction would bring the exodus to an abrupt halt. Britain would then be seen to re-occupy the position of aggressor, and Republican Ireland reunited in defiance of the common enemy.

To a peculiar degree, therefore, the Provisional Government was to be faced with maintaining a firm stand against domestic insurrectionists – to convince the British that the Treaty was home and dry – while no action could safely be taken against them that would swing public sympathy towards them as the victims of an Anglo-Irish junta. Moreover, the departure of the British, vital in reassuring the people of the reality of independence under the Treaty, meant that the Provisional Government would be left in a weak position militarily.

It was hardly to be wondered at, therefore, that Collins, upon whom this dilemma was chiefly to devolve, was forced by degrees into the well-nigh impossible position of having to accommodate the opponents of the Treaty, both political and military, to whom no terms conditional upon it were acceptable, while at the same time satisfying the British Government that in seeking to maintain unity at home he was in no wise betraying the Treaty. Add to this the festering and explosive situation in the North-East and his own over-intense sense of loyalty coupled with a seemingly paradoxical habit of independent action – arising, in fact, from the widely inimical nature of those loyalties – and it will be seen how full of pitfalls was the path upon which Collins was now so resolutely embarked.

The first offices of the Provisional Government were in the City Hall, Dublin. In times past Michael's desk had carried a black velvet cat to whose jauntily-defiant tail he had tied a tricolour bow. On his mantelpiece he now placed a bronze plaque of Theodore Roosevelt, inscribed with his well-known refutation of 'the doctrine of ignoble ease'.

Collins was the head of the first central government in Ireland

[4] Edwards *The Natural History of Revolution* p. 156

that could be fairly termed an Irish Government with international recognition. He did not assume that burden lightly.

The third disadvantage which faces revolutionists become administrators, 'inexperience in government', was modified in the case of the Provisional Government. They had three years of work in the Dail behind them, hampered and limited as its functions had been. In all its major departments, moreover, it now inherited the machinery, and much of the personnel, hitherto controlled by the British. Nevertheless, the accumulated evils of generations of British rule now became apparent. While the lower echelons of the Irish Civil Service had always been filled by well-trained Irishmen and women, the higher positions had almost invariably been English appointments.

Inevitably, Collins became the target for every place-seeker in Ireland. While he disliked importunacy, his criterion was always 'the best man for the job', and it brought him a great deal of criticism. Men who had worked for years for the nationalist cause, often at great personal risk, discovered to their indignation that Collins was equally ready to appoint or promote any man, irrespective of his former attitude, whom he believed to be the most able and whose loyalty he was prepared to take on trust.

Collins, who knew well enough the criticism levelled at him was to write : 'The difficulty, as in everything else, is in getting suitable men. There are undoubtedly many good men, but if a man is appointed for his ability there is immediately a howl that he is not a Nationalist.'[5]

The liberality of outlook which characterized all his dealings undoubtedly smoothed the way enormously for the transfer of power from the British Executive to the Provisional Government. The aspects of administration with which he was concerned were innumerable, ranging from the settlement of an epidemic of industrial disputes to a problem of considerable importance, the re-establishment of an effective police force.

To paralyse the Provisional Government's effective authority was clearly the quickest way to undermine the Treaty. Much of the anti-Treaty section of the Army's opposition to the recruit-

[5] National Library of Ireland: Dr F. S. Bourke Papers. Letter to Tom Donovan dated 1 August 1922

ment of a police force arose nevertheless from a natural enough feeling of indignation that the Army, which had fulfilled police functions honourably and well in the past should no longer be trusted to do so. The return to a stable civil order was indeed to be a long and difficult one.

At such a time Collins might have been forgiven for pushing aside any additional demands. Yet he responded whole-heartedly when, while he was actually forming the Provisional Government, Lady Gregory wrote to him about the controversial bequest by her nephew, Sir Hugh Lane, of pictures to Ireland instead of England in a disputed codicil to his will. On 14 January 1922 she wrote:

'Dear Mr Collins

I would not ask for a few minutes of your time just now to read this but that the Lane picture matter, if not carried through among the Treaty details, may never be settled in our favour – and that Sir John Lavery says you are the man whose request will carry most weight with the London Government. I have been keeping up the fight for them ever since 1915 and got so far when Mr Ian MacPherson was Chief Secretary that he drew up a Bill to legalise Hugh Lane's codicil, and brought it more than once before the Cabinet – where it had been adopted – but for the violence of Lord Curzon – who as a Trustee of the National Gallery is bent on keeping the pictures.

If the Govt. would undertake to carry through that Bill in Parliament it would be the most satisfactory course & simplest, the codicil expressing Hugh Lane's wishes very clearly —

I had already, 2 months ago, sent a statement to the Dail Cabinet, & it was given to the then Minister of Fine Arts with a promise it would be attended to in the Peace terms. But I agree with Lavery that you can best do what he has failed in doing through nearly 7 years.

Yours sincerely (is le meas mise)
A. Gregory.'[6]

Collins replied on 23 January 1922:

[6] Brother Allen's Papers

'With reference to your letter of January 14th, regarding the Hugh Lane Pictures, I would like you to know that I raised this question in London yesterday.

'Some of the advisers of the British Government seem to think that legislation would be necessary before these pictures can be removed, but the opinion was divided. I found, however, that the attitude towards the return was not unsympathetic, and I am raising the matter again after further enquiries have been made. I most sincerely hope that we shall be successful in securing their return.'[7]

A Committee under Collins's chairmanship was formed to draw up a draft Constitution for the Irish Free State. Collins's own part in the Committee's proceedings was by no means a nominal one, as was widely supposed. He realized that the Constitution might be the last chance to restore unity, and was anxious for it to be framed as simply as possible, and in such a way that it would be as suitable for the Republic as for the Free State. He saw the wisdom of consulting those with a knowledge of British constitutional law. He therefore saw Tim Healy, and approached Llewelyn Davies to draw up a specimen draft which he could use as a blueprint by which to measure those of the Constitution Committee. He introduced Davies to Hugh Kennedy and James Douglas, whose joint draft was, in its essentials, that which was finally submitted to the British Cabinet.

Collins had discovered in Hugh Kennedy, the new Attorney General, a man for whose judgement he rapidly conceived considerable respect. At the beginning of February he told Cosgrave with the excited admiration of one who has personally ferretted out a genius: 'I wish we'd had him in London for the Treaty.'[8]

[7] Brother Allen's Papers
[8] In a memorandum dated 17.12.21 Mr Kennedy had given an opinion on the oath in the Treaty. This pointed out that the King was not constitutionally a 'sovereign' but a democratic institution and therefore in and not above the Constitution; it stressed Britain's acknowledgement of the individual national identities of the Commonwealth States, each having its own interpretation of the Constitution. He summed up: 'The proposed Oath is nothing more than a solemn asseveration of, in the first place, the very allegiance which would be due by every Irish citizen, apart from any oath, to the constitution of the Irish Free State . . . and, in the

Opposition to the Treaty was rapidly becoming more widely organized, though real bitterness was to have a tardier flowering. Collins's attitude to the opposition had remained unresentful. With the rising tide of resistance to the Treaty bringing with it a muddy flotsam of abuse for himself, he stuck grimly to his resolve to stand above both party prejudice and personal invective.

He was by no means content merely to assimilate the ideas of those of greater formal education than himself. Later Mrs Davies was to recall :

'He was full of the re-making of Ireland, and the thoughts he expressed were all on this subject. He outlined an immediate programme, and he then allowed himself to dream of a future Gaelic civilization, and he felt his way towards the foundations on which it should be built. . . . He spoke of the possibility of making our provinces – the provincial cities – living centres. He would like to see them given power and responsibility, in the hope that they would flourish, in art, and industry, and education, and become rivals with each other in a healthy competition.'[9]

With such far-reaching plans teeming in his brain it is not surprising that, hearing someone speak of his opponents as the 'extremists' he said quizzically : 'It is *we* who are the extremists.'

For all his desperate determination to regain unity, the gulf was widening remorselessly before the eyes of all. 'Real men are few nowadays, but you are one', wrote one Irish-American, appealing to him, as if it were in his power to prevent it, not to break with de Valera, and Harry Boland whom he himself loved. Collins wrote in reply :

'I am more sorry than you are that the President and Harry are on the other side from myself. I believe they have missed the tide, for, were it not for taking the bold course I am certain

second place, of the very faithfulness which, apart from any Oath, would be due by the Irish Free State and her citizens, if, accepting the Treaty, she accepts a place as a member of the Commonwealth of Nations in the terms and spirit of the Treaty.' (From a copy kindly lent to the author by the late Mr W. T. Cosgrave.)

[9] Llewelyn Davies Papers

this country would have been split by contending factions, whether we liked it or not. If there be but goodwill on all sides I am convinced we may still bring the whole thing to final success. In any case, we are going forward, the English are evacuating this country, and surely no one will claim that we can possibly be worse off when that evacuation is complete.

'As you know Harry Boland so well there is no need for me to tell you what I have thought of him in the past, and I need only to say that my feelings towards both the President and himself are still as cordial as they were.'[10]

II

The British Government, to whom the Provisional Government, set up by the 'Southern Parliament', was the only recognized authority in the twenty-six-county area apart from its own Executive, now proceeded to evacuate its forces, handing over police and military barracks to Irish troops who, in British eyes, were directed by the Provisional Government. To make this assumption more regular Mulcahy explained to the Dail: 'We [the Ministry of Defence, Dail Eireann] have arranged with the Provisional Government to occupy for them all evacuated military and police posts for the purpose of their maintenance and safeguarding. Expense entailed by such occupation is charged to the Provisional Government.'[11]

There was, as yet, no open split in the Army. Throughout the country therefore, whatever their views of the Treaty, the rank and file took over the positions evacuated by the British solely as local units of the I.R.A.

Among their senior officers a very different view prevailed. Immediately after the Dail's approval of the Treaty senior officers opposed to it held meetings to discuss the situation. It was argued that as the majority of Dail Eireann supported the Treaty and was therefore prepared to abrogate the Republic, the Army's oath of allegiance to it was no longer binding; and that the Army was, moreover, bound by the other part of its oath,

[10] Collins Papers
[11] Dail Debates, 1 March 1922, p. 140

'to support and defend the Irish Republic', to resist any attempt by the Dail as by any other body to disestablish it.

In the interests of both Army unity and the Republic, it was proposed that the Army should revert to its old status of a Volunteer body under its own executive. An Army Convention was, therefore, requested so that this might be done. Although Mulcahy argued that the Dail Executive had no power to alter the supreme control of the Army, a Convention was agreed upon. The date for this was fixed as 26 March, and sanctioned by the Dail Cabinet on 27 February.

An Army split was clearly incipient. In Dublin at least the pro-Treaty authorities were able to ensure that troops taking over evacuated positions would remain loyal to whatever government might be elected. When the British handed over Beggars Bush Barracks it became the Headquarters of what was to become known as the National Army. This was maintained as a full-time uniformed force.

While division of loyalty was thus prevented from becoming a major problem for the Provisional Government in Dublin, it was not long before it gave rise to critical incidents in other parts of the country, notably in Limerick, where civil war was narrowly averted. Clearly such incidents could be contained only so long as the possibility remained of finding a permanent agreement under which the Army could remain united and obedient to the elected civil authority without compromising its Republican adherence.

The situation in the North-East had worsened. The Treaty, and in particular its provision for a Boundary Commission, had been received with the hostility of fear by Northern Protestant extremists. The systematic pogroms against the Catholic-Nationalist population of Belfast now flared up again, fanned by the leaders of Orange factionism. In Belfast itself there was a continuous undercurrent of sniping and bomb-throwing of which the Press on both sides made political capital, stirring up further hatreds which took indiscriminate toll of the hapless population, often among the very young and the old who were not quick enough to realize that the streets on which they lived had become battlegrounds. Movements of the I.R.A. over what they still regarded as their territory resulted in clashes with Northern forces.

On 11 January Sir James Craig wrote to Churchill, upon whom responsibility for putting the Treaty into effect had now devolved. He suggested a meeting between himself, Churchill, and the leaders of the Provisional Government, 'so as to ascertain clearly whether the policy of Southern Ireland is to be one of peace or whether the present method of pressure on Northern Ireland is to be continued.'[12]

Such a meeting was fraught with explosive material. Though it did not provide, in Tom Kettle's phrase, 'a bucketful of Boyne to put the sunrise out', Churchill, at least, found it dramatic.

'I lost no time in bringing Craig and Michael Collins to-gether. On January 21 they met in my room at the Colonial Office, which, despite its enormous size, seemed overcharged with electricity. They both glowered magnificently, but after a short, commonplace talk I slipped away upon some excuse and left them together. What these two Irishmen, separated by such gulfs of religion, sentiment, and conduct, said to each other I cannot tell. But it took a long time, and, as I did not wish to disturb them, mutton chops, etc., were tactfully intro-duced about one o'clock.[13] At four o'clock the Private Secre-tary reported signs of movement on the All-Ireland front and I ventured to look in. They announced to me complete agree-ment reduced to writing. They were to help each other in every way; they were to settle outstanding points by personal discussion; they were to stand together within the limits agreed against all disturbers of the peace. We three then joined in the best of all pledges, to wit, "To try to make things work." '[14]

Major Sir Ralph Furse in his autobiography *Aucuparius* has described how he happened to be passing when the 'tactfully introduced' luncheon was about to be borne in. He makes the happy revelation that 'that intriguing etc.' was, in fact, three or

[12] Quoted in Churchill *The Aftermath* pp. 316–17

[13] Collins's timings of the day's work make it rather less of a marathon than Churchill, anxiously waiting without, evidently found it to be. His Appointments Diary notes: '12 Colonial Office; 1 Churchill's Room'. Later in the day he wrote to Kitty from the Jermyn Court Hotel, 'I have just returned @ 3.45 from a four hours interview with Sir James Craig'.

[14] Churchill *The Aftermath* p. 317

four bottles of Guinness, and praises the inspiration that thus regaled the two Irishmen in the search for mutual goodwill. It is disillusioning, perhaps, to reflect that the Craig-Collins Agreement was signed, if anything, in spite of and not as the result of this pleasant thought. Collins loathed the sight of porter. The fate of the bottles of Guiness is, therefore, purely a matter for conjecture.

Michael's comments on the interview hardly go as far as the unconfined *bonhomie* suggested by Churchill. Craig, he reported in Dublin, was less narrow-minded than he had expected, but a dull fellow. And he added, soberly, that 'the North is not in yet by a long chalk'.

By the terms of the Craig-Collins Agreement the Belfast Boycott was to end, Catholics expelled from their jobs were to be reinstated, and relief given to the unemployed. The clause that was to have the most graphic repercussions, however, was that which laid down that the Boundary Commission was to be altered. Each government was to appoint a representative to report to Collins and Craig, who would agree on behalf of their respective governments their future boundaries.

The new commitments demanding reconciliation with old loyalties, and the overriding cruelty of seeing former comrades now standing aside or actively working against him were surely the cause of Michael's writing to Kitty on 27 January: 'I am really and truly having an awful time and am rapidly becoming quite desperate. Oh Lord it is honestly frightful.'

There was worse to come. The Dail Cabinet duly decreed the lifting of the Belfast Boycott on 24 January, and trade was immediately resumed. Yet, almost a week later, scarcely twenty out of the ten thousand or more expelled Catholic workers of Belfast were reported to have been reinstated, and it was doubted whether Craig could bring the Orange shipyard employers to heel. The great blow fell, however, on 27 January. Craig, defending his agreement before an unenthusiastic Belfast audience, declared that it was an admission by the Free State that Ulster was a separate entity, and added: 'I will never give in to any rearrangement of the boundary that leaves our Ulster area less than it is under the Government of Ireland Act.'

In a letter to Kitty, undated, but from internal evidence,

written shortly after Craig's announcement, Michael wrote: 'This is the worst day I have had yet – far far the worst. May God help us all.'

The question of the Boundary had now reached a new crux. The Craig-Collins Agreement had been signed in all sincerity. But upon what misunderstanding had it been based? Craig, though under pressure as extreme as, if less complex than, that on Collins himself, nevertheless agreed to meet him again, this time in Dublin.

After this meeting Collins issued a statement :

> 'Owing to the fact that Mr Collins stands on the Boundary Commission and the Irish Delegation Agreements with Mr Lloyd George that large territories were involved in the Commission, and not merely a boundary line, as Sir James Craig was given to understand privately by several British Ministers and from statements of Mr Lloyd George in the House of Commons, no further agreement was reached, and a very serious situation has consequently arisen.'[15]

Craig and Collins later issued statements accusing each other, somewhat blankly, of a change of front since their London meeting. What was all too clear was that, between North and South, a demarcation line ran as uncompromising as that between the two territories.

The reaction of extreme groups on both sides had become a problem of immediate concern. Having shown little regard for the agreement of the political leaders, they were unlikely to become quiescent in the face of their disagreement. Michael received an urgent summons to confer with Craig and Churchill in London. He wrote to Kitty : 'The Craig business is serious and if we don't find some way of dealing with it all the bravos will get a great chance of distinguishing themselves once more.'

He prepared to meet Craig on 6 February. 'Things do not appear to be very promising', he added, 'but perhaps it's a question of being "the darkest hour before the dawn".'

It was a dawn destined to have no breaking. The London talks left Craig and Collins with their positions unchanged.

[15] *Freeman's Journal* 3 February 1922

The situation in the North-East deteriorated rapidly. A rising tide of hatred and bigotry swept the area, deluging Belfast in particular with carnage and terror. Factionist-led mobs roamed the streets, devastating the Catholic areas, murdering men, women, and children, and driving out families in what was to be the start of a long trek, spread over months, of homeless refugees fleeing in their thousands across the Border or over to Scotland. The 'B Specials', inspired by a far more intense loathing of Sinn Fein than the mercenary infusions of the Black and Tans had ever known, used their armed powers to restore order by eradicating the nationalist minority to the best of their ability.

The I.R.A., whose divisional boundaries knew no political border, retaliated fiercely in support of their Northern brothers, hampered in their guerilla methods by the hostility of the majority of the population in the area, and finding their most rewarding battlegrounds where the boundary line ran through the predominantly nationalist counties of Fermanagh and Tyrone.

Craig and Collins issued public recriminations. North and South were no longer on speaking terms.

III

Collins was unwell once more. He complained of pains in the stomach, and of feeling the cold as he had not done before. As always, he found his cure in work. He wrote a note to Kitty on the subject of Johnny, himself in hospital: 'He is really to be admired in the cheerful way he takes things,' adding magnificently, 'FAMILY FAILING.'

His new position gratified no sense of personal ambition. Power he undoubtedly did enjoy; not for its attendant acclaim, but for its opportunities to fulfil his own and Ireland's destinies. Any triumph he expresses is not for himself but for Ireland. On 17 February he wrote to Kitty: 'The stamp on this was the first Free State stamp ever licked by a member of the Free State Provisional Government.' It is the cry of a young man rejoicing, not so much in his own strength as in that of his country.

The very diffusion of Collins's authority gave the Treaty's opponents the more opportunities for undermining his position as its effective upholder. Consequently it is Collins, and almost exclusively Collins, upon whom we find all the various anti-Treaty forces making unrelenting assault. The history of the remaining months of his life is one of a continual search for unity by the path of compromise, and a steady weakening of the Treaty position, with many shadows, but never the substance, of unity as its result.

The whole Treaty issue turned on the elections. De Valera contended that a decision at the polls that ratified the Treaty would enable Britain to claim that Ireland had bound herself irrevocably within its confines. Griffith and Collins, while anxious to establish the Free State and end the anomaly of rival administrative bodies, thought it prudent therefore to avoid any future charge that they had called an election before the opposition had been given a fair chance to establish its case.

Early in March it was agreed that no election would be held for three months, when the Free State Constitution would also be submitted to the people. There ensued a fury of speech-making up and down the country. Michael attracted huge crowds whenever he appeared on a platform. His dislike of public meetings was never apparent at such times. Naturally given to forthrightness and expansive gesture, he rivetted attention by the sheer force of his appearance and personality, rather than by any skill of oratory. He got the measure of a crowd quickly, and because he never forgot that they were men and women and not merely a collective mind to be harangued, his weapon was plain speaking, never contempt. He played hecklers along to win the crowd, but packed them off with rough and ready dispatch when he had had enough of them.

As a public speaker he had one serious fault. Driven by emotion, he lacked the politician's circumspection. His impulses were always inspired by the desire to do what was best for Ireland; where her various interests conflicted, the impulse of the moment could compromise other commitments.

Wherever he went he would always pause for an old person or a child. Part of the politician's stock-in-trade, with Collins it was a natural trait. Returning from a meeting in Cork just before St Patrick's Day he was met at a wayside station by a little group of ragged children who pressed a bunch of shamrock into his hand, an action which touched him deeply so that he recorded it in a letter afterwards.

Convinced that the people were for the Treaty, he was nevertheless far from complacent about the election campaign. 'Their speeches are not being trounced vigorously enough by our people', he wrote. De Valera's arguments also exasperated him : 'I want to deal with de V's Civil War stuff very sternly & fully. . . . He talked of the Freedom of Australia etc when he was in favour of that – *when* there was *no chance of getting it.*'

In his public utterances he avoided the mistake of condemning the Republic as an impossibilist's dream. He had too much respect for the people's intelligence to resort to the bland argument that although the Republic had been proclaimed to the echo before the Treaty anyone who believed in it now was a fool. His stand attracted hostile attention among the Westminster diehards.

Although the political crisis had been held at bay, that in the Army came to a head in March. Arrangements for the Army Convention on 26 March had gone ahead until 15 March, when the Dail Cabinet decided that it should not, after all, be held.

The anti-Treaty officers could only feel that the pro-Treaty politicians had performed a complete *volte-face* and slammed the door to unity. The Dail Cabinet, no less anxious to reach permanent understanding, can have had little doubt that Republican counsels would prevail at such a convention. Both sides expected the Treaty to be ratified at the elections. The Cabinet could not concede the right of any section of the Army to decide for itself whether it should remain subject to civil authority. Its change of policy undoubtedly lay in the very real danger, forcibly brought home by the Limerick incident, in which pitched battle between rival Army contingents was narrowly averted, that in concurring in the holding of a Convention it would virtually sanction the removal of large sections of the Army from the control of whatever government might be elected.

Despite further efforts to find a solution to the fundamental point at issue, the control of the Army, no agreement was reached, and the anti-Treaty officers summoned the convention for 26 March unilaterally. Its outcome was foreseeable. Within a few days of its decision to maintain itself under its own executive as the Army of the Republic, it had repudiated the authority of the Minister of Defence, and begun operations aimed at undermining the Treaty.

Collins knew that any I.R.A. action in the North to protect the nationalist minority must aggravate the attacks upon them. He also saw that a more effective course was to invoke the co-operation of Britain, whose troops continued to garrison the Six Counties, and who he felt should shoulder her share of the responsibility for its inhabitants which she retained under the Treaty. On 11 March he wrote to Churchill, protesting against anti-nationalist action in Belfast.

Churchill, who was also charged with pacifying Sir James Craig over I.R.A. activities, pointed out in his reply to Collins that the South was still holding as hostages Ulster Constabulary men who had strayed over the Border. 'This hostage business is more suited to the Balkans than to Ireland', he wrote sternly. Clearly, any direct action Collins might undertake in support of the Northern minority would find no favour in Whitehall. Combined action by North and South to restore peace remained the only answer as far as Churchill was concerned.

Craig, like Collins, had his own intransigents. Like Collins too, his sympathies were undoubtedly with their objectives. His actions suggest, however, that, whereas Collins desired the unity of Ireland based on goodwill, Craig himself was not, like Churchill, concerned with 'the interests of Ireland as a whole' but with the cause of Ulster Unionism.

On 15 March 1922 the *Belfast Newsletter* announced Craig's invitation to Sir Henry Wilson to direct the restoration of order in the Six County area. This pronouncement brought a long and strongly worded letter of protest to Churchill from Michael Collins on 21 March. He concluded:

'I must point out to you that the situation in the Six Counties could not be graver. If these offensive *not protective* measures are taken against our people it will fan a flame of indignation and passion amongst the people of the whole country, and I cannot be responsible for the awful consequences that must ensue.

'As it is, it is impossible for me to let this new and undis-guised offensive against our people pass unnoticed and [I] am reluctantly compelled to take immediate counsel regarding the re-imposition of the boycott and other protective measures.

'Once again I wish to remind you before it is too late that I am most anxious for harmony with Belfast, but you will agree, I am sure, it is utterly out of the question under these circumstances.'[16]

Two days later men in uniform entered a Catholic home in Belfast and murdered five members of one family.

Here at least was common ground on which the I.R.A., what-ever its differences over the Treaty, could unite. The I.R.B. had called together its leaders on both sides to seek unity, and the ties of the Brotherhood remained strong. Michael Collins and Liam Lynch in particular had refused to let the last word be said between them, and even after the Army split they continued to meet.

That the 'other protective measures' which Collins had warned Churchill he must take included a planned I.R.A. offensive in the North-East against the Crown forces in which he and Liam Lynch now co-operated must appear startlingly improper in the Chairman of the Provisional Government and a signatory of the Treaty. Collins, however, undertook such a move entirely as a protective measure and only after he had, in Churchill's own words, flooded him with protests about the vendettas and counter-vendettas proceeding nightly in Belfast, and had also given strong warnings against British support for what he regarded as a deliberate offensive by the Northern authorities.

Though he plainly acted from motives of humanity, he trod a perilous path. It is to Lynch's credit, and evidence of his sincerity in mounting the operation as a protective measure, that he did not attempt to hasten the overthrow of the Treaty by promoting British suspicions of pro-Treaty support for the I.R.A. offensive; indeed, he co-operated actively with Collins in con-cealing its existence. Neither he nor Collins wanted to provoke renewed war with the British in the South.

Collins did not abandon his endeavours to bring peace with

[16] P.R.O.: CO 14311

the North by negotiation. A conference in London at the end of March, attended by delegations from the Provisional and Northern Governments and the British Government, resulted in a signed agreement on 30 March, which declared peace between North and South, and called for mutual co-operation in settling differences.

It was all too quickly evident that it was easier to declare peace than to enforce it. Mutual hatreds remained unpurged by politicians' bargaining, and violence flared unabated. Collins's influence over large sections of the I.R.A. operating in the Six Counties was, since the Army split, effective only if exercised towards continued war. Now he responded to the North's disregard of its leader's efforts to find peace by pursuing afresh his secret councils of war with those who, differing from him politically, remained his comrades in arms and at heart.

CHAPTER EIGHTEEN

Resistance

(April – June 1922)

I

The split that had now resulted in the formation of two rival armies was largely shaped by considerations in which the actual terms of the Treaty played little part. These divisions were by no means bitter in these early months of 1922. In some cases, indeed, the split provided the means of settling rather than raising differences. Former officers, returning from internment, found their positions filled by others who, having taken over command, often with considerable credit, during the hottest part of the war, were understandably reluctant to relinquish authority. The breaking-up into pro- and anti-Treaty armies therefore provided an opportunity for the amicable settlement of personal differences.

As Michael had predicted, many released internees felt that they had arrears to make up; these tended to go anti-Treaty in the hopes of gaining a chance to win their spurs against the British. 'Truciliers' whose bellicosity was in proportion to their lack of fighting experience also showed a predilection for last-ditch republicanism.

This great body of Ireland's youth, caught up in the nation's dilemma, was, in fact, the nation's greatest problem; it must also command our greatest sympathy. It had been nourished after 1916 with unadulterated republicanism and the belief that by its arms alone could national freedom be won. The glamour of bearing arms for their country made many reluctant to return to farm, shop counter, or office desk, even when these were available. There was the added fear that to do so might prove an unwitting desertion in Ireland's hour of need.

The older men in the Army, who foresaw far more clearly than the youthful rank and file where this split in the I.R.A.

might lead, took their decisions soberly and in the light of the Treaty's merits as each judged it for himself.

The designation of the two armies was largely a matter of preference. The pro-Treaty forces continued to declare themselves to be the Irish Republican Army, under the authority of Dail Eireann; the anti-Treaty portion of the I.R.A., now recognizing only its own Executive, claimed that title for itself, referring to the pro-Treaty forces as the Free State Army, a style indignantly repudiated by them. No less contentious were the pro-Treaty terms 'Regular' and 'Irregular'. For ease of reference those troops loyal to G.H.Q. will be termed 'Government' forces, or the 'National Army', and those owing allegiance to the Executive appointed on 9 April, 'Republican' forces.

Rory O'Connor, though his was not necessarily the voice of the whole Executive, now announced that the Republican forces no longer recognized any political organization. From now on de Valera's actions appear to have been increasingly influenced by those of the Executive, and not *vice versa*. De Valera's weakness had sometimes been slowness of decision and a consequent reluctance to undertake swift action. The strongest voice raised in the Republican party was that of Cathal Brugha, who was opposed to any move that might result in military dictatorship and an abandonment of civil government.

Positive action was, however, taken not by the politicians, but by the Republican Army Executive, or, more specifically, by Rory O'Connor, whose desire to set up a military dictatorship was not shared by Liam Lynch, the Republican Chief of Staff, for whose authority O'Connor seems to have had light regard.

On the night of 13 April Rory O'Connor, with Liam Mellowes and other Republican Army leaders, seized the Four Courts in Dublin as their headquarters, and proceeded to fortify them.

The challenge of this climacteric defiance of civil authority was inescapable. De Valera, the unquestioned leader of the political Republican party, made no protest. Perhaps, his authority in terms of actual power gone, he feared to weaken the Republican front. It was a sad pass for the man who had once wrought the union of the military and political flanks of the national movement, and a decision which, we are told by Robert Brennan, he was later to deplore.[1]

The reactions of the Irish Ministry, the British Government, the British Army Command in Ireland, and the Irish public generally are revealed or may be inferred in the exchanges between Cope, in close touch with Collins in Dublin, and Churchill at the Colonial Office in London which immediately followed the seizure of the Four Courts.[2]

The relevant extracts run :

Telegram. Cope to Churchill, 14 April 1922. 10.40 a.m.
'Forty armed men entered Four Courts last night. They are still there. They are not attracting any attention.'
2.41 p.m. 'The mutineers are hoping that we will interfere and take a hand in the business and that both sides of the I.R.A. will thereupon unite. The P[rovisional] G[overnment] are most anxious that we should stand aside and I have arranged with Macready accordingly.'

Telegram. Churchill to Cope, 14 April 1922. 2.48 p.m.
'Keep in touch with Macready and let him understand your point of view. I presume you will impress upon the P.G. importance of their acting. Keep me fully informed.'

Telegram. Cope to Churchill, 15 April 1922. 5.49 p.m.
'Four Courts. It is rumoured that the mutineers number about two hundred. Nothing can be seen from the outside except a few sandbags made up as a defence post at one of the doors.

' . . . You will have seen Roderick O'Connor's announcement that the Four Courts were taken over solely as headquarters and not with any intention of a *coup d'état*. This announcement is being received cautiously by P.G. The premises will probably be used as a jumping-off ground for stunts. The P.G. are watching events and do not propose to take drastic measures for dislodgement at present.'

Letter. Churchill to Cope, 17 April 1922.
'Write to me fully by tonight's messenger the kind of action contemplated against the Four Courts Mutineers. I do not

[1] Brennan *Allegiance* p. 337   [2] P.R.O.: CO 19299

understand why they do not ring them round and starve them out.'

Letter. Cope to Churchill, 18 April 1922.

'Four Courts. The situation is unchanged. The mutineers are commandeering food etc from the local shopkeepers and thus making themselves very unpopular. It would not pay the P.G. to take drastic action at the moment. Here again they do not want dramatic effects and funeral orations. They are very active & alert and have done quite a lot to restrict the mutineers' opportunities for creating mischief. Public opinion in Dublin is behind the P.G. & is showing no impatience for more active measures. The P.G.'s policy of waiting is understood & generally approved. Meanwhile the P.G.'s forces are gathering strength & they hold the ascendancy. The P.G. do not want the loss of the Four Courts to be added to that of Custom House. It is probably the finest building in Dublin and its records are invaluable. It may be necessary eventually to take measures to blockade the mutineers but it is better to wait until public opinion demands this as the result of commandeering & other irregularities. There is in fact no practical urgency.'

The arguments which Collins put before Cope against taking any militant action were those which would naturally find the most sympathetic hearing. Churchill had the reputation for impetuosity. Collins undoubtedly resented the necessity that made his decisions answerable to Churchill the imperialist in these transitional days: he certainly had come to trust Churchill the Treaty-maker to stand by the Provisional Government. Nevertheless, he continued to think independently, as an Irishman. His first concern, confronted with the Four Courts situation, was to ensure that the Provisional Government, and not the British, retained the responsibility for dealing with it.

Whether he was wise in taking no immediate action will always be debatable. Churchill's one concern was for the Provisional Government to prove its ability to govern. But Churchill was not an Irishman, while Collins was nothing else. To Collins the Four Courts' leaders were not mutineers, but Rory O'Connor, who had sat at G.H.Q. meetings with him and been his friend, and Liam Mellowes of the gay, punning humour. He was no less determined to see that his Government functioned; he was the more determined that all Irishmen should be convinced of the advantage to be gained by its doing so. The use of force was a last resort not seriously to be contemplated.

The preservation of the Four Courts buildings, while important, was not therefore Collins's primary concern. As long as bloodshed was avoided the chance remained that unity by negotiation might yet be achieved. A blockade to be effective seemed certain to involve sniping, which could trigger off a far worse situation. Another very good reason for not drawing a close picket about the Four Courts and starving the garrison out was that a certain amount of its comings and goings lay in Collins's own direction.

His co-operation with the Executive for a military operation in the North-East was taking positive shape. To combat the Ulster Special Constabulary, 25,000 strong, whose activities in Belfast particularly were outdoing the Black and Tans in terror, Southern officers were to be sent to lead and co-ordinate the Northern Divisions of the I.R.A. The question of allegiance was set aside for the purposes of this one remaining common cause.

The pro-Treaty forces' arms were mostly those supplied by the British to the Provisional Government. Collins arranged with Liam Lynch to exchange a number of British rifles for others in Republican hands. The British Government was unlikely to appreciate the defence of Northern nationalists against British-armed Specials by British-armed Republican troops, should any of these identifiable weapons fall into their hands. It was another case of Collins having so many irons in the fire that his burning seemed inevitable. Yet when every loyalty appeared vital to Ireland, which of them could he renounce?

Rory O'Connor was one of those 'practical men, unfettered by commonsense'[8] who lead extremists into action. He had the zeal of the convert who sweeps aside not only former ideals but also the comrades who once shared and inspired them. His had not been an easy war. While hardly qualifying for Macready's hysterical description as 'the Reds', the Four Courts' garrison were the irreconcilables whom not even Liam Lynch, unswerving

[8] Brinton *The Anatomy of Revolution* p. 173

in his Republican allegiance yet desperately anxious to avert civil war, could deter from their course.

Few cared to contemplate civil war, or accepted its inevitability. Nevertheless, an ugly situation was developing in which guns played an increasing part. Sniping in Dublin was widespread. While the Republican Executive directed such commandeering as it felt necessary for the maintenance of its forces, trigger-happiness was in the air for youngsters upon whom the old discipline and comradeship of the pre-Truce I.R.A. laid no bonds. Their fellows of the Government forces, many of them as raw as themselves, responded to their impetuous fusillades with equal nervous energy.

The proclamation of pro-Treaty pre-election meetings by Republicans showed a more calculated policy, aimed at preventing an election on the Treaty issue. Rail services were disrupted and roads trenched. On 16 April Griffith went to address a meeting in Sligo, despite threats by the local Republican commandant. On the eve of his departure Griffith summoned Collins and Cosgrave to a private meeting. Should anything happen to him he was leaving a written recommendation that Collins should succeed him as leader of the pro-Treaty party. Collins turned lightly to Cosgrave. 'I'll do the same for you', he offered. Walking squarely into the shadows, he continued to laugh them aside. For all his developing faculties, fear and the caution it engenders eluded him to the end.

Faced with the fact that the Provisional Government was establishing itself, and thereby the Treaty, as the proper authority in the people's eyes, the Republicans realized that only desperate measures remained to them. The precedent of Easter Week with its handful of men standing alone for their ideals was sufficient answer to those who declared that the people's will must be sovereign. De Valera condemned military interference with the right of free speech : he could not, unfortunately, prevent it.

As always, Collins remained prone to independent action. At Cabinet meetings, Ernest Blythe recalls, he was wont to ejaculate 'We must fight these b—— fellows' : it was noticeable that he always brought forward a new scheme for negotiating with them instead.

Others believed that he might advance to the edge of the

precipice but not over it. It would be a mistake to over-emphasize his tendency to secret consultation in controversial quarters. None of his colleagues could complain that his loyalties were only for those who opposed him. His days were packed with meetings of Dail Cabinet, Provisional Government Ministry, or G.H.Q. Staff. He was head of only one of these. His opponents labelled him a dictator : in point of respect for his colleagues he was less a dictator than Parnell.

Griffith had never been closely connected with the Army. Lacking Collins's intimate knowledge of it he also lacked a sense of obligation towards it. While Griffith therefore clung to the hope that Collins would renounce militarism in favour of purely constitutional processes, the Republican Army leaders relied no less on Collins to safeguard their interests.

The timing of the election had now become critical. Until agreement on this point could be reached no effort by the peace-makers could succeed. Without some guarantee that the Republic would not be irrevocably ruled out by an election the Republicans refused to agree to one within the limited period laid down by the Treaty party, who were tired of trying to govern by disputed authority, and under pressure from Westminster.

In the North-East, the Craig-Collins Pact of 30 March had not brought the hoped-for response to its brave announcement that 'Peace is declared'. Stiff exchanges between Collins and Craig by letter and telegram ran their course until, by the end of April, any vestiges of personal goodwill between the two men were gone beyond recall, torn to shreds by the divergence of their aims and lost in the gulf which too many of their countrymen had no wish to span. On 27 April Collins wrote to Churchill : 'In all the circumstances I greatly fear that Sir James Craig's Parliament is deliberately creating a situation in which it will no longer be possible to continue the present Agreement. Indeed there is little hope for any Agreement. It is hardly necessary for me to point out how serious the situation has again become.'[4]

Churchill, in reply, urged Collins against allowing himself to be drawn into the tactical courses by which the extremists in both North and South sought to prevent unity on any basis which would deny their full claims.

4 P.R.O.: CO 21011

Collins knew, while he despaired of their recognizing it, that the Ulstermen were his countrymen. But the Southerners, against co-operating with whom Churchill portentously warned him, were more: they were men of his own race and beliefs. The Northern Irish majority might and must be won over with the goodwill of neighbour for neighbour despite conflicting interests. The South's unity lay in the common concerns of brothers, and as long as the Northerners' actions threatened that deep, natural bond, Collins would pawn the Treaty itself to protect it.

He was dangerously overworked, as was Griffith, who, already thinking of retirement from political life once the Treaty was assured, looked increasingly to Collins to assume the burden of the day, probably unaware that the younger man's magnificent physique, like his own now tired and worn-out one, was affected by the long strain of irregular hours and of worry. Michael had had a long succession of colds, and mentioned coughing into the early hours. Of late he had complained more frequently of the stomach pains which had afflicted him for the past three years, and showed an unwonted fussiness about his food, when he bothered to eat at all. 'Am feeling very done up', he wrote on 6 April, underlining the 'very' three times.[5]

He preserved all his old devotion to former comrades with an almost pathetic obstinacy. When Eoin O'Duffy referred lightly to possible civil war Collins castigated him. He wrote to Sean Nunan, now politically divided from him: 'My relations with "the old chargers" remain unchanged.' When someone spoke bitterly of de Valera he was up in arms at once: 'Leave him alone. If you can't say anything good about him, then don't say anything about him.'

At this time a pleasant friendship developed between Michael and Oliver St John Gogarty, whom Chesterton described as being 'like a witty legend of the eighteenth century'. Both men combined a reverence for life with an entirely irreverent approach to it. They also shared a liking for Walt Whitman and sweet tea, and a contempt for danger. Gogarty's son, Oliver, remembers how, as a boy, he answered the door of their house in Ely Place

---

[5] Collins himself told the Laverys that he suspected appendicitis (Lavery *Life of a Painter* p. 216). The late Frank O'Connor suggested to the present author that the symptoms pointed rather to an ulcer.

one evening in those troubled days. In the darkness a soft Cork voice answered the boy's question : 'Never mind who it is. 'Tis good company you're in, anyway.'

In Gogarty's house he met many men with whom he might otherwise never have come in contact. He was to find there a refuge as well as a meeting-place in days to come when death lurked once more in the streets of Dublin.

Fearless himself, Collins rejoiced in the company of all such men. Often it was his admiration for this quality that led him to respect those whose ways were not otherwise his own. Alfred Cope comes to mind. Another man of great bravery for whom he had a developing respect was T. M. Healy. Cosgrave and Collins went together to see Healy on one occasion, at this time of uncertain loyalties. There was a commotion in the hall. Healy broke off his conversation and walked straight out to face a group of armed men. They proved, fortunately, to be Collins's men.

When Sir James Barrie gave his address as rector of St Andrew's on 'Courage' Collins filed a copy of it among his papers. He may, indeed, have inspired part of it himself. 'Go through life without ever ascribing to your opponents motives meaner than your own. Nothing so lowers the moral currency. Give it up, and be great.'

II

'The soldiers get doped by the politicians', was Collins's despairing comment when renewed efforts to solve their accumulating differences failed.

On 20 May the Collins-de Valera Pact was announced to a Dail tensed for failure. The latest meeting of de Valera and Collins had aroused no expectation of more than a formal report of disagreement. When the Dail Cabinet came out of session and took their places in the chamber Collins laid a document on the Speaker's table as he passed. The Pact had come, in the words of the *Freeman's Journal,* like 'a bolt from the blue' and as 'a political miracle'. It added : 'The country has been saved from a situation of horrible possibilities.'

Both Dail and country greeted the Pact with enthusiastic relief. It provided for a Coalition Panel, although any other interest was free to contest the election. A Coalition Government would then be set up, with the anti-Treaty party represented in the Cabinet in the ratio of four to five.

This mood of relief was not shared by those who saw that only the firm establishment of the electorate's wishes on whether Ireland was to work the Treaty or fight on for the Republic would provide any lasting stability in the country. Under the Pact the Treaty was no longer the issue of the election. The advantages to the Republicans were apparent. For the Treaty party the Pact could only appear as a move of grave compromise, jeopardizing all chance of forming a government capable of continuing the task begun by the Provisional Government. A Dail which mathematically reproduced itself and yet declared itself a democratically elected, representative assembly; a Cabinet composed of men diametrically opposed, in which the minority clearly intended that control of the Army should rest in its hands – these were not eventualities to which those who pinned their hopes on the Treaty could look with confidence.

Griffith who, before the Pact was made, had called for elections to be held on 16 June, was visibly shaken by the agreement. At the Cabinet meeting held to make a decision upon it, Ernest Blythe recalls, several members were reluctant to agree but finally did so when a vote was taken round the table. Griffith paused for three or four minutes; adjusted his tie; took off his glasses and polished them with a shaking hand; and finally gave his assent. He had seen the result of a divided Cabinet, and was even then leading a divided Dail. Not least, he must have shrunk from an open split with Collins. It was no less apparent, however, that Griffith believed that, in signing such an agreement, Collins had sold the pass. The British would certainly view the Pact in the gravest light; Griffith himself, by agreeing to recommend it to the Dail, would be held to be answerable equally with Collins by the British, and would probably be required to take the chief part in pleading its cause. Collins, with his emotional attachment to former friends, might find sufficient reason to justify the Pact; Griffith could not. Ernest Blythe noticed that Griffith thereafter ceased to refer to Collins as 'Mick', reserving for him a coldly formal 'Mr Collins'.

Yet in signing the Pact Collins had achieved more than the

national unity which was its primary aim. He had ensured an election; and by his insistence that every interest other than Sinn Fein was to be free to contest it with the Panel candidates he had salvaged something of its democratic character.

Without the Pact it is difficult to see how the election required under the Treaty could have been held. Collins could justifiably argue that by the Pact he had given the opposition a last chance to assume a responsible and constitutional part in restoring the country without losing face by having to accept the Treaty; and that the economic chaos, which obsessed him, and the grave situation in the North-East had now made unity the supreme consideration.

His public declaration that he regarded the Pact as more important than the Treaty was certainly imprudent; since he saw no reason why Pact and Treaty should not be co-existent, it is not, however, evidence of any readiness to dishonour his signature. In private he referred to the Pact as 'a war emergency measure'.

This effort to neutralize political differences in the South had unhappy repercussions in the North-East. Craig immediately announced his Government's refusal to have any dealings with the new Dail returned under the Pact. His Cabinet, furthermore, would not have a Boundary Commission under any circumstances. Heavy shooting and bombing broke out afresh in Belfast, and Catholic refugees once more poured southwards. Curfew was imposed in the city.

Winston Churchill had written to Sir James Craig on 24 May, deploring his defiant statement on the Boundary Commission at a time when the Northern Government was applying for large quantities of money and arms from the British Government. Craig replied on 26 May 1922 :

'Many thanks for your private and confidential scold of yesterday. . . . The Boundary Commission has been at the root of all evil. . . . Hitherto, you and I have been anticipating the Free Staters holding out against de Valera, sweeping the country at the forthcoming Election and placing themselves in a strong position to maintain law and order, in a Free State within the ambit of the British Empire. Now we are confronted with a combination, as 4 is to 5, of out and out Republicans and Free Staters who, through Collins, reiterate that the Treaty is merely a stepping stone to a Republic. . . .

'The constant unparalleled provocation to which our people have been subjected demanded a re-assuring statement and something dramatic to pull them together, and I felt, along with my colleagues, that the appropriate moment had come to free ourselves of the nightmare of the Border Commission. I believe it would have been impossible to have found a more appropriate moment to jettison this preposterous proposal and you, yourself, will, later on, thank God that we got it out of the way so cleverly. . . . If, as I am sure, you will be yourself shrewd enough to take full advantage of this escape from an impossible position, it will clear the air for the defence of Ulster against the Republic. . . .'[6]

Churchill, however, unlike the Northern Prime Minister, had signed the Treaty and, believing that its provisions offered a real basis for a future of trust and co-operation, refused to trim them to favour either political interest in Ireland at the expense of the other. Until the full portent of the Pact became clear he suspended the evacuation of British troops from Ireland and summoned the pro-Treaty leaders to Whitehall.

Griffith and Duggan, with Kevin O'Higgins and Hugh Kennedy, left for London on Thursday 25 May. Collins, while prepared to follow if called upon, was held by work in Dublin. The question of the Constitution was closely linked with that of the Pact; Griffith carried a copy of the proposed draft Constitution with him to London. Churchill was not impressed with Collins's arguments for the Pact by letter, and insisted that he join his co-signatories of the Treaty. Arrangements were made for a full formal meeting to be held at 10 Downing Street on Saturday 27 May.

Long and numerous conferences ensued. Churchill postponed the statement he had promised in the Commons on the Monday. No word of what was passing leaked out to the waiting reporters, who were reduced to noting comings and goings, with nothing more startling to report than that Lord Birkenhead had arrived in a tennis suit and blue sunglasses, and that Kevin O'Higgins

[6] P.R.O.: CO 26434

had a cold and had not arrived at all. On the evening of Tuesday 30 May, however, the news broke that the Crown Law Officers regarded the Pact as an abrogation of the Treaty.

Michael wrote to Kitty: 'Things are bad beyond words and I am almost without hope of being able to do anything of permanent use. It's really awful – to think of what I have to endure here owing to the way things are done by the opponents at home. . . .'

The next day, 31 May, he wrote: 'The weather is awful here and everything is awful – I wish to God someone else was in this position and not I. But that's that.'

Yet, largely because of the unquestionable integrity of Griffith's assurances that he and his colleagues stood firmly by the Treaty, the British leaders at last felt able to recommend to Parliament that the Irishmen be allowed to continue on their new course without interference, if also without British approval.

Collins sat with Griffith and Cosgrave in the Distinguished Strangers' Gallery on Wednesday 31 May, when Churchill addressed the Commons to a gathering in force of the diehard opposition. While undisguisedly critical of the Pact, he put the Irish leaders' arguments as fairly as he could; at the same time he did not spare the Provisional Government for its inability to secure free elections, and gave grave warning of the consequences if the new Government did not carry the Treaty undertaking.

He castigated both Irish Governments for the situation in the North-East. The news of troop infiltration from the South of Belleek and Pettigo on the Border had been received the evening before. The members of the Provisional Government in London had denied responsibility.

Churchill's audience was clearly expecting to hear a great deal more of this critical turn of events. Sir Henry Wilson was strongly in favour of allowing British troops in Dublin to cross into the North should the defence of the frontier require it. He again urged the re-establishment of the Union. Michael Collins, impassively observing the debate, may well have gazed with some intensity at the spare, militant figure of the Field-Marshal, sitting with the other Unionist members for Ulster.

The debate had been weathered by the Government in an

atmosphere of unenthusiastic gloom on both sides of the House. The adjournment for the Whitsuntide recess saw no lessening of activity in Downing Street.

The draft Constitution presented by Griffith was, from the Irish point of view, a promising one. It was, almost certainly, shorter than the original drafts – Collins believed that the less binding it was in detail the better its chances of surviving challenges to it over principles. The definition of the powers of the Crown was purposely left vague; its authority was acknowledged in the Treaty, within the terms of which the Constitution Committee held the draft to be entirely though broadly confined.[7]

'The Republic in disguise' is how Lloyd George described the draft to C. P. Scott on 31 May.[8] It was an impossible proposal and inconsistent with the Treaty. If insisted upon it would mean an end of the Treaty. In that case there would be no attempt to re-occupy Southern Ireland. They would hold the ports and seize the customs. The loyalist minority, in such circumstances, must take their chance. It seemed brutal, but he saw no other way. Though he ruled out arbitration by any outside body, Lloyd George admitted that arbitration by the Dominions, through the Imperial Conference, was more possible.[9]

Negotiations between the Irish, led by Griffith, and the British Government continued almost to the eve of the election, surviving rumours of a British Cabinet appeal to the country and threats

[7] 'A history of rule from above made it essential that the individual Irish citizen should feel in a peculiar manner that the new Government was the Government of the people. . . . The statement that "the sole and exclusive power of making laws for the peace, order, and good government of the Irish Free State is vested in the Oireachtas" (Art. 12) has no precedent in the Dominions Constitutions. It is directed against the supposed power of the British Parliament to super-legislate over the Dominions Parliament. The words "sole and exclusive" were inserted with this intention and were suggested by Professor Berriedale Keith' (Mansergh *The Irish Free State* pp. 87 and 91)

[8] British Museum: Add MS 50906

[9] Even an Irish Government willing to accept the decision of the Commonwealth leaders in conference would not find its ability to act upon that acceptance altogether unimpeded. As Mr W. T. Cosgrave observed to the author: 'We found later that a pronouncement at the Imperial Conference was one thing. The laws of a country were quite another.'

of renewed war, to result in agreement upon a document very different in its approach to the Crown from that upon which Collins had so desperately hoped it would have been possible to achieve permanent unity with the Republicans.

III

Collins's agreement to make common cause with his old Republican comrades had now enmeshed him more inextricably than ever in the agonies of conflicting commitments. It was not perfidy but too many loyalties that had led him so unwisely to seek to solve Ireland's problems by embracing every method employed by those who, from poles apart, were seeking to force their separate solutions.

The Belfast pogroms continued : the combined I.R.A. operations must therefore continue also. On 30 May Sir James Craig invoked and received British aid against armed forces from the South who had, he declared, penetrated his territory in the Belleek–Pettigo triangle between Co. Fermanagh and Co. Donegal.

Collins had shown himself ready to a fault to tolerate challenges at home to the Provisional Government's authority. The British could claim that they were fulfilling their Treaty obligations by defending the Six-County area. In Southern Ireland it was a matter solely of British guns once more being turned on Irishmen.

Churchill countered Collins's telegram of strong protest by reminding him of the denial he and Griffith had themselves heard restated in the Commons that the Provisional Government had any knowledge of raids from their territory. He continued :

'It is with surprise that I read in the Communiqué issued from G.H.Q. Beggars Bush that there were "No other Irish troops" than "our troops" i.e. Free State troops "in the district then or now" and I shall be glad if you will explain the discrepancy. Following on your assurance of Wednesday morning that the Prov. Govt. was in no way responsible for the incursion, orders were immediately issued by H.M.G. to the military authorities to occupy Belleek and Pettigo. . . .'

Churchill concluded with the announcement that the Military had now been ordered into Belleek which lay wholly in the Northern Territory.[10]

What Collins, as a member of G.H.Q. Beggars Bush, thought of this we do not know. As head of the Provisional Government he could hardly object that Churchill's interpretation of 'our troops' as 'Free State troops' should more correctly read 'combined Southern troops'. His protest that Belleek barracks were in Free State territory must have sounded rather thin, even to his own ears, and he suggested an enquiry, not, we may assume, without relief that Griffith was there to fall back on.

Churchill undertook to discuss the Border situation with Griffith next day. Griffith at least, he too may well have reflected with relief, was likely to show a less belligerent determination to back any and every fighting Irishman against the rest, regardless of the obligations of statesmanship. In Churchill's view one firm stand now on the Border was likely to prove a salutary deterrent in the future. On 8 June, having shelled Belleek without much bloodshed, he telegraphed Collins, proposing 'to withdraw Br. troops to Ulster territory as soon as satisfied that F.S. able to prevent further incursion by Irregulars or other persons from F.S. territory.'

Collins was in no mood to accept this diplomatic threat with a good grace. He was sick of the British. He had accepted them as allies under the Treaty because he was convinced that he must if Ireland was to survive in the modern world. To accept their point of view was quite another thing. His public utterances were propagandist and far from conciliatory.

In these pre-election days Collins was not finding the rôle of coalitionist an easy one. For all his reiteration to the external Press that Ireland was ready to unite against outside aggression, he was gravely concerned at home with the need to reconcile his Treaty obligations with the expectations of his allies under the Pact.

On 5 June after an hour-long meeting at the Mansion House between Collins and de Valera an appeal for support for the Panel candidates in the interests of national unity was issued. The electorate's views on this became apparent the following

[10] P.R.O.: CO 27197. Telegram to Collins dated 6 June 1922

day when the nominations disclosed that only thirty-seven Panel candidates were not to be opposed by independent interests.

The Dublin correspondent of the *Daily Mail* observed on 12 June :

'The panel is not a success anywhere. Throughout the country voters dislike the idea of not being able to give a straight vote upon the treaty, and dislike even more the arranging of the affair by political leaders on the grounds that they know best what is good for the people.'

The same correspondent was present at the first of a series of Coalition election meetings in Dublin on 9 June at which Collins and de Valera appeared together. He wrote :

'Mr Collins made a very important speech. I think the best he had made. The gist of it was that if Ireland went on having politics instead of prosperity the country would go to the dogs. He was speaking about the situation being advanced another stage when someone interjected "The Republic". Mr Collins turned on his interruptor, "Don't go tieing [*sic*] yourself to a name like that", he cried, "in a hundred years or more people may be saying that Republics were the worst form of tyranny. Do not put that bar to the progress of the nation". . . .'[11]

Collins, still greatly concerned over the Constitution, left hurriedly for London on the evening of Monday 12 June. The next day was spent in a series of conferences. He started back to Dublin again that night.

On the evening of Wednesday 14 June he went down to his Cork constituency. He was enthusiastically cheered in Cork City. In heavy rain outside Turner's Hotel, and in defiance of shots fired in an attempt to cause a stampede, he made the speech which was generally held to be a repudiation of the Pact.

'You are facing an election here on Friday and I am not hampered now by being on a platform where there are Coalitionists, and I can make a straight appeal to the citizens of Cork to vote for the candidates they think best, to vote for the candidates whom the electors of Cork think will best carry on in the future the work that they want carried on. When

[11] *Daily Mail* 12 June 1922

I spoke in Dublin I put it as gravely as I could, that the country was facing a very serious situation, and if that situation is to be met as it should be met, the country must have the representatives it wants. You understand fully what you have to do, and I will depend on you to do it.'

Collins's intention may well have been merely to redress the emphasis which he felt had been improperly placed by Republican speakers upon the Panel clauses to the virtual effacement of that allowing free voting. But it is more likely that, while having this in mind, he spoke on impulse, and in defiance of the political trimming which had never come naturally to him.

Collins had a deeply rooted sense of respect for the individual. 'The people are our masters', he had cried in the Dail when it was cited as the supreme authority. He had signed the Pact solely to make the country once more a land fit, not for heroes, but for ordinary men and women to live in. With them, he was now declaring, lay the initiative.

He now knew that, no matter how many coalition candidates were returned, such a government as that envisaged in the Pact was unlikely to be formed. The Constitution had been virtually agreed before he started back from London on 13 June. Long negotiations had failed to secure the terms upon which he had hoped against hope to make it acceptable to the Republicans. The oath was made mandatory for all Parliamentary representatives; the Treaty was specified to be the sole basis from which the Constitution was derived; the powers and functions of the Crown were given precise definition. Although the Governor-General, appointed on the recommendation of Irish Ministers, would act upon their advice and not upon that of the Imperial Cabinet, and although the Irish negotiators were sufficiently assured that the formalism insisted upon by the British detracted in no actual and practical way from the independence of the Free State legislature, nevertheless the loss to possible unity in Southern Ireland by Britain's rigidity was incalculable, and, in the event, tragic, since it broke by the letter what the spirit alone could have achieved.

Collins recognized it as the end. Dorothy Macardle wrote later: 'When Republicans consented to a Pact with Michael

Collins it was in the belief that his Party, so strengthened, would now hold out with the utmost firmness for the widest possible interpretation of the Treaty in the interests of Ireland. Only if they did so could a coalition between pro-Treaty and Republican Representatives hope to succeed.'[12]

They had held out, but the point had come at which they believed it was no longer in Ireland's interests to do so. In the choice forced upon them between a State with bitter dissidents within it and the less acerbated chaos of no State at all, they had made their decision, and could only await the outcome with faith that the Irish people would ultimately benefit thereby.

The Constitution was published on the morning of polling day, 16 June. The British, not the Provisional Government, had necessitated its eleventh-hour appearance. On the eve of the election Michael toured his constituency. The people of Cork crowded about him to shake his hand and cheer him. The accustomed warmth of home-coming did not fail him now. But if the people remained unaffected in their love and trust in him, there were those among his opponents who made their differences implacable and personal. These were young men, no doubt, to whom Collins was only a name to be demonstrated against as vigorously as impetuosity and a few guns would allow.

On the night of his speech in Cork Michael went, with Gearoid O'Sullivan and Padraig O'Keeffe, to the Republican Plot in St Finbarr's cemetery. It must have meant not a little to him, in these days of the country's decision, to stand by the graves of such friends as Terence MacSwiney and Tomas MacCurtain. But at the gates armed men barred their entrance. His friends dragged him away.

His rage was terrible. Nor was it, like most of his moments of tempest, quickly to be forgotten. The incident appears to have symbolized for him his rejection in the name of those who had been his comrades; the final breaking of the ties which had made him hold his hand against those who threatened the peace and order, which he believed the Irish people had a right to have restored to them. Ernest Blythe noticed at later Cabinet meetings that he was now inclined to listen to those who were for fighting.

The results of the election were declared on 24 June. Collins's

[12] Macardle *The Irish Republic* p. 719

total of first preference votes, 17,106, headed the poll for the country. Out of a total of 128 seats, 37 of the Panel candidates had been elected unopposed; 58 pro-Treaty Panel candidates and 35 anti-Treaty Panel candidates were returned. The Treaty was not technically the issue at the election; the people had nevertheless shown their support for it by the candidates they elected. The votes have been summarized as: for the Treaty: 486,419, against the Treaty: 133,864.[13] They had also shown, by the number of Independent deputies they elected, their opinion of the Pact. Only a government pledged to uphold the Treaty was now possible.

De Valera, according to Miss Macardle, waited in daily expectation of being invited to submit his Cabinet nominations. One wonders why: he knew the terms of the Constitution. Unless he was in agreement that these held 'the widest possible interpretation of the Treaty' there could be no hope for a Coalition now. Possibly he clung to the hope that Collins and Griffith would follow the letter of the Pact and form a coalition, doomed from the outset, and then call for the election for which it provided should such a coalition fail. But they were realists, and above all the servants of the electorate. The country was plainly against the Pact. To pursue its terms would be to renounce democracy. The Republicans nevertheless continued to affirm that the election result, in that a majority of Panel candidates, irrespective of party, had been returned, was a clear mandate for the Pact.

Collins was now drawing near the point at which even he realized that compromise for the sake of unity must take second place to the people's clear wish to proceed under the Treaty. It was of small satisfaction to him to have their support while those opposed to the Treaty refused them the right to see it put peacefully into operation.

[13] Donal O'Sullivan *The Irish Free State and its Senate* (London 1940) p. 63

CHAPTER NINETEEN

Eruption

(June – August 1922)

I

Attempts to reunify the Army had continued until the election. The Republican Executive itself now split over a proposal to resume hostilities against British troops in Dublin and the Six Counties. Liam Lynch and Cathal Brugha opposed such a move, and the minority, led by Rory O'Connor, closed the gates of the Four Courts upon their colleagues.

Michael Collins must have seen a sudden lightening of the clouds that lowered, big with civil war. The irreconcilables had cut themselves adrift; Liam Lynch commanded the allegiance of considerable forces in the South. Collins may well have hoped that Lynch and his followers might now come to terms with him.

If he did see such hopeful omens they were illusory. Events in the last days of June crowded in to suffocate any prospects of the unification which only he and Lynch, with their deep respect for each other, might have achieved.

On the afternoon of 22 June 1922 Field-Marshal Sir Henry Wilson was shot dead on the doorstep of his London home by two men, later found to be Irishmen. He died as he had lived, with contemptuous courage and a ceremonial sword in his hand.

The death of this extraordinary man shocked the Empire and stirred Britain's allies. A Staff Officer with a brilliant flair for paper strategy, Wilson lacked judgement of actualities. Placed in a difficult field position, he would have been able to state with certainty just which Cabinet Minister's blunder had put him there: of how to extricate himself and his men he would have had little conception.

Indifferent to the mass sufferings of war – he wrote off over a thousand casualties in a single day as 'a nasty little knock' – waspish in his dislikes, vain beyond measure, he was nevertheless a considerate host, a lovable friend, and the reverse of pompous with younger men, to whom he showed a ready sympathy. His friends forgave him his love of backstairs gossip for his unashamed zest in it. He was culpably jealous of Haig and had intrigued to overthrow him; yet that reserved Scot wept to hear of his death.

He was a puckish man, even to his features, delighting in mischief-making, basking in praise, and peevishly vindictive when thwarted. Having Puck's charm, he had also that elfish malevolence which is unconscious of itself. The English, for whom such things have a nursery nostalgia, found him fascinating. The Irish did not. Too many deaths from exploitation and oppression had corroborated the banshee's wail for them to be beguiled.

The Irish are, however, said to be impressed by talk, and Sir Henry Wilson was all talk. When he talked of inflaming sectarian passions in the North and such passions were inflamed, they took his word that he was the manipulator of the strings. How far he was really so, or how far Orangeism merely used his name to strengthen its hand against the British Government is, in the outcome, immaterial. His influence in the past in Irish affairs had plainly been immense. Craig's public invitation to him to take over the defence of Ulster argued strongly that such influence had now become even more direct. The Southern Irish laid the Belfast pogroms at his door. The *Freeman's Journal* satirized him in a series of cartoons as being behind every Unionist move in Ulster.

At the time of his death, it was claimed, there were nearly 4,000 homeless Catholics in Belfast. Thousands more had fled, and the situation in Dublin alone, where the unending stream of refugees had created an appalling problem, had brought home the realities of happenings in the North in ugly fashion to the South.

The assassination of Sir Henry Wilson was, therefore, generally interpreted as being a direct act of revenge by the South for all that Catholic nationalists had suffered at Orange hands.

British reaction was immediate and uncompromising. Westminster was stunned. Unlike the members of Dail Eireann those of the Imperial Parliament were not accustomed to the expectation of having any of their number done to death. 'The debate in Parliament was one of the bitterest I remember', writes Sir Geoffrey Shakespeare.[1] The Englishman's anger is slow to kindle, but once roused it can only be extinguished in action. That anger was now turned against Ireland.

Responsibility for Wilson's death had immediately been laid at the Republicans' door, with little in the way of exoneration for those who had failed to deal effectively with them. Macready, ordered to attack the Four Courts, pleaded that most of the Irish believed that Rory O'Connor had nothing to do with Wilson's death. The Government reconsidered and bade him stay his hand.

Who had commanded the assassination remained unexplained. The two Irishmen, Reginald Dunne and Joseph O'Sullivan, who were tried and sentenced to death for the deed went to the scaffold in silent loyalty to the giver of the order. Both were members of the I.R.A. Rory O'Connor denied all knowledge of their action, as did de Valera. Griffith and his Cabinet were plainly horrified. Later years have ascribed responsibility to Michael Collins, the general opinion being that he gave orders to Dunne before the Treaty and never cancelled them.

Griffith clearly had no suspicion of this. Ernest Blythe, who was present when Griffith drew up his repudiation of 'this anarchic deed', states that Collins went over it with him phrase by phrase. He, Blythe, formed the impression that Collins certainly knew more about the affair than Griffith did, but puts this down to his intelligence contacts. He believed that it had been done as 'a stab in the back for Collins' by those who wanted the Treaty torn up and Collins pulled down. Denis McCullough, however, felt sure he knew all about it.

There can be little doubt that such an order had been given, most probably by Collins, in pre-Treaty days. As C.I.G.S. of the British Army Wilson must have qualified for execution even without his personal Unionist activities. But Collins was not a man who absent-mindedly left execution orders unrevoked. It is infinitely more probable that, far from doing so, he renewed the order to Dunne shortly before it was carried out, when the Belfast pogroms were at their height.

Collins was, first and foremost, an Irish revolutionary. His systematic eradication of Ireland's enemies had provided her

[1] Shakespeare *Let candles be brought in* p. 93

most vital breakthrough. The politician's circumspection came a
poor second to his soldier's instincts. As Chairman of the Provisional Government he can only have agreed with Griffith that
'it is a fundamental principle of civilized government that the
assassination of a political opponent cannot be justified or condoned'. He should also have foreseen – he was presumably blind
to it – that the assassination of Wilson must further weaken the
authority of the Provisional Government. As a physical force
leader he reacted to Wilson's alleged responsibility for the ordering of events in Belfast as he had reacted to those events themselves : as a matter to be effectively met only by the gun. Wilson's
death should prove as salutary a warning to the Ulster Specials
as the deaths of G-men had proved to the detectives of Dublin
Castle.

All the burdens now borne by Collins were rooted in the North-
East. Only by bringing in the North could he reunite Sinn Fein
in the South. Yet every effort to win the North by diplomacy
had resulted in a chaos of mistrust and inflamed hatred, of which,
to the South, Wilson was the embodiment. If Collins could not
shoot Unionism he could at least shoot Wilson.

The Republican forces ensconced in the Four Courts provided
an excellent cover. More important to Collins, there was little
chance that Dunne, London-Irish and a war veteran, need run
any risk of capture.

Neither of these considerations was destined to stand up to
events. Collins cannot have predicted that Dunne would choose
as his companion a crippled man – O'Sullivan had lost a leg at
Ypres – whom he would refuse to desert when the hue and cry
was raised which ended in the capture of both.

The British Government, while it duly fastened blame upon
the Republicans, put the Provisional Government in a disastrous
position by issuing it with an ultimatum. This made the action
subsequently taken on its own initiative by the Provisional
Government appear in Republican eyes as a surrender to British
orders.

Whatever his involvement in Wilson's death, Collins took full
responsibility for the lives of Dunne and O'Sullivan. He sent
Cullen to London to see what could be done, by any means, to
save them. It was McKee and Clancy all over again. He paced

the floor, hurried out to see Tim Healy about legal counsel for
their trial, and brushed aside pressing requests from close colleagues to see them with the curt rejoinder that Dunne and
O'Sullivan were more important.

It was hopeless from the first. The two were tried at the Old
Bailey on 18 July, found guilty, and sentenced to death.

II

Few of the Irishmen who accepted the Treaty can have realized
how much they had so far owed to Churchill. He had staked
his political fortunes upon it and had upheld the actions of its
Irish signatories in the face of bitter attacks at home which had
been fomented by Irishmen, both North and South, who were
not party to it. A resolute believer in nipping trouble in the bud,
he had reluctantly accepted Collins's arguments for delaying
tactics that might dissipate a crisis. But now Collins's most cogent
reason for compromise, the lack of any mandate from the people,
was gone. Churchill undoubtedly felt that unless the Provisional
Government asserted itself quickly he must consider the Colonial
Office's responsibility for upholding law and order in any
Dominion whose administration had shown itself incompetent to
do so. Nor can he have felt bound to sacrifice his own future for
Ireland, a country to which he owed no loyalty beyond that
vested in the Treaty, and for which, it must be added, he had
small affection.

On 26 June, speaking in the Commons, he announced an
ultimatum. Unless the Provisional Government brought the
occupation of the Four Courts to a speedy end, His Majesty's
Government would regard the Treaty as having been violated
and would resume 'full liberty of action'.

When he heard of Churchill's speech Collins, as one of his
colleagues discreetly puts it, 'spoke, raging'. Whatever action the
Provisional Government now took was bound to have the appearance of compulsion by the British Government.

Would the British have moved? It seems far more likely that,
despite that first precipitate order to Macready, later counter-
manded, it would not. The 'ultimatum' seems to have had the

double purpose of pushing the Provisional Government into action which, if taken by the British themselves, would have wrecked the Treaty, not established it; and of muzzling the diehard opposition at home.

Collins, whose view was solely that of Ireland, snarled: 'Let Churchill come over and do his own dirty work.'[2] But he had already realized that the work to be done from now on was the responsibility of the Irish upholders of the Treaty, upon whose shoulders the Irish electorate had placed it.

The Provisional Government had, in any case, come to the end of its tether. Not the least of the Republican forces' moves had been to appropriate a very considerable amount of money from the Bank of Ireland.

On 24 June, the day on which the verdict of the polls was announced, two firms in Dublin were ordered in the name of a Republican leader to hand over sums of money by the following Tuesday. On Monday 26 June, the Four Courts Executive sent one of its members to a Dublin garage to commandeer motor transport. Government troops promptly arrested him.

The Executive had cause for being annoyed: one reason for the cars' seizure was the operations against the North on which G.H.Q. was still, nominally at least, co-operating. That evening members of the Four Courts garrison kidnapped Lieut-General 'Ginger' O'Connell, the Assistant Chief of Staff of the Government forces, as a hostage.

The Provisional Government never accepted that the British ultimatum influenced its decision to attack the Four Courts. General Mulcahy claimed that the decision was 'practically taken' before Churchill made his speech. Among Collins's papers is one headed 'Note for Cabinet Meeting (26.6.1922)' and dated that day. It runs in part: '(a) Internal policy in our own area. The restoration of ordinary conditions. Arrangements for peace and order. . . .'

It was a joint Dail Cabinet and Provisional Government meeting. During its course the raid on the garage was reported. Churchill's speech had not yet been heard. When it was known it almost caused a reversal of the decision which, after the kidnapping of O'Connell, had finally been taken as to

[2] O'Connor *The Big Fellow* p. 177

how the 'restoration of ordinary conditions' was to be attempted.[8]

The meeting at which it was decided to act was very brief. All were agreed before it started that the Four Courts' challenge must be met. The British Government must be approached for artillery. Gavan Duffy raised the only question, that of whether an attack would take long. Gearoid O'Sullivan, present as Adjutant-General, thought it would not. Collins gave no opinion.

He was grimly determined. For the Republican Executive to thumb its nose at the Provisional Government was one thing; the kidnapping of the Assistant Chief of Staff was the first, blatant, attack on the National Army, and quite another. His final words as he left the meeting were those he must have used so often in the past : 'None of you sleep at home tonight.'

The time had come when the Government must either assert its authority or give way to force of arms. It must also have seemed a time when conditions were ripe for taking action with the least possibility of widespread repercussions.

Unknown to Collins, the Republican split was fast healing. With Wilson's death the Northern Catholics could expect only increased violence against them : Liam Lynch was once more in consultation with Rory O'Connor. Collins had no inkling of this – evidence enough of the deep gulf that now finally divided him from his former comrades. Each side had reached the point where it must make its stand.

On Tuesday 27 June the Provisional Government issued a statement which admitted no compromise : ' . . . The Government is determined that the country shall no longer be held up from the pursuit of its normal life and the re-establishment of its free national institutions. It calls, therefore, on the citizens to co-operate actively with it in the measures it is taking to ensure the public safety and to secure Ireland for the Irish people.'

An ultimatum was delivered to the Four Courts' garrison to surrender before 4 a.m. on Wednesday 28 June. Two eighteen-pounder field guns were borrowed from the British Army.

The Four Courts' garrison made no reply and, at 4.7 a.m. the big guns crashed out across the Liffey for the first time since 1916.

[8] Colum *Arthur Griffith* p. 367

Republicans date the commencement of the Civil War from the first shell fired under Collins's orders from a British gun. The Free State supporters point out that a state of civil war had existed from the day the Army Convention repudiated civil authority; that it had hitherto been confined to one side only, and that the Government had now joined battle on ground of the Republicans' own choosing.

The ballad-makers did not spare to lay the primary responsibility at the door of the man who had shown the greatest reluctance to face a contest in arms:

> England blew the bugle
> And threw the gauntlet down,
> And Michael sent the boys in green
> To level Dublin town.[4]

There were no ballads sung for Collins. They are the hereditary weapons of lost causes, of defiance of the Powers that Be. Collins and his companions had no time for singing if the new State was to survive. They could only proceed to establish by guns what they had hoped to achieve by hard work and co-operation. They knew they had abandoned, not the cause for which all had striven, but the means. They knew they had a duty to set up the Treaty.

For both sides the fight against symbols, whether of Republic or Free State, had suddenly and sickeningly become a fight against persons. For Irishmen, drugged for too long by idealism, 28 June 1922 dawned in rude awakening as Dublin shuddered to the labouring guns. 'It had to come', was Collins's comment. But he was no more reconciled to it than if he had spoken of a loved one's death.

Griffith, convinced at last that Collins was not going to sacrifice the Treaty, took comfort as he had done in the past from his support.

On the Friday the Republican garrison surrendered unconditionally. Earlier in the day, by a disastrous combination of Republican munitions and Free State bombardment, the Public Record Office of the Four Courts with its accumulated treasure of centuries had been blown sky-high.

National Library of Ireland

Churchill drafted a telegram on 30 June to Collins, which ended:

> 'The situation in this country is being revolutionized by the action which you have taken & I look forward with increasing confidence to the future. If I refrain from congratulations it is only because I do not wish to embarrass you. The archives of the Four Courts may be scattered but the titledeeds of Ireland are safe.'[5]

Congratulations from the British! For Collins, sorrowing after old comrades, the word must have turned like a knife in the wound. His primary aim now was to restore order in Dublin as swiftly as possible before hostilities spread, and then get on with the urgent administrative work which alone, all guns stilled, could establish Ireland's nationhood.

The Republicans had established themselves in other buildings in Dublin, principally in hotels along O'Connell Street. The Government troops now turned their attention to these pockets of resistance.

The fighting continued throughout Sunday 2 July. Machineguns and rifles alone were used as Government troops advanced to form a cordon round the O'Connell Street area north of the Nelson Pillar. On Monday most of the Republicans managed to withdraw safely from their positions. Brugha remained in the Hammam Hotel with a small garrison. They had orders to hold out as long as possible, then surrender. Heavy guns had now been brought into action. On Tuesday the Republican order to surrender was sent to Brugha, but the door of the building was shut against the messenger.

By noon on Wednesday the Gresham and Hammam Hotels were irrevocably ablaze. In the evening the garrison marched out to surrender. Cathal Brugha was not with them. The barricade was a mass of flame, the narrow lane palled in smoke from the buildings on either side, before his short, resolute figure emerged, a revolver in either hand. Friend and foe joined in cries to him to give in, but he refused, as he had done six years before in Easter Week, and they could only watch as he ran forwards up the lane.

[5] P.R.O.: Colonial Office Papers

'It was a tragedy', a Free State officer has told the author, 'that the Government troops who were waiting for Brugha were not older men who had served with him. They would have held their fire until his ammunition was exhausted and then taken him. But they were youngsters, inexperienced in war. Young fellows are very quick on the draw.'

Brugha fell, mortally wounded by a volley of rifle fire. Yet he would not, after all, have cared to live by the mercy of men whom he considered traitors, in an Ireland governed by them. Two days later he died.

Collins wept unrestrainedly when they told him. 'There was one brave man amongst them', he said.

He and the other Government leaders were hunted men. They were virtually prisoners in Government Buildings, sleeping on mattresses in their offices. Resentful as ever of being confined, Michael broke out and found refuge elsewhere in the city. Those who attempted to track him were more than once put to flight by his sudden, enraged charge. Dr Gogarty gave him a latch-key, and he came and went at the house in Ely Place unobserved.

As Collins had never scoffed at others for their belief in the Republic, so now he did not seek to lay all blame on the other side. Speaking of earlier days he exclaimed: 'Ah, I was young then – and nice. And now I am old and not so nice.' It was a mood of self-disillusionment which many, on both sides, must have experienced. The tarnishing hand of civil strife had touched all of them now, and all had grown old as Collins, not thirty-two, had done.

The Army was all-important now. Joseph McGrath was Director of Intelligence in Portobello, and Collins was constantly in consultation with him. He was soon to return to soldiering himself. Sporadic fighting had begun to spread through various parts of the country. On 12 July a Government meeting appointed a Council of War. Collins was made Commander-in-Chief, relinquishing his post as Minister of Finance. Mulcahy remained Minister of Defence and became Chief of Staff.

General Michael Collins suddenly lost the look of drawn weariness of the past months. His old boyish energy returned. His work lay once more clear-cut before him: restore order and then get back to the job of administration from which civil war had deflected him. He bounded off to set up his headquarters in Portobello, and wrote restively in his notebook next day: 'First day at P.bello. Staff meeting at 4 O'C. Spent morning rather wastefully owing to delay B of Works in fitting up rooms for working in.'[6]

In the South the Republicans were rallying to arms. They had the initial advantage of holding a large proportion of the barracks in Munster and Connaught vacated by the British. From Waterford to Limerick and most of the country to the south was in their hands. The capture of the Four Courts' leaders had, however, resulted in confusion. Despite isolated offensives an overall plan of campaign was lacking. There was little prospect of obtaining arms in any quantity, unless these could be captured from the National Army.

Nevertheless, the Republican leaders under Liam Lynch prepared to hold their line and defend their territory. Seamus Robinson commanded Lynch's former headquarters at Clonmel. It was to Clonmel that Eamon de Valera came, a tall, sombre figure, his arms pledged once more to the defence of the Republic. A man whose star was now in eclipse, he would be given time to lead his country again when those who were now striving to lay the foundations upon which he and others might build were gone.

[6] Collins Papers

CHAPTER TWENTY

The Last Journey South

I

'Be careful not to kill anyone', Collins ordered Dr Thomas Dillon in Galway. He was urgently aware that, once civil war was over, Ireland would need all the finest men of that vital generation to build her as an independent nation.

His transcendent instinct was to create, and the destructive policy upon which the Republicans had embarked filled him with an enraged determination to curb the insensate acts which would leave Ireland impoverished long after hostilities had ceased. The Free State too did not lack its supporters who, like Romulus before them, found only one answer to those who disparaged their ideals. Young men, unnerved by war, soon became brutalized by it, remembering that it had begun with a higher end than itself only when they found a brother among the enemy left dead on the battlefield.

It was clear that while the Republicans could command enough food and money to maintain their troops indefinitely their active resistance would continue. To cut off their food supplies was impracticable since they lived, to a large extent, as in former days, off the land. Revenue sources were more accessible. The Government Council of War determined, therefore, to gain control of key positions in Republican-held areas, stop the seizure of money from banks, post offices and port authorities, and thus break the opposing Army before it could co-ordinate and establish itself.

The administration of the National Army was another task of considerable difficulty with which Collins was faced. Machinery for food supplies and the payment of scattered groups of soldiers would take time to establish. In the meantime the Government forces were in the curious position of being less regularly supplied than the Republicans, who were unhampered by the considerations which prevented Collins's men from raiding shops and revenue offices.

Collins was at his desk day and night in Portobello; his note-book of those July days, crammed with hurried writing, gives some indication of the multitude of concerns which took up his time : prison accommodation, press censorship, medical services, telephone systems, reprieves, engineering, and Intelligence lists for 'Postal Purposes', together with scores of names of the men and women he required to see. When he was not at Portobello or Merrion Square, he was off on tours of military inspection.

He was as impatient as ever of interruption. When Liam O'Briain crept in to give Griffith a message, Collins called him a 'bloody disturber'. Time was running out, and he was in hot pursuit, as if he knew it.

At the back of all his worries lay the North. One of the most tragic aspects of the Civil War was that it drove the Northerners even more determinedly behind the barriers that divided them from their countrymen. Lawless chaos had now wrecked such hope as Collins had had of bringing in the North as a partner in a united Ireland within a forseeable time.

On 7 July 1922 Churchill had written to both Sir James Craig and Collins, bidding them look more hopefully to the future when, once peace was established, broader avenues of approach to unity might be explored. Better relations, he implied, would not best be achieved by recriminations and provocative speeches. Collins replied on 25 July :

' . . . Since I have been entrusted with supreme command of the National Army, I have scarcely a moment for any business other than the urgent business of restoring peace and settled conditions to the country. But I know you will fully appreciate the trying and difficult circumstances of the present position. . . .

'I appreciate very much your observations on the North-Eastern situation and your suggestions for the achievement of Irish unity. Believe me this all-important question is never far removed from my thoughts and were it not for my new obligations and commitments I would be devoting all available time and energy towards its solution.

'In this respect you may recall that practically at my first meeting with Craig I gave it as my opinion that the Boundary Commission would not be regarded as an ideal settlement even if the effect of its decisions were to convey to us the last square foot of our full territorial demand.

'We must seek for a better and more permanent solution, and one which will not be so liable to perpetuate bitter memories amongst neighbours. For this purpose I am most anxious to get back to the very promising position of my first agreement with Craig. . . .'[1]

Churchill, evidently moved, replied hearteningly a few days later. He can hardly have failed to compare the liberality of Collins's approach with the views of Sir James Craig, expressed in the latter's letter of 26 May. His letter to Collins ends : 'I hope that by the time I return in the latter part of August you will have seen that the Irish people are masters in their own house.'[2]

The Provisional Government's first attempt to roll up the Republican line from Waterford to Limerick southwards had failed. Troops sent from Dublin and Wicklow across country were impeded by ambushes, and their striking force was dissipated over a long line. Lacking training, they were unable to gain positions quickly enough to be effective.

Collins determined, therefore, on different strategy. While the Republicans had sufficient arms and deployment to win encounters by land, they lacked artillery and enough men to hold the long coastline at their backs. On 23 July Collins's men landed at Waterford. The next day they took Westport from the sea, and routed the Republicans from Castlebar. From then on the Government forces' advance on Republican strongholds was to prove irresistible.

Peace did not follow in their wake. Wherever a lone man with a gun remained, the unrelenting strife went on. In a small country of close-knit traditions and affections the fall of cities counted as nothing beside that of brothers and neighbours. More deadly than the encounters in the Anglo-Irish War, those now took place

[1] P.R.O.: CO 38573
[2] P.R.O.: CO 38573

in which each side knew the other's secret ways, and tracked them without remorse.

There were moments of great chivalry and others of rank barbarity. Commonly, however, young men used their guns confusedly, bewildered by the crises of war and unable to visualize its restraints.

In one such unguarded encounter Government troops raided the hotel where Harry Boland was sleeping on the night of 31 July. In the uncertainties of darkness shots were fired as they went to take him prisoner, and he fell, mortally wounded, to die two days later.

For every man who experienced the Civil War one incident above all others brought home its full meaning. The death of Harry Boland marked that moment of truth for Collins. He burst into Fionan Lynch's room in a paroxysm of uncontrolled grief. There were those who believed that Collins had ordered his friend's death. Yet Boland's brother, himself a forthright opponent of Collins, does not hold this view. There could be no dissimulation in that devastated reaction.

Michael wrote to Kitty:

'Last night I passed Vincent's Hospital and saw a small crowd outside. My mind went in to him lying dead there and I thought of the times together and whatever good there is in any wish of mine he certainly had it. Although the gap of 8 or 9 months was not forgotten – of course no one can ever forget it – I only thought of him with the friendship of the days of 1918 & 1919. . . . I'd send a wreath but I suppose they'd return it torn up.'

On 4 August he wrote: 'There is no one who feels it all more than I do. My condemnation is all for those who would put themselves up as paragons of Irish Nationality and all the others as being not worthy of concern.'

He wrote bitingly of what he called 'the "diehard" reversion' of those who, having taken no part in the War of Independence, were now eager to kill their fellow-countrymen in the name of the Republic: 'May God help those who are trying to direct big issues on that kind of fickle material. Perhaps not so fickle as variable.'

Government troops were now pushing across Kerry and West Cork from the sea, holding the towns as they went. They occupied Limerick. Amphibious landings were made on 8 August at Passage West. On 9 August Collins wrote : 'Cork is in the melting pot now. We can only wonder how it will get on.'

On 11 August Cork fell to Emmet Dalton. On the same day Liam Lynch and his garrison burned their headquarters in Fermoy and reverted to the countryside as their base for operations.

Henceforward the war was to be a long and bitter mopping-up of the Republican Army flying columns. Marked on one side by burnings, shootings, and intimidation of those attempting to restore settled government, and on the other by large-scale executions and summary emergency powers, the long months that followed the end of regular hostilities lacked the high zeal of former guerilla days, which was replaced by dogged disillusionment.

If Collins and his colleagues could look more hopefully to the time when they could redirect their energies to setting up the Free State, they did so under the shadow of a loss which neither they nor Ireland itself could easily afford.

Arthur Griffith, worn out by the culminating events of a lifetime devoted to the struggle to establish the nationality of Ireland, died suddenly, broken in heart no less than body, on 12 August 1922.

Tributes will be paid to Griffith's work, his scorn of self-seeking, his integrity, and breadth of vision, as long as nationhood counts for anything. All that is best in Ireland's achievements is his epitaph. At the time of his death his friends could only mourn that he had not lived to reap where he had sown, but had to leave the field in those first, unhappy days of troubled harvest.

The loss to Collins of his friend and counsellor was incalculable. 'He had sounder political judgement than any of us', he wrote.[3] There had also been a warmth, known only by his friends and the more valued; and that sheet-anchor quality which had held Ireland on her course when men of lesser judgement hesitated or trimmed dangerously to cross-winds.

Griffith had watched Collins develop in mental stature. Soon

[3] Beaslai *Michael Collins* II, p. 424

Ireland would no longer need his steadying hand upon Collins's stronger, more impetuous one. There were other coming men of sober ability and strength of purpose. His work was done. He had lacked only its rewards.

Collins had been away on a tour of Government-held positions in Limerick, Tipperary, and Kerry. At Tralee he heard of Griffith's death and hurried back to Dublin.

As he headed the long funeral march of the Army through the streets of Dublin, Mulcahy beside him, the crowds jostled to glimpse him. For many it was their first chance to see him. His hurrying figure in earlier months had been hardly noticeable as he dashed, attaché-case in hand, to and from his office. Now they were rewarded by the sight of him, resplendent in the uniform of Commander-in-Chief. The tendency to put on weight which had been evident in the months of relative physical restriction only added to the impression of superb strength. There was no indication of the weariness of body and spirit that still dogged him inexorably. The crowd saw only a hero in the prime of life, whose vitality was a reassurance that Ireland still had a leader to protect and guide her future.

Dr Fogarty, the Bishop of Killaloe, spoke to Collins as he stood alone, gazing long at the grave of his friend. 'Michael, you should be prepared – you may be the next.' Collins turned. 'I know', he said simply. When the long, slow ceremony to Glasnevin was over, with its strain on men unused to processional marching, Michael sighed with relief. 'I hope nobody takes it into his head to die for another twelve months', he said.

These remarks were to return to memory later with the clamour of unheeded prophecy.

On the day that Collins marched to Glasnevin at the head of the Army, Reggie Dunne, for whose life he had fought so desperately, went, with Joseph O'Sullivan, to his execution. One of the gentlest of Ireland's soldiers, his last letter to his mother contains a list of those to whom he wished to be remembered. Among them is the name of 'Micky Collins'. Perhaps it was the same friendly farewell he sent to the others; perhaps it was intended to set the seal on an order accomplished, a word of compassion where no other was possible. As a remembrance, Collins, if he ever received it, can scarcely have needed it. There was no doubting the intention of Dunne's final wish : 'Oh! Pray for our poor country !'[4]

Death searched for Collins in the Dublin streets, and waited about the houses of friends. He dined with the Laverys at the Kingstown Hotel. Hazel Lavery sat between him and the window throughout that evening and cheated the sniper placed there of his quarry.[5] He spoke to a friend on the telephone one evening : 'Did you hear I've been likened to Lincoln? Is it prophetic? Very likely. You know how he ended, and I'm told they mean to get me tonight. They won't tonight, anyway.'

He was a young man with a young man's sense of immortality. Death must come some time. It would never be tonight.

II

Michael's interrupted tour of the south-west had possessed him with a sense of the chaos that reigned throughout the country. He felt that only his presence could set aright much that was amiss, and sustain the morale of the troops for a greater test than the uncomplicated triumph of the capture of a few barracks, when the real demand on their obedience would be made in the need to subjugate militarism to civil law and order.

Especially where Cork was concerned he could not leave someone else to report on the situation. Even more important, he was convinced that if he could meet Liam Lynch and his brother officers on the Republican side a way could be found to halt the senseless slaughter of Irishmen. It was a chance that no one but he could hope to bring off. He strode into Joe McGrath's adjoining office in Portobello and announced his intention of going South.

McGrath was appalled. Griffith was dead, Collins his obvious successor as leader of the Free State. Cork held the hard core of Republican resistance. As Director of Intelligence he was prepared to exert every argument to stop his Commander-in-Chief running recklessly into danger.

Collins scowled. He, Mick Collins, was not going to run from

[4] National Library of Ireland
[5] Lavery *The Life of a Painter* p. 216

his own Corkmen. McGrath lost his temper; Collins shouted back, his determination only increasing. Afterwards McGrath wrote all his objections in a letter, in red ink. He was never to have a reply.

Sunday 20 August was set down for the beginning of Collins's Southern tour of inspection. He went out to Greystones that Saturday morning, to the Leigh Doyles, where he had so often been with the Kevin O'Higginses and other friends. Kitty was staying at the Grand Hotel, and he asked them to take care of her. He had recently had his photograph taken in uniform, and he gave them a copy. He would not sign it : he was in a hurry, would do it when he came back. Never given to studied gestures, he nevertheless turned at the gate as he left, and saluted.

He survived an ambush on the way home from a dinner party that night. A salvo of shots was fired into the car; Collins was more troubled by a pain in his side.[6] He had been unwell all day. Richard Mulcahy was to describe how 'On Saturday, the day before he went on his last journey to Cork, he sat with me at breakfast writhing with pain from a cold all through his body'.

In these last days, too, Liam O'Briain saw him descending the steps of Government Buildings. He wore a military overcoat and went slowly, head hanging, the old dash gone from him. One is reminded of lines from Padraig Colum's *Wild Earth* which Collins had known and loved in the early London days :

> O, man, standing lone and bowed earthward,
> Your task is a day near its close.

The military escort left Portobello early on Sunday morning. A touring car, in which Collins travelled with Fionan Lynch for company as far as Limerick and then Mallow; a Crossley tender with a few troops; an armoured car, the *Slievenamon*. When Oliver Gogarty knew that Collins was looking for a Rolls-Royce driver he had suggested his own former chauffeur. But the man had driven Sir William Orpen through Flanders on his painter's tour of the battlefields, and had seen enough hazardous employment. A Scotsman, McPeake, took his place.

As Collins, coughing and ignoring a heavy chill, prepared to leave, Joe Sweeney made a last-minute attempt to dissuade him.

[6] Lavery *The Life of a Painter* p. 216

It was ridiculous, he told him, for a man in his position to be going about the country in an open car. Collins shrugged it off. 'No one's going to shoot me in my own county.'

There were delays along the road. The further south they went the more evident the signs of depredation. Nevertheless, they reached Limerick safely, where Joe Dolan joined the party. From here they journeyed to Mallow. The viaduct had been blown up, perhaps the most effective Republican ground operation of the Civil War, for it virtually severed Cork from the nerve-centre of Dublin. Like many of the more successful of the Republicans' other activities, this feat had been attributed by the Provisional Government to Erskine Childers. In Griffith's least fine moment he had hailed him as 'a damned Englishman'. The Republicans, in fact, made little use of his wartime officer's experience.

Collins arrived in Cork late in the evening. He strode into the Imperial Hotel to find two sentries asleep. In a gesture characteristic if something less than Napoleonic he seized them both by the collar and banged their heads together before passing on. One of his nephews brought him a cup of tea and asked with youthful eagerness if he might accompany him next day. Michael growled: 'I've got my job to do and you've got yours. Mind your own business and do your own work.'

Next day he spoke with old friends and formed his own estimate of popular feeling. That afternoon, at 3.30, he wrote what was probably his last letter, to Cosgrave. He concluded: 'It would be a big thing to get Civic Guards both here and in LIMERICK. Civil administration urgent everywhere in the South. The people are splendid.'[7]

Despite his illness, this contact with his own people had restored something of Michael's old energy. He was, moreover, looking forward with renewed optimism to an end to bloodshed. He shared a room that night with Joe Dolan. Though it was late when they retired, Dolan remembers the vigour with which the Commander-in-Chief hurled his boots outside the door before taking a flying leap into bed.

They were called very early next morning, Tuesday 22 August.

[7] From the original draft in the possession of Mr Michael Collins, Waterford, a nephew of Michael Collins

Michael rolled out immediately, and called Dolan to breakfast with him. He ate a good meal, and appeared to have shaken off his chill. 'I believe Dev's knocking round this area', he remarked.

Continuing the tour of inspection, they moved off early, shortly after six o'clock. The first stop was Macroom, where Collins had gone the previous day.[8] Republican activity had played havoc with roads and bridges, and only a brief halt was made before the convoy continued on its way, following the maze of back-roads between Macroom and Bandon.

The Government garrison at Bandon was commanded by Sean Hales. Collins was now in the Republican brigade area of Cork No. 3, under the command of Sean's brother, Tom, one of Collins's own most valued comrades of earlier days. The road which the convoy now took ran through the wild and beautiful countryside of hills and little sparsely wooded valleys west of Cork. As they passed the crossroads of the hamlet of Beal na mBlath – the Pass of the Flowers – at about nine that morning they slowed down to ask the road to Bandon of a solitary man strolling nearby. He directed them through Newceston, and the little column drove on.

It had been a fateful moment. The man on the roadside, Dinny Long, had just laid down his rifle and gone for a short walk after doing sentry duty all night outside the house where Republican divisional officers had come for a meeting that day of Cork No. 3 Brigade officers. The meeting had already begun when Long reported the passing of the convoy. In the open touring car he had recognized Michael Collins.

These senior officers decided to lay an ambush a few hundred yards from the Beal na mBlath crossroads on the chance that Collins's column would return that way. The meeting adjourned, and they took up positions to the south of the road, which they barricaded with a cart. It was a warm summer's day. They settled down, prepared to wait, if necessary, till darkness fell.

[8] The sources upon which the author has relied for details of this day's events are the account given her personally by Comdt Joe Dolan; General Emmet Dalton's account, published in Beaslai *Michael Collins*; Eoin Neeson's *The Civil War in Ireland* (Cork 1966); and various personal statements made by Collins's relatives, including his brother Mr Sean Collins, and neighbours who saw him that day.

Collins and his escort reached Bandon, then travelled south-westwards to Clonakilty. There the people crowded out to cheer him, and old friends came to bid him welcome home. He lunched in the house of one of them.

There can have been few days in his life more replete with the simple, everyday things he loved. These were his own people, and they chatted with him, not of the affairs of State or Army, but of their concerns which were his own and had been his father's before him.

Children had always come closest to him, and they came now : the small girl, who never forgot how she ran down into her father's saddler's shop, and saw the splendid figure in uniform filling the whole room before her eyes; the little boy, who pushed past the protective clutter of soldiers, determined to catch a glimpse of the Commander-in-Chief, who turned, and paused in his conversation. 'Well, what does the gossoon want?' 'To see you, sir.' 'How do you do.' The cheerful handshake held six-pence in it.

His roots had always remained where he had been born. He had mastered both Dublin and London, but they were unreal, his achievement of them made in the name of Sam's Cross. He came home now, calling his cousins to fetch his brother Johnny from the fields. They talked together of the work at Woodfield, where, though the house was in ruins, the farming still went on as it had done in the days when he trotted along the furrows after his father. His new responsibilities were an extension, not a denial, of all that had shaped him then. He told Johnny that he had come South to prepare the ground for an end to hostilities.

He gathered his family and friends about him in the Five Alls, where he had gone in the past after a game of bowling on many another summer's evening. Broad-shouldered against the small window beside the bar, he stood them and his escort a pint of Clonakilty Wrastler.

There was the same sense of homecoming when they reached Rosscarbery. After the inspection of the garrison his first thought was to visit an old lady there, a friend of his mother. For him, as for the old men and women he reverenced, the past was all-important, since only its true comprehension could point the right way to use the present.

Next to age he reverenced learning. He walked that afternoon with one of his former schoolmasters at Lisavaird. Years of incalculable development in wide fields had intervened to make him now the head of the Irish Government; but he was unselfconscious in his greeting of the older man as 'master'.

He had come home again to all the things that had been his life's work. Now the time to end his journey had come.

The long day's clear light was fading as they travelled along the deserted ribbon of road that wound towards Beal na mBlath. Ahead of them the Republicans, who had waited in ambush position since morning, had broken up, concluding that Collins's convoy had taken another route.

The road at this point ran between hills, with a small stream to the north of it, the hillside beyond sparsely covered with trees and shrubs. The main ambush party moved on to the road and set off round the bend, intending to resume the interrupted brigade meeting. Four or five men delayed to remove the cart with which they had barricaded the road. As a couple of them dragged it to one side the motor cycle outrider of Collins's escort roared into view. Those on the road dived for cover, their handful of companions opening fire on the approaching column. At least they could warn the main body ahead before the vehicles swept on and into them.

Emmet Dalton, sitting beside Collins, took in the meaning of the shots immediately, and shouted to the driver to 'Drive like hell!' Collins, however, leant forward and commanded him to stop. If only, Joe Dolan was to lament, it had been one of Collins's own drivers, the Hyland brothers, at the wheel. They knew their impetuous Chief and would almost certainly have obeyed Dalton's order and driven on at full speed for a couple of miles before pausing to enquire of Collins, 'What's that you were saying?' But the driver had no such happy disregard for his Commander-in-Chief's wishes, and halted at once.

Ambush positions are not designed to favour the attacked, an elementary principle of war which Collins fatally overlooked, albeit it was a very small group of men who now, as surprised as he, prepared to make a fight of it. Collins also lacked Dalton's experience of ground warfare, having in its place a no less disastrous compensating factor, the urge to take frontline risks.

A Commander-in-Chief does not fling himself on his stomach behind a ditch with a rifle to take pot shots at the enemy. Nor, for that matter, do heads of government. Churchill was to show the same precipitate desire to be in the thick of the fight when, years afterwards, he was prevented from viewing the Normandy landings only by the personal plea of his king. Michael Collins knew no master, and that quality of leadership which had brought him on this last journey south now made him jump from the car to share in the fight.

Joe Dolan, sitting on the back of the armoured car travelling in the rear of the column could, if he leaned out, see Collins sitting in the touring car ahead. Most of the time he did not bother to do so. This part of the countryside was alien to him, its towns and villages unidentifiable. He dozed in the rapidly falling twilight, his rifle planted between his knees. At the first shots he jerked awake. The armoured car halted not far behind the Leyland car.

Collins and Dalton ran back past the armoured car, and took cover as best they could behind a low bank, where Sean O'Connell presently joined them. The Republicans' first fire had been directed from the hillside at the Crossley tender and O'Connell had opened fire with Thompson guns in return. Now the Republicans turned their fire instead on those who had left the touring car. The main body of their force, hearing the shots, had begun to work its way back along the northern hillside.

Collins lay on the road between Dalton and O'Connell. Joe Dolan jumped down from the armoured car and, keeping it behind him, began to fire up the hillside with his rifle. The rest of the little column found positions nearby. McPeake had started off with a burst of machine-gun fire, but after a short time the gun no longer opened properly, but fired single shots, like a rifle. Only later, when McPeake deserted to the Republicans, taking the *Slievenamon* with him, would this failure take on a sinister significance.

The engagement had lasted for almost half an hour. A mist was rising, and this, with the encroaching darkness, reduced visibility. The fire seemed to be directed now from opposite where Collins and those near him were lying. Dolan had the impression that Collins had now knelt upon one knee, and was firing ahead and to the left.

The shot that found him was almost certainly a ricochet, possibly off the armoured car. It penetrated the back of his head, above the right ear. Dolan heard Emmet Dalton's cry of 'The C. in C. is hit!' and his order to keep up a heavy fire. He fired furiously, while Dalton and O'Connell knelt by their Chief. The words of the Act of Contrition said by O'Connell came faintly to him. Death came swiftly and as Collins would have wished, under Cork hills, the Cork sky.

Firing continued a while, then ceased. Six years before it had fallen to Dalton to bury Tom Kettle at Guinchy. Now he supported his dead Chief on his shoulder for the remainder of the journey, described by him as a 'nightmare ride'.

It was far into the night when they reached the city. Back in his rearguard position, with nothing left that he cared to guard, Joe Dolan sat numbed and unbelieving. For him, as for the others, the bottom had dropped out of the world.

CHAPTER TWENTY-ONE

Epilogue

I

The circumstances of Michael Collins's death caused a fierce controversy that has never wholly been forgotten. The temper of the time added rumours of treachery to the jealousies and tragic idealism to which his life had been sacrificed. Later years have heightened certain incidents and distorted others in the memories of those who witnessed his death. Time is an unreliable collaborator.

There can be no value today in dwelling upon a dispute which has, in its time, aroused a bitterness which the generous soul of Collins himself could only have deplored. Only one fact of any importance emerges when all has been said and done: Michael Collins was dead.

Of all the tributes paid him after his death there was none to equal that which, in his lifetime, he had already received, and which he left among his possessions: a hundred door keys, by which he might come and go as he pleased in the houses of his friends in safety and the certainty of welcome.

The numbing shock which had struck first his comrades at Beal na mBlath and then those in Cork in the early hours of Wednesday morning 23 August, spread quickly to Dublin and the rest of Ireland and so to the world. The Army was the first to hear the news. Kevin O'Higgins took the telephone message with the same inability to believe what he heard as those to whom he passed it. Realizing only the terrible aftermath that must come, Richard Mulcahy went away to write, at 3.15 a.m., his call to the Army which was to have an immensely steadying effect upon it.

As the news spread, soldiers whom the chances of the guerilla years had inured to human shocks, gave way to grief.

The Government, like the Army, had lost its leader. Its members were awakened by young Army officers, incoherent with shock, despite their efforts to observe discipline. All the available Ministers gathered, a sober and heavy-hearted little group, and appointed W. T. Cosgrave in Collins's place. He issued his own call to the people that day :

> 'Michael Collins's death is a terrible blow to the Irish nation at the time it stood in greatest need of his wise and courageous guidance, but we are confident that the example of his life impressed on the people's mind by this tragedy will raise their spirit to face difficulties in a great crisis as he faced them, and to triumph over them.
>
> 'His death has sealed his work, and before the tragedy of his death the nation is resolved to bring the work to triumph.'

It was not easy to think of the future's responsibilities without him. Kevin O'Higgins, soon to emerge as the strong man of the Free State Government and to earn thereby Churchill's epitaph of 'a figure out of antiquity, cast in bronze' went down that day to Greystones where his wife was staying. He was weeping openly.

Frank Thornton was one to whom the news was not given. He had fallen, seriously wounded, in an ambush near Clonmel that day. It would be six weeks before they told him. But he must have known. Collins had never failed to come to a comrade in trouble before.

Batt O'Connor was another to whom Army officers came that morning. Tom Cullen and Joe O'Reilly did not want Collins's old friend to be one of those who read the news in the morning's paper.

Many did pick up the paper that day unprepared. Michael's sister Katie, walking down the street in Bohola, saw an old friend coming towards her in tears. She had stopped to condole with him when he thrust the newspaper into her hand.

In London, Hannie was preparing to go on holiday to Ireland. A feeling of heavy unease had been upon her, but on that Tuesday night it suddenly lifted. 'So he is safe', she thought.

To Dublin, as to Ireland generally, Collins's death was a traumatic shock. Men and women who had never met him felt a sense of personal loss. They crowded to Government Buildings, to the newspaper offices, stopping those in the street who might be able to add to the reports in the censored papers. Shopkeepers worked desultorily, or closed their doors completely. Blinds were drawn in many houses as if death had come within. At de Valera's political offices in Suffolk Street the flag hung at half-mast.

Not all Ireland mourned. Young Republican soldiers, who saw only a great victory against the Free State, rejoiced. But those soldiers of the Republic who had been his comrades-in-arms did not share their elation. There can have been few times of war in which the death in battle of the opposing Commander-in-Chief has aroused such personal sorrow as Republicans felt at the passing of Michael Collins. Peadar Kearney, then the official censor in Maryborough (Portlaoise) Prison, broke the news to a Republican prisoner. The man, stunned, cried: 'Good God – no!' then added quietly, 'Ireland is lost'.[1]

Tom Barry had been captured in the Four Courts' fighting and was then imprisoned in Kilmainham Gaol. He writes:

'I was talking with some other prisoners on the night of August 22nd 1922 when the news came in that Michael Collins had been shot dead in West Cork. There was a heavy silence throughout the jail, and ten minutes later from the corridor outside the top tier of cells I looked down on the extraordinary spectacle of about a thousand kneeling Republican prisoners spontaneously reciting the Rosary for the repose of the soul of the dead Michael Collins.'[2]

Frank O'Connor, destined to make his own reparation of love to Collins's memory, was one of the youngsters in arms who rejoiced then to hear of his death. He was with Erskine Childers, and was to recall in later years 'how Childers slunk away to his table silently, lit a cigarette, and wrote a leading article in praise of Collins'.[3] It appeared in *Poblacht na hEireann* on 24 August 1922.

'This supremacy of tragedy', Childers termed Collins's death. Three months later he was himself to die, no less bravely, before a firing squad of Collins's men, his alleged crime the possession

[1] de Burca *The Soldier's Song* p. 219
[2] Tom Barry *Guerilla Days in Ireland* (Cork 1949) p. 180
[3] Frank O'Connor *An Only Child* (London 1961) p. 232

of a small revolver, given him in earlier days by Collins himself, and prized by him long after each had gone his reluctant, irreconcilable way. Of all the tragedies of the Civil War, that which came upon that strangely consorted friendship is perhaps the most moving, for only Collins of all the Free State leaders really understood Childers's sincere devotion to Ireland, even while he hated its negation of the evolutionary processes he himself believed in. Certainly, had Collins lived, he would have saved Childers to serve his espoused country in more comprehending days, as Childers himself found only cause for mourning in the killing of Collins.

Ireland of the days to come was to be full of such tragedies. Perhaps Childers, like Brugha before him, would not have been able to bow to compromise any more than Liam Lynch after him could do. In the natural world those who cannot adapt themselves to evolutionary changes die. Lynch, too, was to die within the year, in a running gun battle on the Southern hills. Much was, after all, spared to Collins. Much more, had he lived, he would have found a way to spare.

Michael's body had been taken to Shanakiel Hospital in Cork on the night of his death. Dr Michael Riordan, young and new to his job at the hospital, saw 'the big dead man on the trolley who I was told was Michael Collins'. In the atmosphere of haste he made only a superficial examination, noting the bullet wound behind the right ear. He saw no exit wound.[4] His findings were later corroborated by Dr Gogarty in Dublin, who recognized the wound as caused by a ricochet bullet.

Even in death Michael was not to remain in his own county for long. Cork now gave him back to the city where most of his life's work had been done. The S.S. *Classic* had arrived that morning from Fishguard. In the evening they carried his coffin aboard, draped in the tricolour, his blood-stained officer's cap upon it. Soldiers stood at attention, rifles reversed. Along the route and at the pierhead at Cobh weeping crowds knelt in prayer. The boat moved out into the bay on its journey to Dublin to the tolling of the bell high in St Colman's Cathedral.

Oliver St John Gogarty has described how he waited through the long hours of darkness until the *Classic* appeared at the North

[4] Letter to the author, dated 10 June 1966

Wall, and how he went with Desmond FitzGerald to carry out
the task of embalming the body for the Lying-in-State. Sean
Kavanagh had just arrived at St Vincent's Hospital when
Gogarty emerged and asked him to fetch the sculptor, Albert
Power, to take a death mask of Collins. In the uneasy dawn, with
snipers active about the streets, this was done.

Collins lay all that day in St Vincent's, past which less than
three weeks before he had himself walked, his thoughts with
Harry Boland lying within. Sir John Lavery now came to work
at his canvas : that depiction of a pallid figure with its latent
smile, peacefully sleeping beneath the tricolour, which he called
'Love of Ireland'.

The public Lying-in-State at the City Hall lasted throughout
Friday until Sunday evening. Under overcast skies a queue a
mile long filed slowly past the bier, lengthening as the day passed,
to dwindle after midnight to the twos and threes who came
during the early hours before dawn; forming again in even vaster
numbers next morning. All Dublin, it seemed, came there where
the men of the Dublin Brigade, the members of the Squad, and
the little group of Collins's Intelligence officers took their proud
turn to guard their dead Chief.

One who came was an old woman; one of those innumerables
familiar to Dublin's back streets, black-shawled, ill-shod. She
pressed forward to stand by Collins's coffin and, in a piercing
voice cried out : 'Michael Collins, Michael Collins, why did you
leave us?'

It was the cry of Ireland, then and for a generation to come.

On the Sunday evening they bore him to the Pro-Cathedral
whence, after Requiem High Mass next morning, the long procession set out to Glasnevin. Not since the death of Parnell, wrote
the editor of the *Irish Independent*, had such a large funeral
procession passed through the streets of Dublin.

Three miles long, the cortège made its slow way to the lament
of pipe and band. Laid on the guncarriage upon which, by bitter
irony, the guns that had shelled the Four Courts had been
mounted, and drawn by six black horses, Collins's body was
borne past hundreds of thousands of people, some of whom had
also come by boat from Cork. The six-mile route to Glasnevin
was crowded. Where there was no space to stand, pavement deep,

people climbed to roofs and windows and up on monuments. They had saluted Arthur Griffith's body twelve days earlier in respect and gratitude to a great national founder. But it was love of a fellow-being, the Big Fellow, the Laughing Boy of the Dublin women, that brought them now to give Michael Collins his last farewell.

They came too as a nation that has lost its leaders in its hour of greatest need. It fell to Richard Mulcahy to sound the call of reassurance in his moving oration by Collins's grave.

One of Collins's pall-bearers was Joe Dolan, who had accompanied his dead Chief to the end of the long road from Beal na mBlath, and now stood near Mulcahy at the graveside. 'We knew there was nothing left', he says, 'that everything was gone. We went back to our normal duties'.

II

Gogarty calls Michael Collins 'the most rapid and bright soul that alien envy in Ireland ever quenched'. He wrote of him in after years :

'Never in our life cycle shall we see the like of Mick Collins. He dwelt among us as our equal. Now that he is dead, we find that we were the familiars of a Napoleon who knew no Waterloo. . . .

'Hundreds of Irishmen in every age were glad to put their necks in risk of England's halter and quick-lime. Collins alone pulled his generation out.'[5]

England paid him her unsimulated tributes when he died. Birkenhead was 'profoundly shocked at the death of Mr Michael Collins. He was a complex and very remarkable personality : daring, resourceful, volatile and merry'. In Belfast Craig expressed his sympathy for the South. When he spoke of the 'terrible calamity' with which the country had met he did not differentiate over areas : the North too had its cause for mourning, as its wisest minds knew.

Statesmen throughout the world paid their tributes; others

[5] Gogarty *Sackville Street* p. 184

mourned him simply as a man. His friend, Bishop Fogarty, said :
'He was big in all aspects, save resentment.'

At least one Republican officer who opposed Collins then
believes now that had he lived Irish history would have been very
different. 'Collins was the ideal man to bring in the North somehow. He was able to see the other man's point of view and consider it in a cool and reasonable way.'

Had Collins lived. . . . Whatever his unfulfilled plans for a
speedy end to hostilities may have been, no other man could have
brought them to fruition, and they died with him. Perhaps they
would only have resulted in further compromise, bringing him
obligations impossible in the end to reconcile. It is more likely
that the resolute Collins of the post-election days, armed with
the people's mandate, would have brought about a *rapproche-
ment* once the Treaty position was firmly established. Some diehards would no doubt have continued to refuse all advances. Yet
he would not have been Collins if he had not found some place
for them also in the new Ireland. He might rage at those who
opposed the Treaty because they impeded his work. He would
never have lost that obstinate regard for them as fellow citizens.

His death brought a new bitterness instead, revealed in the
savage lines scrawled in paint upon a city wall : *Turn over Mick,
make room for Dick, and Willie follows after.*

But Mulcahy and Cosgrave, with Kevin O'Higgins and the
others of that little company of resolute and selfless men, lived to
set up the Irish Free State, upon which foundation the Irish
Republic was to be brought to recognition. With Griffith and
Collins they were, in Churchill's phrase, men 'who feared God,
loved their country, and who kept their word'.

In times of ungovernable strife the ruthless use of force may
alone bring a quick end, and strong men are needed to administer
it. The long toll of executions by which the Free State Government crushed active Republican resistance did not usher in a
reaction like that of 1916, as those hoped who went by them to
brave and scornful deaths. The people were 'worn out, exhausted,
fed up with the experiences of the crusade for the Republic of
Virtue'.[6] They had elected their government after, not before,
those experiences and they were content to abide by their choice,

[6] Brinton *The Anatomy of Revolution* p. 235

not with the fervour by which they had borne forward the first Dail, but with the calmer acceptance, verging on indifference, which normal conditions breed in everyday citizens. The millennium, they had decided, would, after all, be hard to live up to.

Nevertheless, the executions left their tragic scar, borne by each side. Few could believe otherwise who saw Kevin O'Higgins, that cold man of strength, break down as he defended the Cabinet's decision on the day his friend, Rory O'Connor, faced a Free State firing squad.

Had Collins lived, it has been said again and again, there would have been no firing squads. Not because that intensity of love for his friends would have risen up, almost like some debilitating weakness, to prevent them; but because, by its very humanity, it would have found the solution which those who followed him sought desperately in vain.

Collins being dead the scars went deep, but, true to the largeness of heart and vision he had lived and died for, Ireland survived. Revolutions achieve better government, but not usually an essentially different government. Dail Eireann: the Provisional Parliament met on 9 September 1922 to frame the Constitution and to found the Free State. By the amicable dichotomy in which the newly-sleeping dogs of Anglo-Irish relations were at last encouraged to lie, Cosgrave was duly elected Griffith's successor as President of Dail Eireann and chose his Cabinet. The British were left to satisfy their constitutional law by regarding him as Chairman of the Provisional Government, responsible to the Provisional Parliament: a point of view which kept them happy, and enabled the Dail to get on with its work.

The Constitution, introduced by Kevin O'Higgins, was passed. Again, it contained that odd *double entendre* by which its framers intended to relegate formulas to where they could do least harm. Professor Michael Hayes, the first Speaker of the Dail under the Free State, remarks of that Article of the Constitution by which the rôle of the Crown was most closely defined: 'It is a piece of English which is more contradictory than any other piece of English that has ever been written. An endeavour was made to preserve the Crown in accordance with the Treaty and in accordance with what the British wanted, but at the same time to provide that the Dail would have complete power over its own dissolution and its own reassembly. In its reasoning out it defies understanding by anybody.'

Not that this seems to have mattered. In practice it was soon found that the Government could get on with its work without any reference to the Constitution at all. The Irishman had, indeed, become the master in his own house. Whatever the British Crown represented in Ireland, it was not the British Government.

The Governor-General represented the British Crown. The first incumbent of that position was T. M. Healy, the Irishman whose tongue, next to that of the 'Uncrowned King of Ireland' himself, had most exacerbated the Imperial Government in times past. In appointing Tim Healy, K.C., the Irish had, perhaps unconsciously, reverted to their own ancient order which placed learning, represented by a doctor of laws, on an equal footing with royalty and religion.

Had Collins lived. . . . In all the fields where liberality reaches out beyond mere tolerance and seeks to understand, his passing was to leave a gap. Others filled the vacuum as best they could, but the touch of greatness was gone. And he had been barely thirty, and was still developing.

It is difficult to imagine that Michael Collins would have been content with the rôle accorded him in later years as a mere party figure. He was too little the politician, too much the toiler in the wider field of Irish advancement. He deserves better of posterity, which will remember him as the fashioner of Ireland's independence when the parties that grew out of the dissensions of its creation are forgotten.

Collins also presided over the birth of the National Army. His happiest hours were those of his soldiering, with its comradeship and administrative opportunities. Whether he himself would have remained in the Army is doubtful. A non-productive body, once established as he wished, could scarcely have contained his rapidly expanding capabilities. Economics were his abiding interest, and it is more probable that he would have grasped the best opportunity to extend and strengthen the Irish economy. Certainly, wherever the vanguard of Irish progress was he would have been found leading it.

His expectations for the development of the British Commonwealth were to be justified. The League of Free States whose

emergence he had heard foretold and in which he had so courage-
ously believed, came into being under the Statute of Westminster
in 1931. The part played in this realization by Collins's successors,
who had followed his pointing finger, should not be underesti-
mated.

It was Collins's successors who also took Southern Ireland out
of the Commonwealth at the time when national interdependence
was at last being acknowledged as being a greater bond than the
Crown, and Republicanism was no longer regarded as the antithesis of unity. The causes of such a move lie deep in Irish history.
They may be summed up by Balfour's phrase: 'Law without
loyalty cannot strengthen the bonds of Empire.'

Yet it was a step which could only render the problem of Irish
reunification more insuperable. The North, indeed, remains the
paramount dilemma with which Ireland has been faced since
Collins's death: the alpha and omega of the cry 'Had Collins
lived!'

Collins died, but the directions he carved upon the signpost
from Dublin to Belfast are as clear today as when he placed
them there. When Gogarty wrote that 'He was capable of seeing
facts and of adjusting his position in the course of events', he
epitomized not only the essential quality of Collins's greatness,
but also the one ingredient without which no differences of
national outlook will ever be resolved.

The problem of the North-East remains; it should not be
forgotten that to Northern Irishmen it is the problem of the
South. Collins realized it when he first sat down at a table with
Sir James Craig. Extremists may war against the counsels of
tolerance, but the great body of Irish civilized thinking has surely
progressed beyond their battle cries. The Border is a problem
of intolerances that only the Irish themselves can solve, since to
all Irishmen, North or South, and to them alone, belongs the care
of Ireland.

As the years since Collins's death go by, so the achievements
of his life emerge with greater clarity. The host of those who
were his companions dwindles, the entire span of the life of
Ireland as a nation crowding between. Yet even those of his
generation who never met him have a light to the eye when his
name is spoken, and those who worked with him straighten their

shoulders, remembering the man who first told them, often in astonishingly forceful language, that they alone could build a free Ireland.

The building goes on today, as Collins would himself have wished, in the establishment of the Michael Collins Memorial Foundation, with its aims 'the educational, cultural and artistic training and development of Irish men and women from any of the four Provinces, without distinction of creed, class or politics'.

The times in which he lived were the turbulent times of a nation's rebirth. They were not to be set apart from those, less chronicled, that followed them, but were the spring from which that future took its life. They should, therefore, be regarded only in the light of its achievements, as President John Kennedy pointed out when, on 28 June 1963, he addressed Dail Eireann :

' . . . There are those who regard this history of past strife and exile as better forgotten, but to use the phrase of Yeats : "Let us not casually reduce that great past to a trouble of fools, for we need not feel the bitterness of the past to discover its meaning for the present and the future."

'. . . . Great powers have their responsibilities and their burdens, but the smaller nations of the world must fulfil their obligations as well. . . . My friends, Ireland's hour has come. You have something to give to the world, and that is a future of peace with freedom.'[7]

The President of the United States, a young man who, like Collins himself, was to crowd the work of a lifetime lived at full stretch into a handful of years, spoke to the assembled representatives of Ireland who had come together, forgetful of political differences, to hear him. His words were surely words of which Michael Collins, a man, not of party or creed, but of all Ireland, whose stride had lengthened to reach to constantly expanding horizons, would have approved.

[7] *Dail Debates* Vol. 203, No. 14

Bibliography

Andrews, C. S., *Dublin Made Me* (Cork 1979)

Barry, T., *Guerrilla Days in Ireland* (Dublin 1949)

Beaslai, Piaras, *Michael Collins and the Making of a New Ireland* (London 1926)

Beckett, J. C., *Confrontations: Studies in Irish History* (London 1972)

Beckett, J. C., *The Making of Modern Ireland 1603-1923*, 2nd ed. (London 1981)

Bell, J. Bowyer, *The Secret Army: The IRA 1916-79* (London 1979)

Bennett, Richard, *The Black and Tans* (London 1959)

Birkenhead, 2nd Earl of, *F.E.* (London 1959)

Boyce, D. G., *Nationalism in Ireland* (Dublin 1982)

Breen, Dan, *My Fight for Irish Freedom* (Dublin 1924)

Brennan, Robert, *Allegiance* (Dublin 1950)

Brennan-Whitmore, W. J., *With the Irish in Frongoch* (Dublin 1917)

Brinton, Crane, *The Anatomy of Revolution* (London 1953)

Brown, Terence, *Ireland: A Social and Cultural History*, new ed. (London 1985)

Buckland, Patrick, *A History of Northern Ireland* (Dublin 1981)

Darby, John, *Conflict in Northern Ireland* (Dublin 1976)

de Burca, Padraig and John F. Boyle, *Free State or Republic?* (Dublin 1922)

Dwyer, T. Ryle, *Michael Collins and the Treaty: His Differences with De Valera* (Cork 1981)

Caulfield, Max, *The Easter Rebellion* (London 1964)

Churchill, Winston, *The World Crisis: The Aftermath* (London 1929)

Colum, Padraig, *Arthur Griffith* (Dublin 1959)

Dail Eireann, *Proceedings, 1919-21, August 1921-June 1922; Debate on the Treaty between Great Britain and Ireland*

Edwards, Lyford P., *The Natural History of Revolution* (Chicago 1927)

Fanning, Ronan, *Independent Ireland* (Dublin 1986)

FitzGerald, Garrett, *Towards a New Ireland* (Dublin 1972)

Fitzpatrick, David, *Politics and Irish Life 1913-21: Provincial Experience of War and Revolution* (Dublin 1977)

Foster, R. F., *Modern Ireland 1600-1972* (London 1988)

Garvin, Tom, *The Evolution of Irish Nationalist Politics* (Dublin 1981)

Gogarty, Oliver St John, *As I was Going down Sackville Street* (London 1937)

351

Harkness, David, *Northern Ireland Since 1920* (Dublin 1983)

Hopkinson, Michael, *Green Against Green: The Irish Civil War* (Dublin 1988)

Johnson, Paul, *Ireland: Land of Troubles* (London 1980)

Kee, Robert, *The Green Flag* (London 1972)

Laffan, Michael, *The Partition of Ireland 1911-25* (Dublin 1983)

Lee, J. J. and Gearóid Ó Tuathaigh, *The Age of De Valera* (Cork 1982)

Longford, Lord and Thomas P. O'Neill, *Eamon De Valera* (London 1970)

Lyons, F. S. L., *Culture and Anarchy in Ireland 1890-1939* (Oxford 1979)

Lyons, F. S. L., *Ireland Since the Famine* (London 1973)

Macardle, Dorothy, *The Irish Republic*, 4th ed. (Dublin 1951)

McCracken, J. L., *Representative Government in Ireland: a study of Dail Eireann 1919-48* (London 1958)

MacDonagh, Oliver, *Ireland: The Union and its Aftermath* (London 1977)

Mansergh, Nicholas, *Ireland in the Age of Reform and Revolution* (London 1940)

Mitchell, Arthur and Padraig O Snodaigh, *Irish Political Documents 1916-49* (Dublin 1985)

Murphy, Dervla, *A Place Apart* (London 1978)

Murphy, J. A., *Ireland in the Twentieth Century* (Dublin 1989)

Neligan, D., *The Spy in the Castle* (London 1968)

O Broin, Leon (ed.), *In Great Haste: The Letters of Michael Collins and Kitty Kiernan* (Dublin 1983)

O Broin, Leon, *Michael Collins* (Dublin 1980)

O Broin, Leon, *Revolutionary Underground: The Story of the Irish Republican Brotherhood 1858-1924* (Dublin 1976)

O'Carroll, J. P. and J. A. Murphy (eds.), *De Valera and His Times* (Cork 1983)

O'Connor, Frank, *An Only Child* (London 1961)

O'Connor, Frank, *The Big Fellow* (Dublin 1965)

O'Faolain, Sean, *De Valera* (London 1939)

O'Hegarty, P. S., *A History of Ireland under the Union 1801-1922* (London 1952)

O'Malley, Ernie, *On Another Man's Wound* (London 1956)

O'Malley, Ernie, *The Singing Flame* (Dublin 1968)

Owen, Frank, *Tempestuous Journey: Lloyd George, His Life and Times* (London 1954)

Pakenham, Frank (now Lord Longford), *Peace by Ordeal* (London 1962)

Rose, Richard, *Northern Ireland: A Time of Choice* (London 1976)

Rumpf, E. and A. C. Hepburn, *Nationalism and Socialism in 20th Century Ireland* (Liverpool 1977)

Ryan, Desmond, *Remembering Sion* (London 1934)

Ryan, Desmond, *The Rising* (Dublin 1957)

Ryan, Desmond and William O'Brien (eds.), *Devoy's Post Bag* (Dublin 1953)

Shakespeare, Sir Geoffrey, *Let Candles Be Brought In* (London 1949)

Stewart, A. T. Q., *The Narrow Ground: Aspect of Ulster 1609-1969* (London 1977)

Strauss, E., *Irish Nationalism and British Democracy* (London 1951)

Taylor, Rex, *Michael Collins* (London 1958)

Townshend, Charles, *The British Campaign in Ireland 1919-21: The Development of Political and Military Policies* (Oxford 1975)

Townshend, Charles, *Political Violence in Ireland: Government and Resistance since 1848* (Oxford 1983)

White, Terence de Vere, *Kevin O'Higgins* (London 1948)

Younger, Calton, *Arthur Griffith* (Dublin 1981)

Glossary

Act of Union   Passed in 1800, came into force 1801. It stipulated that the Irish Parliament no longer existed as a separate legislature; Irish members were returned for Westminster instead.

Casement, Sir Roger (1864–1916)   Knighted for his humanitarian work in the Belgian Congo while in the British Consular Service. He failed in an attempt to raise a German brigade to fight for his native Ireland in the Rising, though he succeeded in persuading Germany to send the *Aud* with her cargo of arms to Ireland. He was captured after being landed in Co. Kerry by submarine, and was executed for treason on 3 August 1916.

Citizen Army   Formed by James Connolly and James Larkin in 1913 from men and women of the Transport and General Workers' Union to safeguard its members during the Dublin strike of that year.

Clan na Gael   Formed in 1867 to reunite the Fenian movement in America. Organized independently of the I.R.B. in Ireland but it had similar objectives.

Clarke, Thomas J. (1858–1916)   Imprisoned under extremely bad conditions for fifteen years for revolutionary activities in Ireland while a member of the Clan na Gael. After his release he was behind the reorganization of the I.R.B. A signatory of the proclamation of the Irish Republic, he was executed for his part in the Rising on 3 May 1916

Connolly, James (1870–1916)   Born in Ireland and brought up in Scotland, he became an active socialist leader and newspaper editor in America and Ireland. He agreed to join the I.R.B. leaders in organizing the Rising. Although badly wounded in the G.P.O. fighting, he was propped up before a firing squad on 10 May 1916.

Cumann na mBan   Militant women's organization, formed in 1913.

Davis, Thomas (1814–1845)   Irish nationalism's greatest writer. He inspired the newspaper, *Nation*, in 1842. Leader of the Young Ireland movement.

Davitt, Michael (1846–1906)   Founded the Land League in 1879. A Fenian, twice imprisoned, he stood successfully for Parliament while still on ticket-of-leave. Although disqualified, he later took his seat at Westminster, but resigned it in protest over the Boer War.

Dublin Castle Seat of the British civil and military administration in Ireland which was commonly known by this name.

Emmet, Robert (1778–1803) Leader of an insurrection in Dublin in 1803, for which he was publicly hanged.

Fianna na hEireann Founded in 1909 by Countess Markievicz and Bulmer Hobson. A militant youth movement, it took its name from the legendary followers of Finn MacCool.

Gaelic League Founded by Douglas Hyde in 1893 to encourage the revival of the Irish language.

Grattan, Henry (1746–1820) Leader of the Patriotic Party at Westminster. His pressure on Parliament led to the Renunciation Act of 1783, which gave Ireland a free Parliament, though with limited powers. He led the party until the Act of Union. A constitutionalist, he opposed Wolfe Tone's revolutionary methods.

Irish Parliamentary Party Pressed for Home Rule at Westminster. Followed an obstructionist policy in the 1870s, reaching its zenith under the leadership of Parnell. It split over his fall in 1890 and never regained its former effectiveness, despite a brief revival in 1911.

Irish Republican Brotherhood (I.R.B.) Founded in Dublin in 1858 by James Stephens, who also reorganized the American movement in 1859 as 'The Fenian Brotherhood'. The I.R.B. organized the abortive rising of 1867.

Kettle, Tom (1880–1916) One of the most effective members of the Irish Parliamentary Party during its resurgence after 1911. Writer and poet, and a founder of the Irish Volunteers, he was killed in action in France.

Land League Founded by Davitt in 1879 to organize tenant-farmers to campaign for fair rents leading to tenant-ownership and, ultimately, national independence. Suppressed in 1881.

Land War The fight of Irish tenant-farmers for fair rent and fixity of tenure, waged with considerable violence by underground organizations from the Whiteboys (1760s) to Captain Moonlight (1880).

MacDiarmada, Sean (1884–1916) Spent some years in Glasgow as a young man, returning to Ireland to work in every sphere of nationalism. Editor of *Irish Freedom,* 1910. Crippled by polio in 1912, he continued his work undeterred. On the Military Council of the I.R.B. which planned the Rising, he was executed on 12 May 1916.

MacDonagh, Thomas (1878–1916) Poet, and lecturer at University College, Dublin. Joint editor with Joseph Plunkett of the *Irish Review.* Taught under Pearse at St Enda's School. On Military Council of the I.R.B. Executed on 3 May 1916.

O'Connell, Daniel (1775-1847) 'The Liberator'. He achieved Catholic emancipation by constitutional methods, but not the repeal of the Union, which was his primary objective.

An t-Oglach, 'The Volunteer'.

Parnell, Charles Stewart (1846–1891) 'The Uncrowned King of Ireland', and her most famous parliamentarian. He led the Irish Parliamentary Party to its greatest heights, largely by obstructionist tactics. Imprisoned in 1881 for his work with the Land League. He persuaded Gladstone to support Home Rule, but fell from the leadership of his party after the O'Shea divorce scandal, and died the following year.

Pearse, Padraig (1879–1916) Poet and teacher. He founded St Enda's School for boys in 1908 to further his aims of establishing a free, Gaelic Ireland. Co-opted as a member of the Supreme Council of the I.R.B. in 1913, although not in favour of secret societies, he was chosen to be President of the Provisional Government of the Irish Republic proclaimed in Easter Week. He was executed on 3 May 1916.

Plan of Campaign Launched in 1886 by William O'Brien and John Dillon, with the aim of achieving reduced rents by the withholding of all rents. It was successful, but at the cost of much ruthless coercion by Balfour, as Parnell, who opposed it, had foreseen.

Plunkett, George, Noble Count Antiquary and scholar, he was Director of the National Museum of Ireland, and a moderate Home Ruler. He was arrested and deported after the Rising, in which he had taken no part, apparently on account of his sons' participation in it.

Plunkett, Sir Horace (1854–1932) Started a co-operative society in Dunsany in 1879, followed by co-operative creameries. In 1889 he founded the Irish Agricultural Organization Society. A Unionist, he later worked for dominion status for Ireland. A member of the Free State senate 1922–23.

Plunkett, Joseph (1887–1916) Poet, and man of many parts. Joint editor of the *Irish Review.* A founder of the Irish Volunteers, and Director of Military Operations on the I.R.B. Military Council. He was a signatory of the Proclamation of the Irish Republic. He married Grace Gifford in prison on the eve of his execution on 4 May 1916.

Poblacht na hEireann The Republic of Ireland.

Redmond, John (1856–1918) A Parnellite after the split, he led the reunited Irish Parliamentary Party from 1900 until his death.

Tone, Theobald Wolfe (1763–1798) A Protestant, founder of the revolutionary Irish nationalism which led to the Easter Rising. As leader of the United Irishmen, his aim was 'to subvert the tyranny of our execrable Government'. He attempted to secure French aid for Ireland, but such help as came was too late. The rebellion which he led in 1798 was crushed and Tone, on being refused a soldier's execution, committed suicide in prison.

United Irishmen Founded by Wolfe Tone in 1790, its members were both Catholics and Dissenters, united in opposing the penal laws and in lack of faith in the powers of the Dublin Parliament. Inspired by French republicanism, its aims were for a united, independent Ireland. Its plans for rebellion were betrayed by spies planted within the society, Lord Edward FitzGerald was killed, and Tone captured. Though sporadic uprisings took place in the southeast they were savagely crushed.

Index

Abbey Theatre, 15, 70
Act of Union (1800), 177, 274
Active Service Unit, 181
AE (George Russell), 15
Anderson, Sir John, 146, 151, 161, 163, 188, 190, 204
Ashe, Thomas, 44, 75–7
Asquith, H. H., 28–9, 32, 60
Aud, 39, 42
Auxiliaries, 147, 151, 153–4, 164, 169–73, 175, 178, 183, 188, 262

'B' Specials, 289, 299, 318
Balfour, A. J., 10, 349
Bandon, Lord, 205
Barrett, Ben, 128n
Barrie, Sir James, 21, 195, 197, 202, 221–2, 257, 303
Barry, Kevin, 166–8, 171
Barry, Tom, 175, 185, 342
Barton, John (G-Man), 129n
Barton, Robert, and Easter Week, 47; friendship with Collins, 82–3, 126; escapes from Mountjoy, 99; attends Dail meeting (1919), 102; on Collins, 116; imprisoned in Portland, 186; in Dail Ministry (1921), 208; on Collins-Brugha quarrel, 212; delegate to London, 213; on Collins's arrangements in London, 214; on early negotiations, 220; exclusion from full negotiation, 226–7; re-presents External Association, 247; at final negotiations, 250, 252–3;

decision to sign Treaty, 255–6; admits duress, 261; speaks in Treaty debate, 271; parts from Collins, 271; follows de Valera, 276; *passim*, 139, 157, 244, 246, 255, 257, 260
Beaslai, Piaras, 93, 99, 118, 169, 179
Belfast Boycott, 161, 287
Belfast Newsletter, 292
Bell, Alan, 134–5, 138
Better Government of Ireland Bill, 113, 130, 134
Birkenhead, Lord, 218–19, 222, 231–2, 238, 250–1, 256, 268, 306, 345
Birrell, Augustine, 39, 70
Black and Tans, 136–8, 145, 147, 150, 152–3, 156, 162, 164, 175, 177, 183, 189, 257, 289, 299
Blythe, Ernest, 79, 91, 129, 300, 304, 313, 317
Boland, Harry, 75, 88–9, 93–4, 103, 106, 118, 149, 207, 210, 213, 268, 283–4, 329, 344
Botha, Louis, 186
Boyd, Major-General, 144, 163, 172
Breen, Dan, 164
Brennan, Robert, 75, 157, 297
Brennan-Whitmore, W. J., 42–3, 53
Broy, Eamon, 83, 88, 114, 129, 132, 183, 205–6, 214, 217, 223, 243
Brugha, Cathal, and Easter Week, 44; opposes I.R.B., 71, 123; discusses Sinn Fein objectives, 78; Acting President of Dail (1919),

98; Minister for Defence, 122–3; advocates I.R.A. oath of allegiance to Dail, 127; antagonism towards Collins, 157–8, 181, 212, 247; supports move to send Collins to U.S.A., 181; arrest of MacEoin, 186–7; criticizes Collins over Arms Purchases, 188; in Dail Ministry (1921), 208; refuses to negotiate in London, 212; influence on negotiations, 240; Windsor Barracks raid, 240, 242–3; I.R.A. levies, 241–2; Treaty, 259–61; fears Army split, 264; condemns military dictatorship, 296; opposes hostilities against British, 315; dies in Civil War, 323–4; *passim*, 169, 173, 183, 247, 276, 343

Burke, Edmund, 184

Byrne, Vincent, 128n

Cairo Group, 168–70

Cameron, Sir Charles, 60

Camus, Albert, 168

Carson, Sir Edward, 28, 30, 61, 219, 228n

Casement, Roger, 42, 196, 218, 239

Casement, Tom, 196

Chalmers, Lieut, 43

Chamberlain, Austen, 218, 220, 222, 225, 235, 237, 248, 250–1, 253

Chamberlain, Joseph, 146

Chartres, John, 213

Chesterton, G. K., 21, 36, 58, 89, 95, 159, 204, 225, 302

Childers, Erskine, 29, 113, 139–40, 213, 226–7, 228, 244–7, 251, 256, 270–1, 334, 342–3

Churchill, Winston, suggests auxiliary force for R.I.C., 147; British delegate to negotiations, 219–20; host to Collins and Griffith, 231; at final negotiations, 251; on Collins's reactions, 254;

and Craig-Collins meeting, 286–7; arranges further meeting between, 288; on I.R.A. activities in N. East, 292; Collins writes to on N. East, 292–3; correspondence with Cope over Four Courts, 297–8; warns Collins against extremists, 301; rebukes Craig, 305; Collins-de Valera Pact, 306; speaks in Commons on Ireland, 307; Pettigo-Belleek raids, 309–10; ultimatum to Provisional Government, 319–20; telegraphs Collins over Four Courts, 323; writes of hopes for Ireland, 327–8; on Kevin O'Higgins, 341; on Free State leaders, 346; *passim*, 26, 30, 293, 338

Citizen Army, 40, 43

Clan na Gael, 39

Clancy, Peadar, 168–71, 173–4

Clarke, Thomas, 27, 33, 37, 45, 65, 82, 105, 271

Clarke, Mrs Tom, 65–6, 84, 90, 154, 213, 271, 273

Clune, Archbishop, 176–8, 181, 184

Clune, Conor, 169, 173, 176

Cockerill, Brigadier-General G., 166

Cohalan, Judge Daniel F., 105–6, 149

Collins, Helena (Sister M. Celestine), 4, 13, 100, 185

Collins, Jerry, 23, 272

Collins, Johanna (Hannie), 4, 13, 16, 18–19, 21–2, 33, 50–1, 92, 98, 176, 221–2, 230, 341

Collins, Katty (Hurley), 23, 185

Collins, Mary Anne (O'Brien), 4, 6–7, 12, 16, 18

Collins, Maurice, 109, 154, 159

Collins, Michael (father), 3–5, 7–9, 11

Collins, Michael, birth, 5; infancy, 5, 6–9; early nationalism, 9, 11, 13–15, 22, 25–6; schooling, 11–12, 15; love of sport, 12; life

at Woodfield, 12–13, 16; reading, 13; goes to London, 16; in Post Office, 18; anti-clericalism, 19; loyalty, 19; Civil Service examinations, 20; studies, 20–1; joins G.A.A., 22; secretary of Geraldines, 22–3; holidays at Woodfield, 23–4; joins Sinn Fein (1906), 24; extremism, 25; joins I.R.B. (1909), 26; joins Irish Volunteers (1914), 29; with Horne & Co. (1910), 30; Labour Exchange clerk (1914), 30; friendships in London, 31; with Guaranty Trust Co. (1915), 32; conscription threat, 33; returns to Dublin, 34–5; at Larkfield, 35–6, 38; with Craig Gardner (1916), 38; takes part in Rising, 40–7; internment in Stafford, 50–1; and Frongoch, 52–60; returns to Woodfield, 61–2; goes to Dublin (1917), 65; secretary of Irish National Aid, 66–9; N. Roscommon by-election (1917), 69; on temporary Supreme Council of I.R.B. (1917), 71; on provisional Volunteer Executive (1917), 71; organizes gun-running, 72; critical of Sinn Fein, 73; S. Longford by-election (1917), 74; released prisoners, 74–5; helps revise I.R.B. Constitution, 75; secretary of Supreme Council, 75; at Ashe's funeral, 77; speaks at Sinn Fein meetings, 77; walks out of committee meeting, 78; de Valera's presidency of Sinn Fein, 79; on Sinn Fein Executive (1917), 79; Director of Organization, I.R.A., 81–2; Adjutant-General, 82; intelligence work, 82–4, 90–1; work for Sinn Fein, 84; arrested, 84–5; in Sligo Gaol, 85–6; eludes 'German Plot' round-up, 88; Harry Boland, 89; **Kiernan** family, 89; organizes

Volunteers, 90–1, 95, 124–6; *An t-Oglach*, 93; critical of Sinn Fein 'moderates', 93–4, 103–4; has pleurisy, 94; stands for S. Cork, 96; attends pre-Dail meetings, 97; Minister of Home Affairs (1919), 98; rescues de Valera, 98; on the run, 99; Minister of Finance (1919), 99; President Wilson, 101; on raid on Mansion House, 102; Dail Loan, 105, 107–12, 138; develops Intelligence, 114–16, 129; raids Brunswick Street station, 114; President of Supreme Council, I.R.B., 115; Sean Mac-Eoin, 117; moves about freely, 118–19; love of children, 119–20, 143–4; as a leader, 120; moderation, 121; influence, 121; an emotional man, 121–2; arouses dislike, 122; resemblance to Danton, 122; Brugha's distrust of, 123, 127; hopes for American support, 124; opposes I.R.A. oath of allegiance to Dail, 127; administers oath to Dublin Brigade, 127; shooting of G-Men, 128–9; the Squad, 128; shooting of Redmond, 133; price on head, 134; Tomas MacCurtain, 135; hunger-strikes, 137; raids Castle mail, 137; Alan Bell, 138; Erskine Childers, 140; use of bluff, 141; at Mrs O'Donovan's, 142–4; attends Dail session (June 1920), 148; Loan closure, 148; American aid, 150; horror of indiscriminate killing, 152; routine, 154; alertness, 155; gaiety, 155; on success of Dail Loan, 155; estimate of fighting strength of I.R.A., 156; Stack, 157–8; Brugha, 158, 186; on his own failings, 158; hunt for him, 159; arrest of MacSwiney, 161–2; on Belfast Boycott, 161; peace moves,

163; death of MacSwiney, 165; Kevin Barry, 167–8; 'Cairo Group', 168–9; Bloody Sunday, 170–4; Acting President of Dail (Nov. 1920), 174; Kilmichael ambush, 175; Sturgis on hunt for, 175–6; on Terror, 176; Archbishop Clune, 176–7; on Government of Ireland Act, 178; escapes at Gresham Hotel, 178–9; return of de Valera, 179, 180; on dissension in States, 180n; refuses to leave Ireland, 181, A.S.U., 181; unease at hostility within Cabinet, 182, 212; papers seized, 182; escapes raid, 182; renewed illness, 183; Rory O'Connor, 183; arrest of Broy, 183; on Irish aspirations, 184; on British strategy, 184; love of Cork, 185; tribute to dead patriots, 185–6; on his notoriety, 186; on danger to his family, 186; Robert Barton, 186; arrest of MacEoin, 186–8; on hunt for himself, 188; burning of Woodfield, 190; denies hatred for England, 190; stands for Armagh (1921), 191; attempts to rescue MacEoin, 191–2; burning of Custom House, 192; Mary Street raid, 193; denies being 'on the run', 193–4; plans P.O. Savings Bank boycott, 194; some personal letters quoted, 194–5; Queen's University invitation, 195; hopes for peace, 197; doubts Lloyd George's sincerity, 197; on truce terms, 201; on price on head, 201; on J. M. Barrie, 202; on his anonymity, 203; visits Cork, 203–4; Sir Wm Darling, 204; detention of MacEoin, 205; Broy's release, 205–6; on Ulster and settlement, 206–7; weariness, 207; relaxation, 207; Kitty Kiernan, 208, 215; in 2nd Dail Ministry (1921), 208; Army tour, 208; replies to Bishop of Killaloe, 209; Armagh meeting, 209–10; delegation nominations, 211–13; Gairloch letter, 213; chooses staff for London, 214; confers with I.R.B. leaders, 215; arrives in London, 217; at Brompton Oratory, 218, 223, 257; Lloyd George on, 220, 231; distrust of Lloyd George, 220; Cope on, 220; Macready on, 221; some letters to Kitty, 221, 223, 236, 243–4; meets J. M. Barrie, 221–2; depression, 222; writes to a Carmelite, 223; visits Ireland, 224; Dominion status, 225; Childers, 226; unwisdom in handling delegation, 226–7; anger at de Valera's warnings, 227; C. P. Scott, 229, 245; sends for Kitty, 230; evening with Churchill, 231–2; Griffith, 233; his Commonwealth memorandum, 234, 248; Sturgis, 236; on American financial aid, 237; at the Laverys', 238; Mrs Parry, 239; British hopes centred on, 240; views on External Association, 240; on I.R.A. levies, 241–2; I.R.A. gunrunning, 242; Windsor Barracks raid, 243; financial talks with British, 244; optimism, 245–6; argues Dublin Cabinet decisions, 247; refuses to meet British, 247; sees Lloyd George, 249–50; at final negotiations, 250, 252n, 252–4; at Hans Place, 255; signs Treaty, 256; comments on, 257; returns to Dublin, 259–60; supports Treaty in Cabinet, 261; influence on public support for Treaty, 263; importance of Army, 265; speaks in Treaty debate, 265, 269–70, 273–4; opposes private session of Dail, 266; anxieties over Treaty approval,

267–8, 271, 273; on Boland, 268; parts from Barton, 271; appeals to opponents of Treaty, 271, 273; Sam's Cross, 272; opposes de Valera's nomination, 275; proposes Griffith for presidency of Dail, 275; appeals for unity, 276; Army oath of allegiance, 276; release of prisoners, 276; Constitution, 277, 282, 308–9, 312; personal attacks on, 277; Chairman of Provisional Government, 277; takes over Dublin Castle, 277–8; dilemma in government, 279; Civil Service appointments, 280; Lane bequest, 282; on Hugh Kennedy, 282; hopes for a new Ireland, 283; on de Valera and Boland, 283–4; Craig-Collins Agreement, 286–7; failure of, 288; further meeting with Craig, 288; unwell, 289, 302; Election (1922), 290; as a public speaker, 290; protests to Churchill about Belfast, 292–3; co-operates with Liam Lynch, 293–4, 299, 309; Craig-Collins Pact, 294; Four Courts, 298–9; to be Griffith's successor, 300; reluctance to resort to arms, 300; criticizes Craig, 301; loyalty to former friends, 302; Gogarty, 302–3; Barrie's 'Courage', 303; Collins-de Valera Pact, 303–5; goes to London over Pact, 306; attends Commons debate, 307; British military aid for N. East, 309–10; at coalition election meetings, 311; speech in Cork, 311–12; tours Co. Cork, 313; Republican plot episode, 313; heads poll at Election, 314; death of Sir Henry Wilson, 317–18; Churchill's ultimatum, 319; decision to attack Four Courts, 321; Civil War in Dublin, 322–5;

Brugha's death, 324; C.-in-C. National Army, 324, 326–7; hopes for unity with N. East, 327–8; success in Civil War, 328; Boland's death, 329; on war in Cork, 330; Griffith's death, 330–1; escapes assassination, 332, 333; plans to go south, 332–4; Co. Cork inspection, 335; visits Clonakilty, 336; and Sam's Cross, 336; ambushed at Beal na mBlath, 337–8; death of, 339; tributes to, 340–2, 345–6; returned to Dublin, 343–4; lying-in-state, 344; funeral, 344–5; his aspirations, 346–50

Collins, Nancy (O'Brien), 41, 107
Collins, Patrick (uncle), 3–4
Collins, Patrick (brother), 4, 13, 32
Collins, Sean (Johnny), 4, 7, 10, 13, 23, 189–90, 203, 261, 272, 289, 336
Collins, Tom, 3–4
Collins-de Valera Pact, 303–7, 310–12, 314
Colum, Padraig, 21, 333
Congested Districts Board, 10
Conscription Act, 34
Connolly, James, 42–3, 45
Cope, A. W., 146, 151, 196–7, 202, 204, 206, 220, 256, 276, 297–8, 303
Corrigan, Alderman, 66
Cosgrave, W. T., 44, 75–6, 86, 107, 208, 211, 259, 261, 275, 282, 300, 303, 308n, 334, 341, 346–7
Craig, Sir James, 190–1, 196, 198, 202–3, 207, 235, 239, 243, 246, 248–50, 253, 256, 286–9, 292, 301, 305–6, 309, 316, 327–8, 345, 349
Craig-Collins Agreement (January 1922), 287–8
Craig-Collins Pact (March 1922), 294, 301
Crowley, John, 16

Cullen, Tom, 84, 90, 143, 178, 230, 260, 318, 341
Cumann na mBan, 40, 112
Curzon, Lord, 281

Dail Eireann, opening of 1st session, 98; 2nd session, 99; raided, 102; National Arbitration Courts, 105; work of and suppression, 112; authority upheld by Collins, 123n; I.R.A. allegiance to, 127; reliance on I.R.A., 138; Republican Courts, 148; Belfast Boycott, 161; importance in Clune talks, 177; 2nd Dail elected (1921), 191; tacitly recognized by Britain, 202; meets during truce, 205–6, 208; approves delegates for London, 213, 214n; agreement to be submitted to, 214, 246, 258; debates the Treaty, 265, 268–71; adjourns, 271; end of Treaty debate, 273–4; rejects de Valera, 275; Griffith elected President, 276; distinct from Provisional Government, 277; Army and authority of, 284–5; lifts Belfast Boycott, 287; Collins-de Valera Pact, 303–4; Cosgrave becomes President, 347; effect of Constitution on work, 347–8; *passim*, 117, 124, 132, 139, 163, 187, 259–60, 264, 312
Daily Mail, 311
Daily News, 31, 162
Daily Sketch, 185
Dalton, Emmet, 217, 330, 337–9
Daly, Denis, 51
Daly, Paddy, 128n, 133, 152
Danton, Georges, 122
Darling, Sir William, 204
Davis, Thomas, 9, 13–14
Davitt, Michael, 105
Deasy, Liam, 143
De La Rey, Jacobus, 240
Derby, Lord, 190
De Valera, Eamon, in Rising, 44;

elected for Clare, 76; President of Sinn Fein (1917), 79; President of Irish Volunteers (1917), 80; arrested in 'German Plot' round-up, 88; rescued from Lincoln, 98; President of Dail Eireann (1919), 99; goes to America, 105–7; as a leader, 120; favours I.R.A. allegiance to Dail, 127; dissension with Irish-American leaders, 149, 180; Bond Drive, 150; returns to Ireland, 175, 179; suggests that Collins goes to States, 181; meets Lord Derby, 190; and Craig, 196; and Tom Casement, 196; letter from Lloyd George, 197; replies, 198; meets Lloyd George, 202–3; release of MacEoin, 205; rejects British proposals, 206; External Association, 206; corresponds with Lloyd George, 207; President of 2nd Dail (1921), 208; nominations for delegation to London, 211–13; Gairloch proposals, 213; delegates' credentials, 214; telegram to the Pope, 224; 'die-hard' influence on feared, 226; Childers, 226; warns delegates, 227; refuses to go to London, 227; Griffith reports to on Boundary Commission, 235; External Association the only solution, 240; oath of allegiance, 247; Treaty, 259, 261; importance of Army, 264; Document No. 2, 266–7; debate on Treaty, 268–70, 273–4; stands for Presidency of Republic, 275; walks out of Dail, 276; influence against Treaty, 277; Collins's regard for, 283–4, 302; Election, 290; Four Courts, 296; condemns military interference, 300; Collins-de Valera Pact, 303, 310–11; election outcome, 314; death of Sir Henry Wilson, 317; joins Republican Army, 325;

passim, 78, 97n, 124, 140, 182, 203, 215, 232, 239, 246, 252, 258, 265, 291, 305, 335, 342
Devlin, Liam, 116, 123, 179
Devoy, John, 105–6, 149
De Wet, Christian, 240
Dillon, Geraldine (Plunkett), 35
Dillon, John, 96
Dillon, Dr Thomas, 38, 326
Dolan, Joe, 133, 334–5, 337–9, 345
Dominion Home Rule, 153, 156
Douglas, James, 237, 282
Dowling, Joseph, 88, 276
Doyle, Fr P. J., 180
Doyle, Sean, 128n
Dublin Metropolitan Police, 70, 132–3, 160
Duggan, Eamonn, 82, 213, 226, 230, 246–7, 255, 259, 267, 306
Duggan, Mrs Eamonn, 221
Dumont, Mr F. T. F., 162
Dunne, Reginald, 317–9, 331–2

Emmet, Robert, 13, 26
'External Association', 206, 211–12, 225, 240, 247, 255, 260, 266

Fenians, *see* I.R.B.
Fianna na hEireann, 35
FitzAlan, Lord, 278
FitzGerald, Desmond, 107, 155, 160, 229, 261n, 344
Flood, Henry, 274
Fogarty, Most Rev Dr, Bishop of Killaloe, 208–9, 331, 346
Fox, Charles James, 129
Freeman's Journal, 201, 303, 316
French, Lord, 39, 87, 130, 135, 146, 147, 151, 167, 182

Gaelic American, 105
Gaelic Athletic Association, 15, 22–3
Gaelic League, 12, 15, 32, 71, 112
Gavan Duffy, George, 213, 226–7, 245–8, 255–6, 260, 321
Gay, Tomas, 118

George V, H.M. King, 196–8, 210–11, 213, 224, 249
'German Plot', 88, 91
Gladstone, W. E., 10
Gogarty, Oliver St John, 68, 186, 302–3, 324, 333, 343–5, 349
Government of Ireland Act, 177, 190–1, 198
Grattan, Henry, 70, 73, 274
Greenwood, Sir Hamar, 146, 150–1, 161, 175–6, 219
Gregory, Lady, 281
Grey, Sir Edward, 30
Griffith, Arthur, and Sinn Fein, 17, 24–5, 73, 78, 97n, 233; *United Irishman,* 24; in Reading Gaol, 52; returns to Ireland, 65; gives up Presidency of Sinn Fein, 79; I.R.B., 79n; arrested in 'German Plot', 88; Acting-President of Dail Eireann (1919), 105; on Better Government of Ireland Bill, 113; initial support for Childers, 140; on Collins and Dail Loan, 148; in early peace moves, 163, 168; Lloyd George appeals to, 172; arrested, 174; appoints Collins Acting-President, 174; Archbishop Clune, 176; peace moves, 177; in 2nd Dail Ministry, 208; leader of delegation to London, 211; opposes Childers, 213; receives 'instructions', 214n; fears 'die-hard' influence on de Valera, 224; presents External Association, 225; confers with Lloyd George, 225–6; persuades Collins to stay in London, 227; Lloyd George on, 228; at *Beggar's Opera,* 230; at Churchill's house, 231–2; Collins, 233; gives written assurances, 235; Boundary Commission, 235; at the Laverys', 238; at Dublin Cabinet meeting, 246; External Association, 247; at final negotiations, 250–5; after signing Treaty,

257; returns to Dublin, 260; expects de Valera's support, 260, 261n; supports Treaty in Cabinet, 261; influence on public support for Treaty, 263; on Collins, 273–4; speaks in Treaty debate, 274; President of Dail Eireann (1922), 276–7; Election, 290; Sligo meeting, 300; Collins to be his successor, 300; Army, 301; plans retirement, 302; Collins-de Valera Pact, 304; goes to London over Pact, 306–7; attends Commons debate, 307; Constitution, 308; discusses Border with Churchill, 310; death of Sir Henry Wilson, 317; renewed confidence in Collins, 322; death, 330–1; *passim*, 15, 26, 48, 107, 220, 244, 248–9, 267, 269, 278, 309, 314, 327, 332, 334, 345, 346

Haig, Douglas, 316
Hales, Sean, 57, 335
Hales, Tom, 143, 335
Hardy, Thomas, 58
Harte, Christy, 123, 169
Hayes, Michael, 347
Healy, T. M., 55, 212, 228n, 277, 282, 303, 319, 348
Helga, 45
Hewart, Sir Gordon, 219
Hoey, Det.-Con. Daniel, 47, 129
Hogan, Michael, 242–3
Home Rule, 15, 28, 30, 95
Home Rule Act (1914), 30
Home Rule Bill (1912), 28
Hugo, Victor, 159
Hurley, Sean, 16, 29, 34, 46, 62

Irish Convention (1917), 74, 76, 80, 84, 139
Irish Independent, 210, 344
Irish National Aid & Volunteer Dependents' Fund, 65–9, 84

Irish Parliamentary Party, 17, 28, 48, 74, 86, 95
Irish Republican Army (I.R.A.), named by Connolly, 43; reorganization planned, 55, 71, 72; political basis, 72; Ashe's funeral, 77; Convention (1917), 80; obtains arms, 82; effect of Conscription on, 87, 95; 'German Plot' round-up, 88; Collins reorganizes, 89–90; right to defend Republic, 98; Dail Loan, 110; illegal (1919), 112; opposed to R.I.C., 115; construction, 116–17, 124; guerilla methods, 124; organized in England, 126; oath of allegiance to Dail, 127; changes to offensive, 132; burns tax offices, 138; belligerent status, 145; discipline, 146; executes informers, 152; flying columns, 156, 164; captures British military papers, 159–60; British unable to contain, 161; fights in Dublin, 164; Kevin Barry, 168; Clune talks, 176–7; de Valera's policy for, 181; divisions formed, 183–4; south-west activity, 185; MacEoin on, 192; truce problems, 205, 225; levies, 240–2; Windsor Barracks raid, 242–3; Treaty, 264–5, 276; Civil Guards, 281; takes over British barracks, 284; threat of split, 285; N. East activities, 289, 292–3, 299, 309; Convention (1922), 291; attempts to reunify, 315; death of Sir Henry Wilson, 317; *passim*, 49, 147, 163, 184, 187, 188, 224, 297, 300, 304
Irish Republican Brotherhood (I.R.B.), policy of, 11, 26–7, 71; Collins joins, 26; reorganized (1911), 27; behind formation of Irish Volunteers, 28–9; plans Rising, 32, 39, 49; remaining leaders imprisoned, 49, 66; in-

fluence in Frongoch, 55; Collins on temporary Supreme Council (1917), 71; Brugha opposes, 71; influence on Volunteers, 71; Constitution revised, 75; election of Sinn Fein Executive, 79; Griffith on, 79n; Collins President of Supreme Council, 115; recognizes Dail Eireann, 123n; southern leaders confer with Collins, 215; support for Treaty, 264; calls meeting over Treaty, 293; *passim*, 4, 33, 35, 37, 41, 72, 123, 127, 242

Irish Volunteers, 28–30, 32, 35, 37–42

Irish World, 93

John O' London's, 205

Kavanagh, Joe, 47, 83, 132, 183
Kavanagh, Sean, 169, 171, 174, 344
Kearney, Peadar, 31, 342
Keating, Con, 41
Kelly, Ted, 102
Kelly, Alderman Tom, 90, 127
Kelly & Burke & Shea, 24, 272
Kennedy, Hugh, 282, 306
Kennedy, President John F., 350
Keogh, Tom, 128n
Kerr, Neil, 115, 143
Kettle, Tom, 286, 339
Kickham, Charles, 13
Kiernan Family, 89
Kiernan, Kitty, 208, 215, 217, 222, 230, 333
Kirwan, Jim, 109, 116, 123

Land League, 4, 105, 134
Land Act (1887), 10, 14
Land Act (1903), 23
Land War, 4
Lane, Sir Hugh, 281–2
Lavery, Lady, 238–9, 332
Lavery, Sir John, 238, 281, 332, 344
Law, Bonar, 61

Lawless, Joseph, 53
Leader, 15
Leigh Doyle, Mrs, 99, 155, 160, 207, 333
Leonard, Joe, 128n
von Lettow-Vorbeck, 204
Lincoln, Abraham, 332
'Liverpool Lambs', 38
Llewelyn Davies, Crompton, 101, 195, 219, 222, 251, 282
Llewelyn Davies, Mrs, 101, 195, 270, 283
Llewelyn Davies, Michael, 195
Lloyd George, David, Prime Minister (1916), 60; Irish Convention, 74, 80; conscription for Ireland, 85–7, 94; Home Rule measure, 87; Peace Conference, 101; Better Government of Ireland Bill, 113, 134; Ireland an 'unfortunate country', 130; Childers and Irish Convention, 139; finds Irish 'impossible', 148; Greenwood, 150; Cope, 151; favours reprisals, 153; MacSwiney, 162; Griffith distrusts, 168; arrest of Griffith, 174; doubts Griffith's influence with I.R.A., 176; Clune talks, 176–7, 184; Government of Ireland Act, 177, 185; 'double policy', 180; influenced by militarists, 184; in 'yielding mood', 190; cease-fire initiative, 196; George V urges peace, 197; Sinn Fein distrusts, 197; invites Irish to talk peace, 197–8; talks with Craig and de Valera, 202–3; pre-conference exchanges, 206–7, 210, 213; Irish credentials, 214–15; pen-portrait of, 219; on Collins, 220, 231; demands answer on Allegiance, 224; divides Irish in conference, 225–6; C. P. Scott, 228, 244–5; on Irish proposals, 231; Griffith's assurances, 232, 235; on N. Irish

Government, 239; rejects Irish proposals, 239; meets Collins, 248–50; at final negotiations, 250–4; on signing of Treaty, 254, 257; Boundary Commission undertakings, 288; Constitution, 308; *passim*, 191, 218, 229, 233, 246, 258, 260

Lynch, Diarmuid, 75

Lynch, Fionan, 44, 75–6, 84, 91, 96, 213, 329, 333

Lynch, Liam, 215, 241, 293, 296, 299, 315, 321, 325, 330, 332, 343

Lynch, Ned, 22, 38, 241–2

Lynd, Robert, 31, 162

Lyons, Brigid, 187–8, 192

Lyons, Denis, 11, 26

Maguire, Sam, 25–6, 31, 72, 115, 242

Manchester Guardian, 228, 245

Markievicz, Countess, 35

Maxwell, Sir John, 46–7, 61

Mellowes, Liam, 97n, 296, 299

Mirabeau, Honoré, Comte de, 98

Moran, D. P., 15

Morning Post, 210

Mountjoy, Lord, 150

Moylett, Patrick, 74

Mulcahy, Richard, 44, 81, 116, 123, 128n, 143, 169, 173, 187, 188, 224, 241, 276–7, 285, 320, 324, 331, 333, 340, 345, 346

McCabe, Alex, 41

McCartan, Patrick, 106

MacCarthy, Liam, 33

MacCarthy, Miss, 65, 130, 159

McCullough, Denis, 93, 317

MacCurtain, Tomas, 135, 313

MacDiarmada, Sean, 27, 33, 37, 40, 45–7, 66, 76, 92, 129

MacDonagh, Thomas, 40, 76

MacDonnell, Sir Anthony, 135n

McDonnell, Mick, 128n, 129

MacEoin, Sean, 117, 140, 186–8, 191–2, 205, 270

McGrath, Joseph, 66, 79, 85, 109, 213, 257, 324, 332–3

McGrath, Sean, 109, 126

McGuinness, Joseph, 74, 187n

McKee, Dick, 81, 127, 140, 143, 164, 168–74

MacNamara, James, 83, 132, 171, 172, 183

MacNeill, Eoin, 29, 39, 41, 48, 80, 97n

MacNeill, Swift, 84

McPeake, 333, 338

MacPherson, Ian, 281

Macready, General Sir Nevil, 100, 136, 146–8, 151, 160–2, 168, 174, 188, 220–1, 236, 277, 297, 299, 317, 319

MacSwiney, Mary, 274

MacSwiney, Terence, 109–11, 135, 138, 155, 160–2, 165–6, 313

Napoleon, 3

National Army (1922), 285, 296, 299, 320, 321, 326–30, 340, 348

National Volunteers, 32

Nationality, 65

Neligan, David, 170–1, 178, 183

Nelson, Lord, 46

Newman, Major John R. P., 57

Nunan, Sean, 114, 149, 302

O'Briain, Liam, 55, 153, 327, 333

O'Brien, Dan, 9

O'Brien, Johanna McCarthy, 9

O'Brien, R. Barry, 26

O'Coileain, Clan, 3

O Conaire, Padraig, 29

O'Connell, Daniel, 9, 74

O'Connell, J. J., 320

O'Connell, Mort, 51

O'Connell, Sean, 137, 169, 338–9

O'Connor, Batt, 109, 119, 141, 159, 193, 341

O'Connor, Mrs Batt, 141, 155

O'Connor, James, 101
O'Connor, Rory, 38–9, 78, 143, 154, 178–9, 183, 296–9, 315, 317, 321, 347
O'Connor, T. P., 69
O'Donaghue, Daithi, 111
O'Donovan, Mrs J. A., 142, 172, 179, 182
O'Driscoll, Margaret (Collins), 4, 16
O'Duffy, Eoin, 302
O'Farrell, Fergus, 221
O'Flanagan, Fr Michael, 96
An t-Oglach, 93, 126
O'Hegarty, Diarmuid, 31, 37, 44, 55, 70, 110, 116, 167, 213
O'Hegarty, Dick, 75, 172–3
O'Higgins, Kevin, 143, 221, 259, 269, 306, 333, 341, 346–7
O'Higgins, Mrs Kevin, 221
Oisin, 120
O'Keeffe, Padraig, 38, 54, 108, 129, 159, 313
O'Keeffe, Mrs, 130
O Lochlainn, Colm, 38, 40, 110
O'Mara, James, 150, 237
O'Reilly, Joe, 31, 44, 90, 108, 118–19, 142, 144, 171, 192, 341
O'Reilly, M. W., 53, 82
Orpen, Sir William, 333
O'Sullivan, Gearoid, 37, 44, 70, 99, 116, 118, 140, 142–3, 154–5, 178, 193, 230, 313, 321
O'Sullivan, Joseph, 317–19, 331

Parnell, Charles Stewart, 4, 26, 41, 46, 105, 247, 301, 344
Parry, Mrs, 239
Partridge, Sir Bernard, 58
Peace Conference (Versailles), 100–1
Pearse, Padraig, 40, 42–8, 76, 81, 120, 247
Percival, Lt-General A. E., 189
Plan of Campaign, 10
Plunkett, George, 122
Plunkett, George, Noble Count, 34–5, 68–9, 97n

Plunkett, Sir Horace, 15, 148
Plunkett, Joseph, 35–6, 38, 40, 42–3, 45, 53
Poblacht na hEireann, 342
Pope Benedict XV, 224
Powell, Mary (Collins), 4, 8, 186
Powell, Michael, 108
Powell, Sean, 108
Power, Albert, 344
Primrose Commission, 135n
Provisional Government (1922), 275, 277, 279–81, 284–6, 289, 293–4, 297–9, 301, 307, 309–10, 313, 318–21, 328, 334, 347
Punch, 58

Raleigh, Sir Walter, 276
Redmond, John, 26, 28, 30, 32, 68
Republican Army (1922), 292, 296, 299, 323, 326, 328, 330
Resurrection of Hungary, 25, 100
Restoration of Order in Ireland Act, 160
Riddell, Lord, 113, 130, 146, 204, 220
Riddle of the Sands, 140, 256
Riordan, Dr Michael, 343
Robinson, Sir Henry, 278
Robinson, Seamus, 325
Roche, Sergeant, 242
Roosevelt, Theodore, 279
Rosebery, Lord, 114
Royal Irish Constabulary (R.I.C.), 16, 62, 70, 82–3, 115, 117, 128, 132–3, 135–6, 138, 141, 144, 147, 183
Ryan, Desmond, 51, 153, 272
Ryan, Dr James, 50–1, 53
Ryan, Dr Mark, 25
Ryan, W. P., 25

Sankey Commission, 58
Santry, James, 272
Scott, C. P., 134, 150n, 228–30, 239, 244–5, 252, 254, 257, 308

Service, Robert, 58

Shakespeare, Geoffrey, 232, 251, 253, 256, 258, 317

Shanahan, Phil, 118

Shaw, G. B., 21, 58, 158

Sheridan, Katie (Collins), 4, 13, 16, 32, 118–19, 121, 273, 341

Sinn Fein, founded (1905), 17; Collins joins, 24; aims of, 24–5, 73; N. Leitrim by-election, 25; lacks support, 28; believed to be behind Rising, 48–9; N. Roscommon by-election, 68–9; I.R.A. support, 72; S. Longford by-election, 74; Irish Convention, 74; meetings illegal, 76; policy defined, 77–8; Convention (1917), 79–80; 'German Plot', 88; Collins critical of, 93–4, 103–4; fights Election (1918), 95–7; Peace Conference, 100; illegal (1919), 112; MacCurtain's murder, 135; propaganda, 139; British claim a divided body, 147; and without effective leader, 148; Anderson opposes campaign, 151; 'getting upper hand', 153; 'Coercion Act', 160; deputies in prison, 160; moderates look for truce, 163; Clune talks, 177; Government of Ireland Act, 178; distrust of peace moves, 184, 190–1; Craig offers to meet leaders, 190, 196; fights Election (1921), 191; negotiating position, 196; Lloyd George peace offer, 197; Lloyd George on, 228, 244; Scott on, 245; de Valera and unity of, 267; 'B' Specials, 289; Collins and unity of, 318; *passim*, 19, 83–4, 86, 90, 114, 119, 127, 130, 133, 138, 142, 150, 156, 159, 195, 202, 213, 233, 235, 250, 305

Slattery, Jim, 128n

Smith, Det.-Sergeant, 128

Smuts, Field-Marshal J., 112, 182, 196

Squad, 128, 133, 142, 162, 181, 344

Stack, Austin, 76, 91–4, 99, 157–8, 182, 208, 212, 240, 259–62, 261n

Statute of Westminster, 234, 349

Stevenson, Miss Frances, 185

Sturgis, Mark, member of Dublin Castle Executive, 151; *writes on*: self-government for S. Ireland, 152–3, 160; Winter's identification scheme, 160; peace prospects, 162; Dail Loan raid, 166; Bloody Sunday, 170; hunt for Collins, 175–6; failure of Clune talks, 177, 184; seizure of Collins's papers, 182; Lloyd George and peace moves, 185; Craig's Ulster policy, 202; Cope and Macready's views on Collins, 220–1; fears of renewed warfare, 224; meeting with Collins, 236–7; Cope at No. 10, 256

Sweeney, Joseph, 187, 333

Thornton, Frank, 31, 44, 341

The Times, 166

Tobin, Liam, 84, 90

Tone, Theobald Wolfe, 3, 13, 26, 130

Treacy, Sean, 164–5, 174

Treaty of Versailles, 103

Tudor, General Henry, 146, 172, 175, 201

Ulster Volunteers, 28–9

United Irishman, 24

United Irishmen, 28

Vaughan's Hotel, 114, 116, 118, 123, 138, 142, 168–9, 171, 173–4, 178

Walsh, Archbishop, 188

Walsh, J. J., 99, 237

Washington Disarmament Conference, 237

Wedgwood, Col Josiah, 234
Weekly Freeman, 5
Weekly Summary, 162
Whitman, Walt, 21, 204, 302
Wilde, Oscar, 51, 155
Wilson, Sir Henry, 86, 136, 147–8, 153, 292, 307, 315–18, 321
Wilson, President Woodrow, 100–3, 105
Wimborne, Lord, 42

Winter, Ormonde, 146, 160, 170, 188, 193
Woodfield, 3–9, 11–13, 16, 23, 61, 189–90, 203, 218, 222, 272, 336
Worthington-Evans, Sir Laming, 219
Wyndham, George, 23

Yeats, W. B., 15, 21, 48, 73, 120, 350